CANADA AMONG NA

A Fading Power

Edited by
Norman Hillmer
and Maureen Appel Molot

OXFORD
UNIVERSITY PRESS

OXFORD
UNIVERSITY PRESS

70 Wynford Drive, Don Mills, Ontario M3C 1J9
www.oup.com/ca

Oxford University Press is a department of the University of Oxford.
It furthers the University's objective of excellence in research, scholarship,
and education by publishing worldwide in

Oxford   New York

Auckland   Bangkok   Buenos Aires   Cape Town   Chennai
Dar es Salaam   Delhi   Hong Kong   Istanbul   Karachi   Kolkata
Kuala Lumpur   Madrid   Melbourne   Mexico City   Mumbai   Nairobi
São Paulo   Shanghai   Singapore   Taipei   Tokyo   Toronto

with an associated company in Berlin

Oxford is a trade mark of Oxford University Press
in the UK and in certain other countries

Published in Canada
by Oxford University Press

National Library of Canada Cataloguing in Publication Data

The National Library of Canada has catalogued this publication as follows:
Canada among nations

Annual.
1984-
Produced by the Norman Paterson School of International Affairs at Carleton University.
Publisher varies.
Includes bibliographical references.
ISSN 0832-0683
ISBN 0-19-541791-7 (2002 edition)

1. Canada—Foreign relations—1945-   —Periodicals. 2. Canada—Politics and government—
1984-   —Periodicals. 3. Canada—Politics and government—1980-1984—Periodicals. I. Norman
Paterson School of International Affairs

FC242.C345   327.71   C86-031285-2 rev
F1034.2.C36

1 2 3 4 - 05 04 03 02

This book is printed on permanent (acid-free) paper ∞.
Printed in Canada

CONTENTS

The Hemisphere and Beyond

CONTRIBUTORS

Stewart Bell is a national affairs reporter at the *National Post*.

Andrew Cohen is an Associate Professor in the School of Journalism and Mass Communications and The Norman Paterson School of International Affairs, Carleton University.

Jean Daudelin is Principal Researcher, Conflict and Human Security, at the North-South Institute, and Adjunct Research Professor at The Norman Paterson School of International Affairs, Carleton University.

G. Bruce Doern is a Professor of Public Policy in the School of Public Policy and Administration at Carleton University and also holds a Research Chair in Public Policy at the Politics Department, University of Exeter.

John W. Foster is a Principal Researcher at the North-South Institute, Ottawa.

Stephen Gallagher teaches political science at Concordia University.

Monica Gattinger is a doctoral student in the School of Public Policy and Administration at Carleton University.

Norman Hillmer is a Professor of History at Carleton University and Editor-at-Large of *International Journal*.

John Kirton is an Associate Professor of Political Science and Director of the G-8 Research Group at the University of Toronto.

Maureen Appel Molot is a Professor and Director of The Norman Paterson School of International Affairs at Carleton University.

W. David McIntyre is Emeritus Professor of History at the University of Canterbury, New Zealand, and a Research Associate in the Macmillan Brown Centre for Pacific Studies in Christchurch.

Dean F. Oliver is Manager, Historical Research and Archives, at the Canadian War Museum, and Adjunct Research Professor at The Norman Paterson School of International Affairs, Carleton University.

Stephen J. Randall is Dean, Faculty of Social Sciences, University of Calgary.

Martin Rudner is a Professor and Associate Director at The Norman Paterson School of International Affairs, Carleton University, and is Director of the Centre for Security and Defence Studies.

Christopher Sands is a Fellow and Director of the Canada Project at the Center for Security and International Studies, Washington, DC.

ABBREVIATIONS

ART	anti-retroviral therapy
ARV	anti-retroviral (drugs)
ASO	AIDS service organization
CA	Canadian Alliance
CANUKUS	Canada-UK-US intelligence grouping (NATO)
CARICOM	Caribbean Community
CCCS	Commonwealth Committee on Co-operation Through Sport
CCFPD	Canadian Centre for Foreign Policy Development
CCOT	Commonwealth Committee on Terrorism
CCPA	Canadian Centre for Policy Alternatives
CCR	Canadian Council on Refugees
CCRA	Canada Customs and Revenue Agency
CF	Canadian Forces
CFIOG	Canadian Forces Information Operations Group
CFTC	Commonwealth Fund for Technical Co-operation
CHMM	Commonwealth Health Ministers' Meeting
CHPA	Consumer Healthcare Products Association
CIC	Department of Citizenship and Immigration
CIDA	Canadian International Development Agency
CIRRs	commercial interest reference rates
CLUs	Commonwealth Liaison Units
CMAG	Commonwealth Ministerial Action Group
COL	Commonwealth of Learning
CPA	Commonwealth Parliamentary Association
CPHA	Canadian Public Health Association
CPTM	Commonwealth Partnership for Technology Management
CRDD	Convention Refugee Determination Division
CSE	Communications Security Establishment
CSIS	Canadian Security Intelligence Service
DFAIT	Department of Foreign Affairs and International Trade
DND	Department of National Defence
DNP	National Democratic Party (Germany)
DOT Force	Digital Opportunity Task Force
DROC	deferred removal orders class
DVU	German People's Union

EDC	Export Development Corporation
ELN	National Liberation Army (Colombia)
EMBRAER	Empresa Brasileira de Aeronáutica
ETA	Euskadi ta Askatasuna ('Basque Fatherland and Liberty')
EU	European Union
FACT	Federation of Associations of Canadian Tamils
FARC	Revolutionary Armed Forces of Colombia
FATF	Financial Action Task Force on Money Laundering
FDI	foreign direct investment
FOCAL	Canadian Foundation for the Americas
FTA	Canada–US Free Trade Agreement
FTAA	Free Trade Area of the Americas
G-7	Group of Seven leading industrial nations (Canada, France, Germany, Italy, Japan, UK, US)
G-8	Group of Seven plus Russia
G-20	Group of Twenty (international forum of finance ministers and central bank governors representing 19 countries, the EU, the IMF, and the World Bank)
GDP	gross domestic product
GHGs	greenhouse gases
GIA	Armed Islamic Group (Algeria)
HLRG	High-Level Review Group
HUMINT	human intelligence
IDA	International Development Agency
IEA	International Energy Agency
IGOs	intergovernmental organizations
IIRIRA	Illegal Immigration Reform and Immigrant Responsibility Act
ILETS	International Law Enforcement Telecommunications Seminar
IMF	International Monetary Fund
IMFC	International Monetary and Financial Committee
IMINT	satellite imagery intelligence
INCHRITI	International NGO Committee on Human Rights Trade and Investment
INS	Immigration and Naturalization Service (US)
IRA	Irish Republican Army
IRB	Immigration and Refugee Board

KGB	Komitet Gosudarstvennoy Bezopasnosti (Committee for State Security, USSR)
LTCM	long-term capital management
LTTE	Liberation Tigers of Tamil Eelam
MAI	Multilateral Agreement on Investment
Mercosur	Mercado Común Del Sur
MSF	Médécins Sans Frontières
NAFTA	North American Free Trade Agreement
NATO	North Atlantic Treaty Organization
NEP	National Energy Program (Canada)
NEP	National Energy Plan (US)
NFTC	NATO Flying Training in Canada
NGO	non-governmental organizations
NSA	National Security Agency (US)
OAG	Office of the Auditor General of Canada
OAS	Organization of American States
ODA	official development assistance
OECD	Organization for Economic Co-operation and Development
OPEC	Organization of Petroleum Exporting Countries
PCO	Privy Council Office
PKK	Kurdistan Workers Party
PLO	Palestine Liberation Organization
PRI	Institutional Revolutionary Party (Mexico)
PROEX	Programa de Financiamento às Exportações (Program of support to exports - Brazil)
PRS	permanent resident status
RCMP	Royal Canadian Mounted Police
SATCOM	satellite communications
SDF	self-defence forces
SIGINT	signals intelligence
SIN	National Security Organization (Peru)
SIRC	Security and Intelligence Review Committee
TICA	Trade and Investment Co-operation Arrangement
TOA	Treaty of Amsterdam
TRIPS	trade-related intellectual property rights
TWG	Transitional Working Group (for Global Fund To Fight AIDS . . .)
UKUSA	United Kingdom-United States Security Agreement

UNFCCC	United Nations Framework Convention on Climate Change
UNGASS	United Nations General Assembly Special Session
UNHCR	United Nations High Commissioner for Refugees
WHO	World Health Organization
WMD	weapons of mass destruction
WTM	World Tamil Movement
WTO	World Trade Organization

Preface

We began this volume in the early summer of 2001 intensely aware of a crescendo of criticism about the substance and direction of Canadian foreign policy. Resources and bureaucracies had shrunk; the military was on life support; the United States was all too close; and the only real business of external relations was business. Canada seemed to matter so much less in the world, particularly when measured against the glories of the past, real and apparent. There was frustration, furthermore, about a drift in policy following the resignation of Foreign Minister Lloyd Axworthy and a reluctance on the part of the government to engage some thorny issues. At that time, we were aware, the Departments of National Defence and Foreign Affairs and International Trade were both engaged in policy reviews or updates. The terrorist attacks on the US of 11 September brought an understandable delay to the policy updates, but they also gave a new urgency to questions of sovereignty and decline. *A Fading Power* is not a declaration—some of our authors do not accept that it is so—but rather a challenge to our readers to consider the very tough choices that Canadians face.

Canada Among Nations has been published annually by The Norman Paterson School of International Affairs (NPSIA) since 1984. This is the eighteenth volume in the series, which, to our delight, is widely used in Canadian foreign policy courses across Canada and abroad, and has become a publication of record on Canada's policy and actions in international affairs.

The editors acknowledge the indispensable support of the Security and Defence Forum of the Department of National Defence and the Dean of the Faculty of Public Affairs and Management at Carleton University. They underwrote some of the costs of a workshop at Carleton in December 2001, at which the contributors presented their papers and debated the policy issues set forth in the volume. The editors thoroughly enjoyed working with the contributors. We have made new friends and been exposed to new perspectives.

Canada Among Nations could not be produced every year without the assistance and support of our NPSIA colleagues. Brenda Sutherland once again proved how crucial she is as the keeper of the timetable and the maker of the manuscript. Janet Doherty organized the workshop and managed the financial side of the project. Lana Ayyad and Renee Martyna dug out details large and small, and Vivian Cummins made important suggestions for improving the book. We also want to highlight, with real gratitude, the professionalism of Laura Macleod, Mark Piel, and Phyllis Wilson at Oxford University Press. As in the past, we were fortunate to have the very skilled Richard Tallman available to edit the chapters.

We dedicate this edition of *Canada Among Nations* to scholar-commentator James Eayrs, whose critical edge and sparkling prose have informed debates on Canadian foreign policy for five decades. We hope this is his kind of book.

Norman Hillmer
Maureen Appel Molot

11 April 2002

1

The Diplomacy of Decline

MAUREEN APPEL MOLOT AND NORMAN HILLMER

After the terrorist attacks of 11 September 2001 on the World Trade Center in New York and the Pentagon in Washington, Foreign Minister John Manley emerged as the Canadian government's strongest presence. Not since Pierre Trudeau was Justice Minister in the mid-1960s, gushed *Time* magazine in naming Manley its Canadian newsmaker of the year, 'has a politician moved so swiftly or dramatically to orchestrate a transformative moment in Canadian history' (Handelman, 2001–2: 69). Part of the minister's appeal was an extraordinary bluntness, which he applied to Canada's recent international performance. The country, he declared, was 'still trading on a reputation that was built two generations and more ago—but that we haven't continued to live up to'. Canadians had to start paying their share again. 'You can't just sit at the G-8 table and then, when the bill comes, go to the washroom. If you want to play a role in the world, even as a small member of the G-8, there's a cost to doing that.' Manley made his memorable comments to the *National Post* less than a month after 11 September (Wells, 2001). Given the chance to retract them at year's end, he did not do so (Trickey, 2001).

Manley's accusation was explicit. He identified 'glaring' deficiencies in intelligence, the military, and development assistance. Canadians' share in international aid and peacekeeping was decreasing, and a foreign intelligence service simply did not exist, making the government reliant on the Americans and the British for information about what was going on in the world. There was, he insisted, no question of abandoning 'the keys to sovereignty' in immigration policy or in the fashioning of a safer post-11 September Canadian–American border regime. Canada, moreover, could certainly still make an international difference in all kinds of ways. It had global standing as 'a good, honest country', a North American state that was not a superpower or a former colonial master. Canadians had, therefore, a 'unique dimension' on world politics. Added to that was specialized expertise in certain areas. Canada's diplomats were adept at helpful fixing and institution-building in fora such as the North Atlantic Treaty Organization (NATO) and at the fall 2001 Durban Conference on racism. 'We make a lot of things work', Manley told the *Ottawa Citizen*. 'We find solutions' (Trickey, 2001; Wells, 2001).

A pleasant reputation and skilled diplomacy, useful though they might be, could not take the place of the consistent application of real assets. If Canada wanted to maintain its international image, which Manley claimed was 'in some ways better than we deserve', it was simply going to cost more money. Expressing some embarrassment that the Canadian International Development Agency (CIDA) had only been able to raise $6 million in new assistance for Afghanistan, compared to the Americans' $320 million, the minister concluded that Canada was 'borderline in terms of our ability to influence situations that are unexpected'. An apathetic public was only partly to blame for the current pass. Politicians had to lead, and they had not (Wells, 2002; Trickey, 2001).

ONLY CRITICS NEED APPLY

Canadian foreign policy has always had its critics. Now it apparently has little but. The foreign policy of the Jean Chrétien administration seemed from the beginning crass and unheroic. Lester B. Pearson had won the 1957 Nobel Peace Prize with virtuoso diplomacy at the United Nations in New York, and Pierre Trudeau conducted a global peace mission in 1983–4. Chrétien's travel schedule, by contrast, was notable for its Team Canada junkets in pursuit of trade. When the government issued its *Canada in the World* statement in 1995, two years into its mandate, a prominent journalist remarked that 'the new foreign policy of Canada is less idealistic, less engaged, and less empathetic' (Cohen, 1995: 2). Just as that accusation set in, however, Lloyd Axworthy (1996–2000) appeared on the scene, taking a dominant hold on policy. He proved as activist and utopian a Foreign Minister as the country has ever had (Hillmer and Chapnick, 2001).

The disapproval nevertheless continued, and it became denunciation. Axworthy was pilloried for his moralism, rigidity, and stridency, all of them made more suspect by the yawning gulf between rhetoric and resources. Pulpit diplomacy and pinchpenny diplomacy did not mix, the commentators cried, nor did talking loudly when the only weaponry at the ready was a bent twig (Hampson and Oliver, 1998; Nossal, 1998–9; Stairs, 2001a). While luxuriating in lofty prescriptions for a better world, the analysis went on, Axworthy's human security agenda had kidnapped Canadian external policy, crowding out other priorities and appropriating scarce resources in the Department of Foreign Affairs and International Trade (DFAIT). One of Axworthy's own officers reflected a widespread departmental unease about the minister's direction: 'No amount of creativity, soft power, or sanctimony can substitute for the demonstration of conviction through resource allocation, both in terms of seeing to the requirements of those on the front lines and in regard to support of various policy ventures. Yet the minister's apparent disinterest in administrative or institutional reform issues seemed almost complete' (Copeland, 2001: 167–8). But, all the while, did it really matter? The true business of foreign relations was business: 'anything for a buck', with or without Axworthy, in the characterization of one analyst (Sjolander, 1997).

The Manley regime at the Department of Foreign Affairs lasted only a little more than a year and fell into two phases: before and after the terrorist attacks. The first period was quiet. It was marked mainly by the turn away from the Axworthy human security agenda towards an emphasis on economic foreign policy and Canadian–American relationships, as well as for the minister's very public insistence that the case of a drunken Russian diplomat whose car killed one woman and badly injured another on an Ottawa street not be swept under the carpet. Post-11 September, Manley came into his own as a public figure, before rapid promotion (notwithstanding his comments about the government's indifferent record on foreign affairs) to the position of Deputy Prime Minister in mid-January 2002.

The new Foreign Minister, William Graham, encountered his new responsibilities with experience gained from seven years as Chair of the House of Commons Standing Committee on Foreign Affairs and International Trade. He was a respected committee chair, from which he held regular hearings on a wide range of topics, including a series during the fall of 2001 on Canada–US relations in the new security environment. Graham was thought to be in the Axworthy rather than the Manley mould, more skeptical of the United States and more committed to a wide variety of multilateral initiatives (Sallot, 2002; *National Post*, 2002). 'I'm not saying I want the foreign policy to be designed in contradistinction to the United States', Graham said in an early interview, 'but we have to hold our own values' (Martin, 2002). 'The United States has a totally different perspective than we do on the world.' They feel 'that they can have their will' (*National Post*, 2002). From Axworthy to Manley and back again reinforced the impression that foreign relations were adrift from their traditionally stable moorings under a Prime Minister who was either insufficiently committed and knowledgeable or bereft of a clear vision of the Canadian imperative in a threatening world. Or both.

AFTER 11 SEPTEMBER

The challenges for Canadian foreign policy changed dramatically as a result of the 11 September raids, not in nature but in intensity. The international environment was suddenly dominated by an aroused and unsubtle United States bent on revenge, and that put stress on friends as well as enemies. Public attention became focused squarely on a Canadian–American relationship always replete with ambiguities, and more particularly on the frontier between the two countries. There were substantial pressures to ensure the border remained open for trade, yet was secure against the entry of terrorists into the US; the government had to counter rumours that Canada was a prime entry point into the United States for Osama bin Laden's Al-Qaeda cell.

Prime Minister Chrétien reacted uncertainly to the crisis at the outset, causing some annoyance in Canada (and doubtless in the US) when he moved slowly in demonstrating sympathy, and seemed to value sovereignty over solidarity. Into the vacuum moved Manley, who, in the opinion of *Time*'s reporter, assumed the guise of 'Ottawa's most assertive and pro-American figure' (Handelman, 2001–2: 65). Coming to Foreign Affairs from a long stint at Industry Canada, he understood the centrality of the US for Canada. It was Manley who first recognized the enormity of what had occurred and who articulated support for the US fight against terrorism, noting that Canada stood 'shoulder-to-shoulder' with its closest ally (Trickey, 2001). His statements of support were subsequently echoed by the Prime Minister. But that, too, elicited concern, this time from those Canadians who did not want their country to be America's poodle.

The events of 11 September generated an irresistible call to arms against international terrorism. As the cover of this book shows, ships of the Canadian navy—the HMCS *Iroquois*, *Preserver*, and *Charlottetown*—departed for the Arabian Sea from Halifax harbour on 17 October, with Chrétien and Defence Minister Art Eggleton providing the patriotic fanfare. In the Prime Minister's words, 'Canada has never been a nation to sit on the sidelines. We did not pick this fight, but we will finish it, because on the side of justice, in a just cause, there can be only one outcome: victory' (Foot, 2001). The 'doggerel of war' rang false with columnist Christie Blatchford, who compared governmental bombast with a limp defence policy 'that sees Canadian ships still equipped with ageing Sea King helicopters that are every bit as high-maintenance as the average Quebec Liberal.' She added, 'Could anyone but a Canadian general, in this case the Chief of the Defence Staff Ray Hénault, have stood within sight of the weary Sea King choppers and dared brag that the nation was sending the troops off with "the best tools available"?' (Blatchford, 2001).

Combat troops for the land war in Afghanistan followed, with commentators complaining that the forces had the wrong uniforms for the desert and making false claims that the government was surrendering its forces to American command for the first time in Canadian military history. Paul Koring wrote from the Washington bureau of the *Globe and Mail* that 'In the current conflict, Mr Chrétien had a clear choice: either take part in the UN-mandated, multinational peacekeeping force, or to deploy combat troops, under US tactical command, to wage war. The PM opted to salute President George W. Bush's bugle.' The transition was complete from out-of-power Americano-skeptic in the early 1990s to anxious-to-please Prime Minister a decade later (Koring, 2002).

The critiques of Canadian foreign policy accelerated and took on a despairing tone in the aftermath of 11 September. The same themes about Canada's plummeting national independence and international stature were sounded again and again, and in a startlingly similar formulation. Consider the historian Michael Bliss, who asked 'Is Canada a Country in Decline?' and did not stay for an answer (Bliss, 2001). Or Andrew Cohen, a contributor to this volume, whose testimony to the parliamentary Standing Committee on Foreign Affairs and International Trade was excerpted in the *Ottawa Citizen* under the headline, 'The ghost of Canada past: Our global reputation is in decline as we stand on old accomplishments and ignore our present crisis' (Cohen, 2001). Christopher Sands, the most widely quoted of the tiny posse of Canada watchers in the United States, put it succinctly but no less devastatingly: Canada was engaging in the 'diplomacy of decline' (Sands, 2001b).

Where there was decline, could fall be far behind? The *Saskatoon Star Phoenix* greeted the year 2002 with an editorial commenting on the growing number of analysts who were predicting Canada's imminent demise. 'Our complacency in dealing with economic, social and military responsibilities has relegated us to an unprecedented degree of subservience in our own and world affairs. For Canada, this will either be a year of painful rebirth or preparation to face the inevitable' (*Ottawa Citizen*, 2002). Itemizing a scrawny military, an underfunded foreign service, and an unconnected Prime Minister, combined with proximity to 'the most formidable economic and military power in history', the *National Post*'s Paul Wells predicted a Canadian sovereignty emergency. Canada would survive only if 'we give ourselves—and demand from our governments—the tools of a serious country in a serious world' (Wells, 2002). The *Guardian Weekly* pondered the military ambitions of the George W. Bush administration in the Middle East (Iraq in particular) and for the 'homeland defence' of North America in early March 2002. The international newspaper described the Canadian predicament thus: 'In national security terms . . . joined at the hip to the US, yet with a diminishing ability to influence the increasingly volatile colossus at their side' (Borger, 2002).

In a country that had seldom elevated the military to a national priority, Canada's capacity to make a contribution to the fight against terrorism and the way in which that contribution could be made added significantly to the sense of decline. The Canadian Forces (CF), 125,000 members strong in 1960, had fallen to 58,574 by 2000 (DND,

2001). Canada ranks with Spain as the NATO country that spends the least on defence as a per cent of GDP: 1.1 per cent (*National Post Business*, 2002: 74). In her 2001 report, the Auditor General noted that the air force has reduced its activities substantially over the last five years because there are insufficient personnel to keep the aircraft performing at full capacity and urgent requirements for replacement equipment can seldom be met (Laghi, 2001). Even the vaunted image of the CF as the world's peacekeeper *sans pareil* no longer seemed apt (Simpson, 2001). 'We have the rhetoric of peacekeeping but not the capacity', defence expert Douglas Bland stated. The government 'won't spend the money to support it' (Gee, 2002). The December 2001 budget provided resources to enhance domestic security, but little in the way of funds to expand either the size of the CF or their combat readiness. Admittedly, the previous two budgets had contained increases, but the Prime Minister made it clear that little more can be expected. In his view, 11 September had changed nothing 'fundamentally' (Fife, 2002b). The Chrétien government could find $101 million for new Challenger jets to transport its politicians, but nothing to replace the military's antediluvian helicopters (Pugliese, 2002b; Greenspon, 2002).

Contributing to national malaise is the sense that the Canadian economy is faltering relative to that of the United States (Bliss, 2001). Canada did not experience as long a period of growth in the Gilded Age of the 1990s as the US; it recovered more slowly and unemployment numbers never fell as dramatically as they did south of the border. Productivity generally lags behind that of the US, although the gap is lessening as a result of heavy investments by Canadian businesses in information technology (Schwanen, 2000; Little, 2002), and Canadian incomes expressed in terms of purchasing power are falling further behind those of Americans (Statistics Canada, 2000). There is an intimate connection between Canada's economic well-being and the capacity to address post-11 September security and Canada–US border issues.

A fading power, then? That is our subject, and we get at it in various ways. There are chapters relating to the military and to intelligence and development issues, key measures of international capability and commitment. Articles on the G-8 and the Commonwealth test the effectiveness of the country's multilateral diplomacy, the post-World War II cornerstone of Canadian foreign policy activism. Two accounts of hemispheric trade and diplomacy are reminders that, for the first part of 2001, the Free Trade Area of the Americas (FTAA) initiative and the Quebec City Summit, with its anti-globalization demonstrations, loomed large in Canadian thinking. At the book's core, inevitably, is the Canadian–American relationship. Border conundrums, the role of energy, and the Canadian reputation in Washington join studies of terrorism and refugee policy, brought to centre stage by 11 September and raising questions about Canada's capacity to keep its part of the continent safe.

This volume of *Canada Among Nations*, like its predecessors, is structured to review current Canadian foreign policy and provoke debate. Our authors do not agree, and readers will not either. Some, perhaps most, of the evidence in the book adds to and reinforces the Manley indictment, but there are also strong voices in the other direction. Conflicting views of policy in Latin America, for example, suggest that Canada either remains a power with a formidable talent for searching out healing consensus or, as its interests and preoccupations become more confined to the North American continent, has increasingly less to say to the world outside it. The fact that each of those propositions might be true simply hints at the complexity of the problem.

WHEN CANADA MATTERED

Once upon a time, the story goes, no doubts were necessary. In the 1940s and 1950s, fighting Fascism and Communism and building the institutions of a new world order, Canada mattered. The economy was strong, and so, too, was the military for most of the period. The country was unified. Public opinion was activist. It was possible to craft a consensual foreign policy. The Department of External Affairs was led by considerable men—Mackenzie King, Louis St Laurent and L.B. Pearson—and populated by the young and ambitious. Foreigners began to comment on the best bantam foreign office in the world, its diplomats exercising an influence and enjoying a prestige, said *The Economist* (1953), 'out of all proportion to the size of their country or the power it can wield'. After 1945, Britain, Europe, and Japan were devastated; Canada was untouched and bursting at the seams. Given its wealth and prestige, diplomat George Ignatieff recalled in his memoirs, 'Canada had both an obligation and the ability to act as an architect of peaceful solutions to intractable problems. . . . For the first time there was a sense of mission in our foreign policy'(Ignatieff, 1985: 109).

In 1939, against the background of chaotic regionalism, the Depression, and scant military-diplomatic capital, Canada had been definitively a small power. And happily so—foreign policy was trouble. In World War II, however, Canada put a million people in uniform and made an enormous economic contribution to the allied endeavour. By 1944, Pearson was claiming the status of a 'little Big Power' or a 'big little Power'. He clearly preferred the former, but a more appetizing term, 'middle power', was coming into vogue for states that found themselves in between the great and the marginal. The official definition issued by External Affairs in 1947 demonstrated how far the country had travelled in less than a decade: 'The Middle Powers are those which by reason of their size, their material resources, their willingness and ability to accept responsibility, their influence and stability are close to being great powers' (Eayrs, 1975: 20).

Canadians pursued middle powerhood with a vengeance. It was an expandable vessel, speaking to geography and skills at compromise, but most of all to a 'subtle process of nationalist self-promotion' aimed at international status, influence, and manoeuvrability (Chapnick, 2000: 188). The role of the middle power was very consciously carried out in an international system within which Canada 'felt uncomfortably exposed' (Sarty, 1993: 761), occasioning, sometimes in the same breath, alliance solidarity, efforts at brokerage, and what David Haglund terms the use of ideas and ideals as power assets (Haglund, 2000: 102–4). After a three-decade career in External Affairs, Arthur Andrew described the admixture of motives and interests that the concept came to represent in the early Cold War: 'Looking back over the years during which the Department reached the peak of its influence, it seems as if Canada had a destiny to be in all things a Middle Power, an agent of influence for moderation in the geopolitical middle; a crossroads and entrepot, politically, ideologically, culturally, commercially and spiritually' (Andrew, 1993: 181).

Equipoise was crucial. We were America's friend, but also the world's. Canada was a builder of bridges and coalitions, avoiding Washington's 'stifling bilateral embrace' (Eayrs, 1980: 66) in a myriad of multilateral institutions. The high-water mark of the middle power ethos was Pearson's 1957 Nobel Prize.

Escott Reid, another of the ex-diplomats-become-critics, coined the phrase 'the golden decade' for middle powerhood's glory days of the 1940s and early 1950s as he asked for a repeat performance in the 1960s (Reid, 1967). It was not to be, and the image of a Golden Age grew to mythological proportions as a standard against which all subsequent events would be harshly judged. For Reid, a vital ingredient in wartime and immediate post-war diplomatic success had been the intellect, creativity, and determination of senior officials in External Affairs (Reid, 1967: 173). Yet John Diefenbaker loathed the department's 'Pearsonalities'. Pierre Trudeau said he'd rather read the *New York Times*. Brian Mulroney slashed budgets, closed posts, and politicized the foreign service, becoming the record-holder in diplomatic patronage by appointing 36 of his friends to posts abroad (Cohen, 1994). All of this took place, moreover, during decades when the foreign service was becoming a much less attractive employment prospect. Salaries were uncompetitive, morale was low, and officers felt 'underappreciated and underpromoted' (Mackenzie, 2001: 20). Little wonder that an air of disappointment hangs over much of the work of the former members of the Department of External Affairs whose books and articles command the literature of the history of Canadian foreign policy.

Not everyone, to be sure, agreed that Canadian foreign policy was in a state of progressive decline. Trudeau might have insisted in 1968 that 'we should be modest, much more modest than we were . . . in the postwar years' (Eayrs, 1975: 21), but some contemporary analysts were bullish about the country's standing in the world. Peter Dobell promoted Canada from middle to 'minor great power' (ibid., 24), while Peyton Lyon and Brian Tomlin concluded at the end of a 1979 study of 'capabilities' that 'Canada should now be regarded as a major power' (Lyon and Tomlin, 1979: 72). In a much-ballyhooed piece, James Eayrs had no patience with rankings, but he pronounced Canada a 'foremost nation': it had the levers of modern power—technology, resources, and people—in almost sinful profusion (Eayrs, 1975: 24). Building on Eayrs, David Dewitt and John Kirton (1983) have argued for Canada as a 'principal power' that shapes the international order rather than being shaped by it—a 'leader rather than a laggard, and an accomplished principal power practitioner of the diplomacy of concert', as Kirton puts it in his chapter on the G-7/8 in this volume.

None of this could approach the Golden Age in grandeur. Nothing could. Canada was at the global cynosure, but as Reid himself knew, its time was bound to be brief, caused as it was by 'a peculiar and temporary set of circumstances' created by World War II (Reid, 1989:

245). Indeed, this advocate of an expansive diplomacy freely conceded that the resources Canada could devote to foreign policy were always limited (Reid, 1967: 181). Thus the strong popular will for an activist country in the early Cold War was crucial. It has become conventional wisdom to repeat Barbara Ward's flattering assessment of Canada as the 'first international nation' (Ward, 1970; Clark, 1997), but just how deeply did the public backing for a thoroughgoing internationalism run in the decades after the Nobel Prize? John Cruickshank, a keen observer of Canadian external matters from his desk as managing editor of the *Globe and Mail*, wrote in the early 1990s that, 'Except for trade issues such as the deal with the United States and the General Agreements on Tariffs and Trade, foreign policy has not much figured in our national discourse. Our commitments to peacekeeping and foreign aid have been sources of national pride but rarely contentious. On the whole, we have had the luxury of needing to do little thinking about the world' (Cruickshank, 1994).

Governments, then, could reduce the amount spent on the Foreign Affairs Department and the military with impunity, and that in fact is what has happened. Yet the cost has arguably not been great. Cruickshank's contention is that 'the past five decades in Canada have been ones of increasing material well-being, a broadening of democratic rights and growing cultural vibrancy and diversity. In fact, if you consider our key foreign-policy objectives over this period—peace, liberalization of trade and economic development for the least fortunate—there is much to be encouraged by' (Cruickshank, 1994).

The grievance of the Golden-Agers, whose circle extends beyond the former diplomats, goes much deeper. Their recollection is of a period when Canada was finally free of Great Britain and had sufficient distance from the United States to be a moral, objective, and independent citizen of the world, racking up a list of battle honours that included, in a very short compass and all benefiting from a formative and formidable Canadian contribution, the founding of the United Nations, GATT, NATO, and peacekeeping (English, 1998; McCall, 1985: 52; Cohen, 1994). The transition from the St Laurent administration to the Mulroney era, however, seemed from the Golden Age to the age of lead, with plenty of bronze in between (Cruickshank, 1994). In his *Rise and Fall of a Middle Power*, Arthur Andrew lamented the accelerating Americanization of Canadian policy and the move away from the 'precariously-balanced policies required of a Middle Power' into the sphere of 'the safely predictable ally'. Gone is the old Canada, a Canada that may well be irreplaceable in world affairs, Andrew declared in getting to the heart of the tumble-from-the-Golden-Age school of thought: 'Our ability to do good, without being embarrassed by it, our detachment as a peacekeeper and our acceptance among Third World peoples will all diminish as our alignment with the United States becomes more obvious' (Andrew, 1993: 166).

Golden Age thinking misreads history. Against the threats of a dangerous world, Canada stood shoulder to shoulder with the United States in the 1940s and 1950s, no less than it does in the early twenty-first century. The great achievements of Cold War statecraft were done alongside and frequently on behalf of the United States. Canadians practised the diplomacy of 'constraining' the Americans where they could; where they could not (and even where they could), they were the staunch partner, the safely predictable ally (Stairs, 1974). Canada's foreign policy of the Nobel years usually resulted, as since, from reaction, not initiative (Eayrs, 1961: 155). And yet, there was something about the combination of people and circumstance in 'the golden afternoon' that made public and policy-makers alike remember it as a time when Canada successfully battled bilateralism with multilateralism and brandished 'a disproportionate moral influence in the world' (Cohen, 1994). The Golden Age of diplomacy, Christina McCall points out, looks more and more in hindsight like a Golden Age of innocence (McCall, 1985: 49, 52).

THE ENTANGLING CONTINENT

Innocence is harder to come by now, especially after 11 September. At the centre of Canadian concerns about its fading power are the relationship with the United States and the sense of dwindling room for manoeuvre that follows from a complex range of ties with the southern neighbour. Is there a qualitative difference in the relationship since the fall of 2001, or are we witnessing the next steps in the evolution of connectedness that students of economic integration have long been predicting? Very high volumes of trade generate pressures on borders and the need to develop ways to manage the efficient and timely clearance of goods. Similarly, on the defence front, does Canadian participation in the war on terrorism herald something truly new, with new implications for Canadian sovereignty, or is it rather an extension of military co-operation that dates to World War II and that was institutionalized under arrangements such as the North American Air (now Aerospace) Defence Agreement (NORAD)? Even the concerns about the porousness of the border, highlighted in the weeks following the terrorist attacks, and the resulting pressures to be more attentive to the movement of people were not novel, but a repetition, albeit with greater urgency, of the dialogue that flowed from the arrest in December 1999 of Ahmed Ressam, on his way to bomb Los Angeles airport during millennium celebrations.

Since his election in 1993, Prime Minister Chrétien has not confronted the full implications of Canada's growing interdependence with the US. From his perspective, relations with the US were 'excellent'; nothing needed changing (Walker, 1999). Although he prided himself on a close personal relationship with President Clinton, their meetings were at international gatherings, on the golf course, and only occasionally on official visits to the other capital. There were no regularly scheduled meetings of heads of government or ministers, as there had been under the previous Mulroney government. No system or public service function was elaborated to advise on and co-ordinate policy towards the United States.

At its annual retreat at the end of June 1999, the Chrétien cabinet did devote considerable time to a wide-ranging discussion of bilateral relations, with the Ambassador to the United States and favourite nephew of the leader, Raymond Chrétien, present (Hampson and Molot, 2000; Cooper, 2000). Near the end of his tenure as Trade Minister, Sergio Marchi pointed to the need for a consideration of future directions in the bilateral relationship, including the feasibility of a customs union and labour mobility (Cooper, 2000: 42). In addition, a number of senior officials in the Department of Foreign Affairs and International Trade began to consider some of the larger issues in the bilateral relationship, particularly border management, an issue in which Axworthy took an interest. Chrétien displayed a public preference for Democrat Al Gore as Clinton's successor, but with the election of Republican George W. Bush, the Prime Minister continued to insist that relations could not be better. However, priorities lay elsewhere over 2000 and much of 2001, for example on hemispheric questions.

Calls for new thinking emerged from other sources. Business groups and think-tanks in Canada recognized the urgency of the issue and began to organize workshops and sponsor research on the topic. Industry Canada initiated a diverse-ranging research agenda on economic integration (Harris, 2001). Exhibiting the cautiousness of government departments and sensitive to the need for information on which future policy choices could be based, the department called for research on a wide range of issues, from taxes and competition policy to labour mobility. Underlying this agenda was the intensifying economic relationship between the two countries and Canada's increasing export dependence on the US. In 2000, Canada's merchandise exports to the US reached 86.1 per cent of total exports, up from 85.5 per cent the previous year. Exports of services also rose. Canada's trade as a share of gross domestic product (GDP) and its trade with the US as a percentage of GDP were the same, at 45.6 per cent. Canadian exports to the US accounted for 18.8 per cent of total US imports in 2000; US exports to Canada were 22.9 per cent of all US exports (DFAIT, 2001: 4, 6-7).

There was concern, moreover, about Canada's attractiveness as a site for foreign direct investment (FDI). As Richard Harris (2001: 6) comments, FDI is essential for growth, particularly in small open economies, but Canada's share of new North American FDI fell from approximately 26 per cent in 1985 to close to 16 per cent 12 years later. By 2000 it was 13 per cent. A recent Industry Canada discussion paper suggests that Canada has made 'scant progress' in attracting foreign investors. Another study concludes that 'Canada is ranked third in a three-horse race', losing ground to both the US and Mexico as a destination for FDI (Toulin, 2002a).

The vulnerabilities of a small country were evident in the latest incarnation of the now ancient dispute about Canadian exports of softwood lumber to the United States. This affair has its roots in complaints by US lumber producers, going all the way back to 1982, that Canadian stumpage fees (the rates provincial governments charge forestry firms for the right to cut timber) were unfair subsidies to production. Canada's position that its lumber producers were not unfairly subsidized was upheld by GATT and the Canada–US Free Trade Agreement (FTA) panels. Despite vindication of its position by panel decision and the existence of a trade agreement that is supposed to promote free rather than managed trade, the softwood lumber fray demonstrates Canadian dependence on the US market and its vulnerability to US trade remedy practices, which thus far have not been tamed by bilateral or multilateral arrangement. In 1996, as a means to buy temporary peace, Canada and the US signed a five-year softwood lumber pact that capped duty-free exports at an annual level of about 15 billion board feet. Exports over this amount would be assessed an export tax. Anticipating the end of this agreement in 2001, US lumber producers filed petitions claiming unfair Canadian subsidies to exports. Once again, the US Department of Commerce upheld their claim and imposed an export tax on Canadian lumber. When the two countries could not reach an agreement to manage levels of Canadian lumber exports to the US by 21 March 2002, the export duties became permanent (Herman, 2001).

Canada adopted two different strategies—one legal, the second involving bilateral talks—in an attempt to resolve the controversy. In January 2002 Canada asked the World Trade Organization (WTO) to expedite the selection of panellists to hear Canada's complaint, begun in December 2001, against the US imposition of duties on imports of Canadian softwood lumber. Canada has also filed two NAFTA challenges under Chapter 19, questioning the countervailing duty portion of the tariffs imposed by the US government on Canadian softwood and the anti-dumping portion of the duties. Both moved ahead when no agreement was reached by the 21 March deadline (Chase and Kennedy, 2002). Officials from both countries worked for many months to find an arrangement that would satisfy all parties, but a deal could not be finalized by the time Chrétien and Bush met in Washington on 14 March (McKenna, 2002), and a temporary resolution buying the negotiators additional time was not possible either (Jack and Morton, 2002).

Energy is highly significant in Canada's exports to the US, and this, too, frequently generates bilateral controversy. Canada remains the largest overall energy trading partner with the US, and is the leading US supplier of oil, natural gas, and electricity. Though overshadowed at the moment by more pressing issues, Bush's determination to ensure US energy security through the development of Arctic oil reserves worries environmentalists throughout North America. Chapter 4 in this volume, by Bruce Doern and Monica Gattinger, points to the domestic Canadian complexities of possible bilateral discussions, noting the demand of Alberta for participation.

The way in which energy relations are unfolding in North America may be a metaphor for the complexities of the broader continental relationship. Clearly, there is a trilateral dimension to the sector, since both Canada and Mexico supply energy to the US. Recognizing that demand and environmental considerations are creating a de facto continental energy market in North America, President Bush, Mexican President Vicente Fox, and Prime Minister Chrétien agreed to form a North American Energy Working Group. Comprised of senior officials from each country, the group met for the first time at the end of June 2001 (DePalma, 2001). At the same time, however, Canada has agreed to co-sponsor, with the US, the first-ever summit of G-8 energy ministers in Detroit in early May 2002. This venue for multilateral discussions will rule out Mexican involvement, reinforcing the recent trend towards bilateral Canada–US co-operation in a range of areas, energy among them (Sands, 2002).

When free trade was debated in the 1980s, opponents argued strongly that a deal with the US would start Canada down the slippery slope to greater continental entanglement. At one level, they were correct: the dynamics generated by free trade agreements have long been understood by analysts of economic integration. The history of integration in Europe demonstrates that domestic stakeholders generally pressure their governments to take steps to ensure that the benefits from the preferential trading arrangement continue, if they are not enhanced. Even prior to the Canada–US Free Trade Agreement, the economic linkages between the two economies were intense and growing more so. The 1989 FTA and then the 1993 NAFTA gave new structure to what was already a clear example of investment-led integration. Nor are trade arrangements between economies with a high degree of interdependence static. Just as it was Canada that proposed the FTA and Mexico the NAFTA, one or both of these states are likely to take the lead in framing the next steps in North American integration. Comments by the Mexican President and his Foreign Minister, Jorge Castenada, illustrate that serious thinking along these lines has begun in that country.

Reflecting a sensitivity to 'the Mexico factor', there was pique at Bush's decision in 2001 to make his first post-election foreign trip to Mexico, not Canada, producing a lightning visit by Chrétien to Washington to pre-empt the President's trip to see Vicente Fox. Anxieties materialized as well that, within a decade, Mexico might overtake Canada as the most important trading partner of the US. In reality, neither of these concerns is very important. More critical are Mexico's heightened ability to make its case in Washington and across the US, a factor emphasized by Andrew Cohen in Chapter 2, and the willingness of American leaders to take a longer-term view of ways in which NAFTA might evolve. Prior to his election, Fox talked of extending NAFTA, and he pressed Chrétien on the issue in a visit to Canada in the summer of 2000 (Teichman, 2001).

Whether the US would be receptive to Mexican proposals for changes to NAFTA is not the issue. In fact, Sands believes (2001a) that the US was strongly committed pre-11 September to trilateralism and to not pushing the pace beyond what Mexico could reasonably manage; however, since that date Washington is clearly prepared to deepen its relationship with Canada beyond that with Mexico, as discussions about the border, energy, and continental defence demonstrate. The top political leadership in Mexico, however, is considering the future of North America and thinking about ways in which NAFTA might be strengthened. Moreover, Mexico is seeking Canadian support in its efforts to promote democracy and improve its economy. Canada may thus have to take some decisions about the importance of Mexico in Canadian foreign policy priorities, decisions that can not be separated from those with respect to Canada–US relations and the future of NAFTA.

In the Age of Integration, more than (Cdn) $1.5 billion in goods traverses the Canada–US border daily, some 70 per cent of it by truck. On 13 September, the lineup waiting to cross the Ambassador Bridge at Windsor–Detroit stretched for 36 kilometres (Hart and Dymond, 2001: 7). Any interruption in border clearance has immediate economic impact in both countries, but because of Canada's trade dependence, there are much more serious consequences for the smaller country. In the auto industry, a sector of enormous importance to both economies, the costs of tighter border security were evident immediately because just-in-time delivery was interrupted. In the week following 11 September, Ford temporarily closed three engine assembly plants in Windsor, and fewer vehicles were produced at Ford's St Thomas, Ontario, location. General Motors and DaimlerChrysler were also affected, although because of poor sales the former had already decided to close its engine plant during the week of 17 September (Brieger, 2001). Across both countries, automakers assembled 47,000 fewer vehicles in September-October than anticipated by their production plans (Kachadourian, 2001).

Firms and industry associations appear to be ahead of the Canadian government with respect to border management. In the months after 11 September, business groups in Canada were active in pressing their concerns to Ottawa about the importance of finding ways to ensure the reliable movement of goods and people. A survey of 250 Canadian chief executive officers in October revealed that three-quarters of those polled were prepared to accept common rules for visitors, immigrants, and refugees if this would protect access to the US market for Canadian exports (Kuitenbrouwer, 2001). A group of more than 45 business associations and companies, the Coalition for Secure and Trade-Efficient Borders, is pushing for a comprehensive bilateral review of the issue. While shying away from the term 'security perimeter' because of its suggestion of an American squeeze, the coalition has put forward a number of proposals, among them common clearance of goods and people at entry points to the continent rather than as they cross the border, customs inspection at the point at which cargo is loaded, and pre-screening of people, freight, and shippers posing a low risk (Coalition, 2001).

The Canadian Trucking Association is an additional lobbyist, and the Big Three auto manufacturers have proposed dedicated lanes and pre-registration for parts shipments and pre-certification of drivers (*Financial Post*, 2001). If firms cannot be assured that their output will reach US customers in a timely manner, Canada's position as a destination for foreign direct investment will decline still further; companies will be reluctant to establish or expand operations in Canada (Coalition, 2001: Appendix 1).

The delays at the border underlined a problem that had long been in evidence. The demands for efficient clearance of trucks and their goods exceed the capacity of the infrastructure, physical and human. The two countries certainly discussed border management strategies pre-11 September, but desultorily, and Canadian officials claimed that the lack of drive was on the US side. The Canada–US Partnership (CUSP) Forum, launched in October 1999 by Chrétien and Clinton, is evidence of official recognition of the importance of the problem, but the December 2000 CUSP Forum report is long on description of the complexities and short on concrete proposals (CUSP, 2001).

With 11 September and the very strong link between prosperity and security that it exposed, both governments turned intently to the border. On 3 December 2001, they issued a Joint Statement of Co-operation on Border Security and Regional Migration. Nine days later, Canada and the US signed a declaration for the creation of 'a Smart Border for the 21st Century' (DFAIT News Release 192). By early March 2002, they were close to an understanding on the most controversial aspects of the 'smart border' program, among them pre-clearance for companies that regularly carry goods across the border by truck. Also agreed upon were joint inspection by Canadian and US customs officials of cargo and containers in five major ports (Vancouver, Montreal, Halifax, Seattle, and Newark), the reintroduction of pre-clearance of passengers travelling to the US by US customs and immigration officials in Vancouver, and the expansion of the NEXUS fast-track border crossing program for frequent travellers at three border crossings in BC, with the expectation that this will be extended to other locations later in 2002 (Trickey, 2002c; Department of State, 2002).

Many Americans, in Congress and the US Justice Department not the least, have become convinced that their northern border was 'very porous' (Miller, 2002) and that Canada did not have the capacity or the will to take security concerns with the seriousness they deserved. Stewart Bell, in his discussion of terrorist fundraising in Chapter 8, maintains that the critics are right. Virtually every major terrorist organization in the world, he asserts, operates in Canada under the nose of an indifferent and negligent government. They use Canada as a base to raise funds, act as a bureaucracy for larger international networks, and hijack cultural institutions and religious groups within Canadian refugee communities. Post-11 September, Ottawa passed anti-terrorism legislation, but 'so late into the game that terrorist groups are now deeply entrenched into Canadian society, so deeply that ridding them from the country may well be impossible'.

Stephen Gallagher, in Chapter 5, connects Bell's analysis to refugee policy, pointing out that there is probably justification for the frequent American charge that 'the openness of Canada's system might be providing a haven and springboard for terrorism.' Despite sophisticated barriers to keep migrants at bay, asylum-seekers who manage to get to Canada are treated benignly. They can stay for extended periods, receive generous social benefits, and are likely to be granted permanent resident status. Gallagher describes a refugee structure that is complex, expensive, and inefficient. It is also highly politicized. The Liberals paint their policies as tolerant and humanitarian in the best Canadian tradition; they garner huge support in ethnic communities; they tread lightly into the refugee arena.

As a consequence of 11 September, the border was transformed into an exigent national defence issue and, inevitably, a problem with continental dimensions as well. Questions of perimeter defence and its military-strategic implications for Canada were not new (Jockel,

2002). What is more novel is the public discussion of joint defence beyond that enshrined in NORAD. The Canadian Forces are clear on the need for a new defence relationship: they and their minister have been engaged in preliminary talks with the US about the possible shape of an integrated continental defence system. From the outset in the 1950s, a Canadian has been deputy commander of NORAD, and that model for continental defence might give Canada a significant role. Other options, such as an arrangement with a regional commander-in-chief for US defence, might not need Canadian participation (Koring and Leblanc, 2002). An early 2002 report in the *Guardian Weekly* referred to a post-11 September Pentagon proposal for a unified 'homeland' defence 'continental command' under which the CF would serve (Borger, 2002). Defence Minister Eggleton is on the record as favouring an integrated NORAD-like defence structure; that is the way to maintain influence, not lose it, he says (Fife and Alberts, 2002; Naumetz, 2002). John Manley is less convinced of the necessity of a single command, 'but if there's a way, maybe I could be persuaded' (Trickey, 2001).

Canada will also have to make a decision on participation in national missile defence (NMD) in the relatively near future, certainly before 2004. Although Eggleton maintains Canada has yet to be asked to join the NMD system, the US is moving to implement it. The control systems for the experimental missile shield are to be installed at the site of the NORAD command in Colorado (Pugliese, 2002a). Dean Oliver, in Chapter 6, notes the necessary caution: there is a deep-seated political animus against closer military integration with the United States.

After 11 September Manley was given the chair of the Cabinet Committee on Security and Counter-Terrorism. The Committee was set up as 'ad hoc' rather than as a permanent one, perhaps to avoid the sense that a World War II-style 'war cabinet' was being created to meet a major emergency. The Committee, made up of the ministers of Transport, Finance, National Defence, Justice, National Revenue, Citizenship and Immigration, Intergovernmental Affairs, and the Solicitor General, is supported by a team of senior deputy ministers, a core group that includes the deputy ministers of Finance, National Defence, Foreign Affairs, Canada Customs and Revenue, Justice, and Citizenship and Immigration, as well as the Director of the Canadian Security and Intelligence Service (CSIS), the Commissioner of the Royal Canadian Mounted Police (RCMP), the

Chief of the Defence Staff, and other senior officials as needed. When Manley was appointed Deputy Prime Minister in the cabinet shuffle of 15 January 2002, he took his responsibilities for security and the border with him.

THE HEMISPHERE AND BEYOND

Foreign Minister Bill Graham, then, may have less manoeuvrability and a more limited set of issues to oversee in the immediate future than any minister since Mark MacGuigan in the early 1980s. This will allow Graham to pursue subjects he believes significant in human security, development, human rights, and the relationship with Latin America, areas less essential than Canada–US relations but nonetheless vital as means to balance and offset the overwhelming force of the continental pull. It is in the diplomacy beyond North America that a strong case can be made that Canada remains a country that matters.

For the first third of 2001, Canada was preoccupied with the hemisphere. Quebec City hosted the Summit of the Americas, the last of a series of summits of hemispheric organizations held in Canada since 1999. Stephen J. Randall, in chapter 11, reviews the history of Canada's involvement in Latin America since it joined the Organization of American States (OAS) in 1989. His is a very positive assessment of Canada's contribution to that body, particularly its unit for the promotion of democracy, and of the part Canada has played in promoting a peaceful change of regimes in Peru. Although activity in the FTAA working groups continues, the hemisphere appeared to recede from Canadian foreign policy priorities after the San José summit of foreign ministers that followed on from the Quebec City meeting.

It is arguable that Canada's ties to the hemisphere are supported more by values than by hard domestic interests. Values are important; they can reinforce, but they cannot build a relationship. Indeed, Latin Americans can quickly grow tired of a discourse that makes a claim for the superiority of Canadian values of peace, order, and moral governance. What remains to be seen is whether the base of support for a sustained connection to the region can be developed, particularly after 11 September, and how Canada will define the next stage in its relationship with the countries of Latin America (Molot, 2001).

Jean Daudelin, in Chapter 12, situates his analysis of the long dispute between Canada and Brazil over subsidies to aircraft production in the context of the different ways in which the two countries have inserted themselves into the global economy. Brazil has opted for global engagement, while Canada has definitively become a North American player. The aircraft dispute could set a pattern for future Canadian commercial quarrels, particularly with developing countries, insofar as the trade relationship could become a hostage to Ottawa's support for its multinational firms. As Canada's continental connection intensifies, its ties with countries outside the region become less significant. This narrowing of the Canadian arena is very damaging, Daudelin suggests, for an already fading power that cherishes its multilateralist tradition.

By contrast, in Chapter 10 John Kirton perceives Canada as a principal power in G-7/8 summitry that engages effectively in the 'diplomacy of concert'. He provides a glowing assessment of Canada's contribution to summit deliberations, arguing that its record in meeting commitments is consistently impressive and that skilful summitry has allowed the country to exercise considerable influence over outcomes. One of the key deliverables at the 2002 summit meeting in Kananaskis, Alberta, in June 2002 is an aid package for Africa. In its December 2001 budget, the Chrétien government announced an increase in foreign aid of $1 billion over the next three years, half of which will be devoted to an 'Africa Fund'. 'Should Canada be able to maintain the momentum', Kirton avers, 'and act as a national principle pioneer to create a new North-South paradigm for development, it would . . . produce a vision for a new global order designed on Canadian ideals.'

It is worthwhile to read this assessment alongside John Foster's sombre discussion of international health in Chapter 9, which focuses on the HIV/AIDS pandemic in Africa and the response of the international community. Foster sees Canada as 'a leader in the global response to the challenge of AIDS': the $150 million over three years pledged by the government ranks favourably with the donations of others (Scoffield, 2001). Yet, overall Canadian spending on development assistance is low, 'far below our capability', and the country's stance is ambiguous at best on the crucial issue of access to essential drugs for the millions of sick and disadvantaged with little money or hope. Foster argues forcefully that health is a human right, and that the international economic system as currently constituted undermines the immune capacity of large populations and restricts the fight against disease in poor populations the world over.

The importance Prime Minister Chrétien attaches to a successful G-8 summit may well have helped shape Canada's stance towards Zimbabwe's rogue government at the early March 2002 Commonwealth heads of government meeting in Australia. Perhaps because of an upcoming April trip to Africa to seek endorsement from some of the continent's leaders for an initiative tying economic assistance to democratic and legal reforms, Chrétien was not prepared to support a summit proposal by Britain, New Zealand, and Australia to impose immediate sanctions against Zimbabwe, whose President Robert Mugabe, an icon of the anti-colonialist movement, was engaged in stealing a national election. Although there was some disagreement about the centrality of his role (Fife, 2002a), Chrétien actively promoted a compromise postponing any decision on sanctions until after the Zimbabwe election of 9–10 March. Canada was prepared to join in the condemnation of Mugabe and cut off all direct bilateral aid to Zimbabwe, but only after a report of a trio of Commonwealth members—South Africa, Nigeria, and Australia—charged with reviewing the election (Sallot, 2002a).

The desire for a blockbuster G-8 meeting at Kananaskis also explains two other spring 2002 Chrétien initiatives. The first was a commitment Canada made at the UN Conference on Financing for Development in Monterrey, Mexico, in late March 2002 to augment Canadian official development assistance (ODA) by at least 8 per cent annually. It is not clear whether this increase in the $2.4 billion budgeted for 2002–3 was planned—reports suggested the PM surprised even his own officials by departing from his prepared text—or whether it will last beyond Chrétien's tenure as Prime Minister (Scoffield, 2002). Without question, Canada was under pressure from other conference participants to be more generous in its ODA, evidence perhaps of John Manley's dictum that Canada has to pay its way to be taken seriously by other major actors.

The second Chrétien undertaking was the trip to Africa, planned to ensure that Canada could come to the G-8 table with evidence of a commitment to reform from heads of major African states. He discussed with a number of African leaders the New Partnership for African Development (NEPAD), an Africa-led proposal (developed by the leaders of Algeria, Nigeria, and South Africa) intended to encourage countries to adopt democratic reforms in exchange for increased aid. The Africans and the G-8 were trying, in advance of Kananaskis, to create a peer review system to determine eligibility for NEPAD funding. Chrétien has put considerable effort into what will be the last summit in Canada under his leadership. Journalist Edward Greenspon was scathing about the Prime Minister's 'fin-de-regime junket to Africa. Helping this misbegotten continent pull itself up by its bootstraps is a laudable enough goal, if one can get past the understandable skepticism that Africa is merely the flavour of the month and that good money will be thrown after bad. But rightly or wrongly, a first-term Mr Chrétien would not have expended this kind of effort on an initiative with such a small political constituency at home. Good works are usually the sign of a leader winding down. Remember Pierre Trudeau's peace initiative? You can bet Mr Chrétien does' (Greenspon, 2002).

The Commonwealth is Canada's oldest multilateral forum, and there is little doubt that this country's role as a facilitator and funder (of one-quarter of the organization's working budgets) has been central to its growth and significance. In Chapter 13, David McIntyre makes Canada's importance clear, but concludes that Chrétien has been less of a Commonwealth activist than previous prime ministers such as Trudeau and Mulroney, who set great store in the sprawling multiracial collection of states of all shapes and sizes and capacities. McIntyre worries that the Commonwealth is avoiding confrontation with its 'basic dilemmas', primary among them the manner in which Mugabe-style violations of Commonwealth principles can be constructively punished. He sees, however, a possibly encouraging shift in institutional balances, with the development of a 'peoples' Commonwealth' threatening to outstrip the 'official Commonwealth' in energy and imagination.

Does the Commonwealth still resonate as an important locus for Canadian foreign policy? If so, was Canada's recent stand, siding with African leaders in opposition to Britain, Australia, and New Zealand over Zimbabwe, a classic application of Canada's curative diplomacy and long-standing unwillingness to see black Africa isolated? Or was short-term peace an expedient only, won at the expense of human rights in Zimbabwe and the legitimacy of the Commonwealth?

As a highly trade-dependent country, Canada has historically been active in the various rounds of negotiations under the GATT and later the WTO. Membership in a range of international groupings—the Quadrilateral Group, the Commonwealth and la Francophonie, the Cairns Group of agricultural exporters—has enabled Canada to take a large share in international trade negotiations. Curtis and Wolfe

(1998: 129) suggest that Canada can build coalitions on international trade issues because its policies occupy 'a middle ground' between those, primarily the US, who champion freer trade and those, led by Europe, who are more interventionist. Thus it was 'no accident' that the creation of the WTO was the result of a Canadian initiative, that of Canada's then Trade Minister, John Crosbie.

The Canadian culture of brokerage was in evidence at ministerial meetings in Doha, Qatar, in November 2001, where the 142 members of the WTO reached agreement to launch a new round of global trade negotiations, to be concluded by 1 January 2005. Trade Minister Pierre Pettigrew, at WTO Director-General Moore's request, was responsible at Doha for co-ordinating discussions on investment, competition policy, transparency in procurement, and trade facilitation. Whether the round is finished on time is less important than agreement on its launch, and following the debacle in Seattle in November 1999, that was by no means certain. The agenda for the new round is ambitious, including negotiations to reduce agricultural subsidies (a victory for the Cairns Group), on services under clear timelines, on trade and the environment, and on anti-dumping, subsidies, and countervailing duties. As well, this round aims to improve the institution's transparency and to assist the developing world to benefit more from the global trading system and adapt to WTO rules at a pace appropriate to needs.

Canada has acted to implement the Doha commitment to help developing countries to prepare for the next round of talks by pledging $1 million to the WTO's Global Trust Fund, one purpose of which is to enhance the negotiating capacity of developing and least-developed countries. The government also contributed $300,000 to the WTO Training Institute, which provides training for officials from the least-developed countries (DFAIT, 2002). The heavy lifting during the next WTO round will be done by the major traders—the US, the European Union (EU), Japan if its economy improves, Brazil and India as leaders of the developing world, and possibly China. However, there may be space for Canada's aptitude for bridge-building, especially in sectors such as agriculture.

Doern and Gattinger note in Chapter 4 that Canada was one of the 150 states signing the 1997 United Nations Framework Convention on Climate Change at Kyoto. The Kyoto Protocol binds industrialized countries to reduce their greenhouse gas emissions by 6 per cent below their 1990 levels over the period 2008–10. Although

Canada prides itself on environmental sensitivity, its participation in a group of states, among them the US, Japan, Australia, and occasionally New Zealand, which have acted to weaken international conventions on climate change, has earned it (to adopt the words of one academic observer) the epithet of an environmental rogue state (Broadhead, 2001). The Chrétien government has indicated that Canada intends to comply with Kyoto, but the date for a decision on ratification is being pushed back. At one point there was talk of an announcement of ratification to coincide with the G-8 summit (Mittelstaedt, 2002), but by the end of March 2002 the goal was simply a 'ratification decision in 2002' (Toulin, 2002c).

If Canada decides to ratify the accord, fulfilling the Kyoto commitments will not be easy. Because Canada has done almost nothing thus far to reduce its greenhouse gas emissions, the level of reductions now required to meet Kyoto is far higher than it was in the late 1990s. Moreover, the provinces disagree about the implementation of Kyoto, with Alberta and Ontario the most critical of its terms. Environment Minister David Anderson has said the 'provinces can't stop Kyoto' (Toulin, 2002c), meaning that they cannot prevent Ottawa from deciding to ratify the agreement. The federal-provincial division of powers, however, mandates that provincial co-operation will be needed to develop and implement Kyoto's policies. Canadian industry opposes Kyoto ratification, fearing that the added costs necessary to meet the target will make Canadian exports less competitive in the US (Toulin and Benzie, 2002). Adding to the pressures on governmental decision-making are the opposing positions of the EU, which has indicated it is prepared to be bound by Kyoto, and George Bush's US, which refuses to adhere to the treaty.

AS URGENCY FADES

The terrorist attacks of 11 September shattered the myth that North America was invulnerable to serious attack. The challenges for Canadian foreign policy intensified dramatically as a result of the events of that day, and they were put into much stronger relief: military and intelligence capabilities, terrorism, refugees, development assistance, and, at the heart of it all, the full panoply of the Canadian–American relationship. Led by then Foreign Minister Manley, academics, and some members of the press, Canadians debated the nature of their foreign policy and the country's capacity to fulfill its international obligations. Issues of sovereignty, the border, and the gap between international commitment and national will were all suddenly and intensely part of the public conversation.

By early 2002, however, the urgency had dwindled. Warnings of another Al-Qaeda attack became commonplace, part of the background noise of busy North American lives. It was still frequently said that the world had changed irrevocably on 11 September, but just what that meant was difficult to articulate, as were the extent and implications of the threats to Canada of a new kind of international conflict. Barebones stories about Canadian Forces personnel serving in Afghanistan generated only limited interest, particularly when suicide bombers in Israel and an Israeli incursion into the territory of the Palestinian Authority grabbed hearts and headlines.

Reviews of foreign policy and defence are underway, but such documents have rarely lived up to their billing as serious expressions of Canadian interests. They are often redundant on publication and, because of the politics of their preparation, rarely inspire the making of hard choices (Malone, 2001). The Prime Minister seems permanently on the road, having tripled his expenditure on foreign travel over his years in power to $12.7 million (*Public Accounts Canada*, 1995–2001), and it is unclear how much authority and resources Deputy Prime Minister Manley has in his absence to get on with the tough planning and hard thinking that have been missing, Lloyd Axworthy apart, from Canadian statecraft. Manley's replacement as Foreign Minister by Bill Graham in January 2002 has hinted at a return to the old verities of Canadian policy, with perhaps less attention being paid to the new and crucial Canada–US relationship.

If exigency has departed, anxiety has not. By the standard of the Golden Age, Canadian diplomacy has long been in decline. That halcyon period left its mark, firmly embedding foreign policy as an ideal and a symbol, part of a modern Canadian identity. However, as Peter Dobell (1972: 143–4) has written sagely, 'many Canadians came to believe that their country was uniquely qualified to mediate the world's problems and to act as the planet's conscience'; and when the remarkable attainments of the immediate post-war years dried up, 'politicians began to try to substitute artful pretense for that which had formerly come naturally.'

Through the long Cold War, Canadian leaders struggled to keep up with their reputation while maintaining an uneasy balance between national independence and North American partnership.

The 1990s were a hard decade, with the recrudescence of American power, civil strife in Africa and the Balkans, rampaging North American integration, and an economy that never seemed robust. The aftermath of 11 September brought out all the doubters. Roy MacGregor (2002) said it well: 'For Canada, it was almost as if it had sailed through a radioactive fog and become The Incredible Shrinking Country—at least in perspective, if not in fact.' John Manley, indeed, became his own government's most trenchant critic, underscoring the seriousness of the problem and the pressing necessity of a realistic assessment of Canada's diplomatic constraints and capabilities.

NOTE

We thank the Social Sciences and Humanities Research Council for the support of relevant research, and necessarily anonymous government officials for granting us interviews about their work. Grant Dawson, Hector Mackenzie, Ryan Shackleton, Susan Whitney, and Greg Wigmore provided much helpful information.

REFERENCES

Alberts, Sheldon. 2002. 'Review Takes Aim at Defence, Foreign Policy', *National Post*, 23 Feb., A6.

Andrew, Arthur. 1993. *The Rise and Fall of a Middle Power: Canadian Diplomacy from King to Mulroney*. Toronto: James Lorimer & Company.

Blanchfield, Mike. 2002. 'Canadian Warships Take Prisoners in Al-Qaeda Hunt', *Ottawa Citizen*, 2 Mar., A1-2.

Blatchford, Christie. 2001. 'Our Heroes Suffer, Even Before Leaving', *National Post*, 18 Oct., A9.

Bliss, Michael. 2001. 'Is Canada a Country in Decline?', *National Post*, 30 Nov., A18.

Borger, Julian. 2002. 'Canada Gripped by a New Identity Crisis', *Guardian Weekly*, 28 Feb.–6 Mar., 6.

Broadhead, Lee-Anne. 2001. 'Canada as a Rogue State', *International Journal* 56, 3 (Summer): 461–80.

Brieger, Peter. 2001. 'Auto Sector's Outlook Turns Bleak, Experts Say', *Financial Post*, 4 Oct., B6.

Canada-US Partnership Forum (CUSP). *Building a Border for the 21st Century*. 2001. A report submitted to President William J. Clinton and Prime Minister Jean Chrétien by Secretary of State Madeleine K. Albright and Foreign Minister John Manley, US Department of State, Bureau of Western Hemisphere Affairs. Available at: <http://www.state.gov/www/regions/wha0012_cusp_report.html>.

Chapnick, Adam. 2000. 'The Canadian Middle Power Myth', *International Journal* 55, 2 (Spring): 188–206.

Chase, Stephen, and Peter Kennedy. 2002. 'Canada Files Second NAFTA Challenge in Softwood Row', *Globe and Mail*, 28 Feb., B9.

Clark, Joe. 1997. "'The First International Country'", *International Journal* 52, 4 (Autumn): 539–45.

Coalition for Secure and Trade-Efficient Borders. 2001. *Rethinking Our Borders: A Plan for Action*. Ottawa, 3 Dec.

Cohen, Andrew. 1994. 'The Diplomats Make a Comeback', *Globe and Mail*, 19 Nov., D1-2.

———. 1995. 'Canada in the World: The Return of the National Interest', Canadian Institute of International Affairs, *Behind the Headlines* (Summer).

———. 2001. 'The Ghost of Canada Past', *Ottawa Citizen*, 4 Dec., A15.

Cooper, Andrew. 2000. 'Waiting at the Perimeter: Making US Policy in Canada', in Maureen Appel Molot and Fen O. Hampson, eds, *Canada Among Nations 2000: Vanishing Borders*. Toronto: Oxford University Press, 27–46.

Copeland, Daryl. 2001. 'The Axworthy Years: Canadian Foreign Policy in the Era of Diminished Capacity', in Fen Osler Hampson, Norman Hillmer, and Maureen Appel Molot, eds, *Canada Among Nations 2001. The Axworthy Legacy*. Toronto: Oxford University Press, 152–72.

Cruikshank, John. 1994. 'Diplomatic Mettle', *Globe and Mail*, 26 Feb.

Curtis, John, and Robert Wolfe. 1999. 'Providing Leadership for the Trade Regime', in Fen Osler Hampson and Maureen Appel Molot, eds, *Canada Among Nations 1998: Leadership and Dialogue*. Toronto: Oxford University Press, 119–42.

Dawson, Grant. 2001. 'Fading Here, Fading There? Some Thoughts on Canada's International Role in 2001', paper prepared for the Canada Among Nations 2002 Workshop, Carleton University, 13–14 Dec.

Department of National Defence (DND), Directorate of Policy Development. 2001. 'Canadian Armed Forces Total Military Strength 1960–2000'.

Department of Foreign Affairs and International Trade (DFAIT). 2001a. *Trade Update 2001: Second Annual Report on Canada's State of Trade*. May.

———. 2001b. 'Canada and the United States Sign Smart Border Declaration', News Release 162, 12 Dec. Available at: <http://www.dfait-maeci.gc.c.>.

———. 2002. 'Canada Contributes $1.3 million in Trade-Related Assistance to Developing Countries', News Release 25, 10 Mar. Available at: <http://www.dfait-maeci.gc.ca>.

DePalma, Anthony. 2001. 'From Alberta, Energy's Good Guy (and Bad Guy)', *New York Times*, 14 Aug., electronic edition.

Dewitt, David B., and John J.Kirton. 1983. *Canada as a Principal Power: A Study of Foreign Policy and International Relations*. Toronto: John Wiley and Sons.

Dobell, Peter C. 1972. *Canada's Search for New Roles: Foreign Policy in the Trudeau Era*. London: Oxford University Press.

The Economist. 1953. 'Canada's Diplomats', 166, 17 Jan., 154–5.

Eayrs, James. 1961. *The Art of the Possible: Government and Foreign Policy in Canada*. Toronto: University of Toronto Press.

———. 1975. 'Defining a New Place for Canada in the Hierarchy of World Power', *International Perspectives* (May–June): 16–25.

———. 1980. *In Defence of Canada: Growing Up Allied*. Toronto: University of Toronto Press.

English, John. 1998. '"A Fine Romance": Canada and the United Nations, 1943–1957', in Greg Donaghy, ed., *Canada and the Early Cold War, 1943–1957*. Ottawa: Department of Foreign Affairs and International Trade.

Fife, Robert. 2002a. 'Zimbabwe "Bloodbath" Predicted', *National Post*, 5 Mar., A1, A15.

———. 2002b. 'No More Money for Defence: PM', *National Post*, 19 Mar., A1, A13.

——— and Sheldon Alberts. 2002. 'Eggleton Pushes for Joint Defence', *National Post*, 31 Jan., A1, A8.

Financial Post. 2001. 'Big Three Propose Border Solutions', 6 Nov., FP8.

Foot, Richard. 2001. 'Sailors' Families Line Docks as Warships Head Out', *National Post*, 18 Oct., A9.

Freeman, Alan. 2002. 'Canada Shuns Minor Peace Role', *Globe and Mail*, 4 Jan., A1, A7.

Gee, Marcus. 2002. 'Canada's Peacekeeper Image a Myth', *Globe and Mail*, 4 Jan., A6.

Graham, Bill. 2002. 'Affirming Canadian Sovereignty in an Independent World', speech at Canadian Institute of International Affairs, Toronto, 4 Apr. DFAIT E-mail Subscription Service.

Greenspon, Edward. 2002. 'On Jean's Watch: Third-Termitis', *Globe and Mail*, 6 Apr., A15.

Haglund, David. 2000. *The North Atlantic Triangle Revisited: Canadian Grand Strategy at Century's End*. Toronto: Canadian Institute of International Affairs/Irwin Publishing, Contemporary Affairs Number 4.

Hampson, Fen Osler, and Dean F. Oliver. 1998. 'Pulpit Diplomacy: A Critical Assessment of the Axworthy Doctrine', *International Journal* 53, 3 (Summer): 379–407.

Handelman, Stephen. 2001–2. 'Border Guardian', *Time*, 31 Dec.–7 Jan., 65–73.

Harris, Richard G. 2001. *North American Economic Integration: Issues and Research Agenda*. Ottawa: Industry Canada Research Publications Program, May.

Hart, Michael, and William Dymond. 2001. *Common Borders, Shared Destinies: Canada, the United States and Deepening Integration*. Ottawa: Centre for Trade Policy and Law, Carleton University.

Herman, Lawrence L. 2001. 'Softwood Lumber: The Next Phase', *Backgrounder*. Toronto: C.D. Howe Institute, 6 Dec.

Hillmer, Norman, and Adam Chapnick. 2001. 'The Axworthy Revolution', in Fen Osler Hampson, Norman Hillmer, and Maureen Appel Molot, eds, *Canada Among Nations 2001: The Axworthy Legacy*. Toronto: Oxford University Press, 67–88.

Ignatieff, George. 1985. *The Memoirs of George Ignatieff: The Making of a Peacemonger*. Toronto: University of Toronto Press.

Jack, Ian, and Peter Morton. 2002. 'Summit Seen as Softwood War Truce', *Financial Post*, 7 Mar., FP7.

Jockel, Joseph T. 2000. 'US National Missile Defense, Canada and the Future of NORAD', in Maureen Appel Molot and Fen O. Hampson, eds, *Canada Among Nations 2000: Vanishing Borders*. Toronto: Oxford University Press, 73–92.

Kachadourian, Gail. 2001. 'Shutdowns Likely to Continue', *Automotive News*, 17 Sept., 1, 43.

Koring, Paul. 2002. 'Is PM Changing His Mind on Waging War Against Iraq?', *Globe and Mail*, 15 Mar., A9.

———— and Daniel Leblanc. 2002. 'Canada Aims to Join "Americas Command"', *Globe and Mail*, 29 Jan., A1, A4.

Kuitenbrouwer, Peter. 2001. 'Perimeter Will Save Trade: CEOs', *National Post*, 29 Oct., A1–2.

Laghi, Brian. 2001. 'Disrepair in Military Deplored', *Globe and Mail*, 5 Dec., A1, A9.

Little, Bruce. 2002. 'Tech Spending Narrows Productivity Gap with U.S.', *Globe and Mail*, 2 Mar., B4.

Lyon, Peyton V., and Brian W. Tomlin. 1979. *Canada as an International Actor*. Toronto: Macmillan.

McCall, Christina. 1985. 'End of an Era', *Saturday Night* (June): 49–52.

MacGregor, Roy. 2002. 'Canada Is Just Like High School', *National Post*, 19 Jan., B5.

McKenna, Barrie. 2002. 'Lumber Deal Pledged', *Globe and Mail*, 15 Mar., A9.

Mackenzie, Hector M. 2001. 'Appointment to Level in the Foreign Service of Canada: Historical Background', paper presented at conference of L'École nationale d'administration publique, 'The Administration of Foreign Affairs: A Renewed Challenge?', Hull, Que., 1–3 Nov.

Malone, David. 2001. 'Foreign Policy Reviews Reconsidered', *International Journal* 56, 4 (Autumn): 555–78.

Martin, Sandra. 2002. 'Flamboyant MP Takes His Post and Prepares to Represent Canada before the World', *Globe and Mail*, 22 Jan., A4.

Mittelstaedt, Martin. 2002. 'Canada May Ratify Kyoto Accord by June', *Globe and Mail*, 7 Feb., A11.

Miller, Bill. 2002. 'Plugging a Very Porous Northern Border', *Washington Post*, 8 April.

Molot, Maureen Appel. 2001. 'Canadá y América Latina: amigos por siempre?', *Foreign Affairs en Español* 1, 3 (Otono-Invierono): 126–40.

———— and Hampson, Fen O., 2000. 'Does the 49th Parallel Matter Any More?', in Fen O. Hampson and Maureen Appel Molot, eds, *Canada Among Nations 2000: Vanishing Borders*. Toronto: Oxford University Press, 1–23.

National Post. 2002. Editorial, 'Axworthy's Heir?', 23 Jan., on-line version.

National Post Business. 2002. 'The Weakest Link?', Jan., 74.

Naumetz, Tim. 2002. 'Canada Begins Talks with US over Joint Defence', *National Post*, 9 Feb., A2.

Nguyen, Lily. 2002. '66% Back Canada's War Role,' *Globe and Mail*, 14 Jan., A1, A8.

Nossal, Kim Richard. 1998–9. 'Pinchpenny Diplomacy: The Decline of "Good International Citizenship" in Canadian Foreign Policy', *International Journal* 54, 1 (Winter): 88–105.

Ottawa Citizen. 2002. 'Short Cuts', B7.

Public Accounts Canada. 1995–2001. Volume II, part 2.

Pugliese, David. 2002a. 'U.S. to Install Missile Shield at NORAD Base', *National Post*, 2 Mar., A2.

————. 2002b. '"No Need" to Replace Jets for MPs', *Ottawa Citizen*, 6 Apr., A1, A14.

Reid, Escott. 1967. 'Canadian Foreign Policy, 1967–1977: A Second Golden Decade?', *International Journal* 22, 2 (Spring): 171–81.

————. 1989. *Radical Mandarin: The Memoirs of Escott Reid*. Toronto: University of Toronto Press.

Sallot, Jeff. 2002a. 'PM Gets Tough with Mugabe', *Globe and Mail*, 15 Mar., A1, A7.
———. 2002b. 'Graham Pushes Nuclear Cutbacks', *Globe and Mail*, 20 Mar., A17.
Sands, Christopher. 2001a. Testimony before the Standing Committee on Foreign Affairs and International Trade, Minutes of Proceedings, Meeting No. 45, 27 Nov.
———. 2001b. 'The Relevance of Borders in North America', presentation to the Canada Among Nations 2002 Workshop, Carleton University, 13 Dec.
———. 2002. 'Canada', *Hemisphere Highlights Americas Program* 1, 3 (Mar.) Washington: Center for Security and International Studies.
Savoie, Donald. 1999. 'The Rise of Court Government in Canada', *Canadian Journal of Political Science* 32, 4 (Dec.): 635–64.
Schwanen, Daniel. 2000. 'Catching Up Is Hard To Do: Thinking About the Canada-US Productivity Gap', in Maureen Appel Molot and Fen O. Hampson, eds, *Canada Among Nations 2000: Vanishing Borders*. Toronto: Oxford University Press, 117–44.
Scoffield, Heather. 2001. 'Canada Set to Donate $150-millions for AIDS', *Globe and Mail*, 11 July, A1, A5.
———. 2002. 'Canada Boosts Aid to Poor Countries', *Globe and Mail*, 22 Mar., A8.
Simpson, Jeffrey. 2001. 'The Peaceable Kingdom Abroad', *Globe and Mail*, 22 Aug., A13.
Sjolander, Claire Turenne. 1997. 'International Trade as Foreign Policy: "Anything for a Buck"', in Gene Swimmer, ed., *How Ottawa Spends 1997–98. Seeing Red: A Liberal Report Card*. Ottawa: Carleton University Press.
Stairs, Denis. 1974. *The Diplomacy of Constraint: Canada, the Korean War and the United States*. Toronto: University of Toronto Press.
———. 2001a. 'Canada in the 1990s: Talk Loudly and Carry a Bent Twig', *Policy Options* (Jan.–Feb.): 43–9.
———. 2001b. 'The Changing Office and Changing Environment of the Minister of Foreign Affairs in the Axworthy Era', in Fen O. Hampson, Norman Hillmer, and Maureen Appel Molot, eds, *Canada Among Nations 2001: The Axworthy Legacy*. Toronto: Oxford University Press, 19–38.
Statistics Canada. 2000. 'Income Inequality in North America: Does the 49th Parallel Still Matter?' Available at: <http://www.statcan.ca>.
Teichman, Judith. 2001. 'Mexico under Vicente Fox: What Can Canada Expect?', in Fen O. Hampson, Norman Hillmer, and Maureen Appel Molot, eds, *Canada Among Nations 2001: The Axworthy Legacy*. Toronto: Oxford University Press, 270–93.
Toulin, Alan. 2002a. 'Closer Ties to U.S. Needed to Attract Capital: Study', *National Post*, 15 Feb., A6.
———. 2002b. 'We're "Third" in a 3-Horse Race: Ottawa', *National Post*, 14 Feb., A1, A12.
———. 2002c. 'Canada Won't Buckle to Kyoto Pressure: Minister', *Financial Post*, 30 Mar., FP8.
——— and Robert Benzie. 2002. 'Kyoto Plan is "Foolish": Chamber', *National Post*, 4 Mar., A1, A8.
Trickey, Mike. 2001. '"We Have a Better Image than We Deserve"', *Ottawa Citizen*, 26 Dec., A1–2.

————. 2002a. 'New Foreign Minister's Views Fall between Those of Predecessors', *Ottawa Citizen*, 25 Jan., A5.

————. 2002b. 'Defence, Foreign Affairs Rift Grows over U.S. Plan', *National Post*, 30 Jan., A6.

————. 2002c. 'Canada, U.S. Close in on Smart Border', *National Post*, 9 Mar., FP8.

United States, Department of State. 2002. White House Hails Progress with Canada on Smart Border Action Plan: Program for low-risk travelers to be expanded by summer of 2002. Washington File, 8 Mar. Available at: <http://www. usembassycanada.gov/content/content.asp?section=can_usa&subsection1= borderissues&document=borderissues_030802>.

Walker, William. 1999. 'PM Seeks Freer Trade in Americas', *Toronto Star*, 30 June, A1.

Ward, Barbara. 1970. 'The First International Nation', in William Kilbourn, ed., *Canada: A Guide to the Peaceable Kingdom*. Toronto: Macmillan, 45–8.

Wells, Paul (with files from Sheldon Albert). 2001. 'We Don't Pull Our Weight: Manley', *National Post*. 5 Oct., on-line version.

————. 2002. 'What is the Worth of Canadian Sovereignty?', *National Post*, 5 Jan., B2.

2

Canadian–American Relations: Does Canada Matter in Washington? Does It Matter If Canada Doesn't Matter?

ANDREW COHEN

On 20 September 2001, George Walker Bush appeared before a Joint Session of Congress to deliver the most important speech of his fledgling presidency. Nine days earlier, on 11 September, the United States had come under terrorist attack in Washington and New York City, causing a loss of life unseen on its soil on a single day since the Civil War. Suddenly, America was at war, and the somnolent, leaden-tongued Bush was commander-in-chief, mourner-in-chief, and orator-in-chief. His address had several purposes: to comfort a stunned people innocent of terrorism; to show his resolve to find and destroy the sponsors; to thank friends and rally neutrals, trying to consolidate the fragile coalition the United States was forging to prosecute this new, unfamiliar war.

Bush had delayed his appearance, worried about tone and timing. His speech writers had not begun to craft the speech that would define his presidency until two days earlier. Yet there he was, at nine o'clock that Tuesday evening, standing in the well of the House of Representatives, reading those 6,107 carefully chosen words. The hope, at least for this momentous evening, was to turn George Bush into Winston Churchill, mobilizing the English language and sending it into battle, as John Kennedy once put it.

The President ran down his rhetorical checklist. Salute the courage and charity of the American people. Pay homage to the leadership and unity of their lawmakers. Issue a call to arms to the civilized world. Assure Muslims this is not about them. Proclaim measures for 'Homeland Security' and introduce the man to implement them. Exude confidence. Show resolve. Invoke the law. Don the vestments of morality and rectitude. Thunder 'freedom and fear at war' and declare 'God isn't neutral.'

Bush reserved a few of the 41 minutes of the speech to acknowledge the outpouring of sympathy from abroad. Americans would remember the playing of 'The Star-Spangled Banner' at Buckingham Palace in London, he said, on the streets of Paris, and at the Brandenburg Gate in Berlin. They would remember Korean children praying outside the American Embassy in Seoul, Egyptians at a mosque in Cairo, and moments of silence in Australia, Africa, and South America.

Bush went on to name many of the 80 countries whose citizens had died in the collapse of the World Trade Center: 'dozens of Pakistanis; more than 130 Israelis; more than 250 people from India; men and women from El Salvador, Iran, Mexico, and Japan; hundreds of British citizens'. He then saluted Tony Blair, the Prime Minister of Great Britain, who was seated in the Visitors' Gallery next to the First Lady.

'America has no truer friend than Great Britain', Bush said. 'Once again, we are joined together in a great cause—so honored that the British Prime Minister has crossed an ocean to show his unity of purpose with America. Thank you for coming, friend' (Bush, 2001).

So there it was. Points made, bases covered, message sent. Mr Bush stepped down to a rapturous ovation and glowing reviews. Well, not from everywhere. Amid all the hosannas, there was one gnawing question for those 31 million souls watching from the other side of 'the 49th parallel': What about Canada? Bush had not mentioned Canada, America's ally and neighbour, even as he thanked a dozen others. Paris and London we could understand;

Pakistan, Egypt, and India, too. But El Salvador? Japan? Iran? Mexico? 'No truer friend' than Britain? Oh, Canada, ignored and insulted. How had it come to this?

The Great Snub was sure to raise a fuss in Canada and it did. To a people lacking in self-confidence, this could only be deliberate. The opposition in Parliament thought so; it argued that the United States was unhappy that Prime Minister Jean Chrétien had not offered uncategorical support on 11 September, especially in his ambivalence on invoking Article Five of the North Atlantic Treaty. Ignoring Canada, they said, was a subtle rebuke.[1]

Among Canadians, though, the response was incredulity. After all, Canada had taken in some 33,000 passengers from 224 flights diverted north when the United States closed its air space. In cities across the country, Canadians fed and housed their guests, sometimes for days. In Gander, Newfoundland, for example, 12,000 visitors descended on a community of 10,000 (DFAIT, 2001). On 14 September, an estimated 100,000 people gathered on Parliament Hill in Ottawa to show their solidarity. Canadians raised money, waved the Stars and Stripes, and gave blood. Brigades of firemen and policemen went to New York City to comb the ruins of the World Trade Center. Newspapers urged solidarity. 'Let's rally round our American friends', editorialized the *Globe and Mail* on 13 September.

The Americans, realizing the affront, moved quickly to contain the damage. The day after the speech Colin Powell, the Secretary of State, heaped lavish praise on Canada in the presence of John Manley, then Minister of Foreign Affairs. A few days later, when Bush met Chrétien at the White House, the President outdid his Secretary. 'I didn't necessarily think it was important to praise a brother', the President explained. 'After all, we're talking about family. There should be no doubt in anybody's mind about how honoured we are to have the support of Canadians, and how strong the Canadian Prime Minister has been.' Taking aim at Chrétien's critics at home, Bush added: 'I suggest those who try to play politics with my words and drive wedges between Canada and me [should] understand that at this time, when nations are under attack, now is not the time for politics' (Diebel, 2001: A1). That was that, then. Canada was family, immediate rather than extended. When tossing bouquets, you don't need to praise family, do you?

Bush's warm assurances may have soothed the *amour propre* of Canadians and silenced the critics. When it was over, there were two truths to ponder. The first is that the ripple in Canadian–American relations in September was different from the one in January, when Bush decided to visit Mexico before Canada, which appeared to reverse tradition. At root, did it really matter who visited whom when? Seen in that light, the contretemps then said more about our insecurity than their insensitivity. Ultimately, though, it was our problem, and we'd have to get over it.

The second time, though, it said more about them than about us. By the same logic that would make it their problem, but of course, given the asymmetrical nature of the relationship, it is still our problem. Ultimately, as junior partner, whatever the Americans think of us is always our problem.

The second truth is that the 'slight' was most likely an oversight, whatever the fantasists said. In a lengthy analysis published in the *New York Times*, D.T. Max wrote: 'Only the Canadians, of all people, were piqued. their mention, as part of the OAS, was cut so the speech wouldn't sag' (Max, 2001). Indeed, Canada may never have been mentioned by name in any draft of a seminal speech that was given an 'extraordinary going over', vetted by the State Department, the National Security Council, and the White House. If the Americans were concerned about offending allies, apparently Canada was not among them.

The speech was not a rebuke, as the critics said, but a reflection of Canada's loss of stature in Washington, the hub of the universe, where we are there but not there. As Joe Clark, the leader of the Conservative Party, put it. 'I wouldn't consider this a snub. I consider it, in fact, an indication that Canada is off the radar screen.'

The speech is important only in so much as it is a tidy, telling metaphor of a shifting relationship. If the association between Canada and the United States remains special, which is what it was once called, it may now be becoming less special. Canada has always struggled for attention in Washington, but it will now have to work harder to remain on 'the radar screen'. The danger is that as Canada fades as a power in the world—in the reach of its military, the impact of its foreign aid, the influence of its diplomacy, the absence of foreign intelligence-gathering—it risks becoming a fading presence in Washington, too.

It is not unusual for Canadians to worry about their standing with Americans; it is a function of who we are, who they are, and the disparity between us. The US is a superpower, stronger now than at any time in its history of 225 years. The American Empire dominates the world unlike any empire since Rome. Economically, militarily, diplomatically, culturally, and technologically, it has no equal. No one even comes close.

Canada is a middle power, a regional power without a region, as someone pointedly put it. As the US grows stronger in the world, Canada becomes relatively weaker. Its military, among the world's largest at the end of World War II, is now among the smallest of industrialized nations; as a peacekeeper, under the auspices of the United Nations, it has fallen from being one of the world's most active peacekeepers to way down the list among nations in its contribution of personnel and material support(Gee, 2002: 6). Its foreign aid, once an emblem of pride, has plunged to 0.24 per cent of gross domestic product, one of the lowest of the nations of the OECD (Trickey, 2001b: A10). Its diplomatic service, once considered among the world's best, has been diluted by underfunding and the loss of senior officers. Despite successes in recent years—such as brokering democracy in Peru or helping ban the spread of landmines—Canada is no longer the force it was the post-war era, especially under Lester Pearson. As for its foreign intelligence-gathering, it has none at all (see Chapter 8, this volume).

That the United States is a superpower while Canada is not does not in itself marginalize Canada in Washington. That may make us less visible there, perhaps, especially as a military partner or a gatherer of intelligence. But the threat to our presence in Washington—that danger of falling off 'the radar screen', as Joe Clark put it—probably has more to do with a clutch of other factors. Let us consider them.

ECONOMIC

Canada and the United States have the largest commercial relationship in the world. The value of trade between the two countries was $412 billion (US) in 2000, or $1.1 billion a day, and this figure was likely to increase by about 10 per cent in 2002. With the exception of some highly publicized disputes like softwood lumber, the commercial relationship is without acrimony, which is remarkable considering the exponential increase in the volume of goods and services crossing the border in recent years (USTR, 1999: 6.).

The danger for Canada is that 85 per cent of its exports go to the United States, an increase from about two-thirds a quarter-century ago. At the same time, only about 25 per cent of US exports go to Canada. It means that Canada has to care more about its interests in Washington—always worried about the rise of a protectionist Congress—than Washington has to care about its interests in Canada, which is not to say that its trade and investment in Canada are not significant. They are, especially in some sectors, but such trade and investment are not necessarily fundamental to America's material well-being.

Moreover, there are signs that commerce between Canada and the US may be overtaken by commerce between Mexico and the US. Between 1994 and 1999 US exports to Mexico increased by 70 per cent and to Canada by 45 per cent. Imports from Mexico increased 121 per cent and from Canada by 54 per cent. In other words, Canada is in danger of losing its status as the largest trading partner of the world's most formidable economy. The consequences of this are uncertain, but it could weaken our latitude in Washington.

POLITICAL

If Canada is worried about its prominence in Washington, it begins with the political leadership. While George Bush has learned much about the world in his first year in office—as almost all presidents do—his natural inclination, when thinking about North America, is to look toward Central America. When Bush chose to visit Mexico and its new President, Vicente Fox, before he visited Canada, it was because he was governor of a southwestern state that borders Mexico and is home to millions of its natives. Indeed, whatever Bush knew initially about foreign policy was shaped by what he knew about Mexico and his relationship with Fox, who was Governor of Guadalajara when the American President was Governor of Texas.

What Bush knew about Canada before coming to office was said to be minimal, presumably shaped by his exposure to Brian Mulroney, who in all likelihood had little nice to say about Jean Chrétien. Chrétien, by contrast, maintained a close relationship with Bill Clinton in the seven years and a half years their terms of office coincided, a warmth that Chrétien will be hard-pressed to replicate with Bush.

In political terms, then, Canada has geography and history against it in Bush's Washington. The President came to office knowing less about Canada than Mexico, which is now led by a friend. And if the past is any measure, the President is not likely to have a close relationship with the Prime Minister because Liberal prime ministers and Republican presidents seldom do, though it is not always so.

That notwithstanding, Bush and Chrétien have apparently established a good working relationship. Certainly there are similarities in style and temperament; both are folksy, instinctive, and inarticulate, unencumbered by great vision or big ideas. Neither has been accused of being an intellectual. Both are plain and practical.

In Bush's first year in office, Canada and the United States disagreed on softwood lumber, drilling for oil in Alaska, national missile defence (NMD), and the Kyoto Treaty on global warming. But after 11 September, in the face of the anti-terrorism agenda, those differences have seemed to fade in prominence. In the anti-terrorism effort, Mexico is a minor international player of little help to the United States. For its part, Canada tried to be a significant participant in the American-led anti-terrorism campaign.

The other threat to Canada's stature in Washington is Congress. While the Democrats control the Senate, the Republicans control the House of Representatives. Many of its leaders are from the Southwest, where economic and political power has shifted markedly. Increasingly, the centre of political gravity in the United States lies not in the Northeast but in the Sunbelt—in states such as Texas, Arizona, Louisiana, and New Mexico—all of which look to the southern hemisphere. It is not accidental, either, that four of the last five presidents have come from the South: George W. Bush (Texas), Bill Clinton (Arkansas), George H.W. Bush (Texas), Jimmy Carter (Georgia). Al Gore, who nearly became president in 2001, is from Tennessee, and John McCain, who pressed Bush for the nomination of the Republican Party, is from Arizona.

DEMOGRAPHY

Another danger for Canada in the United States is the rise of Hispanic Americans. Latinos from Mexico and from Central and South America are displacing black Americans as the country's largest visible minority and as a new electoral force. Of those, an estimated four to five million come from Mexico (Rodriguez, 2002: 6).

The government of Mexico takes its expatriates seriously. It has appointed a special envoy with joint citizenship to represent them in the United States and created a huge diplomatic presence to promote its economic and political interests. Beyond its embassy in Washington, Mexico has 47 consulates and offices, some in little-known places such as Calexico, California, and Douglas, Arizona. While many address immigration exclusively, Mexico's legations serve a vocal, visible diaspora. Mexican Americans are becoming so significant politically in the Southwest that both Republicans and Democrats courted them intensely in the 2000 presidential election, an effort that will intensify in 2004 and beyond.

In contrast, the estimated 680,000 Canadians living in the US are largely assimilated. Beyond its soaring neo-classical embassy in Washington, which occupies the most prestigious spot in the imperial capital, Canada has consulates in New York, Los Angeles, Atlanta, Boston, Chicago, Dallas, and San Francisco. On the map of the United States, there is really no contest in representation; the sombrero far outnumbers the Maple Leaf.

MILITARY

The United States does not rely on Canada as a military power, which is just as well, because Canada can offer little help anyway. The decline of Canada's armed forces is beyond dispute except by the generals who bravely lift their heads out of their foxholes to dismiss yet another mocking report. All observers reach the same sad conclusion: Canada's forces are ill-equipped, undermanned, and underfunded. The government is increasing military spending, but it would not be enough to arrest decades of erosion.

A weak military means that Canada can make only modest contributions to international coalitions, such as the ones formed in the Persian Gulf, Kosovo, and Afghanistan. In terms of peacekeeping, which was one of its foremost military roles, it is no longer as prominent as it was. The United States knows this and lives with it. Washington was happy to enlist Canada in the war in Afghanistan if only to say, for diplomatic consumption, that it had an international coalition; in truth, militarily, it would have preferred to act alone (Friedman, 2002: 15). Still, the absence of military clout hurts our credibility in America. Tony Blair was taken seriously when he made a ringing statement of support for the US on 11 September not only because he felt keenly the moral issue at stake, but because he could supply troops. He could put his military where his mouth was. In contrast, Jean Chrétien could not field an expeditionary force. That seemed to come through in his fumbling response to the news from New York. He equivocated on NATO's role and later mused about keeping Canadians out of harm's way, as if soldiers should not be exposed to danger. It underlined the predicament Canada now faces. 'We suddenly realize that the coinage of sovereignty is military power', says Michael Ignatieff (2002). 'Canada made the mistake of assuming that we could have sovereignty without substantial military expenditure. That illusion is over. We must wake up and make some public policy choices.'

DIPLOMATIC

Americans may not be enamoured of our championing of 'soft power' under former Foreign Affairs Minister Lloyd Axworthy (which itself is said to have been a creative response to the country's diminishing resources, leading it to practise diplomacy on the cheap). Canada supported the Landmines Treaty, the International Tribunal on War Criminals, and the Kyoto Treaty. The United States opposed all of them and they won Canada little goodwill in Washington. As one Canadian observer in Washington put it privately, 'it (the US) didn't like having a stick pointed in its eye.' This is not to say that Canada should not have embraced those causes, just that they came at a cost in terms of relations with Washington that cannot be ignored.

DOES IT MATTER?

All these factors—the personal orientation of President Bush, the shift in political power, the rise of Mexico, the erosion of Canada's military, the thrust of our diplomacy—have contributed to a loss of presence in the US, a loss that manifests itself in other ways. It is doubtful Canada has ever had much of an enduring impact on Americans beyond the occasional moment of fame, such as the Iran hostage crisis of 1980. If Canada ever evoked public recognition, it does not appear to now, despite our occasional appearances on CSPAN. Knowledge of Canada has never been a strong suit among Americans, and nothing demonstrable has changed that in recent months. Canada is there, as it always been, as neighbour, friend, or even 'brother'. But even if we trade, work, and visit with each other more than we ever have, as reflected in myriad official and unofficial relationships, the reality remains: Americans are staggeringly ignorant of Canada.

It is not just those clever screenwriters who write *The West Wing*, where they place the border between Vermont and Ontario. How would they know otherwise? The truth is, there is almost no mention of Canada in the American media. None of the major television networks has a correspondent in Canada, and only a handful of newspapers, including the *Washington Post* and the *Boston Globe*, maintain a presence here. Astonishingly, in the mid-1990s, the *New York Times* covered Canada with a correspondent based in Colorado. If the *Times* does carry stories on Canada, as do the *Post* and *Globe*, it is an exception. Americans read or watch little about Canada, and little as it is, it may be even less than they used to. Moreover, there is no awareness of Canada taking place in the universities, where there are fewer programs in Canadian Studies than there were.

It did not require a $77,000 survey commissioned by the Department of Foreign Affairs and International Trade (Thompson, 2001: 20) to reveal that Americans are 'clueless' about the identity of Canada's Prime Minister, who was elected in 1993. If it is any consolation, more could name Pierre Trudeau, Brian Mulroney, and celebrities Wayne Gretzky, Céline Dion, and Shania Twain, the last three of whom work in the United States. Nor did the government have to commission that survey to learn about the stereotypes of Canada. 'Canadians are described as nice, fun people', it found. 'They are frequently described as people who like to party and like their beer.' It found that 'Canadians are known for their interest in and ability at hockey . . . . Many are also aware that there are a lot of Canadian comedians, with some saying that Canadians therefore must have a good sense of humour.'

Given this perception, a little knowledge can be a bad thing for Americans. When it was popular to accuse Canada of being a haven for terrorists, which was not true, Americans were inclined to believe it. When they saw a rebroadcast of a CBC National Town Hall on CSPAN, for example, 12,000 viewers called to complain of the anti-American views, assuming those views represented those of most Canadians. Polls show they do not, and the CBC ombudsman found that the opinions expressed on the broadcast were disproportionately anti-American.

The misperception about Canada is so great that some analysts have urged Canada to launch a major advertising campaign south of the border 'to brand itself' a friend and ally of the United States (the Canadian Embassy did run a modest campaign in Washington last fall) (Trickey, 2001a: A1). They also suggested putting in place a truth commission or a war room to refute falsehoods in the media. But Canadians should not feel aggrieved or alone. The fact is that the US knows little about the rest of the world, a studied ignorance that has not changed all that much since 11 September. America is not discriminating against Canada; it knows as little about anyone else as it does about Canada.

Context matters here. For years, the United States has been wary of the world at the very moment it stood atop it. Up until 11 September, less foreign news was presented in America in recent years, as measured in minutes on television news and space in newspapers and magazines, than was the case in the past. By one measure, *Time* magazine ran fewer cover stories on foreign subjects in the 1990s than it did in the 1960s. In Congress, it has been said that almost a third of representatives do not have passports. In the Clinton years, the US refused to pay its dues to the United Nations on time and in full (though it eventually recanted), rejected international treaties, was slow to enter Bosnia and Kosovo, withdrew hurriedly from Somalia, and avoided Rwanda altogether. If the US is not practising isolationism, it is engaged in unilateralism, a narrow view of the world and America's place within it.

All this may have changed now. Undoubtedly the United States appeared to be less unilateralist as it repaid its outstanding dues to the United Nations and as Bush rushed to form an international coalition, appointed an envoy to the Middle East (a job vacant since the President came to office), and no longer talked about abandoning peacekeeping in Bosnia. On the other hand, the US showed no compunction over withdrawing from the Anti-Ballistic Missile (ABM) Treaty. The simple truth is that it is too early to say if a new era of American multilateralism has dawned.

In the new world, Canada faces new questions about its relationship with the United States. How does Canada assure its prosperity in the face of a newly defended border? How does it assure its security in a climate of terrorism? And, most pointedly, how does Canada maintain and affirm its sovereignty as it joins the US in military campaigns overseas, an embrace that calls for greater integration, harmonization, and dollarization? In 2002, all these issues were shaping the national agenda, filling Parliament and the newspapers. The fate of Taliban prisoners in Afghanistan? The fire sale of Canadian energy firms? The falling dollar? Overnight, national sovereignty was again a part of the national discourse. As John Godfrey, an outspoken parliamentarian, argues, sovereignty will become the great cause of this generation.

For Canada, these questions are opening a new debate on its view of the United States, animated by a familiar chorus of threats, cries, and laments. From the predictable voices, the predictable response: if the government moved forcefully to address the 'porous' border, its liberal immigration and refugee policies, and its weak public security, it would be shamefully continentalist, kowtowing to Uncle Sam. If it were reluctant to seal its border and align immigration and refugee policy with that of the Americans, it would be parochial, timid, and characteristically anti-American. In Canada, both the nationalists and the continentalists, or the rejectionists and the appeasers, could draw on a rich history. Of course, this dreary conversation is as old as the country itself. Which is precisely the problem.

Canada sent mixed messages. That the Prime Minister could offer fulsome support to Mr Bush in the Rose Garden and warn about impetuous measures to his critics in the House of Commons suggested an inconsistency sure to be noticed in Washington. Rhetoric aside, the government did act after 11 September. It sent troops to Afghanistan; it toughened refugee and immigration laws; it enacted an anti-terrorism law; it strengthened security at airports and utilities; and it moved to ensure the free flow of commerce across the border.

In much of this, there was a curious psychological game at play. At first, it seemed the Prime Minister worried about being seen as too pro-American in a country he thought traditionally wary of Americans; hence, his guarded public statements in the early hours. Then, having realized that public opinion was running ahead of the government in support of the US, he agreed to virtually everything the United States asked.

There was, in Canada's response, an eagerness to please, even a kind of 'me-tooism'. Lawrence McCauley, the Solicitor General, just could not resist crowing in the House of Commons that it was Canada that had tipped off the Americans about an imminent threat. This might have been better left unsaid but, of course, you do not get credit if you do not announce it. If the smug Mr McCauley won a pat on the head in Washington, he got a slap on the wrist in Ottawa from the opposition.

That desire to satisfy showed itself most forcefully in our military intervention. In some quarters, it was said that Canada had begged to serve with US forces in Afghanistan (the report was that the Minister of Defence 'asked to be asked') even if we did not have the planes to ferry our heavy equipment or the uniforms to camouflage our soldiers. To critics, it was about currying favour.

In the world after 11 September, we had to ask ourselves once again: Is there a way to be true to our friends and true to ourselves, to be both an independent nation and a reliable ally? In the past, Canada found ways to differ with the United States over critical international issues, such as over Cuba and the Vietnam War. We had greater confidence then; our military was larger, our diplomacy stronger, our dollar higher. But in the last three adventures—the Gulf War, Kosovo, and Afghanistan—we could not dissent, and there was not much debate over these foreign policy issues, either. To the nationalists, this suggested that we had sold out to the Americans. To the continentalists, such objections were a renewal of enduring anti-Americanism.

Is there a way to break the cycle, to shift the paradigm, so to speak? The idea of an independent foreign policy, the one Canada trumpeted in the 1960s, is wholly unrealistic now, given our integration with the United States. To protect our prosperity, we have no choice but to implement measures on the border that will satisfy the US, to let commerce in and keep terrorists out. We will also have to follow other measures, such as airport security (our planes cannot fly to Reagan National Airport in Washington without sky marshals) and some on immigration, to assure the United States we can defend the continent. These will be the requirements of living in the neighbourhood. They are inescapable and they will earn trust and credibility for Canada in Washington.

But the challenge for Canada, for its self-respect and integrity, is greater than that. It is to be an effective power that would win both trust and respect. The way to do that is to reclaim old assets: a strong, credible military; an efficient, exemplary aid program; an effective diplomatic service and a first-class intelligence service. With these tools, Canada could speak more confidently on the world stage. We would be taken more seriously. It would give us the moral authority not only to say no to the United States, if that is where we thought our interests lie, but to say yes. And saying yes to the US—in Kuwait or Kosovo or Afghanistan—is no shame if that is where we see ourselves rather than where we would like the United States to see us. But those choices should be made from strength. We ought not say no to the US because we have to pull the tail of the Eagle out of some adolescent act of independence, but because it is the right thing to do. We would respect ourselves more, and we would hope the United States would respect us, too. For Canada, the unfinished country, it would be part of growing up.

The United States will remain Canada's most important relationship. That will not change. But Canada will never be America's most important relationship. A strong, self-confident Canada will not care if we are noticed in Washington, which might even have advantages if the Americans keep forgetting that it is they who have a trade deficit, not us. We might learn not to care if we are a fading power in Washington—if we are confident that we are a good neighbour at home and a good ally abroad, pursuing our agenda as a warrior, peacekeeper, humanitarian, and diplomat, true to ourselves. And in that balance we just might find our purpose and place as a true nation of the world.

NOTE

1.   The conspiracy theorists even saw in this the hand of David Frum, the outspoken conservative from Canada who was a speech writer in the White House. They were sure he had personally withdrawn any reference to Canada out of pique. For this they produced no evidence.

REFERENCES

Bush, George. 2001. 'Address to a Joint Session of Congress and the American People', 20 Sept. The White House. Available at: <www.whitehouse.gov. news'releases/ 2001>.

Chrétien, Jean. 2001. 'Address by the Prime Minister Jean Chrétien on the occasion of a Special House of Commons Debate in response to September 11', 17 Sept. Available at: <www.pm.gc>.

Copeland, Daryl. 2001. 'The Axworthy Years: Foreign Policy in the Era of Diminished Capacity', in Fen Osler Hampson, Norman Hillmer, and Maureen Appel Molot, eds, *Canada Among Nations 2001: The Axworthy Legacy*. Toronto: Oxford University Press, 152–72.

Department of Foreign Affairs and International Trade. 2001. 'Canada's Actions Against Terrorism Since September 11', Nov. Available at: <www.gc.com>.

Diebel, Linda. 2001 'Not Important to praise "brother"', *Toronto Star*, 25 Sept., A1.

DePalma, Anthony. 2001. *Here: A Biography of the New American Continent*. New York: Public Affairs.

Friedman, Thomas L. 2002. 'The End of NATO?', *New York Times*, 3 Feb., 15.

Gee, Marcus. 2002. 'Canada Peacekeeper Image a Myth', *Globe and Mail*, 4 Jan., A6. *Globe and Mail*. 2001. 'Let's rally round our American friends', 13 Sept.

Ignatieff, Michael. 2002. *Maclean's*, Canada Section, interview, 4 Feb.

May, Kathryn. 2001. 'Canada's Non-Canadian Foreign Service', *Ottawa Citizen*, 22 Oct., A1.

Max, D.T. 2001. 'The Making of a Speech', *New York Times Magazine*, 7 Oct.

Rodriguez, Gregory. 2002. 'Where the Minorities Rule', *New York Times*, 10 Feb., 6.

Thompson, Elizabeth. 2001. 'Americans clueless about Canada', *Ottawa Citizen*, 27 Nov., A20.

Trickey, Mike. 2001a. 'Analysts say Canada must clear its name', *Ottawa Citizen*, 28 Nov., A1.

———. 2001b. 'Budget expected to do little for world's poor', *Ottawa Citizen*, 8 Dec., A10.

United States Trade Representative, *1999 Annual Report*. 2000. Washington.

3

Fading Power or Rising Power: 11 September and Lessons from the Section 110 Experience

CHRISTOPHER SANDS

The border between Canada and the United States is the natural flashpoint for bilateral disputes, and was violated regularly in the nineteenth and twentieth centuries: by US troops until 1815; by Fenian raiders; by agents of the Confederate States during the US Civil War; and by rum-runners during Prohibition. In recent years, the Canada–United States Free Trade Agreement and the North American Free Trade Agreement (NAFTA) gave many Canadians and Americans the hope that border barriers to the free flow of people and commerce between these two countries would gradually fade away thanks to economic integration. A previous volume in this series captured this spirit with the theme *Vanishing Borders* (Hampson and Molot, 2000).

Until 10 September 2001, scholars continued to wonder whether this border was relevant anymore. The following morning, the border made a comeback.

In just three months following the terrorist attacks on the World Trade Center in New York and the Pentagon in northern Virginia, the governments of Canada and the United States established new security procedures at the border between the two countries and took steps to improve co-operation between their respective law enforcement and national security agencies. The US Congress and the Canadian Parliament voted to authorize new funding for the wide array of officials—from customs inspectors and immigration agents to police and intelligence services—responsible for managing borders and conducting domestic counter-terrorist activities, and on 12 December 2001 US Homeland Security Director Tom Ridge and Canadian Foreign Minister John Manley met in Ottawa to endorse a joint action plan (Office of Homeland Security, 2001) further committing the two governments to negotiate on an additional 30 separate areas of potential bilateral co-operation, designed to reduce if not eliminate the risk of future terrorist attacks.

This chapter addresses three questions about the joint response of the United States and Canada on border-related issues after 11 September 2001. First, how was it that the two governments were able to agree on a common agenda so quickly? This was particularly surprising to many who saw relations between the George W. Bush administration and the government of Jean Chrétien begin awkwardly and remain relatively poor (Sands, 2001). Second, what does this experience suggest about the prospect for improved Canada–United States relations? Is Canada perhaps entering into a new period of constructive partnership with the United States? Third, how do the Chrétien government's choices now affect Canadian interests in the longer term? Is this episode in the aftermath of the 11 September attacks on the United States an aberration, or does it have lasting significance for Canada's relations with the United States and the world?

To answer the first question, the two governments were able to agree on a consensus agenda for action on the border because they had been engaged in a vigorous debate over border management that dated back to 1993, yet had received relatively little public attention. This debate belied the widespread impression that the border was becoming less important due to trade liberalization. A succession of bilateral agreements was signed between 1993 and 2001 to improve cross-border co-operation. These agreements were negotiated partly in response to the attempts of the Congress to reform US immigration policy following the passage of the Customs Modernization Act of

1993—both measures designed to address concerns raised by members of Congress and their constituents during the debate over NAFTA. The Canadian government viewed one provision of the US legislation as potentially harmful to its trade with the United States: the Section 110 requirement that the US Immigration and Naturalization Service (INS) develop an automated entry and exit record system to track non-US citizens crossing all US borders, including the land borders.

The debate over Section 110 coincided with the emergence of serious terrorist activity in North America that gradually began to colour the US perception of the urgency and necessity of stricter measures to control access across its land borders. In order to appreciate the reaction of the governments to the 11 September attacks, it is necessary to trace these three strands: congressional attempts to reform US immigration policy; Canadian attempts to engage the US government in a bilateral dialogue on border management, which Canada hoped would divert the US from implementing the Section 110 provision; and the growing penetration of both societies by Al-Qaeda terrorists that culminated in the 11 September attacks. The connections between these three efforts grew more intense over time, and together explain the swift reaction of the two governments to border security after 11 September. These recent events also offer the best indication of the likelihood of success of post-11 September co-operation and suggest something further about the future of bilateral relations in the years to come.

INS MODERNIZATION AND THE SHARED BORDER ACCORD

The Customs Modernization Act of 1993 grew out of the concerns of many in Congress that the policing of US borders required improvement in order to cope with the growing pressures of trade and individuals crossing in and out of the United States with increasing frequency. Its passage was an important precursor to the congressional ratification of NAFTA and related implementing legislation in November of that year. At the time, modernization of the INS, along with that of the US Customs Service, the other major border enforcement agency of the US government, was also considered necessary and individual representatives and senators crafted language for an INS modernization bill. President Bill Clinton, seeking to stave off concerns related to the potential for a flood of immigration and trade once NAFTA took effect (and thereby to win over enough members of Congress to get NAFTA and related implementing legislation passed), ordered the temporary transfer of one-third of the Customs, INS, and Border Patrol agents working on the northern border with Canada to serve on the southern border with Mexico.

On 26 February 1993, the first attack on the World Trade Center in New York resulted in the death of six people and the injury of 1,042. A rented van packed with explosives was detonated while parked in a garage beneath one of the towers. The US Federal Bureau of Investigation (FBI) launched an investigation that linked the attack to a group of individuals recruited by Sheikh Omar Abdel Rahman, a blind Egyptian Muslim cleric who had been accused by the Egyptian government of involvement in the assassination of Egyptian President Anwar Sadat. Abdel Rahman sought asylum in the United States from what he claimed was political persecution by the Egyptian government related to these unproven charges, and the US approved his application in 1989, permitting Abdel Rahman to settle in New Jersey.

The FBI investigation of the first attack on the World Trade Center uncovered evidence that followers of Abdel Rahman were actively plotting to bomb a series of New York City landmarks, including the United Nations headquarters building, the George Washington Bridge, and the Lincoln and Holland tunnels. These plans were thwarted when Abdel Rahman and nine of his associates were arrested on 23 June 1993.

Tracing Abdel Rahman's movements from his arrival in the United States, the FBI discovered that he had travelled extensively to cities across North America from 1990 to 1993, preaching in mosques and Islamic community centres in Los Angeles, Chicago, Detroit, and also in Montreal and Toronto. The FBI sought and received help from the Royal Canadian Mounted Police (RCMP) in investigating Abdel Rahman's activity while in Canada. Both the FBI and RCMP suspected that Abdel Rahman had used these trips to recruit followers for terrorist attacks, seeing the sheikh as the organizer of both the first World Trade Center attack and the plot to bomb New York City landmarks. Neither the FBI nor the RCMP yet suspected these incidents were linked to the larger Al-Qaeda terrorist network, and the focus remained on Abdel Rahman as the key figure.

On 14 September 1993 the first World Trade Center bombing trial began, and on 4 March 1994 four individuals connected to Abdel Rahman were convicted on all charges. On the strength of testimony and evidence presented in this trial, federal prosecutors indicted fugitive Ramzi Yousef as the ringleader who had planned the attack on the World Trade Center. There was insufficient evidence at the time to indict Abdel Rahman in the World Trade Center attack, but he remained in custody and was brought to trial on 9 January 1995 with nine others for participation in the plot to bomb New York City landmarks. On 7 February, Ramzi Youssef was arrested in Pakistan and subsequently extradited to face charges in the United States related to the first World Trade Center attack.

Two years after the shock of the first attack on the World Trade Center it appeared that all of those involved had been caught and were being brought to justice. If US officials had been surprised by the extent of the terrorist network they had uncovered in the United States, they still believed that they had uprooted it completely and that key figures Abdel Rahman and Ramzi Yousef would soon be in prison.

In February 1995, during a state visit by President Clinton to Ottawa, Clinton and Prime Minister Chrétien signed the US–Canada Shared Border Accord. This agreement included a series of measures to improve co-operation between customs and immigration officials in both countries. The emphasis of the Shared Border Accord was on customs, however, since the main challenge the two countries faced at the border was facilitating rapid growth in commercial traffic, and Canada Customs hoped to observe and even consult with their US counterparts on the implementation of the Customs Modernization Act with a view to developing common commercial documentation and electronic data interchange standards so that firms could minimize the amount of paperwork required on shipments moving across the border.

SECTION 110 AND THE BORDER VISION INITIATIVE

On 4 August 1995 the Immigration in the National Interest Act of 1995 was introduced in the US House of Representatives as HR 2202. The bill was intended to become the counterpart of the Customs Modernization Act of 1993, reforming an array of regulations and procedural requirements in the legislation governing the INS. When several amendments caused passage of the bill to be delayed, it was renamed the Illegal Immigration Reform and Immigrant Responsibility Act of 1996. The colourful title of the new bill reflected the style of the new Republican majority in the House in the 104th

Congress, led by Speaker of the House Newt Gingrich of Georgia. The 104th Congress was elected in 1994, at the same time that California voters approved Proposition 187, restricting some public services to US citizens and excluding thousands of illegal immigrants, mainly from Mexico. California's tough new mood on immigration was reflected in the 104th Congress, which was determined to legislate significant immigration reforms as quickly as possible.

One key amendment to the immigration reform bill established the Section 110 provision, which required the INS to develop a system to document the entry and exit of non-US citizens at all border crossing points. The initial purpose of the Section 110 provision was to allow authorities to keep track of those individuals who attempted to cross into the United States illegally and repeatedly, some of whom were thought to be human smugglers who charged substantial fees for aiding individuals seeking to evade lawful immigration procedures. Documentation of those exiting would allow the INS to determine that court-ordered deportations had in fact taken place; the agency had no way to be certain whether such orders were complied with except in extreme cases where individuals were escorted to the border in custody—and in such cases, there was no way to tell if these individuals re-entered the United States subsequently.

The Section 110 provision was to apply to all non-citizens crossing the US borders. The language of Section 110 allowed for the development of an automated system to track entry and exit, but no new funding was appropriated for this purpose. To give the INS time to develop and put in place an adequate system to comply with Section 110, the legislation required that Section 110 be implemented within two years after the immigration reform bill was signed into law.

The principal concern of members of Congress sponsoring the immigration reform bill was illegal migration across the US border with Mexico, by both Mexicans and Central Americans who crossed through Mexico in the hope of entering the United States (Krouse and Wasem, 1998). However, there was also concern in Congress about illegal entry from Canada. The INS estimated that 15,000 people attempted to enter the United States from Canada illegally in 1995. Acknowledging that there were illegal immigration flows from the United States into Canada as well, the INS nonetheless estimated that 75 per cent of the illegal migration across the Canada–US border went from Canada into the United States and consisted mainly of third-country nationals (not Canadians) who passed through Canada always intending to end their journey in the United States (Beltrame, 1997).

Canadian government officials insisted that the Section 110 provision was not intended to affect those entering from Canada, and solicited statements from individual sponsors of the legislation to support this contention. The Canadian government argued publicly that the effect of implementation would be long lines at busy border crossings and the loss of billions of dollars in trade to the economies of both countries (Cooper, 2000). Congress did not exempt the Canadian border from the application of Section 110, and did not agree to exempt Canadians from the documentation requirement for non-US citizens. On 21 March 1996 the Illegal Immigration Reform and Immigrant Responsibility Act of 1996, including the Section 110 provision, was passed by the House of Representatives by a vote of 333–87. Senate passage followed in May 1996, and after a House-Senate conference in September worked out differences between the two versions of the bill as passed by each chamber, the immigration reform legislation was signed into law in October, establishing the deadline for full implementation of Section 110 as October 1998.

Just one year before the Act became law, in October 1995, Abdel Rahman and nine others were convicted of plotting to bomb New York landmarks. During the course of their trial, it was revealed that one of the accused, El Sayyid Nosair, was also the assassin of New York Rabbi Meir Kahane in 1990, and that Abdel Rahman himself had indeed played a part in the assassination of Anwar Sadat, for which both were also convicted. All 10 individuals received lengthy prison terms.

Less attention was paid to the case of Ahmed Saied Khadr, an Egyptian-born Canadian citizen who was arrested in Pakistan in connection with a truck bombing of the Egyptian embassy in Islamabad that killed 16 and wounded 50 people. Khadr held computer science degrees from the University of Ottawa and headed up the Canadian branch of Human Concern International, based in Gloucester, Ontario. He had travelled to Pakistan en route to Kabul, Afghanistan, where he sought to arrange the marriage of his daughter to Khalid Abdullah, an Egyptian guest of the Taliban regime. Prime Minister Chrétien raised Khadr's case with Pakistani Prime Minister Benazir Bhutto during a visit to Islamabad in January 1996, and requested his release given the weak case against him for direct involvement in the embassy bombing. In March 1996, the Pakistani government released

Khadr, who returned to Canada where he faced no charges (Dahlburg, 1996).

On 17 July 1996, TWA Flight 800 exploded above the Long Island shoreline, killing all 230 passengers and crew shortly after the plane left New York's Kennedy Airport. Crash investigators suspected a link to terrorism, given the suddenness of the explosion, and lawyers for Ramzi Yousef feared that the TWA incident would prejudice the jury in his trial against him. Yousef was charged in a plot to place bombs on at least a dozen US passenger aircraft bound for Asia. Prosecutors claimed that there was ample evidence for conviction even without the TWA 800 tragedy, and on 5 September 1996 Yousef and two associates were convicted. Yousef went to prison while the prosecutors built a case against him for masterminding the 1993 World Trade Center attack.

The Canadian government did not ignore the US immigration policy debate. Two bilateral agreements in 1997 demonstrated Canada's willingness to be part of the solution to US immigration concerns anywhere there was a proven link to Canada. In February, Canadian Solicitor General Herb Gray and US Attorney General Janet Reno announced the formation of two groups, the Canadian Anti-Smuggling Working Group and the Northeast Border Working Group, which would co-ordinate an intensified campaign by national immigration and law enforcement resources in each country to combat human and contraband smuggling through Ontario and Quebec into New York and some New England states. Gray and Reno indicated that the two working groups would share information and attempt to co-ordinate intelligence information between them. In addition to the smuggling of individuals from third countries such as India and China, the two countries shared a concern over illicit movement of small arms (mainly handguns from the United States to Canada) and illegal drugs (flowing in both directions).

In April 1997, the governments of Canada and the United States announced a new Border Vision Initiative during Prime Minister Chrétien's first state visit to Washington as Prime Minister. This joint effort aimed to facilitate greater information-sharing and co-ordination between Citizenship and Immigration Canada (CIC) and the INS, particularly at the land border, through intelligence-sharing on illegal migration. The Border Vision Initiative also began a dialogue between CIC and INS on the potential for co-ordination and consolidation of lookout lists, third-country visa requirements, joint overseas operations, and intelligence exchanges for background checks on third-country applicants. Consensus formed on many of the technical issues addressed by the two agencies under the aegis of the Border Vision Initiative, but action did not immediately follow on some of the most far-reaching items under consideration for want of either funding (particularly for new technology) or political support (where sovereignty concerns were flagged by either side). Nonetheless, both 1997 agreements represented progress towards bilateral immigration policy reform, nudged along by new legislation in the United States.

'BOMBS IN BROOKLYN' AND THE CROSS-BORDER CRIME FORUM

The harmonious mood of co-operation that followed the Chrétien-Clinton meeting in April 1997 gave rise to hopes that the Section 110 provision could be waived for Canada, or perhaps eliminated entirely. The era of good feeling on immigration was undermined by revelations from a US Department of Justice investigation less than a year later.

On 31 July 1997 New York City police raided a Brooklyn apartment and caught two men, Ghazi Ibrahim Abu Mezer and Lafi Khalil, in the act of preparing explosive devices that they intended to detonate in the New York City subway system. The police had been tipped off by an Arab-American neighbour who disliked the two and heard them talking in Arabic about their plans. It was clearly a lucky break that led to the prevention of the attack, rather than effective intelligence. Days later, a furious New York Mayor Rudolph Giuliani and US Senator Alphonse d'Amato wrote an open letter to President Clinton demanding that the INS explain how Abu Mezer and Khalil got into the United States.

At the US Department of Justice, of which the INS is a part, the department's Office of the Inspector General began an investigation of INS handling of the Abu Mezer and Khalil cases. Members of Congress voted in November 1997 to extend the deadline for the implementation of the Section 110 provision by a full year to October 1999, compromising with the Clinton administration and US business groups, which had advocated removing the deadline entirely (Krouse and Wasem, 1998).

Canada and the United States expanded their bilateral co-operation at the border with the establishment of the Cross-Border Crime

Forum, which held its first meeting in Ottawa on 30 September 1997. Where the Border Vision Initiative fostered co-operation in immigration cases, the Cross-Border Crime Forum was created to encourage law enforcement agencies in both countries to work together more effectively to combat transnational crime, including smuggling, telemarketing fraud, money laundering, missing children, and cybercrime. Two concrete steps were taken as a result of dialogue at the Cross-Border Crime Forum. First, a procedure for binational threat assessments was established. Second, a proposal to create Integrated Border Enforcement Teams (IBETs) was tested along the British Columbia–Washington border, where Canadian and US law enforcement personnel working for federal, state, and local governments could conduct investigations and enforcement operations, as well as training exercises together, overcoming jurisdictional issues pragmatically and prompting a heightened degree of information-sharing among all of the participating organizations.

The need for cross-border co-operation was underscored in February 1998, when Walter Cadman, INS Counterterrorism Coordinator, testified before the Senate Judiciary Committee that in 1996, illegal immigrants from 118 countries had attempted unlawful entry into the United States from Canada, and that Canada was becoming an important 'alternative gateway' for illegal migration (Cadman, 1998). Cadman also told senators that established human smuggling operations were being used by international terrorist and organized crime groups to obtain entry for their members to the United States, thereby eluding new measures to screen applicants and detect forged documents more thoroughly that had been instituted by the INS in response to the 1996 immigration reform legislation passed by Congress.

Cadman's testimony anticipated the findings of the investigation into INS handling of the Abu Mezer and Khalil cases by Michael Bromowich, the inspector general of the US Department of Justice (Bromowich, 1998). The Bromowich report, titled 'Bombs in Brooklyn', confirmed that Abu Mezer was a Palestinian born on the West Bank who had been arrested several times in Israel, which believed him to be a member of the Hamas organization. Abu Mezer received a student visa from the government of Canada in 1993, and shortly after arriving in Canada he applied for political refugee status based on fear of persecution in Israel, admitting his connections to Hamas members but denying participation in any terrorist activity. At that time, he also applied for a visa to enter the United States at the US Consular Office in Toronto but was denied. Subsequently, he began attempting to enter the United States illegally, and was arrested on three occasions in 1996 and 1997. On his third try, when US officials sought to return him to Canada, Canada refused him entry due to two felony convictions (for assault and credit card fraud, respectively) during his time in Canada. The Border Patrol then began deportation proceedings and the case went to court. Had Abu Mezer's connection to Hamas been established at the time of his asylum hearing, Bromowich argued, he would have been swiftly deported. However, the INS had not conducted a thorough check on Abu Mezer through available databases on international terrorists (where it would have found the Israeli charges that Abu Mezer was a Hamas member), and the State Department responded to the immigration court judge's request for information with a routine reply that the department had no information concerning the individual in question.

Bromowich's report shed unflattering light on the state of co-operation at the Canada–US border by immigration and law enforcement agencies:

[T]his case exposes pervasive and long-standing weaknesses in the immigration process that are not unique to this matter. First, Mezer's easy entry to Canada and his ability to remain there while he repeatedly attempted to illegally enter the United States demonstrates part of the difficulty in controlling illegal immigration into the United States.

Second, Mezer's case also shows the inadequacy of INS resources for preventing illegal immigration along the northwest border. With an average of four Border Patrol agents in the Lynden and Blaine stations covering 102 miles of the northern border, and no coverage of the border from midnight to morning, it is surprising that Mezer was apprehended once, much less three times, within approximately six months.

Third, the virtual impunity from prosecution that aliens face when they are caught illegally entering the United States is also made apparent by Mezer's case. Border Patrol statistics show that most illegal aliens who are apprehended entering the United States from Canada are voluntarily returned without any criminal or immigration consequences. Despite twice being caught attempting to enter the United States illegally within one week, Mezer was simply returned voluntarily to Canada each time. INS and law enforcement authorities do not normally prosecute or even detain aliens who are

caught attempting to enter the United States, and they are typically returned
to Canada voluntarily, able to try again any time (Bromowich, 1998).

The Bromowich report's findings in the case of Khalil were equally
disturbing, but did not relate to Canada.

Meeting in Washington in May 1998, participants in the second
Cross-Border Crime Forum could hope for no better case study of
the challenges that the two countries faced in improving co-operation and co-ordination among law enforcement and other agencies
within, and across, the border.

SECTION 110 AND THE CUSP

On 7 June 1998 Ramzi Yousef was convicted and sentenced to life
in prison for his role in the first World Trade Center attack. Two
months later, US embassies in Dar es Salaam, Tanzania, and Nairobi,
Kenya, were bombed. President Clinton accused Al-Qaeda, the terrorist organization led by Osama bin Laden, of carrying out the
attacks, and ordered cruise missile strikes on suspected Al-Qaeda targets in Sudan and Afghanistan. US officials who previously considered Sheikh Abdel Rahman and Ramzi Yousef the masterminds
behind past attacks on the United States began reviewing the evidence for possible links between these attacks and Al-Qaeda. When
Swissair Flight 111, originating at New York's Kennedy Airport and
bound for Geneva, crashed off the coast of Nova Scotia on 2
September 1998, killing 229, investigators naturally looked to terrorism as a possible cause.

The summer of 1999 saw an easing of concern over illegal immigration into the United States. In July, citing the progress of federal
immigration policy reform, California Governor Gray Davis announced
that he was dropping an appeal of an earlier federal court ruling that
had found much of the state's Proposition 187 unconstitutional
(Nieves, 1999). That same month, Congress lifted the October 1999
deadline for implementation of the Section 110 provision of the 1996
immigration reform legislation as part of the Border Improvement and
Immigration Act of 1998. The new Act belatedly provided the INS with
rather modest funding for the development of an automated entry and
exit control system to implement Section 110, and at the same time
called for a study of the impact entry and exit controls would have on
traffic facilitation at the major border crossing points—a concession to

critics of Section 110 in the business community. It was a partial retreat from Section 110 implementation, although Congress revived the prospect that Section 110 controls might be imposed at a later date.

US and Canadian officials continued their joint efforts to improve the management of the border. In December 1998 the US Department of Justice and Canada's Justice Ministry announced the successful conclusion of a joint operation (called Project Othello in Canada and Operation Over the Rainbow in the United States) to break up human smuggling rings operating across the New York border with Ontario and Quebec.

The growing number and range of such initiatives, from focused enforcement operations to co-ordinated planning for border management and infrastructure, combined with concern over the potential collateral damage to the economies of border communities if Section 110 were implemented, resulted in the mobilization of local leaders to demand a role in the discussions that had largely remained exclusively between federal officials on both sides of the border (Meyers and Papademetriou, 2001). Ottawa and Washington responded with the Canada–United States Partnership (CUSP) Agreement, signed during President Clinton's state visit to Ottawa in October 1999, during which he dedicated the new US Embassy building. The CUSP pledged both governments to initiate a series of stakeholder consultations that would solicit ideas and input on border management from communities, interest groups, and businesses. The explicit purpose of the CUSP process was to redress a perceived imbalance towards security and enforcement improvements with renewed attention to traffic facilitation in the spirit of the 1995 Shared Border Accord, while bringing local input into the security dialogue as well. CUSP consultations were planned for 2000 in the east and west (CUSP, 2000).

Before the first CUSP meetings could be held, international terrorism would again touch North America. On 31 October 1999 EgyptAir Flight 990, bound from New York to Cairo, crashed in the waters off Nantucket killing all 217 aboard. Although 'pilot error' was ruled the probable cause, US investigators again considered terrorism a potential factor in the crash. Then, in December 1999, Ahmed Ressam was arrested attempting to enter the United States with a carload of explosives and, he subsequently confessed, a plan to attack the Los Angeles International Airport to coincide with millennium celebrations. Ressam was an Algerian who had resided in

Montreal since 1994 while his application for political asylum was adjudicated. His application was denied in 1998, and he was ordered deported, at which point he went underground and adopted a new identity with forged documents that indicated that he was Beni Antoine Norris, a Canadian citizen.

The Ressam case received more attention than any previous incident involving terrorism and the Canada–US border. In part, this reflected the growing concern in the United States over international terrorism and attacks on US targets. Canadian officials initially downplayed the significance of the Ressam case, arguing that he had been caught—proof that existing security measures were adequate. But many Americans noted that the arrest of Ressam owed more to luck and a sharp-eyed US border inspector, and his plan could very easily have succeeded. CIC officials claimed that at no stage were they aware of the connections between Ressam and Algerian terrorist groups or Al-Qaeda—an admission that drew American public attention to the Canadian immigration and refugee system and to the limited financial and intelligence resources available to CIC officials, whose decisions on immigrants were now viewed as affecting the safety of US citizens as never before (Farley, 1999).

The heightened public anxiety in the United States that followed Ressam's arrest quickly led to fierce political recriminations. In Washington, the Federation for American Immigration Reform (FAIR) held a press conference on 20 December 1999 to attack congressional leaders who had voted to waive the deadline for Section 110 implementation for increasing the risk of terrorist attacks on US citizens (FAIR, 1999). The group singled out Senator Spencer Abraham of Michigan, the lone Arab American in the US Senate, for his efforts to repeal the Section 110 provision. 'It is gross negligence that national lawmakers, led by Senate Immigration Subcommittee chair Spencer Abraham, have been actively working to undermine effective border security', charged FAIR executive director Dan Stein in a press release. 'A measure enacted by Congress in 1996 would have required the Immigration and Naturalization Service to collect records on all arriving foreign visitors and match them with departure records. But it has been attacked and buried by Sen. Abraham and a handful of other politicians who put the interests of border merchants and ethnic communities ahead of the security of the American public' (FAIR, 1999). FAIR subsequently produced television ads attacking Abraham's position on immigration reform that ran during his 2000 campaign for re-election, in which he was defeated.

In January 2000, the Subcommittee on Immigration and Claims of the House Judiciary Committee held a hearing on Canada's immigration and border control policies and their affect on the United States. Representative Lamar Smith (R-Texas), one of the key sponsors of the Section 110 provision, chaired the hearing. In addition to three American witnesses (including this author), the Subcommittee heard from a roster of Canadian critics of the Chrétien government's security policies who testified to the chronic underfunding of the RCMP and the Canadian Security and Intelligence Service, and charged that the Liberal government was too beholden to support from immigrant communities in Canada to restrict immigration to meet US security concerns.

The increasingly ugly debate over US immigration policy and borders, which now included a debate over Canada's immigration and security policies, cast a shadow over the first and second rounds of stakeholder consultations under the CUSP, which were held in April 2000 in Niagara-on-the-Lake, Ontario, and Buffalo, New York, and in June 2000 in Vancouver, British Columbia, and Blaine, Washington. Participants in these sessions were briefed on the increased degree of bilateral co-operation by federal agencies along the border and raised a number of concerns, including the importance of maintaining a secure yet relatively open border for tourism, trade, and local economies (CUSP, 2000). Perhaps the most important outcome of the CUSP process was the demonstration of the strength of the grassroots constituency in both countries for improvements at the Canada–US border.

It was with the same positive spirit that Representative Lamar Smith introduced the Immigration and Naturalization Service Data Management Act of 2000 on 18 May; the bill won wide support, passed both houses of Congress, and was signed into law by President Clinton on 15 June 2000—less than one month later. The new Act built on the immigration reform legislation of 1996 and 1998 by authorizing significant new funding for the development of information technology solutions for implementing the Section 110 provision, attempting to improve the quality of information gathered by those entering and exiting the United States to permit US Customs and INS inspectors at the border to implement better risk-management, focusing enforcement resources where the risk was higher, while facilitating the flow of low-risk individuals and commerce. The 2000 immigration law also expressed 'the sense of Congress that the Attorney General, in consultation with the Secretaries of State, Commerce, and the Treasury should consult with affected foreign governments to improve border management', an acknowledgement of the importance of consultation with neighbours in developing border management policies; it was a message Canada had wanted to hear.

In November 2000, test-implementation of a new electronic system called NEXUS began at the Blue Water Bridge crossing between Sarnia, Ontario, and Port Huron, Michigan. Under the NEXUS program, US Customs, the INS, CIC, and Canada Customs developed a common data form, allowing travellers and shippers in both countries to file the same personal information form. Individuals would then receive a NEXUS card with biometric support that would enable the bearer to access an expedited inspection and clearance lane, since NEXUS participation allowed the four agencies to confirm the individual as low risk and in the process gather more information about the person than was possible in the normal inspection interview. The program test was suspended in the wake of the 11 September attacks.

THE LESSONS OF THE SECTION 110 EXPERIENCE

The most contentious aspect of US immigration policy reform from the perspective of Canada–US relations was the Section 110 provision, and charges that the failure to implement this provision contributed to the vulnerability of the United States to terrorist attacks before and on 11 September itself were the most incendiary of many levelled against proponents of improved co-operation between Canada and the United States in managing the border. On 10 October, Representative Virgil Goode (R-Virginia) introduced a bill calling for the immediate implementation of the Section 110 provision by the INS along both US land borders (introduced as HR 3077).

Yet the Section 110 provision was a failure from nearly every perspective. For its proponents, Section 110 failed because it was never implemented; its design had proven too controversial, too cumbersome and expensive to administer, and too extreme a response to what generally seemed to be the problem of illegal immigration and not terrorism. For its critics, including Canada, the flaws of Section 110 were immediately apparent. But even today the provision is not dead, despite the considerable time and energy spent by the broad coalition of government officials, business groups, and non-governmental organizations to stop it. After 11 September, the shadow of terrorism is certain to colour the US immigration policy debate, making the revival of the debate over Section 110 or a successor measure a possibility.

On 12 December 2001 the two governments endorsed the 30-point Smart Border Declaration (Office of Homeland Security, 2001). In it, the governments of Canada and the United States pledge to improve co-operation, develop new, joint procedures, share more intelligence information, and implement specific reforms to immigration, inspection, and traffic management practices at the border. It is a complex and ambitious agenda, but as can be seen from the foregoing discussion, the Smart Border Declaration is not a new beginning so much as a new commitment of political will and adequate funding to follow through on good ideas that had languished for want of both prior to 11 September.

Will the Smart Border Declaration succeed in improving the security and efficiency of the Canada–US border while decisively forestalling measures like Section 110, where previous efforts have met with only partial success? It is still too early to answer this question, but the success of current efforts will depend to a considerable extent on whether or not leaders in both Canada and the United States have learned key lessons from their Section 110 experiences. Specifically, there are four important lessons for each side.

US Lesson 1: Security measures cannot ignore economic concerns. After 11 September, the desire of the US Congress that the INS better document who is crossing US borders does not appear to have been so unreasonable. Yet domestic US economic interests, including some of the largest US corporations, rely heavily on cross-border production and resisted the Section 110 mandate. If the proponents of Section 110 had been able to accommodate the concerns of the business community, the requirement might have been successfully implemented. In other words, powerful economic interests can and will fight back if security measures come at a disproportionate economic cost.

US Lesson 2: Underfunded mandates are more difficult to implement. When the US Congress ordered the INS to develop a plan to implement the Section 110 requirement, it did not make significant new funding available to the INS to finance implementation. As a result, the INS had to consider the lowest-cost options for implementation—even paper forms, similar to those handed out to passengers arriving by air and sea. Critics of Section 110 pointed out that technologies already developed would allow the required information to be transmitted electronically for frequent border crossers through transponders or smart cards issued by the two governments. In fact, US and Canadian border agencies were experimenting with such systems on a limited basis throughout the debate over Section 110—ultimately leading to the test implementation of the NEXUS program. But in fairness to the INS, lack of funding for a major expansion of such programs prevented consideration of viable high-tech alternatives that would permit better data collection without sacrificing border facilitation.

A further barrier to successful Section 110 implementation was inadvertently created through understaffing by US agencies at the Canadian border. The Clinton administration in 1994 ordered the temporary reassignment of one-third of the personnel at the Canadian border to the US–Mexican border to handle the anticipated surge in traffic prompted by NAFTA. Subsequently, these staffers were not replaced, and so US agencies working on the Canadian border were forced to inspect growing traffic volumes with a shortage of trained personnel. At busy ports, such as Detroit–Windsor and Buffalo–Fort Erie, college students and schoolteachers seeking supplemental income were hired to staff US inspection booths in order to reduce backups. Stretched as they were by understaffing, US agencies at the border were in no position to cope with the additional requirement of individual entry and exit documentation imposed by Congress.

US Lesson 3: Canada and Mexico are not the same. Since NAFTA took effect, there have been frequent attempts by Washington policy-makers to approach certain issues with one US policy for both Canada and Mexico. In Congress, the need to build coalitions in support of legislation often requires representatives and senators from northern and southern border states to work together, further encouraging the harmonization of practices at both borders. Yet the relative openness of the Canada–US border permits firms to employ just-in-time inventory management practices that make manufacturing and service operations vulnerable to border delays to a far greater extent than at the US–Mexico border, where longer inspection and clearance times are the norm. Failure to account for different border conditions and concerns was a key flaw in the design of the Section 110 provision of the 1996 immigration reform.

US Lesson 4: Unilateral approaches are more difficult to implement. Underscoring the previous lesson, the requirement that the INS record individual exit data at the borders as well as entry data effectively doubled the potential effort required to implement the Section 110 provision. Had the United States sought Canadian co-operation from the outset, Canadian officials might have been persuaded to gather entry data that could be shared with the United States—effectively allowing Canada to collect exit data for the US along the land border. As the series of bilateral agreements between 1993 and 2001 indicate, Canada was willing to work with the United States to improve border security throughout this period, making it reasonable to expect that Ottawa would have been willing also to co-operate with the United States in data collection at the border—something that the 2000 immigration reform legislation belatedly acknowledges. As it was, Canada fought the implementation of the Section 110 provision and many Canadians viewed the measure with hostility.

The Chrétien government, which encountered considerable US resistance in its attempt to turn back Section 110, also stands to learn important lessons from the Section 110 experience.

Canadian Lesson 1: Economic concerns do not trump security concerns. The mirror image of the US lesson, it became clear to Ottawa that despite the value of bilateral trade to both countries, members of Congress and US officials responsible for security at the border would not be deterred by economic arguments alone. One analysis suggests that the US is concerned mainly about security at the border, while Canada is concerned mainly about the economic impact of border management (Shea, 2001). This is too simplistic: in reality both countries are concerned with both goals, and the Section 110 debate proved that the two concerns could stalemate action if not reconciled.

Canadian Lesson 2: Canada has a credibility gap on security issues in the United States. Canadians did not consider themselves to be lax when it came to security, even after several incidents suggested that international terrorists were abusing Canadian openness and tolerance to gain access to the United States. The tendency of Canadians to respond to US criticism by touting Canada's supposedly superior tolerance of diversity further undermined Canadian credibility with Americans, who interpreted such rhetoric as evidence that their northern neighbours did not understand the extent of the danger posed by terrorism. Throughout the debate over Section 110 the American stereotype of Canadians as well-intentioned but naive Boy Scouts collided with Canadian stereotypes of Americans as gun-toting Rambo clones, and yet instead of cancelling one another out, the effect of these two shallow generalizations, when combined with increasing evidence of terrorist activity in North America, was to erode Canadian credibility on security questions. The result was that Canada repeatedly found itself placed on the defensive by critics in the United States who questioned Canada's resolve to fight terrorism.

Canadian Lesson 3: Trilateral solutions are problematic for Canada, but tempting for the United States. For some Canadians, the contrast between the US–Canada border and the US–Mexico border is so stark that there does not seem to be a polite way of pointing out the differences, since comparisons are inevitably so unflattering to Mexico. Yet in the face of a US tendency to trilateralize issues following NAFTA, Canada runs the risk of seeing the United States opt for the lowest-common-denominator approach to its borders rather than seeking to duplicate the 'best-practice' policies of the Canada–US border on the US–Mexico border. With the majority of congressional leaders now representing the populous southern states, the mental image of borders for many in Congress is the US–Mexico border. The Section 110 debate demonstrated the extent to which Canada must be prepared to educate US leaders about the US northern border.

Canadian Lesson 4: Participation in US domestic debates is open to the Canadian government and its domestic critics. The Canadian government was pleased to forge alliances with US business and border community groups with a common interest in blocking implementation of the Section 110 provision. It was less pleased to discover critics of its policies could just as easily win a hearing in the United States. The Section 110 debate provided both governments with a foretaste of the complex political dynamics that will accompany deepening bilateral economic integration. Participation in the US political arena will work for and against Ottawa's agenda at different times— and frequently, in a concurrent fashion. This will make conflict resolution with the United States more difficult for Ottawa to manage.

While it is important not to judge either government too harshly on whether it has learned these lessons in the immediate aftermath of 11 September, given the enormity of the attacks and the psychological and emotional impact they have had on citizens of both countries, there are encouraging signs in the Smart Border Declaration and the conduct of Canada–US relations since then that leaders in both countries have indeed adapted their approach to consider some of these lessons.

First, the two governments have adopted a reasonably balanced approach to improving security while remaining sensitive to the economic impact of new security measures. The constituency tapped by the CUSP process, mobilized by the Section 110 debate, is quick to praise or challenge measures that do not meet this test. So, on the first lesson, Canada and the United States both earn high marks.

Second, both countries are approaching the border with the understanding that they must establish their respective bona fides. The United States is demonstrating a new seriousness by committing to the full funding of border improvement measures, rather than mandating that the INS and other border agencies somehow manage to do more with less. Canada, for its part, has acted quickly to redress the underfunding of its immigration courts and domestic security services, and has closed loopholes in its immigration laws that were exploited by Abu Mezer and Ressam. On this second lesson, Canada and the United States also receive high marks. However, the United States has thus far earned an incomplete grade—the old congressional practice of announcing the authorization of funds, to which significant preconditions are attached, and then appropriating far less can still not be ruled out. For the US to win applause, the promised money must actually be spent.

Third, since 11 September the two governments have clearly rediscovered room for bilateralism in their relationship. They have done so generally without precluding Mexico from participation in new border management practices, but recognizing at the same time that Canada and the United States have a stronger foundation of bilateral co-operation at the border on which to build, as well as established security and intelligence-sharing relationships through NATO, NORAD, the Permanent Joint Board on Defence, the International Joint Commission, and other institutions. Here, too, Canada and the United States deserve credit for appearing to have learned something from the Section 110 debate.

The fourth lessons remain problematic for both countries, for different reasons. It is not at all clear that the United States has abandoned its preference for managing the border unilaterally since 11 September. Indeed, in the absence of any clear Canadian initiatives

or counterproposals for improving border security and fighting terrorism in North America, the bilateral co-operation since 11
September is impossible to distinguish from a combination of US unilateralism and Canadian acquiescence to the US agenda. At the same
time, while Canada has sought to establish its good faith as a partner to the United States rather than assuming it is viewed by
Americans as a reliable security partner, Ottawa continues to react
with evident shock when comments declaring Canada's determination to resist US pressure, made by Canadian politicians for domestic consumption, are interpreted by US policy-makers as evidence
that Canada is an unreliable ally.

These suggested lessons from the Section 110 experience will
remain important as the 30 points of the Smart Border Declaration
move from rhetoric to implementation. So soon after the events of
11 September, no judgement on whether these lessons have been
learned can be deemed final—the early good marks can be rescinded
and the areas where improvement still seems necessary can yet be
turned around.

11 SEPTEMBER AND CANADA–US RELATIONS: WHAT NEXT?

Thucydides observed that in human relations and affairs of state, the
strong do what they can and the weak accept what they must. This
is an apt description for Canada–US relations over border management issues since 1993. The United States government sought to institute a series of immigration policy reforms, while gradually awakening
to the threat posed to its citizens by international terrorism on US soil.
The Canadian government adopted a strategy of attempting to substitute bilateral dialogue and co-operation for unilateral US actions,
often fighting a rearguard battle to stop Section 110 implementation.
However, in the aftermath of 11 September, Canada's strategy seemed
to change.

It seems obvious that, in this bilateral relationship, the United
States will always be the strong state and Canada the weak state. Yet,
as Keohane and Nye argued 25 years ago, the interdependence of
Canada and the United States, which has grown with deepening economic integration, alters the power balance between the two countries (Keohane and Nye, 1977). Interdependence renders Canada
stronger and the United States weaker vis-à-vis one another. Canada
is one of the few states in the international system to have a choice

of whether it will act as a strong state or a weak state in its approach to the United States.

A strong state strategy for Canada would involve improving Canadian domestic security and implementing a creative counter-terrorism effort taken with or without US participation, simply because Canadian citizens are threatened by international terrorism, as is their way of life as part of the civilized world. Canada's national interest lies in maintaining the best possible relations with the United States, and so a strong Canada would naturally secure its borders and aggressively enforce its laws in all areas. To paraphrase Pierre Trudeau, to those who do not like the sight of men with guns and who wonder how far Canada will go, just watch and see.

A weak state strategy for Canada would consider the threat of international terrorism largely a US concern, and seek to placate US pressure with minimum efforts while husbanding Canadian sovereignty and avoiding commitments to undertake new responsibilities with regard to the defence of North America. To paraphrase William Lyon Mackenzie King, full security co-operation with the United States *if* necessary, but not necessarily full security co-operation with the United States.

Whether Canada opts for a strong state strategy or a weak state strategy will have a decisive impact on its relationship with the United States as the campaign against global terrorism continues, both in North America and overseas. From the US perspective, a Canada following a strong state strategy is a desirable partner; a Canada following a weak state strategy is an obstacle to progress towards greater security. Washington will approach Canada in coming years based on the posture Canada adopts towards the United States. The strategy that Canada chooses will determine whether the US learns the final lesson of the Section 110 experience and approaches the border in the spirit of bilateral co-operation or with non-negotiable demands. At the same time, Canada's choice will indicate whether it has learned from the Section 110 experience—that in the face of deepening integration the vulnerability of Canadian interests to the United States will continue to grow and that a weak state strategy, while appearing to preserve Canada's ability to take decisions independently within its own sovereign jurisdiction, will further weaken Canada's ability to defend its interests in the United States.

The theme of this volume in the *Canada Among Nations* series describes 'a fading power'. Readers will be tempted to see in this theme an indication that Canada will inevitably opt to continue pursuing a weak state strategy with regard to the United States, as it did in the debate over the border from 1993 onward, once the residual effect of the 11 September attacks has faded and the politics of Canada–US relations revert to a new normalcy. The Section 110 experience, however, suggests another possibility.

The turbulent nature of the Section 110 debate, and the high stakes for Canadian interests in particular, mobilized an array of new participants in the debate over border management. Many border communities, transnational firms, and non-governmental interest groups demanded a voice in a policy debate that seemed too important to be left to the federal governments—and many felt that the federal governments were making a mess of things instead of co-operating. State and provincial governments, too, came to question the way that Ottawa and Washington were bickering over the management of the border, and sought a role for themselves to defend their own interests. The federal governments responded with the CUSP process, which further encouraged new players to become involved and demand to be heard.

In the weeks after 11 September, when Ottawa appeared to hesitate to declare its unconditional support for the United States, Canadian citizens, firms, and communities reacted instinctively to demonstrate their support in words and deeds. Provincial governments stepped forward to offer emergency relief and to co-ordinate with state law enforcement and security counterparts in homeland defence preparations. For millions of Canadians, Americans are friends, family, and business partners. The choice between international terrorists and helping a neighbour was simple, and most Canadians made it without equivocation or calculation of national interest.

Thanks to deepening interdependence through economic integration, Canada is not a fading power in the United States. It is instead a rising power, more important to Americans and their prosperity today than ever before in US history.

No, it is Ottawa that risks becoming a fading power today. If it continues to adopt a weak country strategy it will fade in its ability to represent and defend Canadian interests in the United States, while fading in its attractiveness as a partner for Washington in the management of cross-border issues. The lessons of the Section 110 experience and the debate over the border in recent years indicate that Ottawa does have a choice. So, too, do Canadians.

REFERENCES

Beltrame, Julian. 1997. 'Canada to help stop illegal entry into U.S.: Illegal immigrants cross porous border from Ontario, Quebec', *Ottawa Citizen*, 8 Feb.

Bromowich, Michael. 1998. *Bombs in Brooklyn: How Two Illegal Aliens Arrested for Plotting to Bomb the New York Subway Entered and Remained in the United States*. Washington: Office of the Inspector General, US Department of Justice, Mar.

Cadman, Walter D. 1998. Prepared Testimony of Walter D. Cadman, Counterterrorism Coordinator, Office of Field Operations, Immigration and Naturalization Service, before the Senate Committee on the Judiciary, Subcommitee on Technology, Terrorism and Government Information Regarding Foreign Terrorist Activities in the United States, 24 Feb.

Canada-US Partnership Forum (CUSP). 2000. *Building a Border for the 21st Century: CUSP Forum Report*, Dec.

Cooper, Andrew F. 2000. 'Waiting at the Perimeter: Making US Policy in Canada', in F.O. Hampson and M.A. Molot, eds, *Canada Among Nations 2000: Vanishing Borders*. Toronto: Oxford University Press.

Dahlburg, John-Thor. 1996. 'Legacy of Fear: Afghanistan's Mix of Faith, Terror—A Global Scourge', *Los Angeles Times*, 6 Aug.

Farley, Maggie. 1999. 'Canada's Lapses Kept Algerian Suspect Free', *Los Angeles Times*, 23 Dec.

Federation for American Immigration Reform (FAIR). 1999. 'Sen. Abraham's Activities Have Increased the Risk of Terrorist Penetration, Says FAIR', Press Release, Washington, 20 Dec.

Hampson, Fen Osler, and Maureen Appel Molot. 2000. 'Does the 49th Parallel Matter Any More?', in Hampson and Molot, eds, *Canada Among Nations 2000: Vanishing Borders*. Toronto: Oxford University Press.

Keohane, Robert, and Joseph Nye. 1977. *Power and Interdependence: World Politics in Transition*. Boston: Little, Brown.

Krouse, William J., and Ruth Ellen Wasem. 1998. 'Immigration: Visa Entry/Exit Control System', Congressional Research Service Report for Congress. Washington. Library of Congress, 26 Aug.

Meyers, Deborah Waller, and Demetrios G. Papademetriou. 2001. 'Self-Governance Along the US-Canada Border: A View from Three Regions', in Meyers and Papademetriou, eds, *Caught in the Middle: Border Communities in an Era of Globalization*. Washington: Carnegie Endowment for International Peace.

Nieves, Evelyn. 1999. 'California Calls Off Effort to Carry Out Immigrant Measure', *New York Times*, 30 July.

Office of Homeland Security. 2001. 'Action Plan for Creating a Secure and Smart Border', Washington: Executive Office of the President of the United States, 12 Dec. Available at: <www.whitehouse.gov/news/releases/12/20011212-6.html>.

Sands, Christopher. 2001. 'Canada and the Bush Challenge', *Canada Focus* 2, 1. Washington: Center for Strategic and International Studies, Jan. Available at: <www.csis.org/americas/canada/focus/focus0101.html>.

Shea, Andrew. 2001. *Border Choices: Balancing the Need for Security and Trade*. Ottawa: Conference Board of Canada.

4

Another 'NEP': The Bush Energy Plan and Canada's Political and Policy Responses

G. BRUCE DOERN AND MONICA GATTINGER

The election of the Bush administration in the United States elevated Canadian, continental, and global energy issues to their highest level in some time. Energy issues were bumped up a notch further in the aftermath of the 11 September 2001 terrorist attacks when the security of energy facilities was added to the normal concerns about security of supply. Indeed, one of the first things the Chrétien Liberal government had to do following its own 2000 election victory and that of the Bush administration was to create a reference cabinet committee on energy.[1] In essence, the Chrétien cabinet had to re-educate itself about energy policy because for most of the previous 15 years energy policy seemed to tick along in a familiar way, sheltered by the pro-market consensus and low and stable oil and gas prices.

The Bush administration's National Energy Plan (Government of United States, 2001), ironically another 'NEP',[2] and high gasoline prices in 2000–1 changed the politics of energy in several respects. The Bush NEP report is titled *Reliable, Affordable, and Environmentally Sound Energy for America's Future*, and the three goals in the title are in order of priority. The Bush Republican administration is concerned about reducing US dependence on oil from the Middle-East. It faces electricity shortfalls and power outages in California caused by a less than ideal adoption of electricity deregulation combined with failures, partly due to environmentalist pressure, to build new power plants. It deeply opposes the Kyoto Protocol and, hence, stands against measures to reduce greenhouse gas emissions. It favours a supply-side solution centred on its own untapped Alaska reserves located in ecologically crucial lands populated by wildlife. But it also seeks secure long-term access to Mexican and Canadian energy, including Alberta's natural gas and its vast tar sands supply. There are environmental and conservation components to the Bush NEP but they are clearly not central to it, all the more so in light of the events of 11 September.

On the Canadian side of the political-economic and energy-environment equations sits a Chrétien Liberal government, returned to power for a third majority mandate but with serious political fences to mend in western Canada, where it won only a handful of seats. Mindful of not wanting to repeat the sins of the 1980 National Energy Program (the NEP), which was deeply despised in western Canada, the federal Liberals this time are determined to make gains in Alberta by supporting western Canadian energy producer ambitions rather than restraining them. But the Canadian record on Kyoto is little better than that of the US and hence the macro political-economic stage is set for a considerable re-politicization of energy in Canada, albeit in ways that are quite different from the last era of energy policy conflict in the late 1970s and early 1980s.

The purpose of this chapter is to examine the Bush NEP and Canada's political and policy responses, actual or likely. Our central argument is that mainstream energy politics and policy are unlikely to regard the main Bush energy initiatives as being troublesome to Canada. Indeed, quite the contrary: they may be seen as an opportunity for Canadian energy industries. But the growing and inevitable links with climate change and the obligations of the Kyoto Protocol are likely to make energy and climate change policy quite divisive within Canada, and especially between the federal government and

Alberta. To explore this central argument, we first set out the Bush energy plan and its rationale. The second section places the US plan in the context of past continental energy politics as a whole, and of the current continental energy political environment. This is followed in the third section by a brief assessment of the extent to which the Mexican equation in continental energy politics and policy affects Canada or changes the nature of bargaining and negotiation. The final section then switches to the core dynamics of the Canadian response. It examines the macro politics of energy, focusing first on the federal-Alberta equation and then on other key federal-provincial/regional dimensions.

THE BUSH NEP: WHAT IS IT?

In many respects, until the Bush NEP was announced in May 2001, Canadian energy policy as such might well have stayed on the back-burner of federal priorities. The high gasoline and heating prices of early 2001 have ameliorated somewhat. Nothing is more ironic than an American 'NEP' bringing energy policy back with a primacy not seen since the demise of Canada's NEP over 15 years ago But the Bush plan undoubtedly has major implications for pan-Canadian energy policy. Drafted by Vice-President Dick Cheney in a Bush administration whose cabinet contains several ex-energy industry executives, the Bush NEP is unabashedly a supply-driven and supply-dominated policy (ibid., viii–xviii; McGregor, 2001: 8). The policy was crafted in early 2001 in the midst of rapidly rising gas prices both at the pump and in home heating fuel and in the midst of the electricity crisis in California, where electricity prices were soaring and blackouts were frequent in a then still booming Internet-driven knowledge economy.

The central features of the Bush NEP aim to:

- ease restrictions on oil and gas development on public lands;
- open part of the Arctic National Wildlife Refuge in Alaska for drilling;
- reconsider requirements for 'boutique' gasoline blends that contribute to supply shortages;
- streamline the approval process for siting power plants;
- affirm government authority for the takeover of private property for power lines;

- provide tax breaks for developing clean coal technologies;
- ease regulatory barriers, including clean-air rules, to speed up expansion of or build new plants;
- speed nuclear safety reviews in the relicensing of reactors and the licensing of new plants;
- limit industry liability from a nuclear accident.

The Bush NEP also includes some tax breaks for renewable energy and conservation, but these are decidedly secondary to the plan as a whole (McGregor, 2001: 8).

The Bush plan received mixed reaction in the United States. As Hart and Tomlin (2002) point out, initially, its proposals to open up drilling in part of the Arctic National Wildlife Refuge (ANWR) in Alaska were sure to face opposition in the Senate, where the Democrats were in control. In the post-11 September political and economic climate, however, the prospects for drilling in the ANWR appear much more favourable, in order to reduce US dependence on oil supplies from the Middle East.

This plan has an impact on Canada simply because it affects the full North American energy industry. But the Bush plan also speaks of energy security for the US in terms of North American energy supply and thus Canada's oil and gas reserves are a key part of the continental plan. With a US Senate controlled by the Democratic Party and a House of Representatives controlled by the President's Republican Party, there is no guarantee that the US NEP will be approved in its entirety, but it is clearly the agenda to which everyone is now reacting. However, President Bush's political hand has undoubtedly been strengthened by his soaring popularity in the wake of the 11 September attacks.

Some of the added security emphasis was in evidence when Paul Cellucci, US Ambassador to Canada, spoke in terms of the need for a new continental energy pact. This seemed to be left at quite a vague level because what it appeared to mean in the short run was that Canada and the US should streamline their approvals process 'so that we can get the energy to where it is needed quickly' (Church, 2001:B2). The Canadian government's response to this kind of extra emphasis from the US side has been that the energy provisions in the North American Free Trade Agreement (NAFTA) and the earlier Canada–US Free Trade Agreement (FTA) are more than sufficient as a macro energy agreement.

The Bush administration's aggressive opposition to the Kyoto Protocol process and its above-mentioned supply-side energy policy focus create for Canada a curious mixture of both high and low politics. On the one hand, Canada can and has played the card of rhetorically criticizing the Bush US policy on Kyoto as the height of international arrogance and has pronounced that Canada will continue to support its Kyoto commitments. This kind of 'look good, feel good' foreign policy stance is contradicted, however, by the larger reality that Canada's energy policy has scarcely begun to comply with its Kyoto commitments (Schwanen, 2000) and faces a challenge of a magnitude similar to its American neighbour. Moreover, there is an overwhelming urge to sell more and more Canadian oil and gas to the energy-starved American economy and consumers.

HOW DO THE NEW CONTINENTAL ENERGY POLITICS DIFFER FROM THE PAST?

The new continental energy politics and context are similar in two major respects to 20 years ago, but different in at least four ways. The first similarity is the endurance of two unalterable facts: the United States has 10 times the population of Canada and Canada's resources are mainly located in the more sparsely populated parts of the country. This has meant that Canadian energy decisions are almost always simultaneously American decisions (Canada, 1988). Practically any major energy development, beyond the exploration stage and decisions regarding the financing and building of production facilities, involves not only American influence but decisions by American authorities and regulators. Over 40 per cent of oil and gas transported from one part of Canada to another traverses the US. While hydroelectric development was for a long period somewhat isolated from these continental realities, it, too, has increasingly been tied to the desire of provincial governments, which own these utilities, to export increasing amounts of electrical power to the United States (the huge James Bay projects in Quebec typify this trend). The fact that the Canadian oil and gas industry has been extensively American-owned only adds to this energy market dependence. Foreign ownership has been as high as 70 per cent; it was reduced in the 1970s and 1980s to about 40 per cent but edged upward again in the last decade and has recently increased as a result of a spate of takeovers of Canadian firms by US firms.

The second similarity with 20 years ago is that Canadian energy development has always been influenced by US policy, whether the latter is protectionist or market-oriented. It has been adversely affected in the past by US energy protectionism. This has come in the form of import taxes and fees, regulatory rules, and outright prohibitions (Doern and Toner, 1985). To a significant extent, when US energy policy changes, Canadian energy policy changes, too, albeit not always in lockstep. For example, the partial deregulation of natural gas in the US in the late 1970s and early 1980s certainly helped precipitate the Canadian effort to deregulate in 1985 and 1986, but then Canada's deregulation of gas actually proceeded much more quickly than that of the US. On the other hand, the introduction of electricity competition in the 1990s advanced more slowly in Canada (Natural Resources Canada, 2000).

If these first two features are examples of the continuing continental reality, the next point of reference is the first aberration. Contemporary continental dynamics will not likely include a Canadian exhibition of nationalist energy policy to match that of 20 years ago. In its budget in the fall of 1980 the Liberals announced their National Energy Program. The NEP was a massive act of federal intervention premised on the Liberals' campaign promise of fair 'made in Canada' prices. This involved 50 per cent Canadian ownership of the oil and gas industry and a promise to promote energy security, including self-sufficiency in oil by 1990. The NEP was premised on absolutely bullish expectations about rising future energy prices that failed to materialize (Doern and Toner, 1985; Desveaux, 1995).

The NEP was barely underway, however, when many of its underpinnings fell away. High interest rates and the 1982 worldwide recession dealt it an initial blow. Oil prices softened due to reduced demand caused by the recession itself, by political splits in the Organization of Petroleum Exporting Countries (OPEC), and by the cumulative effects of past conservation programs and the discovery of new world supplies. When combined with the new energy taxes and the uncertainties of the new NEP regime, the energy industry in Canada nose-dived. By mid-1982 the Liberal government was already prepared to change the policy.

The NEP did increase Canadian ownership and did produce a level of exploration in the frontier areas that increased knowledge of existing reserves. The gas industry infrastructure was expanded further into Quebec, and Petro-Canada became a formidable and symbolic presence in the consciousness of Canadians. But the great majority of professional energy policy opinion was that the NEP was a mistaken and seriously flawed policy. The view increasingly was that energy issues were too volatile economically and that no policy could anticipate or encompass all possible eventualities. Massive intervention only made things worse. The stage was set politically and economically for the return of a pro-market energy policy, as was undertaken by the Mulroney Conservative government.

Although the NEP was dismantled in 1985 under the Conservatives, the bitter distrust it produced in the relations between central and western Canada endured. The NEP became the quintessential example, especially in western Canada, of how not to make policy. It was seen as a combative unilateral act by an unsympathetic eastern-dominated government. This lesson was a major contributing factor in discussions in 1987–8 when energy free trade was secured through the Canada–US FTA (Doern and Tomlin, 1991). From the western Canadian perspective, the FTA ensured that there could never again be 'another NEP'. However, debates over the Kyoto Protocol on climate change provoked concern in the West that Kyoto would be 'another NEP', that is, another unilaterally imposed policy by eastern governments over western oil and gas. In effect, free trade has been the dominant reality of Canadian energy policy since the mid- to late 1980s and energy regulation has been affected both directly and indirectly by the free trade juggernaut (see more below).

Another key difference in the current period is the growing integration of the Canadian and US economies in the wake of free trade and other globalization pressures. Here the attention has shifted away from western oil and gas producers and their desire to entrench energy free trade, to Ontario-centred mainstream industries. From the early 1990s to the present, Canadian businesses have become more and more sensitive to their costs and competitiveness relative to American firms with which they compete in the US, Canadian, and global markets. Canadian firms have had the advantage of the lower Canadian dollar but have suffered from much lower productivity than their American counterparts and hence have paid ever greater attention to any area of cost advantage or disadvantage, including energy costs (Ontario, 1996). The most direct manifestation of such concern was in the cost of electricity, and this, along with concerns about

Ontario Hydro's managerial faults and nuclear plant difficulties, led to the establishment of the Macdonald Committee in 1996 by the province of Ontario and then to the eventual restructuring and deregulation of the Ontario electricity industry by the Harris Conservative government. Other threads of this issue are picked up later in this chapter.

The provisions of free trade agreements that now make nationalist policies virtually impossible are a third difference in the current era. The Canada–US FTA of 1987 greatly liberalized Canada–US trade; its energy chapter essentially prevents any actions by the federal government such as those that were at the core of the 1980 Liberal NEP, including two-price systems for oil and gas. The FTA also eliminates any realistic basis for Canada to shut off supply to the US, should Canadians need more of their own energy in an emergency. Some of the latter provisions for emergency sharing also exist under Canada's larger obligations through the International Energy Agency (IEA) and thus they are not just a free trade agreement provision. In essence, therefore, the Canada–US FTA did entrench oil and gas free trade in particular. The later 1993 NAFTA deal, which added Mexico to the now continental free trade area, did not significantly alter Canada's energy rules. It should be noted that Mexico, with its largely state-owned energy industry and constitutional prohibitions against foreign ownership in the petroleum sector, did fight for and retain some powers that Canada had ceded in 1987 (for example, foreign investment is not permitted in the Mexican oil and gas production and petrochemical services industries) (Cameron and Tomlin, 2000).

DOES THE MEXICO EQUATION MATTER?

There is, of course, a further difference in the contemporary era of energy continentalism—now it is truly continental. The North American energy market is increasingly integrated, indeed, truly continentalized. Energy market continentalization (especially of gas and electricity) has been enabled, on the one hand, by the FTA and NAFTA, and, on the other, by deregulatory reforms in all three countries, industrial convergence in gas and electricity, and developments in information technology that permit instantaneous market exchanges to take place (Dukert, 2000). The question for Canada is whether the Mexico equation matters. The answer undoubtedly is yes, but in quite uncertain ways. There are three elements of the equation that the Canadian government will have to factor in: (1) the so-called 'Tex-Mex' alliance between a US President from Texas, George W. Bush, and Mexico's new pro-market President Vicente Fox; (2) Mexico as a trade and energy market competitor to Canada but also as a source of economic opportunity; and (3) the nature of trilateral continental energy bargaining compared to bilateral Canada–US bargaining. We discuss each of these in turn.

When Vicente Fox, a pro-market enthusiast and former senior executive of the Coca-Cola Corporation, won the Mexican presidential election in July 2000, the victory ended 71 years of one-party rule in Mexico under the Institutional Revolutionary Party (PRI) and signalled that Mexico was poised for major change. When George W. Bush was elected President of the United States shortly thereafter, it was apparent that one dimension of change in Mexico might be closer bilateral relations with the United States. Bush, a former Texas governor, already possessed intimate working knowledge of Mexico and Mexican–American relations, and was personally acquainted with Fox. Perhaps because of his familiarity with Mexico, the newly inaugurated American President scheduled his first foreign visit to the country. The first meeting of the two presidents, the so-called 'cowboy boot' summit (in recognition of the two leaders' shared passion for Western footwear), was heralded on both sides of the Mexican–US border as a sign of closer relations between the two countries. In Canada, meanwhile, some interpreted the event not as cause for celebration but as a disturbing symptom that Canada's 'special relationship' with the US was deteriorating.[3] Because Bush's three predecessors had come to Canada for their first foreign visit, the cowboy boot summit was interpreted as an ominous sign that America was redirecting its attentions from Canada to Mexico. Regardless of whether President Bush's decision to head south rather than north on his first foreign trip signals an unfavourable turn in Canadian–American relations, it has served as an important reminder to Canada that Mexico is indeed a player in continental politics, and perhaps an increasingly powerful one. While Canada's two-way trade with the United States is still about twice that of Mexico's, the latter possesses a substantial voter community within the US (some 20 million Hispanic Americans) and Mexican–American trade is on the rise.

The second aspect of the Mexican equation is Mexico as energy competitor but also as a market opportunity for the Canadian energy sector. As energy competitor, Canada and Mexico are rivals in the American marketplace, especially in certain segments of the oil sector, because the US is a key export market for both countries. And under Bush's NEP, competition with Mexico could increase, as the US looks to Canada and Mexico for natural gas supplies (Mexico has large untapped natural gas reserves). But Mexico is not only a rival for the Canadian energy sector; the country is also increasingly a market opportunity. Mexico is currently a net importer of natural gas and electricity, and there is evidence that energy market continentalization has enabled Canada to sell gas and electricity into the Mexican market (Dukert, 2000: 350). In the oil sector, meanwhile, energy services contracting is a profitable market for foreign firms. Pemex, the state-owned oil and gas monopoly, is the only entity permitted by the Mexican constitution to extract oil and gas, but it contracts foreign firms to undertake virtually all construction, maintenance, and drilling work. Since the inception of NAFTA, this energy services market has been quite lucrative.

Moreover, with Vicente Fox now at the Mexican presidential helm, additional market opportunities are emerging for foreign firms. Fox is charting a new course for Mexico, including deregulatory reforms in the energy sector. While crude oil production will remain 'off-limits' to private investment, among Fox's reform plans are opening up electricity generation and certain components of the natural gas and petrochemicals sectors to direct private investment (Shields, 2001). Canadian firms are well positioned to capitalize on these upcoming investment opportunities, in part because Mexico looks to Canada as a key partner and to some extent a model for the political, social, and economic reforms it seeks to undertake, but also because Mexico's market access commitments through NAFTA accord Canadian companies privileged access to the Mexican market and because the Canadian government supports companies in their pursuit of market opportunities in Mexico (Mexico was the Export Development Corporation's second largest market for business volume in 2000) (Hough, 2001: 22–5).

The third dimension of the Mexican equation is the nature of trilateral continental energy relations in comparison to bilateral Canada–US relations. While there has always been a trilateral aspect to North American energy relations, bilateral US–Canadian and US–Mexican relations have tended to supersede trilateral relations. In more recent times, however, this hub-and-spoke configuration appears to be giving way to a more truly continentalized relationship, propelled in part by NAFTA, but also by the other drivers of market integration mentioned earlier—domestic deregulatory reform, industrial convergence, and developments in information technology. Perhaps the most visible manifestation of the move to energy trilateralism is the newly minted North American Energy Working Group, announced following the April 2001 meeting of Presidents Bush and Fox and Prime Minister Jean Chrétien during the Summit of the Americas in Quebec City. The Working Group was formed to explore continental energy co-operation. While Canada's Minister of Natural Resources maintains that the Working Group will not be negotiating a formal international agreement (quoted in Jeffs, 2001: A8), the trilateral talks may mark the beginning of a new era of energy trilateralism. The election of Vicente Fox may also signal a stronger trilateral—versus hub-and-spoke—approach to North American energy relations, since Fox has said he envisages a vastly expanded relationship with Canada (*St John's Evening Telegram*, 2000: 23).

FEDERAL LIBERAL ENERGY POLICY AND THE GENERAL POLITICS OF THE CANADIAN RESPONSE

The Liberals argue that since 1993, federal energy policy has been 'guided by the principles of sustainable development' and that its 'sustainable energy policy framework' consists of three main objectives:

- to develop a competitive and innovative energy sector—by implementing a framework that promotes the long-term development of Canadian energy resources, encourages wise use of energy resources, and maximizes economic opportunity in the energy sector for Canadians (which reflects the government's goal of promoting jobs and growth);
- to encourage environmental stewardship—by addressing the environmental impacts of energy development, transportation, and use and by integrating environmental objectives into all policies and programs;
- to establish secure access—by ensuring that current and future generations of Canadians have enough competitively priced energy and by taking measures that make efficient use of existing resources and provide reliable energy services to Canadians (Natural Resources Canada, 2000: 9).

The Liberal government's insistence that the principles of sustainable development underpin Canada's energy policy more closely resembles rhetoric than reality, however. Climate change policy is often seen as the acid test of whether sustainable development is being practised, and, as we have already noted and will discuss again shortly, Canada is seriously lagging in its Kyoto commitments to reduce greenhouse gas emissions. Without doubt, Canada's energy policy is certainly contextualized by the principles of sustainable development, but this is a decidedly different thing from being guided by such principles.

Within its very broad and complex notion of energy policy, the Chrétien Liberals see energy regulation, like all regulation, as having evolved considerably in the last 20 years, 'driven by the same global trends—globalization, deregulation, increased environmental awareness, and the overall theme of reliance on markets' (ibid., 137). Federal energy policy views energy regulation as being quintessentially federal and provincial in nature, and increasingly continental and global as well, and perceives the management of energy markets to mean 'more markets–less government'. But in the very next breath the same statement says that 'environmental concerns are growing' and that 'contrary to the trend towards trusting markets and competition, environmental concerns, particularly those related to energy, often call for more regulation' (ibid., 138). The federal view also stresses that energy commodities are 'no longer considered "unique" or "special"' and that contemporary energy regulation must be contrasted with the 1970s and early 1980s when it was driven by several different precepts.

- A perception of scarcity—the world's energy resources were finite, while demand for energy would inevitably rise. The demand for energy needed to be regulated.
- An emphasis on security—Western countries were susceptible to disruptions in their supply.
- An emphasis on self-sufficiency—Canada sought to reduce its vulnerability by protecting and increasing its domestic supply of energy.
- An expectation of rising prices—with scarcity came the belief that prices for energy would rise.
- A perception of market inadequacy—oil markets, in particular, were distorted and concentrated, which led to oligopoly control (ibid., 137).

If these are the core Liberal views of energy policy, then how do domestic energy politics in Canada align or conflict with the core elements of the Bush NEP, some of which depend on increased government intervention within the US and vis-à-vis its continental neighbours? Two elements of these political forces need to be canvassed: the Chrétien agenda vis-à-vis Alberta and Alberta's own response domestically and internationally; and the response of other energy consumer and producer regions/provinces in Canada, including the reconfigured politics of energy in the North, the interests of Aboriginal peoples, and the building of new pipelines for Canadian and US gas supply routes to the United States.

The Chrétien Liberals and the Wooing of Alberta

The Chrétien agenda regarding Alberta and the Bush NEP is quite straightforward. Perhaps with an eye on his place in history, Chrétien has made a determined bid to woo Alberta since the 2000 election when the Liberals won only a handful of seats in western Canada. He seems determined to make future electoral gains in that province and in western Canada more generally. Right from the time of the announcement that Vice-President Cheney would head up a US energy committee, Chrétien has personally stressed the great business opportunities that US energy markets represent for Alberta and the West. Former federal Minister of Natural Resources, Ralph Goodale, whose political base is in Saskatchewan, and new Minister Herb Dhaliwal of BC also ensure that a pro-western Canadian position is being developed. As Goodale stated in April 2001, 'Canada expects that a continental energy market will result in billions of dollars of US investment in Alberta's tar sands and proposals for a new gas pipeline through Canada's north within the year' (Fife, 2001: A1). Chrétien has also made several speaking trips to Alberta and has gone out of his way to praise Alberta Premier Ralph Klein's contributions to national unity. Some of this wooing, of course, coincided with the implosion of the Canadian Alliance under its first leader, Stockwell Day. These combined developments have undoubtedly suggested to federal Liberal strategists that Alberta was 'up for grabs' politically in a way that would not have been foreseen in the immediate aftermath of Chrétien's 2000 election victory. In late August 2001, the federal Liberal caucus held a pre-autumn planning caucus meeting in Edmonton, and energy development was the focus of a Chrétien speech on 23 August. Perhaps as a trial balloon, but in the same speech, Chrétien indirectly suggested that Albertans might have to share their wealth with other less fortunate Canadians by noting that 'You're in an extremely fortunate situation in Alberta, but it's creating pressures on the neighbouring provinces' (*Globe and Mail*, 2001: A1). Some of his reference to other provinces dealt with the fact that a richer Alberta could pay higher salaries to doctors and nurses and thus attract them to Alberta, but as a result create severe shortages in the exporting provinces. Following an immediate backlash from Albertans about any federal moves along these lines, Chrétien quickly clarified that this comment did not mean 'another NEP' was in the works. Indeed, he said the 'NEP is long dead' (McCarthy and Mahoney, 2001: A1).

Another way that the Chrétien Liberals sought to assuage western concerns was by stating that a new continental energy pact was not necessary because NAFTA's energy chapter was functioning well. Thus it was the only deal required and the key was therefore to work within it and ensure, through the new cabinet reference committee on energy chaired by then Foreign Affairs Minister John Manley, that the government had a co-ordinated approach on pipelines and related issues.

Meanwhile, Ralph Klein's Alberta government, also freshly elected with a third mandate in March 2001, was leaving nothing to chance. Klein immediately sought and obtained a right to meet directly with Cheney and with US officials to remind them that Alberta and other provinces were the owners of oil and gas resources. The Chrétien Liberals agreed to this and put no obstacles in his way. The Klein government's political calculus was crafted not just with memories of the 1980s NEP in mind. While the Bush plan was very positive news for the Alberta economy, the Alberta government had been experiencing severe political criticism over soaring energy prices in the province. Both natural gas and electricity prices had increased sharply in the winter of 2000–1, which forced the Alberta Tories to create a rebate scheme to assist Albertans with their home heating bills. Alberta's natural gas price increases were driven by national increases and by heavy US demand. Together, these forces combined to push Alberta's prices even higher than the average Canadian price hikes. Alberta's electricity prices and some experience with power shortages were attributed to problems with Alberta's deregulation of electricity markets, a market-based reform where Alberta led the way in Canada. Because California was experiencing even more serious electricity problems, there was an easy media linkage about the excesses of rely-ing on markets. Alberta's electricity problems were not parallel to those of California, but the overall climate was such that Premier Klein had to be careful about his own energy politics. In any event, Klein easily won a third term.

In addition to these direct Ottawa–Alberta dynamics on the Bush NEP are Ottawa–Alberta relations on the Kyoto Protocol. The Kyoto Protocol on the United Nations Framework Convention on Climate Change (UNFCCC) was agreed to in December 1997. Under its terms, Canada undertook to reduce its greenhouse gas (GHG) emissions by 6 per cent below their 1990 levels averaged over the 2008–12 period (Natural Resources Canada, 2000: 159–65; Schwanen, 2000). But given a serious lag in action, that commitment now amounts to a 26 per cent reduction. However, as Schwanen stresses, the problem is how to achieve it:

> Unfortunately, the Kyoto targets were set without reference to the cost of meeting them (or to their potential benefits relative to those of following alternative scenarios of emissions reductions and time frames). Considering how far Canada is from reaching its Kyoto target and how closely the emis-sions of the principal GHGs resulting from human activity are linked with the growth and type of economic activity the country has typically enjoyed, a serious attempt at meeting the commitment within a given timetable would likely involve significant changes in the economy and even in Canadian lifestyles (Schwanen, 2000: 1).

After the 1997 Kyoto Protocol was negotiated, Prime Minister Chrétien and the premiers directed the federal, provincial, and terri-torial ministers of energy and environment 'to examine the impacts, costs and benefits of implementing the Kyoto Protocol, as well as the options for addressing climate change' (National Climate Change Process, 2000: 2). They were to do so under 'a guiding principle that no region should bear an unreasonable burden from implementing the Protocol' (ibid.). Thus, at the political level, Canada recognized the central importance of equity considerations among the country's regions, analogous to the larger 'equity' debate in the global negoti-ations among countries. Such a principle was undoubtedly needed in an overall national unity sense, but it was especially imperative for accommodating Alberta. Alberta was already rhetorically casting Kyoto as 'another NEP' and, of course, it knew that it was the province at the heart of the carbon-producing part, albeit not the core carbon-consuming part, of the Canadian economy.

One further element of Canada's approach to the Kyoto Protocol negotiations and implementation, nationally and internationally, is the issue of carbon sinks. Canada sought, and at Bonn in 2001 eventually obtained, agreement for the crediting of carbon sinks for removing carbon dioxide from the environment. This was based on the fact that plants and trees 'breathe in' and store CO_2 from the atmosphere; thus, forests and agricultural soils that absorb and store CO_2 are known as 'carbon sinks' under the Kyoto Protocol. Canada wanted credit for enhancing sinks (Canada, 2001). Crediting for carbon sinks became a key negotiating issue on several levels: moral, political, and economic. The European Union and many non-governmental organizations (NGO) sought to exclude them on the grounds that they did not represent real greenhouse emission reductions and that indeed they were not based, in the view of some, on 'credible science'. Canada and other countries with large forests, such as Australia, Japan, and Russia, supported the inclusion of carbon sinks. In the end the Bonn 2001 agreement included them under certain conditions.

The carbon sinks element of the Kyoto story is complex in its own right, but it is of particular import to the domestic regulatory politics of the eventual national position and of the core regulatory bargain. For Canada, a forest sinks provision had to be part of the package or else the country would have had to impose rather draconian direct emission control targets in a way that would undermine national unity (as defined partly by provincial governments) and would violate federal-provincial principles, such as not imposing undue burdens on any one region.

The above discussion of some key international and national elements of Kyoto certainly suggests that while the Protocol is ultimately regulatory (given its dependence on targeted emission reductions when it comes into force and is implemented), the Alberta equation is central to Canadian action and inaction. During the Bonn negotiations in July 2001, Alberta's Environment Minister, Lorne Taylor, praised Ottawa initially during the negotiations for moving away from the 1997 Kyoto accord by pressing for credits for forest sinks. The difference in Alberta politics was that even its Environment Minister went out of his way to say Alberta is a 'Kyoto agnostic' and Taylor, moreover, returned to the NEP rhetoric by saying that Kyoto would do more harm to his province's economy than the hated NEP of two decades earlier and that it would 'shut our economy down' (McKinnon, 2001: A1). Thus, Ottawa–Alberta relations on the Bush NEP are both affected by and impact on Ottawa–Alberta relations on Kyoto and on federal political aspirations in the West.

Other Regional–Provincial Energy Politics

Compared to 20 years ago, other regional–provincial energy political configurations are also more complex. This complexity, however, is still anchored by the fact that in comparison to other Western federal countries, Canada probably has the most divided and decentralized jurisdictional framework for energy. This arises primarily because of the extensiveness of direct provincial ownership of lands containing energy resources and as a result of strong provincial managerial powers over resource extraction (Pratt and Richards, 1980). The federal government also has jurisdictional capacity that can directly and indirectly influence energy development. Provincial powers are derived from section 109 of Canada's Constitution Act, 1867, which assigns control of all lands, mines, minerals, and royalties to the provinces. Provincial ownership is reinforced through the property and civil rights clause, s. 92(13), the power to levy direct taxes, s. 92(2), and the authority over management and sale of public lands, s 92(50). Federal power resides in the trade and commerce clause, s. 91(2), which confers powers over interprovincial trade, and s. 91(3), which enables the federal government to tax by any mode or means, as well as in the federal government's emergency and declaratory powers and treaty powers. The federal government also has direct ownership of the vast Canada Lands (the North and offshore) over which it has all the powers of a province as well as the powers of the owner. Some of these latter powers have been in dispute in two senses: in some cases, offshore areas, such as those off Newfoundland, raise provincial-like disputes; and in some cases Native peoples' land claims are in dispute.

Divided jurisdiction means that energy policy-making is always a process of federal–provincial bargaining. This has been most intense over oil and gas issues. In the realm of hydroelectric power, which is also a traditional area of monopoly economic activity, provincial ownership has been the norm. Moreover, with only limited interprovincial trade in electricity, it has generally escaped significant federal–provincial dispute. With regard to uranium and aspects of nuclear power development, the federal government has the upper hand, mainly due to powers granted at the dawn of the nuclear age during World War II. Even here, however, there are important elements of shared power. For example, Ontario is by far the largest producer and user of nuclear power and Saskatchewan has huge uranium reserves (Doern et al., 2001).

Canada's vast spatial imperatives also ensure that most energy developments involve large transportation-pipeline links to bring energy supplies to market. Individual projects, usually megaprojects, therefore become very visible because of their cost and risk. Both political and business careers are 'on the line' with the full glare of national and regional media coverage. Governments at the federal and provincial levels have both risen to and fallen from power on the basis of the promises, successes, and failures of such projects. And with the political emergence of an environmental movement in the late 1960s, the linkage between energy and environment has only intensified and become both more complex and more specific. The increased political visibility of the moral case advanced by Aboriginal peoples for their land claims in energy-rich areas has also enhanced the links. Environmental-energy issues first peaked on the national political-economic agenda in the mid-1970s when a major commission of inquiry, the Berger Inquiry, examined the desirability of building the huge proposed Mackenzie Valley gas pipeline. Because of the Berger hearings and the sensitivities they raised, the project was put on hold (Bregha, 1980).

However, central to immediate Canadian policy in response to the Bush NEP (but also to expanded energy free trade with the US) is the selection of the route and then the planned construction of a massive $20 billion pipeline to bring Alaska (and Canadian) natural gas to the US market (Toulin, 2001: A1). The Alaska gas reserves are estimated at 100 trillion cubic feet, enough to supply the American market for 50–60 years. There are two routes under consideration. One route, the Alaska Highway project, would travel down an existing land route in Alaska, across Yukon, and into Alberta. The other route, the Mackenzie Valley route, is based on a pipeline buried in a trench across the Beaufort Sea, which then would move south along the Mackenzie Valley to Alberta. Either route would require a new pipeline from Alberta on to Chicago.

The Canadian political preference appears to be the Mackenzie Valley route, but the Chrétien government has said it will rely on the private sector to pick the most economical route. Nonetheless, the politics will be complex because the Alaska government is pushing hard for the Alaska route. Pipelines always bring the highly visible politics of megaproject choices, including spinoff benefits and local employment.

While these are in some overall sense similar to earlier pipeline debates, a key difference from 30 years ago is in the politics of Canada's North and its Aboriginal peoples. In the past, Aboriginal peoples were fiercely opposed to pipeline development, in part on environmental grounds but also because Aboriginal land claims and treaty rights were only beginning to be addressed. This time around, Aboriginal peoples and the territorial governments are generally supportive of pipeline and energy development, provided there is partial Aboriginal ownership of the pipelines and supporting businesses and that local employment preferences are built into the projects. There are difficult negotiations ahead on these questions, but it is nonetheless true that the northern and Aboriginal political culture has changed since the Berger era of 25 years ago.

With regard to other core provincial–regional interests and orientations, the broad picture is also supportive of continental energy accommodation. British Columbia's new Liberal government is decidedly pro-business and anxious to take advantage of burgeoning natural gas development and also of BC's role as supplier of residual electricity to California as that state's crisis is resolved. British Columbia also has a vested interest in the developing Ballard hydrogen fuel cell technologies, which are now attracting major investment and are intended to help decarbonize the economy.

For Ontario, the core political-economic instinct is to ensure low oil and gas prices in Canada's largest energy-consuming province. As mentioned earlier, this is now not only a raw consumer instinct but also an Ontario instinct of industrial competitiveness as Ontario's industries become ever more sensitive to competitive energy and other business costs compared to their US competitors and markets. Ontario's policy of restructuring its electricity industry also makes it more sensitive to natural gas supplies and needs, in part because it wants to encourage new gas-fired technologies for electricity generation.

In addition, Ontario relies on nuclear power to a greater extent than any other province, and its response to the Bush NEP is complex in this respect. On the one hand, Ontario's restructuring policy seems to be moving away from its nuclear CANDU reactor reliance; on the other hand, the nuclear service industry sector (including the federal Crown corporation, Atomic Energy of Canada Limited) and Ontario's management of its own reactors may be able to gain from the Bush NEP, which sees the possible need for new reactors in the US or significant refurbishment programs to extend the life of existing reactors.

Atlantic Canada also sees opportunity in the continental agenda, since offshore oil and gas development in Nova Scotia and Newfoundland is now more extensive and energy exports to the US are seen as pivotal. These two provinces have used the Bush agenda and its attending political climate as a way to press Ottawa to hand over more of the oil and gas revenues to the two provinces. At present, these are jointly shared through the offshore co-management agreements between each province and Ottawa. Alliances with Alberta and other provinces were fostered on this point in the summer of 2001 to increase pressure on the Chrétien Liberals.

CONCLUSIONS

This chapter has examined the Bush administration's National Energy Plan and Canada's political and policy responses to the initiative. Our central argument is that mainstream energy politics and policy are unlikely to regard the main Bush energy initiatives as being troublesome to Canada. Indeed, quite the contrary: they are seen as an opportunity for Canadian energy industries. But the growing and inevitable links with climate change and the obligations of the Kyoto Protocol are likely to make energy and climate change policy quite divisive within Canada, and especially between the federal government and Alberta. It is also quite possible that the evolving energy developments will spur on debate and conflict over contending definitions and senses of security (security of sources of supply, the physical security of pipelines and power plants, and the security of the planet's climate). Accordingly, these developments may produce quite different ways of debating about what actually constitutes Canada's energy 'reserves'. This, of course, cuts to the heart of the debate about the carbon versus non-carbon economy and about the mixed carbon and non-carbon economy we are increasingly likely to have.

Broadly speaking, the Canadian response to the Bush energy plan has been one of accommodation, though with some care taken to indicate that no new continental energy pacts are needed from the

Canadian perspective. The Bush NEP is largely a supply-driven plan, seeking energy security through expanded resource development in the US and by securing access to North American energy supplies. While the Canadian government has been critical of the US record on Kyoto and President Bush's opposition to the Protocol, the Chrétien Liberals have given a positive reception to the Bush NEP and have fudged their own dubious record on greenhouse gas emission reductions.

The Canadian federal government has been supportive of Western producer ambitions and cautious to tread lightly in Ottawa–Alberta relations. In part, this reflects the institutional context of continental energy politics, where free trade agreements render impossible a federal interventionist strategy along the lines of the former National Energy Program. But to a greater extent, Ottawa's support for the West is probably based on the prospect of future electoral gains in Alberta and western Canada. The Bush NEP also arrives at a time when Ottawa–Alberta relations are already strained over the eventual implementation of the Kyoto Protocol. The Bush plan has enjoyed an equally receptive response in other provinces and regions in Canada, from support in the North for new pipeline development, to opportunities for Ontario in the nuclear services market, to anticipated sales of oil and gas and resultant royalty revenues for Atlantic Canada.

Energy has ascended rapidly on the political agenda in both the United States and Canada, and is likely to continue to be an important political priority in the aftermath of the 11 September terrorist attacks, as energy security concerns are bound to intensify. Those attacks, and American responses to them, may serve to broaden and deepen support for the Bush NEP within both the United States and Canada. In the US, growing energy security concerns may even help to overcome congressional resistance to opening up the Arctic National Wildlife Refuge in Alaska for drilling, and will likely deepen President Bush's commitment to secure access to Canadian and Mexican energy reserves. In Canada, the existing urge to capitalize on new opportunities in the American energy market will likely multiply as both federal and provincial governments look to energy resource revenues to fill government coffers at a time of extreme economic uncertainty and new military, security, and other expenditure requirements in the aftermath of 11 September. The terrorist attacks in the United States are likely to result in the Canadian government extending a positive reception to the US National Energy Plan, but the same plan is likely to trigger important debates about exactly what energy security means in an era of climate change and with regard to real or alleged policies on energy policy guided by sustainable development.

NOTES

1. This committee, chaired by John Manley, also included Ralph Goodale and Anne McLellan, two westerners who at the time chaired the two major cabinet committees on economic and social policy.
2. By 'another NEP', we are referring to Canada's ill-fated 1980 National Energy Program, an energy initiative that ironically bears the same acronym as the Bush NEP. Canada's NEP, as we will elaborate further on in this chapter, was hated in western Canada, and the enduring political dynamics it unleashed are crucial to understanding Canada's current political and policy responses to the Bush NEP.
3. Perhaps the most vocal proponent of this view was former Foreign Affairs Minister Lloyd Axworthy. See Lindgren (2001: A1).

REFERENCES

Bregha, François. 1980. *Bob Blair's Pipeline*. Toronto: Lorimer.

Cameron, Maxwell, and Brian Tomlin. 2000. *The Making of NAFTA: How The Deal Was Done*. Ithaca, NY: Cornell University Press.

Canada. 1988. *Energy and Canadians into the 21st Century*. Ottawa: Minister of Supply and Services.

———. 2001. *Canada's Position on Forests and Agriculture Sinks*. Ottawa: Natural Resources Canada.

Church, Elizabeth. 2001. 'US Ambassador Raises Energy Integration', *Globe and Mail*, 31 Oct., B2.

Desveaux, James. 1995. *Designing Bureaucracies: Institutional Capacity and Large-Scale Problem-Solving*. Stanford, Calif.: Stanford University Press.

Doern, Bruce, Arslan Dorman, and Robert Morrison, eds. 2001. *Canadian Nuclear Energy Policy: Changing Ideas, Institutions and Interests*. Toronto: University of Toronto Press.

——— and Brian Tomlin. 1991. *Faith and Fear: The Free Trade Story*. Toronto: Stoddart.

——— and Glen Toner. 1985. *The Politics of Energy*. Toronto: Methuen.

Dukert, Joseph M. 2000. 'The Evolution of the North American Energy Market: Implications of Continentalization for a Strategic Sector of the Canadian Economy', *American Review of Canadian Studies* 30, 3: 349–59.

Fife, Robert. 2001. 'PM Touts Canada as US Fuel Tank: Working with Cheney on Plan to Supply Energy from Canada's West and North', *National Post*, 6 Apr., A1.

Government of United States. 2001. *Reliable, Affordable, and Environmentally Sound Energy for America's Future*. Washington: US Government Printing Office.

Hart, Michael, and Brian Tomlin. 2002. 'Inside the Perimeter: The US Policy Agenda and Its Implications for Canada', in G. Bruce Doern, ed., *How Ottawa Spends: 2002–2003*. Toronto: Oxford University Press, ch. 3.

Hough, Marvin. 2001. 'Mexico Inc.: Under New Management', *ExportWise* (June): 22–5.

International Energy Agency. 1998a. *Energy Policies of IEA Countries: The United States 1998 Review*. Paris: OECD/IEA.

———. 1998b. *Natural Gas Pricing in Competitive Markets*. Paris: OECD/IEA.

———. 1999. *Energy Policies of IEA Countries: 1998 Review*. Paris: OECD/IEA.

Jeffs, Allyson. 2001. 'Provinces not invited to negotiate energy policy: Alberta may have to give up its demand to participate in continental talks', *Edmonton Journal*, 22 June, A8.

Lindgren, April. 2001. 'Canada stuck in "time warp": Axworthy on foreign policy: "We can't do business as usual"; "Special relationship" with US has been taken for granted', *Ottawa Citizen*, 15 Feb., A1.

McCarthy, Shawn, and Jill Mahoney. 2001. 'PM's Talk Infuriates Albertans', *Globe and Mail*, 24 Aug., A1.

McGregor, Deborah. 2001. 'Plan Fuels Flames of War between Two Parties', *Financial Times* (London), 18 May, 8.

MacKinnon, Mark. 2001. 'Kyoto Pact Would Destroy Economy, Alberta Says', *Globe and Mail*, 20 July, A1.

National Climate Change Process. 2000. *Canada's National Implementation Strategy on Climate Change*. Ottawa: Government of Canada.

Natural Resources Canada. 2000. *Energy in Canada 2000*. Ottawa: Natural Resources Canada.

Ontario. 1996. *A Framework for Competition. Report of the Advisory Committee on Competition in the Ontario Electricity System to the Ontario Ministry of Environment and Energy*. Toronto: Province of Ontario.

Pratt, Larry, and J. Richards. 1980. *Prairie Capitalism*. Toronto: McClelland & Stewart.

Schwanen, Daniel. 2000. *A Cooler Approach: Tackling Canada's Commitments on Greenhouse Gas Emissions*. Toronto: C.D. Howe Institute.

Shields, David. 2001. 'Mexican Pipeline: The Future of Oil Under Vicente Fox', *Report on the Americas* 34, 4: 31–7.

St. John's Evening Telegram. 2000. 'Mexico's new leader seeks stronger Canada-Mexico ties', 21 Aug., 23.

Toulin, Alan. 2001. '$20 Billion Pipeline to be Biggest Private Project Ever in N. America', *National Post*, 27 July, A1.

5

The Open Door Beyond the Moat: Canadian Refugee Policy from a Comparative Perspective

STEPHEN GALLAGHER

Canada is the easiest country in the world for an immigrant to gain 'convention refugee' status. It is also the easiest country in the world for a failed refugee applicant to gain permanent-resident status (PRS). In addition, Canada agrees to 'resettle' a large number of refugees from overseas and, on a per capita basis, operates the largest resettlement program in the world. While a debate rages on whether this is in the national interest, the objective here is to provide an overview of the logic, operation, and impact of Canada's refugee policy.

To begin with, there are two types of refugee claimant. The first makes an application to come to a resettlement country such as Canada. Often, the Office of the United Nations High Commissioner for Refugees (UNHCR) facilitates these applications from camps it operates. The host country reviews the claim, accepts it, and 'resettles' the refugee. Canada, the United States, and Australia are countries that have resettlement programs, and Canada in particular has a proud history in this regard. The focus of this study is the second type, the self-selected refugee claimant who chooses a country and travels there to submit a request for asylum. This phenomenon of 'asylum-seeking' is of recent origin, facilitated by the emergence of globalized transportation and communications links. An asylum-seeker arriving in a country can make a claim directly to a specialized administration established for reviewing in-country claims. In the US, claims are heard by the Immigration and Naturalization Service (INS), in the United Kingdom by the Immigration and Nationality Directorate (IND) of the Home Department, and in Canada by the Immigration and Refugee Board (IRB).

Canada is obligated to hear such claims because it has signed the 1951 Geneva Convention on the Status of Refugees. The fundamental commitment embodied in the Geneva Convention is not to return individuals fleeing persecution to the area of their flight (*non-refoulement*). Currently, all developed countries, with the exception of Japan, face a significant flow of asylum-seekers arriving from post-Communist countries and the developing world.[1] Some are clearly economic migrants, but turmoil is endemic in many parts of the world and large numbers have a clear claim to Geneva Convention protection.

In response to asylum-seeking, migratory flow countries in the developed world have established means of blocking passage. Canada is no exception to the effort to block migratory movements. Canada imposes visas on over a hundred countries and imposes fines on transportation companies that even inadvertently carry refugee claimants to Canada.

Canada is unusual, however, in the generosity of its in-country refugee determination system and its treatment of failed claimants. This is to say, Canada's refugee policy provides a relatively effective means of entering and remaining in Canada for extended periods. Second, it provides immediate access to generous social benefits, including employment. Finally, the majority of claimants eventually gain PRS and, one presumes, go on to become Canadian citizens. The reason for this lies in the fact that Canada's interpretation of what constitutes a convention refugee is relatively broad and Canada does not resort to regulatory practices that cause large numbers of asylum-seekers to be turned away from other countries without a hearing or after an expedited process.

That Canada has sustained such policies while all other developed countries are more restrictive can be attributed to a number of factors. These include a powerful 'anti-populist norm',[2] the impact of partisan electoral interests, the effect of interest groups, and the existence of a large and relatively uncontroversial immigration program. The result is an inconsistency between the efforts of the government to block asylum-seekers before they reach Canadian soil and their treatment if access is gained. In effect, the door is open for asylum-seekers to enter Canada, but they have to cross a moat of entry controls to reach it.

CANADA'S REFUGEE POLICY AND INTERNATIONAL COMMITMENTS

Canada's refugee policy includes internal and external government programs that affect people who choose or are forced to leave their existing living space in order to make a claim of asylum in Canada. We can speak of 'push' factors that force people to leave their existing living space. This may involve some form of 'persecution'. There are also 'pull' factors, which relate to the pursuit of a better life elsewhere. When coupled with a flight from persecution, some pull factors might be considered legitimate reasons to seek refuge in a particular country. These might include reuniting a family, seeking out a country with a liberal refugee determination system, or wanting to relocate in a country perceived to have a fair legal system. In the past two decades, the cumulative effect of these forces brought about approximately 560,000 'humanitarian' arrivals in Canada (CIC, 2000: Figure 1). The vast majority of these people were 'spontaneous arrivals', that is, self-selected in-country refugee claimants. It should be kept in mind that although push and pull factors are important to understanding asylum-seeking behaviour, efforts to weld the concepts to a determination on whether a person is a legitimate 'convention refugee' are fraught with difficulty.

Canada's in-country, or what the government calls 'landed', system of convention refugee determination, is currently administered by the Convention Refugee Determination Division (CRDD) of the IRB. With the passage of the Immigration and Refugee Protection Act in 2001, this Division will soon become the Refugee Protection Division and a new Refugee Appeal Division will be added. The obligation to establish and maintain a refugee determination system derives from the fact that Canada is one of approximately 140 countries to have signed the 1951 Geneva Convention on the Status of Refugees along with its 1967 protocol. These international commitments are embedded in the Immigration and Refugee Protection Act and grant a right to refuge to individuals arriving in Canada who have fled their country 'owing to well-founded fear of being persecuted for reasons of race, religion, nationality, membership of a particular social group or political opinion'. Geneva Convention signatories must establish a 'determination' process to evaluate 'claims', and if the 'persecution' test is met the individual is designated a 'convention refugee'. In Canada a convention refugee is given the opportunity to apply for permanent resident status, which grants access to an extensive range of social benefits as well as a right to apply eventually for Canadian citizenship.

Unlike its colleagues in the club of rich nations, Canada has not responded to the rising tide of asylum-seekers by moving to make, or reinforce, hard decisions that compromise liberal humanist values (Boswell, 2000). The underlying reason for the development of exclusionary policies is wrapped up in the significance of the Geneva Convention obligation. By signing the Geneva Convention, a national government chooses to protect the human rights of foreign individuals regardless of the interests of its own citizens. This is because convention refugee status grants residence within the host country and access to some social benefits. If the influx is large, the costs may be high. The host country might even be destabilized. For most countries, there are practical limits, or at least perceived limits, on the number of convention refugees and asylum-seekers they are capable of hosting. For this reason, the debate over the Geneva Convention tends to pit nationalists against rights advocates.[3] At times the debate creates strange bedfellows because socialists and unionists might oppose an open-door refugee policy on the grounds that it could weaken the state's capacity to provide generous benefits to its own workers.

With respect to the important points, Canada's in-country regime for refugee determination was fixed for the whole of the 1990s.[4] A major rewriting of legislative controls was tabled in Parliament early in 2000 (Bill C-31), but was allowed to die when a federal election was called for October 2000. After the election, a modified version of the legislation, Bill C-11, the Immigration and Refugee Protection Act, was introduced in Parliament in February 2001 and passed by the end of the year.[5]

It is unclear how the new law will affect the final disposition of asylum-seekers entering Canada. There is an assumption, however, that Canada's refugee determination system will be significantly tightened. This is by no means assured. First, the IRB retains its independence of decision-making and the case law on which its decisions are made is unaffected. Second, the new legislation does not significantly limit judicial review of IRB and Citizenship and Immigration Canada (CIC) decision-making. When the US, UK, and Australia (among others) reformed their refugee systems during the 1990s, significant limitations on judicial appeals were core elements of reform. Finally, if determination (and post-determination) policies were significantly tightened, failed refugee claimants would have to be removed in numbers not previously seen. It is doubtful that the political will or interest exists to sustain such reform. For example, when regulations related to the new Act were announced in January 2002, Liberal backbenchers attacked their own minister, who has since been replaced, for endangering the party's 'bedrock immigrant support' (Aubry, 2002: A1). Alternatives likely will be considered, and there has already been a call to expedite the review of the substantial backlog of refugee claims that has built up in the existing system in preparation for the new regulatory environment. When the IRB was first established in 1988, it was thought necessary to expedite the process of refugee determination for as many as 122,000 claimants who had arrived between May 1986 and December 1988. This group was reviewed by a 'backlog administration' using significantly lower standards and the vast majority were granted PRS.

What has changed, however, is Canada's attitude to border security, which could have a significant impact on asylum-seeking. This is especially the case if Canada reaches an agreement with the US on treating each other as 'safe countries' for the purposes of refugee determination. This is because more than half of Canada's refugee claimants enter from the US. There were US–Canada negotiations in the mid-1990s to reach such an agreement, but the negotiations failed for the likely reason that asylum-seeking flows are essentially one-way north while the flow south is made up of economic migrants seeking to avoid detection. Put simply, the US has no 'burden' to share with Canada. The potential exists for a deal, however, if Canada were willing to reform its visa policies. Such reform would crack down on economic migrants using Canada as a transit point to gain entry to the US, and in return the US might be willing to intercept asylum-seekers passing through the US to make a refugee claim at the Canadian border. Canada might also refuse to hear the cases of those who pass through the US on their way to Canada to make a claim (i.e., introduce a safe third-country policy). These claimants could be turned over to the Americans for the purpose of refugee determination. This would constitute a 'safe third-country' policy whose logic is that once a refugee reaches safety, subsequent movement constitutes economic migration (asylum shopping).[6] Of course, when such policies were introduced in Europe (Dublin Convention) asylum-seekers began evading entry controls and once inside the target country they would destroy their travel documents and deny knowledge of how they arrived. Without proof of origin it is difficult to return asylum-seekers to third countries.

Recently there has been movement towards a border security agreement. On 3 December 2001, Canada and the US signed a statement entitled Joint Statement of Cooperation on Border Security and Regional Migration Issues (DFAIT, 2001). One of the objectives was to intercept illegal migration. Two measures set out in the agreement were a visa 'policy review' and developing a 'safe third country agreement' (CIC, 2001b). Later in December, Canada added a visa requirement for several countries that had a history of 'passport-issuing irregularities' and 'irregular migration'. Not among these countries, however, was South Korea, whose nationals require a visa to enter the US but not Canada. South Korea has been identified by the US as the source of a steady stream of illegal migration.

FORTRESS FIRST WORLD

The flow of asylum-seekers to Canada must be viewed in a context of global migration. The post-World War II era opened with the flow of immigrants and 'guest workers' into America and Europe being encouraged by government policy. In Western Europe the economic miracle of the early post-war period, coupled with a shortage of young men, meant wages were rising and work was available. Government policy in West Germany encouraged workers to come from Southern Europe and Turkey, while the UK and France did not discourage the inflow of colonials pulled by the same forces. When the first marginal downturns in the economy occurred in the 1970s, policies were modified but families continued to arrive and there was little backlash in the general population to the continued presence of large numbers of foreigners. In the US, Canada, and Australia, immigration levels were significant and, aside from the issue of race-related controls, immigration was not especially controversial.

As Western Europe cut back on legal migration, it began to receive large numbers of asylum-seekers. Western Europe, which received approximately 30,000 asylum-seekers a year during the 1970s, saw the number rise above 100,000 in the early 1980s and reach 400,000 a year by the end of the decade (Edminster, 2000). The US saw numbers rise from nearly 6,000 in 1979 to 101,000 in 1989 (US Department of Justice, 1999: Table 1). Canada's numbers went from under 2,000 annually in the 1970s to hit a high of 80,554 in 1989. This trend was a function of numerous factors, including the vastly increased availability of transportation, especially air transport. At the same time, a communications revolution spread word of opportunities in the West and disseminated information on how the meagre entry controls that did exist could be defeated. Finally, growing communities of expatriates were available to shelter and aid the assimilation of asylum-seekers.

When Europe's buffer to the arrival of large numbers of asylum-seekers from the East weakened in the late 1980s and then disappeared with the collapse of Communism, the flow of asylum-seekers began to accelerate with perceived, if not actual, adverse social and economic consequences. Political extremism, not previously a strong force in post-war continental European politics, began to surge in lockstep with this influx (Ignazi, 1997: 59–60). In Germany, extremist parties such as the Republikaner, the National Democratic Party (NPD), and the German People's Union (DVU) arose and grew in electoral support. The annual number of refugee claims continued to rise in the unified Germany, reaching half a million by 1992. Social harmony was strained as anti-foreigner and skinhead violence was met by militant demonstrations against racism. In this increasingly explosive atmosphere, the major parties in Germany came together to amend the Constitution in 1993 to allow 'return to safe third countries' (Merkl, 1997: 30). Agreements were quickly reached with countries on Germany's eastern approaches and the asylum-seeking flow slowed considerably, falling below 100,000 annually after 1995. With these controls in place, support for the extreme right has ebbed (ibid., 32).

In France during the same period, the National Front led by Jean-Marie Le Pen rose to great prominence, first in the National Assembly elections of 1986, then in the presidential race of 1988. The rhetoric was solidly anti-immigrant and anti-foreign and Le Pen's diatribes against the influx of asylum-seekers struck a resonant cord with the electorate (Cohen, 1999). In the early 1990s the party gained a degree of legitimacy that shook the mainline parties, causing them to move to the right and introduce measures to restrict access to France from the South.

Elsewhere in Europe, including the UK, where the neo-fascist British National Party formed in 1982 actually won a seat in a 1993 local election, the influx was also met by growing extremism and tighter controls on asylum-seekers. Scandinavian countries and later the Netherlands, which in the 1980s and early 1990s had experienced the creation of what Piero Ignazi describes as Post-Industrial Extreme Right Parties that showcase anti-immigration platforms, strengthened their barriers to asylum-seekers and began recognizing fewer convention refugees as the 1990s wore on.

Early on European countries recognized that asylum concerns could be addressed effectively only through co-ordinated action, and therefore European Union (EU) institutions became central to the effort to find solutions. The 1997 Treaty of Amsterdam (TOA) initiated a process to harmonize internal immigrant and asylum policies in order to promote 'responsibility-sharing' and combat 'asylum shopping'. The ultimate objective, which is currently well advanced, will see the implementation of a Common European Asylum System that is mandated to be fully operational by 2005 (Gallagher, 2002).

The United States also received increased flows of asylum-seekers, beginning in the mid-1980s and peaking in the mid-1990s. The influx prompted criticism that economic migrants were abusing the system. Critics also pointed to the ease with which suspected terrorists such as Sheik Omar Abdel-Rahman, implicated in the 1993 World Trade Centre bombing, could use the system to remain in the US. The US INS, an arm of the Justice Department, reacted vigorously by introducing sweeping changes to regulatory controls in 1995. American legislators were not persuaded this was sufficient, however, and passed the Illegal Immigration Reform and Immigrant Responsibility Act (IIRIRA) a year later. This new regime, which streamlined the determination process and limited appeal possibilities, had an immediate impact on the number of asylum cases filed with the INS. They fell from 154,464 in 1995 to 85,866 in 1997. This trend continued to the end of the 1990s and the backlog of cases built up under the old system was being reduced in the new.

In comparison to other developed countries, asylum issues appear to have had relatively little impact on Canadian policies. Put simply, there has been little populist opposition to Canada's refugee system. This cannot be seen as a result of firm government action to remove the issue from the public's mind. Unlike Japan or the US, Canada has no existing law or practice that guarantees to executive authorities the power to turn back the majority of asylum-seekers. In comparison to European countries, there has been neither major popular agitation nor the development of extremist parties to force the government to put in place similar policies. This is the case despite the fact that Canada's rate of asylum-seeking influx of approximately 1 per 1,000 inhabitants is comparable to the UK's 1.66, Germany's .96 and France's .65 (Canada's rate for 2001 is close to 1.5).[7] Canada's rate is many times greater than that of the US. Furthermore, these numbers do not include refugees accepted as part of 'resettlement policies', under which Canada accepts approximately 10,000 annually.[8] Overall, Canada stands out as the only developed country where the influx of large numbers of asylum-seekers has not had a great impact on national agenda-setting and led to the adoption of powerful exclusionary practices or policies. But this is not to say Canada is wide open to asylum-seeking flows.

AN ARSENAL OF HURDLES

Canada's major defence against international migrations, refugee or otherwise, is an arsenal of guard posts and barriers that screen travellers. To some extent, these screens have always existed, but when large numbers of asylum-seekers first began reaching the West in the 1980s, they were mightily reinforced. James C. Hathaway (1996) identifies these barriers as mechanisms of *non-entrée* and all developed countries have them. The imposition of a visa requirement on states that are likely to produce asylum-seekers was a first step. For this strategy to be effective, immigration control personnel must be moved out into the field. They must be posted at transit points and especially at airports where asylum-seekers are known to depart. These personnel can double as instructors and monitors of private-sector transportation employees. The ticket agents of airlines, for example, comprise the front line because they are expected to identify 'improper documentation'. Penalties are always part of the system and carriers are routinely fined for transporting illegals.

Once the direct routes from asylum-producing areas, generally in the 'South', are blocked, the next task involves the creation of buffers to overland routes. The rich countries of Western Europe have worked out agreements with their poorer neighbours so that in return for development assistance and other benefits the poorer countries make passage across their territory difficult for migratory flows. In the United States the 'Puebla Process' was created with the same objective in mind. Mexico and other Latin American countries were pressured to discourage the northward migration of Central Americans. In 1999, after Hurricane Mitch caused extensive damage in Central America, Mexican officials (funded by the US government) contained and turned back large numbers of migrants at the Guatemala–Mexico border (Nezer, 1999).

Even with the success of this form of blockage, large numbers make it to the West because of their resourcefulness and ingenuity. They also use people smugglers. The club of rich nations must therefore process a steady flow of in-country arrivals. In fact, the numbers are such that most countries employ controversial means to speed the review of certain types of claims.

A first practice is simply to list countries considered 'safe'. If an individual comes from a country on the list, the claim can be dismissed or expedited. Second, claimants frequently are returned to 'safe third countries'. Although refugees are protected from return to the place of persecution, because of travel restrictions they have usually crossed a 'safe' country on the road to the rich targeted country. Although this safe third country may have signed the Geneva Convention, its interpretation of convention requirements may be narrow. In addition, in terms of work, health, and social services, its practices are not likely to be as generous as the original targeted country. For example, many if not most of Canada's refugee claimants pass through the US to arrive in Canada. An asylum-seeker in the US cannot work for six months after submitting an asylum claim and receives no welfare or medical coverage. Third, if the persecution is viewed as localized within a source country, the asylum-seeker might be repatriated using the argument that there is an 'internal flight option'. An area within the country of persecution is identified where the individual is safe and to which he or she can be returned. Fourth, the Geneva Convention might be interpreted as solely a protection against state-sponsored persecution (e.g., Germany and France take this view). Many arriving in the developed

world are claiming asylum based on persecution that their governments are actively working to eradicate. Finally, a receiving country
might resort to an extensive list of administrative practices to speed
the review process. These policies are invariably disadvantageous to
the asylum-seeker and include denying legal representation, detention without access to counsel, allowing a short period to prepare
for a hearing, limiting access to resources for claimants to make
themselves aware of their own rights, and limiting possibilities for
appeal.

CANADA'S EXTENDED REFUGEE REVIEW MAZE

Canada does not resort to any of these 'internal' practices, although
the laws exist to employ them. As a result, the vast majority of asylum-seekers who arrive in Canada have access to the full regular in-
country refugee determination process, which is undertaken by the
IRB. Although most observers tend to focus on the first step of 'convention refugee' determination, in fact this is only the first stage in a
complex extended review process. To the asylum-seeker, the real
prize is permanent resident status, which comes with being recognized as a 'convention refugee' but can also be obtained in other
ways. Although the majority who follow through with a convention
refugee application receive it, the bulk of those who fail and choose
to stay on eventually gain PRS in other ways.

Technically, the Canadian system has three stages of review
before a claimant is deported. The first is the convention refugee
determination process, which begins when a senior immigration official assesses the 'credibility' of the claim and can recommend the
granting of immediate convention status. If the case is found credible, as 95 per cent are, the individual goes on to a review by one or
two IRB judges. If the IRB rejects the claim, a process that can take
some time, the decision can be challenged in the courts, further
lengthening the process. The next stage is a 'risk of return' assessment administered by the CIC. Here, failed convention refugee applicants argue that return to the country of origin would put them in
danger. If this claim is rejected, a third review can be initiated where
the applicant asks to be allowed to stay in Canada on humanitarian
grounds. CIC then assesses whether removal of the individual would
create excessive hardships, for example, on a family begun in or
brought to Canada.

Even refusal at this point may not extinguish hope for securing PRS. For example, the government set up the 'Deferred Removal Orders Class' (DROC) in 1994, allowing individuals who had managed to avoid removal for three years to gain PRS. This program was cancelled in 1997 for the obvious reason that '[i]n the Minister's opinion, the regulations had encouraged some people to try to delay their removal so that they could eventually qualify for landing as a member of the class' (Young, 1999: 15). In addition, Canada has resorted to a backlog clearance exercise in the past and there is a possibility that this mechanism could be employed to dispose of the existing backlog.

The hardly surprising consequence of this regime can be seen in the Auditor General's 1997 report on refugee determination, which concluded that in the four years between February 1993 and March 1997 the number of confirmed departures of individuals who claimed refugee status in Canada was 4,300, even though 31,200 had been refused status out of a total caseload of 95,500 (Auditor General, 1997: 25: 34). This means that 95 per cent of those who made refugee claims during this period had succeeded in their objective of remaining in Canada or using it as a transit point to enter the US. The Auditor General did a 'follow-up' in 2001 and reported that, although the government was 'actively taking steps' and had made 'satisfactory progress in addressing most recommendations related to refugee determination', the government's full response was embodied in new legislation that was not yet in place. The Auditor General went on to state that 'Citizenship and Immigration Canada could not provide information on removals of failed refugee claimants from the country that would indicate whether its processes were more effective' (Auditor General, 2001: 12: 69).

THE PULL FACTOR

Many aspects of Canada's refugee determination regime strongly pull asylum-seekers. First, once an asylum-seeker has arrived in Canada, the process of being denied convention refugee status is slower than is the case in other developed countries. When this length of time is coupled with the prospect of gaining PRS though other avenues, which can be equally time-consuming, Canada represents a relatively secure, and thus inviting, destination. Second, Canada's interpretation of what constitutes a convention refugee is the most liberal among the club of rich countries. Canada's post-determination regime, which includes 'risk of return' and 'humanitarian' grounds for gaining PRS, cannot be compared to policies in other countries because Canada's is an immigration policy, not 'temporary protection'. Other countries do not have immigration policies, are unwilling to funnel failed refugee claimants into their immigration programs, or are reluctant to regularize a process of granting permanent residency to anyone, even convention refugees.[9] Third, Canada does not generally detain claimants, nor is it harsh on the asylum-seeking tactic of destroying documents. Fourth, most if not all state benefits, including the right to work, are available to the claimant in short order. Fifth, Canada does not resort to practices, such as return to a safe first country of asylum, to weed out claims. Sixth, decades of high levels of immigration, refugee acceptance, and resettlement have created a web of expatriates and relations to welcome and absorb newcomers. Finally, Canada is genuinely sympathetic to the plight of refugees, justly proud of its accomplishments and manifestly willing to err on the side of humanitarianism.

For all these reasons, the asylum-seeker may be pulled to Canada. Still, the number of claimants is not huge. This can be attributed to the fact that so few can reach Canada past the visa restrictions, buffer countries, and formidable geographic obstacles. These barriers filter out the vast majority, regardless of their desperation. Most must resort to professional people smugglers to make the journey. In addition, as the case of the many Chinese who abandon their claims in order to move on to the US shows, reaching Canada means in effect reaching the US. As an Australian study of asylum-seeking bluntly states, Canada is 'increasingly viewed as part of a single migration zone with the USA . . . [and] would appear to be seen by many asylum-seekers as more generous and receptive than the US, but a less desirable place to live' (Millbank, 1999).

To begin with, Canada's refugee process has been positively glacial compared to that in other countries. The US, for example, sets a target of six months for determination and appears to have allocated the resources to hit the mark. Failure leads to immediate removal for those in detention. Of those refused who were not in detention, most fail to report for removal, thereby joining the ranks of the more than 6 million who live in the US illegally. In Europe, determination times differ, with the current UK system in the greatest disorder. France and Germany generally complete their process in a year, and although the vast majority of claims are rejected in all countries, individuals are not for the most part sent packing. At the same time, they are not left wondering whether they meet the convention refugee criteria in the eyes of the host country. In Canada the Auditor General found that the average IRB processing time was 13 months in 1996–7 (Auditor General, 1997: 25: 33). But if only failed claimants were included, it is very likely this average time would be much longer; in fact, a recent government report identified what it called a 'worst case scenario' of 5.4 years (CIC, 2001a). In terms of a pull factor, the calculating asylum-seeker or a people smuggler is likely to consider this more important than an 'average' time that would presumably include accepted claims.

Second, it is not difficult to show that Canada has a liberal interpretation of 'convention refugee' that turns on assessing whether there has been a flight from 'persecution'. As interpreted by Canadian law, a woman fleeing China because she would be 'persecuted' for having a second child can be considered a genuine convention refugee. A woman with two children was given convention refugee status because in the country they came from they would be 'subjected to the Sharia law'. An Immigration and Refugee Board document on refugee case law notes, 'Serious economic deprivations may be components of persecution.' Another passage reads, 'Education is a basic human right and a nine-year-old claimant who could have avoided persecution only by refusing to go to school was deemed to be a Convention refugee' (IRB, Legal Services, 1999). In all of these areas, Canada is viewed as a trend-setter, but probably the most important area where Canadian practice is most generous is in its willingness to grant convention refugee status to civilians facing generalized violence and civil war situations.[10]

Arguably, all of these types of claims represent a genuine need for refuge and deserve convention refugee status. Although the most effective way to show that other countries do not share so liberal an understanding of Geneva Convention obligations would be to examine the case law, this is beyond the scope of this chapter.[11] However, an examination of convention refugee recognition data using UNHCR statistics provides an approximate indicator of the liberalness of convention refugee determination. It also provides an indication of the degree to which various practices are used to expedite or dismiss applications.

Because Canada is willing to examine such a wide range of types of persecution, it is not possible simply to designate or consider certain countries 'safe' and therefore to dismiss claimants from these countries prior to a hearing, as is the practice in many other countries. It is not surprising, therefore, that data for 1999 show Canada as the only country to recognize refugees from Chile, Costa Rica, Djibouti, Czech Republic, Hungary, Jamaica, Poland, Tanzania, and the Republic of Korea (these are figures for in-country determinations and a minimum of 100 decisions were required to appear in these UNHCR tabulations). Furthermore, because of the breadth of Canada's understanding of 'convention refugee', individuals from countries not generally perceived internationally to produce refugees can more easily gain convention refugee status. Thus, Canada is listed as the country that recognized the most (in absolute numbers) convention refugees from Argentina, Bangladesh, Colombia, Guinea, Lebanon, Libya, and Nicaragua. In the cases of Algeria, Bulgaria, Chad, Israel, Kazakhstan, Mexico, Pakistan, Romania, and Sri Lanka, Canada was not only the country that recognized the most convention refugees but it also recognized more in total than all the other countries combined (UNHCR, 2000b: Table IV.3). Over time, such policies can have a significant demographic effect. For example, since civil war erupted in Sri Lanka in the early 1980s, Canada has become home to over 200,000 Sri Lankan Tamils.

Canada's liberal interpretation of the Geneva Convention can also be seen in the aggregate number of refugees it recognizes. According to UNHCR statistics, during the 1990s Canada recognized 61.8 per cent of its in-country refugee claimants as convention refugees. This compares to the UK, at 12 per cent, Germany, 9.1 per cent, France, 20 per cent, and the US, 43.9 per cent (ibid., Table V.16). In terms of absolute numbers of positive in-country convention refugee decisions during the 1990s, UNHCR figures show that Canada's refugee determination system recognized the second highest total number after Germany (131,000 compared to 157,000). It should be noted that only 277,000 claims were made in Canada compared to 1.8 million in Germany (ibid., Table V.4). It is also noteworthy that Canada's total was greater than that of the US (approximately 120,000). These numbers translate into a comparatively large refugee recognition figure for any given year. Statistics show that for 1999 Canada recognized four times more 'in-country' convention refugees on a per-capita basis than European countries and seven times more than the US. Furthermore, unlike other countries, Canada routinely funnels substantial numbers of failed convention refugee claimants into immigration categories.

With respect to detention and the treatment of asylum-seekers without documentation, Canada is far and away the most generous. Since the passage of IIRIRA in 1996, it has been mandatory for US immigration officials to detain undocumented asylum-seekers until they can prove a 'credible fear' of persecution. Without documents it is hard to make the case of credible fear, and failure to do so leads to immediate deportation. Even if credible fear can be shown, the claimant can be and often is detained until a final decision is rendered on convention status. This could take six months. The situation is such that Amnesty International has singled out US practice for special criticism (Amnesty International, 1999).

In Europe, detention at entry points is a common occurrence. Arriving at a German airport without documentation invites detention in what is termed an 'international zone' where one is deemed not to have entered the country. These individuals face long odds in a vastly expedited determination process. Given rules on safe third countries, Europe-bound asylum-seekers are faced with a perilous decision on whether or not to destroy documents. If documents are destroyed, it speaks against the credibility of the 'convention refugee' claim, but if documents are retained, they likely show how entry to the target country was secured, facilitating return to a safe 'transit' country. In the UK, which is less capable of returning asylum-seekers to safe third countries, large-scale detention is being considered to discourage entry. In the case of Italy, where claimants can reach its borders directly, undocumented individuals have been turned back at the Italian border with Slovenia and Italy has reached agreements with Tunisia, Albania, and Morocco for these countries to act as buffer states blocking the departure of undocumented ships (US Committee for Refugees, 2001).

In Canada, detention of asylum-seekers is highly unusual. In the summer of 1999, several hundred Chinese were detained after the ships carrying them were intercepted off the west coast. Lawyers seeking their release had no trouble establishing that detention was an unusual practice in Canada. In fact, of the 1,100 refugee claimants who arrived in Vancouver by air in 1999, none was detained for more than a day (Skelton, 2000: A1). The standard procedure is to give newly arrived refugee claimants forms to fill out and then release them, often to waiting friends and relatives.

With respect to making an application for refugee status in Canada without documentation, this has its costs. Instead of satisfying one IRB board member, in some cases two must be satisfied. If convention status is obtained, the wait for PRS could take longer. On the other hand, it can be advantageous not to have one's claim muddied by documentary detail when one makes one's case at the IRB's non-adversarial 'hearing' stage. The Auditor General states in his report on the processing of claims that 'the non-adversarial hearing takes place in a context where the very nature of the claim poses major challenges of availability and quality of information', and 'while in theory the burden of proof is on the claimant, Canada has decided to give claimants the benefit of the doubt' (Auditor General, 1997: 25: 59).

The Auditor General reports that more than half of Canada's in-country refugee claimants arrive without valid documents and many without any documents whatsoever. There is much evidence to support the belief that many of these people destroyed their documents in a calculated attempt to improve their chances for gaining PRS at some stage of Canada's extended refugee determination process. This is especially the case with respect to claimants who arrive by air. Of course, many of these documents were forgeries in the first place and, according to the Canadian Council for Refugees (CCR), a refugee rights group, asylum-seekers might destroy documents because 'they have been led to believe that they should for their own protection' because 'this may be an effective way of preventing themselves being returned to persecution' (CCR, 2001).

REFUGEE POLICY

How do we explain the generosity of the Canadian refugee process in comparison to those of all other developed nations? Certainly Canada's humanist impulse is strong and Canadians are justifiably proud of their record. But are these virtues unique to Canada? At the same time, the absence of an anti-immigration party and of anti-refugee rhetoric seems surprising, given the existence of such political movements and popular attitudes in Europe, which has roughly similar levels of per capita intake. Arguably, this is mainly a result of two characteristics of the Canadian situation.

First, the visibility of the refugee inflow is obscured by a larger immigration flow that is generally viewed as beneficial and therefore does not generate significant opposition. During the 1990s the number of refugees Canada accepted (landed and resettled) ranged from a high of nearly 47,000 in 1991 to a low of 20,400 in 1997. Through the 1990s Canada's intake of immigrants was usually between 150,000 and 200,000 annually. Put simply, the refugee component does not stand out when the two inflows are totalled.

Second, there is a clear political interest on the part of the federal government to tread lightly in areas of policy, such as refugee determination, that affect new Canadians. New Canadians tend to vote Liberal and to congregate in urban areas. Urban ridings in Canada's largest cities are very important to the electoral fortunes of the governing Liberal Party. In addition, large and well-funded interest groups have arisen in the immigration/refugee policy area, and they are almost exclusively supportive of a more open refugee policy. Groups, such as the Canadian Chinese Congress, represent the various ethnicities in Canada. In addition, numerous human rights groups and refugee support organizations, such as the Canadian Council for Refugees and Project Genesis, can be vocal opponents of government policy. A lucrative industry made up of immigration lawyers and consultants has developed around assisting individuals to gain permanent resident status in Canada. This group is politically active and well connected to all the political parties and is represented by such associations as the International Association of Immigration Practitioners and the Organization of Professional Immigration Consultants. On the other side, individuals and groups who express concern about Canada's refugee and immigration programs appear to carry less weight than those found in other countries. For example, Canada has no organization comparable in status or influence to the US Federation for Immigration Reform (FAIR), which describes itself as the 'leading advocate for a sensible immigration policy'.

As a result, during the mid- to late 1990s the government was not strongly pressured to reform refugee policies, regardless of glaring deficiencies in the refugee determination system. Bill C-31, legislation introduced after lengthy consultations, seemed more a result of state-centred policy planning than a grassroots initiative with strong political backing. Bill C-31 would have streamlined the refugee determination process, limited court appeals, and clarified the government's capacity to remove failed claimants (Young, 2000). Although numerous bills were rushed through the legislative process in the dying days of the 36th Parliament, Bill C-31 was not among them. The legislation faced strong opposition from a range of interest groups when it was tabled and Liberal policy planners could have been concerned about losing crucial urban electoral support if the Liberal Party was viewed as 'anti-immigrant'.

Electoral calculus may provide an explanation for why the Canadian Alliance (CA) was also unwilling to challenge the refugee policy status quo. When a CA candidate in Winnipeg, Betty Granger, made disparaging remarks about what she described as an 'Asian invasion' of the Canadian west coast, senior members of the party pressured her to resign and she eventually did so. When asked if the CA had pressed her, Granger responded: 'You could say that. . . . I was told that the voters on the West Coast—the Asian voters were, of course, livid with my comments—that several ridings could fall either way because of my remarks, that it involved 10 seats. Ten seats could be put in jeopardy. Money was being withdrawn from the campaign. I mean I'm small potatoes compared to 10 seats on the West Coast' (Roberts and Scoffield, 2000). In addition, having spent much of the 2000 federal election fighting accusations of 'extremism', a foray into the emotional field of refugee policy would not have been in the interest of the CA. One of the leaders in such attacks was Liberal Immigration Minister Elinor Caplan, who 'accused the Alliance of harbouring supporters who are racist and bigoted' (McCarthy, 2000).

THE DANGER AND COSTS OF CANADA'S REFUGEE POLICY

There is a dark side to Canada's mediated humanism that can be argued on several levels (see also Gallagher, 2001). First, at an administrative level it is hard to justify the utility and expense of a system with so many potential appeal routes and end runs. The IRB and other refugee determination costs amount to more than $120 million annually and this is a fraction of the cost of supporting refugee claimants in Canada while their cases are being heard. Even without the extraordinary possibilities embodied in a minister's intervention or the DROC noted above, success at any of the three stages results in the same outcome: PRS. Thus, at least the first stage seems redundant. The third stage of humanitarian review is bound to be problematical because so many of the cases take years to complete and claimants often set down roots in a community such that everyone's sensibilities are jogged by their removal.

Second, corruption is the inevitable consequence of a refugee determination system in which a claim made in Canada provides such a direct path to citizenship. The pressure on Canada's gatekeepers

abroad and even in Canada is tremendous. Canadian visas, ministerial permits, and other travel documents are very valuable, and there
have been numerous cases of theft, fraud, and corruption.

Third, Canada's refugee system can be criticized for encouraging
the whole industry of 'people smuggling' that internationally is
reported to earn US$10 billion and move 4 million people across bor-
ders annually. While Elinor Caplan has described the Chinese boat
people as 'naive' and the tendency is to portray smuggled people as
'victims', the result of Canada's liberal refugee review processes is that
people smugglers often do deliver their clients to a better life.

Fourth is the assertion that, because of lax screening and end-
less judicial appeal possibilities, Canada constitutes a potential safe
haven for perpetrators of human rights abuses and other criminals
whose fortunes in their home countries have soured. Among numerous cases that might be identified are those of a former Rwandan
official accused of inciting genocide and of two Bangladeshi military officers accused of mass murder (Stevenson, 1999: A3). The case
of Mahmoud Mohammad Issa Mohammad, who made a refugee
claim in 1988, is another. As a Palestine Liberation Organization
(PLO) terrorist, he participated in an attack on an El Al aircraft, yet
after years of judicial appeals he has not been deported. With a reference to the UN Convention Against Torture embodied in the new
Act, it may be even more difficult to deport foreign criminals, spies,
and assassins.

Finally, the openness of Canada's system might be providing a
haven and springboard for terrorism, as has often been charged by
Americans. In March 2001, Reid Morden, former Deputy Minister of
Foreign Affairs and Director of CSIS, argued that the Liberal government was unwilling to take a strong stance against the activities of
many ethnic community groups that had been identified as supporting international terrorism because of what he described as a 'very
large political calculation'. The government is unwilling to jeopardize
the support of new Canadians (Fife, 2001: A1). The events of 11
September highlight this issue as never before. Border security is now
a central policy concern.

CONCLUSION

Canada's policy on refugees is often viewed as an example of
Canada's humanitarian tradition, along with peacekeeping, medicare,

and multiculturalism. The reality is less heart-warming. Canada imposes a visa restriction on over 100 countries, including just about every country that is perceived to be a source of refugees. When several hundred of the Czech Republic's Roma minority were granted convention refugee status, a visa requirement was placed on the Czech Republic and large numbers were blocked from coming. In December 2001 Zimbabwe was added to the list of countries from which all entrants to Canada must carry visas after large numbers began arriving to request asylum. It is fair to say that, in order to reach Canada from a refugee-producing area, some form of subterfuge or the use of a smuggler is required. Of course, Canada is not alone in its efforts to stop the inflow of asylum-seekers. All developed nations have similar policies.

In Europe there has been remarkable social opposition to the arrival of large numbers of asylum-seekers. Such attitudes can be directly linked to the rise of extremist political parties and other manifestations of intolerance. In response, European governments have moved vigorously to block access to Europe and a process is well underway to erect more effective ramparts for fortress Europe in the form of the Common European Asylum System. In the US, when the number of asylum-seekers rose alarmingly from some perspectives, legislation and regulations were overhauled to streamline the in-country convention refugee determination process. The determination process is now swift, with few appeals. An 'illegal alien' arriving at a border and requesting asylum can expect to be detained. Destroying one's documents is not advisable and failure to meet the 'credible fear' test leads to removal in short order.

What makes Canada unique among advanced industrial nations is that it does not have in place policies or practices that give the government the power to control and remove the majority of asylum-seekers who do arrive. Absent are such practices as identifying safe countries of origin, safe third countries, and areas of internal flight. Furthermore, Canada's rate of positive decisions at the convention refugee determination stage is relatively high. In addition, Canada has many mechanisms of appeal and alternate means by which failed convention refugee claimants can gain PRS and eventually citizenship. There appears to be relatively little societal opposition to these policies, which can be seen in the comparative absence of extremist rhetoric or the rise of anti-immigrant parties. This is the case even though the inflow of asylum-seekers is comparable to that of such

European countries as the UK, where social opposition to such migration is alarmingly significant.

The tendency is for Canada's political leadership to view these facts as evidence of Canadians' openness and tolerance. Elinor Caplan (2000) has suggested that Canada's refugee determination system is 'one of the most important ways in which Canada has earned its reputation as a humanitarian leader in the world'. There are crucial factors at play in the Canadian environment, however, the absence of which would surely lead to retrenchment and policy reform, likely along the lines of the American model. First, Canada believes it needs newcomers and, although the total number of refugee claims made in Canada is large even compared to that made in European countries, the number of refugees has been around only 15 per cent of Canada's annual intake of immigrants. Given electoral concerns, it simply has been expedient for governments not to challenge the acceptance of the majority of asylum-seekers as convention refugees and to channel large numbers of failed claimants into various immigration categories. In addition, Canada has shown a unique lack of interest in policies of detention and removal, which in other countries are primary tools in the effort to discourage asylum-seeking.

Second, the governing Liberal Party has a political interest in not angering 'new' Canadian voters and the range of interest groups and advocacy organizations that inhabit the policy field. Opposition parties have not targeted the policy for focused criticism. With respect to party interests, new Canadian populations tend to live in urban ridings, which were crucial to the re-election of the Liberal party in the run-up to the 2000 federal election. Bill C-31, An Act to Amend the Immigration Act, was destined to die with the dissolution of the 36th Parliament. Similar legislation, the Immigration and Refugee Protection Act, was introduced within months of the election and passed late in 2001. At this point, however, it is too early to assess the impact of the new law or of various border security and anti-terrorism initiatives. Until then, we can conclude that Canada remains relatively generous to asylum-seekers, although at the same time it maintains a sophisticated ring of barriers in an effort to block the arrival of migrants, as do all other advanced industrialized nations.

NOTES

1.   Japan granted convention refugee status to 50 individuals out of 1,050 applications from 1990 to 1999.

2. This is a term developed by Gary Freeman to describe the tendency of elites to de-emphasize the diverse ethnic origin of contemporary immigration, to seek consensus on immigration matters, and to keep them from becoming a partisan question. See Joppke (1998: 270).
3. For an examination of the ethical and humanitarian questions surrounding the antinomy of state interest and human rights, see Gibney (1999).
4. For a short review of the evolution of Canada's refugee policy, with summaries of the policy reforms embodied in Bills C-55, 86, and 44, see Young (1999).
5. For an examination of the changes, see Young and Sinha (2001).
6. In refugee policy terminology, the 'first' country is the home country; the 'second' country is the country of first asylum, from where the asylum-seeker moves on to a 'third' country.
7. Canada's applications are calculated at an annual rate of 30,000 asylum-seekers, although for 2001 as many as 45,000 arrived in Canada. Europe's numbers are found in UNCHR (2001: Table 2).
8. Canada's resettlement policies are the most generous in the world on a per capita basis. Resettlement numbers for 1999: US, 85,010; Canada, 17,077; Austria, 8,330; Norway, 3,940; New Zealand, 1,140; Sweden, 550 (UNHCR, 2000a: 11).
9. The Geneva Convention provides for 'cessation', which means that if the persecution is deemed to have ended, convention refugee status may be revoked and individuals returned to their homeland. Canada does not use these provisions.
10. Compare, for example, 'Joint Position on the Harmonized Application of the Definition of the Term: "Refugee"', adopted on 4 March 1996 by the European Union, with 'guidelines' on refugee determination published the same year by the IRB (1996).
11. For an examination of some of the issues surrounding the definition of 'convention refugee' in international law, see Nicholson and Twomey (1999); Selm-Thorburn (1998); Carlier et al. (1997).

REFERENCES

Amnesty International. 1999. 'United States of America: Lost in the Labyrinth: Detention of Asylum-Seekers', Report—AMR51/51/99, Sept.

Aubry, Jack. 2002. 'Liberals complain that tougher rules could cost party its bedrock immigrant support', *National Post*, 14 Jan., A1.

Auditor General of Canada. 1997. 'Citizenship and Immigration Canada and Immigration and Refugee Board—The Processing of Refugee Claims', Dec.

———. 2001. 'Follow-up: Citizenship and Immigration Canada and Immigration and Refugee Board—The Processing of Refugee Claims', Dec.

Boswell, Christina. 2000. 'European Values and the Asylum Crisis', *International Affairs* (July): 537–58.

Canada, Immigration and Refugee Board. 1996. 'Guidelines Issued by the Chairperson Pursuant to Section 65(3) of the Immigration Act, Civilian Non-Combatants Fearing Persecution in Civil War Situations', 7 Mar.

———, Legal Services. 1999. 'Interpretation of the Convention Refugee Definition in the Case Law', 31 Dec.

Canadian Council for Refugees (CCR). 2001. 'Comments on CIC Paper "New Regulations to Accompany Bill C-11"', 1 May.

Caplan, Elinor. 2000. Notes for an address, Minister of Citizenship and Immigration, to the Maytree Foundation Forum, 'Economic Migrants or Refugees? Trends in Global Migration', Toronto, 12 Jan.

Carlier, Jean-Yves, D. Vanheule, and K. Hullmann, eds. 1997. *Who Is a Refugee? A Comparative Case Law Study*. The Hague: Kluwer Law International.

Citizenship and Immigration Canada (CIC). 2000. *Facts and Figures 1999: Overview of Temporary Resident and Refugee Claimant Population*. Ottawa, Dec.

————. 2001a. 'Backgrounder #5—Timelines: Worst Case Scenario', Mar.

————. 2001b. 'News Release: Canada-United States Issue Statement on Common Security Priorities', 3 Dec.

Cohen, Mel. 1999. 'The National Front and Burden of History', *Contemporary French Civilization* 23, 1 (Winter/Spring): 24–46.

Department of Foreign Affairs and International Trade (DFAIT). 2001. 'Canada and the United States Sign Smart Border Declaration', news release 162, 12 Dec.

Edminster, Steven. 2000. 'The High Road or the Low Road: The Way Forward to Asylum Harmonization in the European Union', *World Refugee Survey*. Available at: <www.refugees.org/world/articles/wrs00_highlow.htm>.

Fife, Robert. 2001. 'Politics Trumping Security: Ex-Spy', *National Post*, 9 Mar., A1.

Freeman, Gary. 1994. 'Can Liberal States Control Unwanted Migration?', *Annals, AAPSS* 534 (July): 17–30.

Gallagher, Stephen. 2001. 'Canada's Dysfunctional Refugee Policy—The Case for Reform from a Realist Perspective', *Behind the Headlines* 58, 4 (Summer): 1–17.

————. 2002. 'Towards a Common European Asylum System: Fortress Europe Redesigns the Ramparts', *International Journal* (forthcoming).

Gibney, Matthew J. 1999. 'Liberal democratic states and responsibilities to refugees', *American Political Science Review* 93, 1 (Mar.): 169–81.

Hathaway, James C. 1991. *The Law of Refugee Status*. Toronto: Butterworths.

————. 1996. 'Can International Refugee Law Be Made Relevant Again?', *World Refugee Survey*. Available at: <www.refugees.org/world/articles/intl_law_wrs96.htm>.

House of Commons, Standing Committee on Citizenship and Immigration. 2000. *Refugee Protection and Border Security: Striking a Balance*. Ottawa, Mar.

Ignazi, Piero. 1997. 'The Extreme Right in Europe: A Survey', in Merkl and Weinberg (1997).

Joppke, Christian. 1998. 'Why Liberal States Accept Unwanted Immigration', *World Politics* 50, 2 (Jan.): 266–93.

McCarthy, Shawn. 2000. 'Alliance candidate quits over remarks', *Globe and Mail*, 20 Nov., A1.

Merkl, Peter H. 1997. 'Why Are They So Strong Now? Comparative Reflections on the Revival of the Radical Right in Europe', in Merkl and Weinberg (1997).

———— and Leonard Weinberg, eds. 1997. *The Revival of Right-Wing Extremism in the Nineties*. London: Frank Cass & Co.

Millbank, Adrienne. 1999. 'Boat People, Illegal Migration and Asylum-seekers: in Perspective', Current Issues Brief 13 Parliamentary Library, Parliament of Australia, 14 Dec.

Nezer, Melanie. 1999. 'The Puebla Process: US Migration Controls Move South of the Border', *World Refugee Survey*. Available at: <www.refugees.org/world/articles/wrs99_migrationcontrols.htm>.

Nicholson, Frances, and Patrick Twomey, eds. 1999. *Refugee Rights and Realities: Evolving International Concepts and Regimes*. Cambridge: Cambridge University Press.

Roberts, David, and Heather Scoffield. 2000. 'Candidate says she was "manipulated" into quitting', *Globe and Mail*, 21 Nov. A9.

Selm-Thorburn, Joanne. 1998. *Refugee Protection in Europe: Lessons of the Yugoslav Crisis*. The Hague: Martinus Nijhoff Publishers.

Skelton, Chad. 2000. 'Twice as many illegal migrants arrive here by air as by sea, statistics show', *Vancouver Sun*, 7 Jan., A1.

Stevenson, Mark. 1999. 'Second Bangladeshi Officer Claims Refugee Status', *National Post*, 8 Dec., A3.

UNHCR. 2000a. 'Refugees by Numbers', Geneva, 1 Jan.

———. 2000b. *Refugees and Others of Concern to UNHCR: 1999 Statistical Overview*. July. Available at: <www.unhcr.ch/cgi-bin/texis/vtx/home/opendoc.pdf?tbl=STATISTICS&id=3ae6bc834&page=statistics>.

———. 2001. 'Asylum Applications Submitted in Europe, 2000', Jan. Available at: <www.unhcr.ch/cgi-bin/texis/vtx/home/opendoc.pdf?tbl=STATISTICS&id=3b937bc4100&page=statistics>.

US Committee for Refugees. 2001. *Country Report: Italy*. Available at: <www.refugees.org/world/countryrpt/europe/italy.htm>.

US Department of Justice, INS. 1999. 'Asylees: Fiscal Year 1997', July.

Young, Margaret. 1999. 'Canada's Refugee Status Determination System', Library of Parliament, Canada, July 1993; revised, Sept. 1999.

———. 2000. 'Bill C-31: The Immigration and Refugee Protection Act', Library of Parliament, Canada, 25 Apr.

——— and Jay Sinha. 2001. 'Bill C-11: The Immigration and Refugee Protection Act', Library of Parliament, Canada.

6

How Much Was Never Enough?
Canadian Defence and 11 September

DEAN F. OLIVER

In at least one important way, the tragedy of 11 September 2001 was not unique in the post-Cold War history of the Canadian Forces (CF). Though perhaps heralding, as Thomas Homer-Dixon and others have suggested, the onset of 'complex' terrorism, 11 September also continued familiar debates about Canadian defence policy, military capabilities, and bilateral and alliance obligations (Homer-Dixon, 2002). The disaster broadened the scope of that debate and heightened, at least temporarily, the sense of gravity and imminent peril surrounding it. However, most of the substantial questions, from the mobility and readiness of Canada's army to the capacity of its reserves, had long since featured in the public discourse. It was not exactly the rhetorical business as usual in the weeks and months after 11 September but at times it was eerily close.

Such reactions were also representative of more deeply rooted Canadian preoccupations—such as the relationship with the United States and the appropriate balance between guns and butter in the national defence budget—but in tone and substance the post-11 September debate still tracked more closely recent disputes wherein, more often than not, a federal government sensitive to the pitfalls of overspending on defence had allegedly left Canada bereft of military capability. Consequently, Canada sometimes found itself less able to act effectively in response to unexpected situations. For critics of Canada's defence effort, 11 September and the types of responses it might entail for Canada's thinly stretched armed forces therefore capped a longer period of gradual military decline, but it was hardly the first evidence of that unwelcome demise.

This is hardly to diminish the human or geopolitical import of the terrorist attacks. Future structural and strategic changes spawned in part by this catastrophe might well alter in substantial ways the size, composition, and commitments of Canada's military and the course of its foreign policy, but the immediate challenge posed to Canadian officialdom by the attacks was of a piece with past security challenges like East Timor, Kosovo, and the Gulf War. In short, how should Canada respond and, more importantly from a CF perspective, with what?

This new challenge was of a piece, too, with other recent events in raising further questions about certain concepts of international security, war, and the role of military force popular in the nation's foreign policy establishment since the early 1990s. 'Soft power' and 'human security' might not have been altogether contradicted by the actions of the North Atlantic Treaty Organization (NATO) in Kosovo, but they were—at the very least—seriously challenged. Canadian non-governmental organizations previously supportive of, and influential in, the foreign policy direction of former Foreign Minister Lloyd Axworthy certainly thought as much. In this as well, the debate over a potential military response to 11 September, and the subsequent onset of operations in Afghanistan, continued a trend. A concern for addressing the 'root causes' of disorder with broadly based socio-economic palliatives conflicted with the apparent requirement for enhanced security, intelligence, and military capabilities.

This debate will continue to lie near the core of any review of defence affairs arising from the terrorist attacks. Not only must Canadians ask whether existing resources and commitments are sufficient for a reasonable level of national protection at home, but they must also ask seriously, perhaps for the first time since the early 1950s, what capacity does or should exist to forestall, disrupt, or destroy the military potential of the nation's new non-state enemies abroad. In this dialogue, ideological carping on the declining utility or outright illegitimacy of a nation's armed forces is a hoary fiction Canadians would be wise not to indulge. At the same time, the indecent haste with which 'I told you so'—the academic incarnation of 'gotcha' journalism—echoed easily, and unreflectively, from some defence intellectuals is scant justification for precipitate and profligate activity. Either way, the seductive resemblance between the current debate and those of recent years should not hide an important possibility: that Canadian defence post-11 September might—and perhaps should—yet move far from its traditional, self-satisfied moorings. The times have rarely been more propitious for innovation, or more demanding of the necessity for caution.

SOMETHING OLD, SOMETHING NEW

Peacetime armed forces are supposed to do precisely that which Canada's are now doing: prepare for a range of bad things in the unfortunate and sometimes unlikely case they may actually happen, and then to rely on professional and effective people, good equipment, and realistic plans to respond when they do. Of course, not all components of a military's planning and response mechanism will work with equal success when the moment for action arrives. Nor do all militaries plan for uncertainty in similar or equally successful ways. The literature on military effectiveness and lessons learned is replete with the seeming oddity of supposedly professional, resilient military organizations being astonished, overwhelmed, and physically pummelled in military situations of which their training, doctrine, or mindset had left them unaware. In this sense, the Cold War dictated the development and acquisition of weapons systems, and the doctrines for their use, that flowed logically from the nature of the global stalemate, the strategic geography of the conflict, and the balance of power, yet in no two NATO countries did national military policy follow precisely the same lines. Nor did fixation on the Central Front and the North Atlantic air-sea battle preclude combat deployments by participants in places as diverse as Vietnam, the Falkland

Islands, or Chad. Still, while flexibility remained inherent even within the confines of the Cold War standoff, especially in the aftermath of NATO's adoption of flexible response and the American fixation on counter-insurgency warfare, both dating from the 1960s, the end of the Cold War raised the curtain on an unprecedented period of flux and soul-searching in the defence establishments of most NATO nations. The struggles of NATO to redefine its post-Cold War role, and the criticism the alliance faced from those arguing that its only conceivable mission had ended with the collapse of the Soviet Union and Warsaw Pact, were therefore symptomatic of a broader intellectual and structural post-Cold War malaise. Having fought and won the 'war without battles' (Maloney, 1997), what was left for a victor's army to do?

In the Canadian case, the electoral process returned in the midst of this debate a Liberal government publicly dedicated to providing answers. Long insistent, even as early as the 1990–1 Gulf War, that the Canadian defence team was too firmly hitched to the American military wagon, the Chrétien Liberals inherited easily the slightly rebellious but avowedly reformist cloak first cut by Pierre Trudeau over 20 years before. Having promised in the campaign to cut loose Canadian defence and foreign affairs from their familiar Cold War anchorage, the new government, at some political (and financial) cost, immediately cancelled in the fall of 1993 a major contract for the purchase of helicopters to replace the CF's fleet of Labradors and Sea Kings. It also soon plunged into an extensive and public defence and foreign affairs review that resulted in new policy White Papers in late 1994 and early 1995, respectively (DND, 1994; DFAIT, 1995).

The defence component of that review was a stark contrast to the hawkish admonishments of the Progressive Conservatives' 1987 version, *Challenge and Commitment* (DND, 1987), a document that the course of international events soon rendered obsolescent. Liberal policy would instead be founded not on the certainty of struggle against a common and widely acknowledged foe—there was none, after all—but on the future dangers faced by Canada in a disordered and uncertain future. In this, it is true, the new government made a virtue from fiscal necessity, embracing, within a considerably reduced base budget, concepts like planned uncertainty, flexibility, and multi-purpose forces in an effort doctrinally to make shrinking resources cover a wider range of eventualities. (The military's own adoption of capabilities-based planning, as opposed to assessments based on specific risks, regions, or standing commitments, later to become strategic holy writ, likewise accentuated the more generic and malleable nature of the post-Cold War Canadian defence effort.) But this was also sensible politics in an environment in which advocates for a more substantial defence posture were crowded increasingly from the stage by impassioned and well-funded lobbyists for less robust, less expensive alternatives.

Squeezed between the political imperative of defence reduction and the marginal good sense of standing fast, the White Paper carved out an ambiguous middle ground. Building intellectually on the good foundations of professional, highly motivated personnel and the demonstrable utility (in alliance counsels, for instance) of armed force, it shielded residual capabilities against deeper cuts by the logic of their inherent flexibility, even while promising that in a less imminently threatening security environment Canada could continue to meet its commitments with a smaller force.

Sterner critics, from left and right, have never been swayed by the virtues of this compromise, claiming, respectively, either that the Liberals caved in to pressure from the military-industrial complex or that the government sold out the military by reducing it below the operational level at which it could remain effective and internationally respected. These were hardly disinterested critiques, but they nonetheless had some basis in fact. Post-1994 force and budget reductions and continuing demands on the CF added strong evidence that the Liberals' post-Cold War status quo had institutionalized, if not aggravated, the old commitment-to-capability gap, but it still remained true that the apocalyptic tinges infusing the defence debate came frequently from the domestic defence industry or those quasi-independent organizations with which it was publicly affiliated. The Conference of Defence Associations, the service lobby, and other conservative groups were frequently correct in their predictions of the shape of wars to come, and Canada's role in them, but this mattered little to peace groups for whom the pro-defence lobby was a rather unfortunate blight, and there was high irony in the frequently stony reception accorded such pro-defence views in the high towers of National Defence Headquarters. There is a good study yet to be written of the relationship between the Defence Department and the pro-defence lobby in this period, but the 1994 White Paper and the inadequacies it allegedly enshrined had set erstwhile natural allies at odds without the compensatory advantage of having substituted new friends in the bargain.

It is seductively easy now, with nearly a decade of reflection, scholarship, and international history in hand, to poke critically at the process and content of the White Paper. The truth is that credible prophets for the future of armed conflict were in short supply in the early 1990s, most having been caught unawares both by the speed of Soviet Communism's collapse and by the explosion of ethno-nationalist violence that followed. The quality of strategic assessment folded by the Defence Department into the White Paper's planning assumptions was at least as good as that emanating from academic and other non-government sources of the day, and in many important ways it was a great deal better. When viewed against the political and strategic backdrop of 1993–4, in other words, the White Paper's effort to make necessity a virtue while also protecting critical resources for future emergencies appears far less untenable than either line of public criticism might warrant.

The government's general approach to defence was laudable in other ways, too. A country almost completely lacking in contemporary conventional foes and publicly sustainable levels of long-term funding, and under domestic political attack for making even a minimal effort in the direction of defence, can be forgiven for cashing a substantial peace dividend, even if one can still skirmish on the margins over scale, selectivity, and coherence. On the other hand, prudence and partnership continued to dictate substantial expenditures. A country about whose defence effort its allies and domestic foes complain bitterly and for which some forms of international military commitment have supposedly reaped international rewards in the end protected residual and 'multi-purpose' capabilities across a broad spectrum of options. A foreign policy establishment in which constabulary multilateralism, especially under United Nations auspices, is widely viewed as an expected, essential, and preferred token of international legitimacy also proved not to be predisposed to a more radical defence reorganization. In the latter case, the only uncertainty *is* uncertainty itself, and the variety of demands placed on military assets remained as multifarious as the regions of the world in which they were called upon to operate.

The cascading demands of this kind of international ticket-punching imposed dangerous burdens on the readiness and agility of the military institution and placed at great risk the lives and mental well-being of its members and their families. But calls for firm criteria by which peacekeeping or peace support missions could be categorized, judged, and possibly refused, thereby easing the personal and institutional burden on the CF members, were intuitively counteracted by the multiplicity and uniqueness of the situations from which such demands arise. In this, too, the White Paper offered wisdom if little solace. The post-1994 military, it promised implicitly, would be ready for nearly anything, nearly anywhere, nearly anytime, if at levels much reduced from the heyday of the Cold War. But the White Paper rejected quite pointedly the all-peacekeeping force proposed by several influential participants in the debate. This was hardly the first time in Canadian military history that the competing demands of practicality, sufficiency, and the ideological certitude that often masqueraded as both had wrestled for policy space on a defence issue (Mackenzie King would have understood the dilemma all too well, whether in 1935 or in 1945), but it may have been the first time that the sparring was conducted so openly, so vigorously, and, despite criticisms of the review process, so democratically. It may even have been, as embattled defence spokespersons sometimes averred, the first time in which the voice of reasonable preparedness had actually, unfathomably, won.

The structured ambiguity that resulted was far from completely repugnant to Canada's military caste. The Liberals had at least protected some military capabilities for which slim contemporary demand might otherwise have existed, most notably in the armoured corps, the submarine fleet, and the CF-18 fighter squadrons. This eased the legitimate concerns of environmental commanders and, albeit with less success, the political sensitivities of the service associations and honorary colonels. But, as the debate had also demonstrated, preserving residual and reduced capabilities across the board was not the only option. The minority chorus that had warned of Liberal predations on the armed forces before 1993 was scarcely mollified by the rump CF that survived the 1994 review. Canada's still underfunded military, they argued, had long since been scraping by on decades of governmental neglect. The end of the Cold War offered no opportunity to slice further into already marginal resources, but simply allowed the international demand side of the security equation to fall more closely into line with Canada's unarguably modest supply. This argument, perhaps more than any other, recurred in the post-1994 defence debate, epitomized by the string of crises in former Yugoslavia, central Africa, and elsewhere that continued to call dwindling numbers of Canadian troops abroad.

Whether or not the 1994 exercise had framed the right questions, in the right process, and thus had preserved a sufficient mix of forces to make good on the nation's promises, commitments, and expectations was an important component of the debate. But it was also increasingly irrelevant. Subsequent crises, not theoretical strategic or bureaucratic navel-gazing, provided the real litmus test for Canada's defence forces and reasonable, if ambiguous, standards for judging their effectiveness. Having rejected for obvious reasons the platitudes and assurances of Cold War deployments, to what extent did the post-review CF actually retain the capacity to guard against those forms of global uncertainty that had featured so prominently in the White Paper's articulation? Did that capacity decline as the decade advanced or, as Defence officials often maintained, had new equipment offset quantitative declines and led to similar, or greater, increments of combat power? How much was enough, in other words, and against what set of missions or possibilities could such sufficiency (or insufficiency) be judged? When uncertainty crystallized into UN or NATO requests for battalions of troops, transport planes, and warships, or when the evening news and the letters to the editor columns filled with public insistence on Canadian action, the adequacy and preparedness of the CF were no longer the issues of a theological debate.

A familiar question therefore came bluntly in the aftermath of 11 September, a most unfamiliar event. If, as US President Bush and British Prime Minister Blair promised, the perpetrators of the attacks could be identified, found, and punished, what exactly could the Canadian Forces contribute as part of the expected international effort? And if Canada's options in the face of this challenge proved limited, what might be done to rectify matters in the future?

Defence watchers had heard much of it before. The debate continued the long-running skirmish over general purpose versus niche or closely tailored assets; it highlighted the parlous state of Canadian intelligence, counter-intelligence, and counter-terrorist capabilities; it raised questions over the CF's ability to participate in ground combat missions abroad; and it infused the long-simmering debate over the organizational ability of the government and cabinet to reply coherently and quickly to complex security emergencies. Such questions would have been even more pointed had the terrorist attacks occurred in Montreal, Toronto, or Vancouver, but they were broad, sometimes condemnatory, and all-encompassing just the same. That they played into ongoing internal deliberations about readiness, integration with American forces, and the replacement of several key assets, including replenishment ships, airlift, and naval helicopters, added urgency, if not originality, to the discussion.

Consensus on most fronts proved as elusive as ever, although public opinion and expert commentary did appear almost uniform in critique of the neglected state of domestic security precautions, both generally and in the nation's airports. More importantly, the discussion as a whole, made so poignant by the immediacy of human loss and the blanket news coverage of rescue operations, challenged directly the broad philosophical underpinnings of Canadian defence and foreign policy. What, for example, did the event and the nature and timing of Canada's response reveal of the flexible, multi-purpose military instrument through which, since 1994, Canadian military policy was supposed to have been actualized? In what ways did the crisis speak to the current nature of international security and to the likely credentials and protections needed for states to operate safely therein? What did it say of military alliances and their utility in the twenty-first century, or of the sometimes tawdry exchange, in which many of us so gleefully participated, over soft versus hard power, human security, 'new' security, or humanitarian intervention? What of the future of US–Canadian defence and security relations, whether Liberal MP David Pratt's reinvented World War II-era 'Devil's Brigade' writ large, or the long-discussed missile defence program? More ominously still, and not necessarily to reinvigorate, as Robert Kaplan (Kaplan, 2001) has recently done, the musings of Samuel Huntington on the 'clash of civilizations' (Huntington, 1997), what might this mean for Canadian policy towards the Middle East in particular and terrorism in general?

While 11 September therefore roiled the familiar waters, it also returned the debate to a discussion of first principles in ways not seen even in the aftermath of the Somalia affair. What this might ultimately mean for Canadian defence is far too early to say, but the discussion would initially be well served by exploring the nature and intentions of Canada's first comprehensive post-Cold War policies and their evolution since 1994. Quite simply, if the basic purpose of the original policies remains sound, with ample means available to protect or advance the interests enunciated therein, then the impending defence review must be tinged with the essential adequacy of the resources at hand and the search for amelioration can be redirected elsewhere. If, on the other hand, the current challenges seem poised to outstrip Canada's ability to respond effectively, then revisiting the basics constitutes due diligence and the essential springboard for future reform or reorganization.

This is true despite the risks of political liability, institutional instability, and inflated expectations that a more thoroughgoing review can create. Unlike past crises, 11 September at least appears temporarily to have obviated the legitimacy of the political status quo and the bland assurances of sufficiency with which it has all too often been cloaked. The more robust critics of Canada's defences, sometimes disingenuously (as most know better, often having served in the military or the civilian bureaucracy), have downplayed the dangers implicit in such invasive procedures, but this hardly excuses the faint smugness and lack of interest with which calls for reform have all too often been met. Whether the post-Somalia advocates of changes in peacekeeping training, the technological aficionados enamoured of the 'revolution in military affairs', or the press corps pursuing a more consistent and open public relations policy, ensuring a hearing from Canada's defence establishment has been the labour of Sisyphus for far too many well-intentioned souls. It need not be so. As Tony Blair noted in the fall in announcing the development of a new chapter in Britain's Strategic Defence Review (Blair, 2001), and, significantly, not a new review itself, the first task must be 'to stop and assess if 11 September represented a fundamental change in the strategic context and, if so, how serious a change?' It is no shame to stand behind existing policy that is sound or, conversely, to admit that the world has changed. It is obviously a greater leap to deduce from recent events that the emperor might always have had no clothes, but missing the opportunity to know the difference would be monstrous.

REFLECTIONS AND PROJECTIONS

Canada's post-Cold War defence policy protected most of the essential components of 50-year old security commitments, including links to the North American Aerospace Defence Command (NORAD) and NATO, but this policy made important changes, too. The military instrument shrank in size and budget, spent more time training for and operating in multilateral peacekeeping and peace support missions, and, in the aftermath of Somalia and other scandals, submerged institutionally in an all-consuming and painful self-assessment of personnel, infrastructure, professional ethics, and leadership. The Liberal government for several years served up quantitatively thin gruel to an already struggling defence establishment, but in the wake of the Warsaw Pact's demise, Somalia, and the long series of hazing rituals, sex scandals, and official misdemeanours that marked the 1990s, that establishment might be seen as preternaturally lucky not to have endured a far worse political fate. Indeed, over the past several years, in the face of improved government finances, the defence budget has actually grown. Widespread public indignation over the social conditions affecting CF personnel and their families, the fast pace of overseas rotation, and the perceived linkages between indifferent federal support and subsequent bad behaviour combined with the celebration of historic anniversaries, support for Canadian war veterans, and renewed interest in remembrance and commemoration to lay the groundwork for modest but important changes in military funding. There had been at least mild incongruity in the spectacle of public celebration of the country's military past while fiscally motivated governments cut deeply into its military future, but the gap between these nodes of civic interest—public support on the one hand versus public willingness to fund on the other—has narrowed somewhat in the last several federal budgets.

The long-term significance of the government's conservative management of this file might well earn it higher marks from future scholars than has heretofore been the case. It is seldom recalled clearly, less than a decade after the fact, that the defence debate of 1993–4 included large and vocal elements for which merely the continued maintenance of a conventionally armed, alliance-dedicated Canadian military with general-purpose combat capability—of whatever magnitude and competence—was little less than political pornography. The Canada 21 Council, more reasonable though no less passionate than such groups, seemed poised, with substantial support from within the governing party's ranks, to push firmly the stumbling CF in the direction of a lightly armed constabulary force with domestic security and traditional peacekeeping missions (Canada 21, 1994). There may have been worse fates, and the CF as an institution has itself in subsequent years embraced more openly its peacekeeping destiny, but the armoured corps, the artillery, the navy, and the air force (especially the fighter community) might have been forgiven a certain difficulty in envisioning them. Canadian withdrawal from permanent commitments to NATO in Europe likewise affected not at all the strategic balance of post-Cold War Europe, but it did affect public—and political—perceptions of why the country continued to need what some commentators derisively called 'war-fighting' forces when, clearly in their view, there was no longer any 'war' to be fought.

To be sure, many such military savants would also have been found a decade previously making precisely the same complaint, irrespective of the strength of the Soviet forces in Germany or the growing naval menace in the North Atlantic and North Pacific, but, regrettably, the strategic bankruptcy of the Cold War peace movement was no hedge against its post-Cold War longevity. The Gulf War, the Yugoslav debacle, and now Afghanistan added to the weight of argument against such strategic myopia, but a full accounting of the tenor of the Canadian debate in these years must acknowledge the logical and fiscal attractions in reducing substantially a military instrument with important components that seemed no longer to be required.

But if the Chrétien Liberals are to be credited with seeing the CF through a turbulent and uncertain decade more or less intact, much to the chagrin of those who effectively 'lost' the fight for Canada's military in 1994, the size, effectiveness, and disposition of the rump force that remains is a dubious laurel. Current military operations in Afghanistan, no less than other recent missions, speak both to the increasingly contestable value and logic of the country's minimal force structure and to the rhetorical underpinnings of soft power, human security, and the new international order that have come to inform Canadian diplomatic practice in the intervening years. The events of 11 September and their aftermath are neither the budget-affirming elixir of Canada's pro-defence lobby nor, in the form of 'blow-back' or unexpected consequences, the delightful comeuppance that fuels the oratory of diehards like Sunera Thobani.

Instead, as the Canadian navy sailed with the pomp of Nelson to an air-land battle against an enemy having neither warships nor coasts and as the army legitimized the elite rapid reaction, air-portable light infantry role it partially eviscerated some years ago in disbanding, on political orders, the Airborne Regiment, September's events suggested a need to revisit the appropriateness of Canadian defence policy in the first post-Cold War decade, especially the military capabilities and arrangements with which the country had been left. In that context, too, the assumptions girding such concepts as capability-based planning, the political animus against closer military integration with the United States, and the continued viability and utility of the CF's current asset mix and structural organization might also fall under the microscope. Air-to-air refuelling, strategic life assets, air assault, the strength and firepower of light infantry units, the government's capacity for strategic assessment, policy planning and co-ordination, and alliance relations are not far down the list.

The semantic vigour with which Defence officials insisted for some months after 11 September that a program review, not a policy review, would suffice to address any issues or imbalances arising from Afghanistan had undoubted technical and bureaucratic merit, but it was difficult not to discern in their defence of the status quo more a fear of the unexpected consequences of the process, which is to say a fear of being unable to manage it, than a rejection of the need. The previous review could have left no one overly sanguine as to the potential for mischief-making in a policy free-for-all of the kind likely to ensue if the review were conducted against the backdrop of ongoing operations. But the hastily added epilogue to *Strategic Assessment 2001*, two short pages compiled in the fall by the Directorate of Strategic Analysis, was suggestion enough that, even on first glance, the implications of 11 September might be radical and far-reaching for Canadian security interests (DND, 2001). If the events 'may be a harbinger of a much more hostile and dangerous international environment' wherein 'transnational terrorism will likely be regarded as the primary threat', one through which other problems, security issues, and military capabilities might well be judged, the challenges posed by such potentially revolutionary developments become not just unlikely to be addressed within a mere program review but positively dangerous. Thus, while there may be few things new under the sun, it is also plausible to entertain the possibility that 11 September and its implications do indeed constitute just such a new thing.

The opening, none too subtle, gambit in such a thoroughgoing re-evaluation has also been mooted numerous times in the press and in the Defence Department's periodic policy consultations with the academic community: neither flexible nor multi-purpose anymore, the Canadian Forces, by gradual but incessant reductions, have been ushered in the direction of the glorified sovereignty protection and peacekeeping roles its fiercer critics had for a decade and more demanded. The air war in Kosovo and the navy's wisely articulated co-operation with its American counterparts aside, the 1990s witnessed a near-endless series of highly publicized embarrassments for the CF wherein minimal or token Canadian commitments were shown up by the more robust and capable contributions of allies. The attentive public through most of the decade heard a virtual drumbeat of criticism directed at the CF and the Defence Department such that the capacity to disbelieve the bromides of ministers and generals grew to rather vast proportions. The good works done by the military in response to domestic floods and environmental emergencies, international humanitarian crises, and the never-ending series of peacekeeping missions offered occasional solace to a beleaguered defence establishment, but the tenor of commentary remained noxious most of the time, stoked by the sad state of relations with the national press corps.

In reality, of course, the honours of the 1990s were far more even, despite pressing questions about the size, missions, and overall capacity of the force. Afghanistan, no more than Kosovo or the Great Ice Storm, showed the Canadian military entering the next century in a role worn familiarly in the last: underfunded and scarcely appreciated at home but competent, professional, and highly reliable abroad. But many commentators, most notably Joseph Jockel, have noted that even in relation to the quantitative performance and commitment benchmarks of the government itself, the CF remained in trouble, with shrinking human resources compounded by aging equipment, a high operational tempo, and the failure to define a comprehensive vision of itself that would integrate all services. The recent report of the Canadian Council on Security, the 'Strategic Assessment' produced in 1999 by the Defence Policy Committee of the Conference of Defence Associations, periodic reviews by the Auditor General, and other third-party assessments all point in this direction (CDA, 1999). Together, they capture a sense of the malaise into which the bulk of informed commentators believe the CF and its political overseers have sunk.

This general consensus is far from a unanimous or unidirectional critique, but the march of events since 1994, even since September 2001, has probably moved the centre much further to the right than was evident in the policy review of that year. It is an odd enough legacy of the first post-Cold War decade in a country iconoclastic enough to have been dubbed, many years ago, the Yugoslavs of NATO. The maelstrom of Somalia and the investigations that followed affected substantially this divide, in some ways fracturing the community of defence intellectuals itself into two rather distinct camps— those who believed the increasingly incredible explanations of the defence establishment for its sins and those who, quite frankly, did not. But the period was also one in which international crises—in the Balkans, in the Indian subcontinent, and lately in the skies of North America—repeatedly contradicted the assurances of some opinion-makers as to the novelty, but manageability, of the new international system and called into question the philosophical assumptions that underlay, for example, human security and soft power.

These years, especially the tenure of Lloyd Axworthy as Foreign Affairs Minister, were ones of deep reflection and spirited public debate on Canada's global role. They also witnessed substantial internecine squabbling over the connections between defence and foreign affairs and the articulation of a broader, more closely co-ordinated international security framework. In last year's version of this publication, Defence official Vincent Rigby argued that the participants in that exchange, this author included, had exaggerated the gulf between defence and foreign affairs in ways not especially helpful to either the government or the Canadian Forces. The latter, he noted, had always been central to the human security dimensions of Canadian foreign policy and would continue to be so, their performance in that role, as in so many others, merely requiring the resources and training appropriate to the task. It was an important, and courageous, reminder, if a highly contentious one, as the anti-personnel landmines case indicated, but also one ever so subtle in its implications. The new nostrums, like the old, demanded a familiar laundry list of personnel and material resources in order to rise above the irrelevancy of simple rhetoric. Human security was a military project, too.

This is undoubtedly twisting Rigby's careful argument to a slightly mischievous degree, but the consensus between human security's would-be critics and its would-be defenders, at least in this particular instance, is worthy of note. The critics, after all, had complained less of the harbingers of biblical doom hiding subliminally in the Foreign Minister's verbiage than of the illogic in an intellectual and political project the scope of which widened the gap between CF capabilities and CF missions and whose diplomatic consequences ranged from the disillusionment of the Canadian public to the disgruntlement of key allies. It also appeared to do so even as the world view on which it was based denied validity to the defence establishment in the performance of many, if not most, of its traditional roles. A world in which the threat of conventional war or of interstate conflict has largely receded is a world in which much of the Canadian military, its doctrine, expertise, and leadership skills could—ultimately—be discarded. It is also a world in which the viability of international defence arrangements, such as NATO, maintained in large part as a precaution against such dire events, can also systematically be revisited. One need not be Chicken Little and run from the falling sky to query the longer-term implications of such a policy for the CF. A healthy challenge it might be, but it is a challenge nevertheless, and not the happy marriage of fellow travellers well met.

The waning resource base and the challenge posed the CF by the human security agenda or, more broadly, by competing conceptions of the new international order were not the only things contributing to the defence debate as Kosovo and 11 September marked the century's turning. As the parliamentary hearings on the 'social and economic challenges' facing members of the CF demonstrated, the rank and file seemed in all but open revolt against higher authority for the sins of low pay, inadequate benefits, and stressful occupations. The message of corporate wellness may fervently have been believed at the top, though even there former Chief of the Defence Staff General Maurice Baril led heroically in its abandonment, but the hearings proved that much was being lost in translation. Some CF officers testified, interestingly enough, to their belief that the new foreign policy agenda made their roles and responsibilities irrelevant, linking their conception of an unclear mission to the financial realities of the pay packet.

CONCLUSION

The very interconnectedness of these events—the fusing of the foreign policy debate with the periodic security challenges of recent years and the growing disquiet, publicly and institutionally, over the state of the military—is the essential preliminary to any understanding of how 11 September will affect the future of Canadian defence. The playing field on which for many years the CF has made necessity a virtue by doing more with less has undoubtedly changed, and a typology of actions for which it has never adequately prepared has just been added to its list of missions. It is surely not the last irony of the post-11 September period that in Afghanistan the methods by which the new war will be fought appear to involve many of the same assets of the Cold War now thought, and hoped by many, to have been the stuff of history. Even a short list would include power projection, forced insertion capability, rapid reaction forces, commando or special forces, strategic airlift and sealift assets, intelligence, light artillery, ground-attack aircraft, precision-guided munitions, helicopters, and offshore replenishment. Not all pre-emption or response to the terrorist challenge will, of course, enlist military means, the complexity of the threat having already provided a historic thrust to multinational and multi-agency co-operative efforts, but the extent to which—in the skies over New York or the mountains of Afghanistan—the military instrument has emerged as a critical policy tool is nevertheless striking. It is also, no doubt, a great discomfort to those who would have interred the conventionally armed, professionally trained CF in the grave of the Cold War.

This is hardly to suggest that transnational terrorism has brought us back to the traditional future of international conflict. But it is to argue that the compromise approach to Canadian defence that created and sustained the defence consensus of the mid-1990s, rickety and under intermittent siege though it was, has frayed with the passage of time. The shift in geopolitical understandings in the wake of 11 September is not the first challenge to Canadians' assumptions about the world and their place in it, but it may be the greatest in the past half-century or more. Not since Japanese balloon bombs and German submarines during World War II has North American security been so obviously at risk, the self-evident dangers of the nuclear balance notwithstanding. Not since the Gulf War has Canada faced—and this time accepted—the risks of high-tempo ground combat for its considerably diminished ground forces. Not since the Cuban Missile Crisis have continental defence and joint command with the United States been a subject of such intense public scrutiny. If revisiting the fundamental basis of Canada's military risks were to mean all but disestablishing the Canadian Forces, as some commentators have argued, then that, to be fair, is perhaps a point in favour of avoiding the effort. If, on the other hand, Canadians are serious in wanting to provide the CF with relevant and realistic strategic guidance to take the military well into the next century, then it is altogether difficult to envisage the game as not being worth the candle.

Some strategic shibboleths might well be jettisoned as a result of this inquiry. Others might be found seasoned with age and of continued utility. Regardless, as the late Nick Stetham wrote in a brief to the Special Joint Committee in 1994, 'we must avoid the temptation to dress up the results of financial constraint as the product of strategic wisdom', for in the end, 'there is a vital caution: don't fake it.'

> In the past, nestled within a powerful alliance in a more stable world, we have indulged in a degree of policy fraud when it came to defence, pretending to capabilities we did not have and deploying strategic arguments which bore little or no relationship to the real world. In chaotic, unpredictable times such as these, that is a national self indulgence that we cannot afford. The cost of fraud now may turn out to be measured in human lives, the most precious dimensions of our investment in the armed forces.
>
> In any case, such deceptions never fooled our adversaries or our allies. They saw what was really there, as they will in future. The only people liable to be fooled are Canadians. The return on an investment in faking it is nothing more than self delusion (Stetham, 1994).

Canadians might yet view recent events as a fitting opportunity to recalibrate ends and means, to revisit their fundamental assumptions about the world and the security threats it contains, as Defence Minister Art Eggleton appeared to imply in his 22 February 2002 remarks to the Conference of Defence Associations (Thompson, 2002). Or they might simply and cursorily view the status quo as a flexible vessel into which all spirits can flow. Either way, Canadian military power and influence are fading no more demonstrably now, in the aftermath of 11 September and Afghanistan, than they did during the past decade and more. The relative dimness of Canadian military capability post-11 September, however, might just be that much easier to see, and the relative consequences of inattention to this fact that much easier to grasp.

REFERENCES

Blair, Tony. 2001. Speech at King's College, London, 5 Dec.

Canada 21. 1994. *Canada 21: Canada and Common Security in the Twenty-first Century*, Toronto: Centre for International Studies, University of Toronto.

Conference of Defence Associations Institute. 1999. *A Strategic Assessment: Canada's Response to the New Challenges of International Security*. Ottawa.

Department of Foreign Affairs and International Trade (DFAIT). 1995. *Canada in the World*. Ottawa: Government Communications Group.

Department of National Defence (DND). 1987. *Challenge and Commitment: A Defence Policy for Canada*. Ottawa.

———. 1994. *1994 Defence White Paper*. Ottawa: Minister of Supply and Services.

———. 2001. Directorate of Strategic Analysis, Policy Planning Division, Policy Group. *Strategic Assessment 2001*. Ottawa, Sept.

Homer-Dixon, Thomas. 2002. 'The Rise of Complex Terrorism', *Foreign Policy* (Jan.–Feb.). Available at: <www.foreignpolicy.com>.

Huntington, Samuel P. 1997. *The Clash of Civilizations and the Remaking of World Order*. New York: Touchstone.

Kaplan, Robert D. 2001. 'Looking the World in the Eye', *Atlantic Monthly* 288, 5 (Dec.): 68–82.

Maloney, Sean M. 1997. *War Without Battles: Canada's NATO Brigade in Germany, 1951–1993*. Toronto: McGraw-Hill Ryerson.

Rigby, Vincent. 2001. 'The Canadian Forces and Human Security: A Redundant or Relevant Military?', in Fen Osler Hampson, Norman Hillmer, and Maureen Appel Molot, eds, *Canada Among Nations 2001: The Axworthy Legacy*. Toronto: Oxford University Press.

Stetham, Nicholas. 1994. 'The Construction of Canadian Defence Policy', submission to the Special Joint Committee on Canada's Defence Policy, 17 June.

Thompson, Allan. 2002. 'Major defence and foreign policy reviews planned', *Toronto Star*, 22 Feb.

United Kingdom Ministry of Defence. 1998. *United Kingdom Strategic Defence Review: Modern Forces for a Modern World*. London: Ministry of Defence, July.

7

Contemporary Threats, Future Tasks: Canadian Intelligence and the Challenges of Global Security

MARTIN RUDNER

Canada's intelligence community consists of an intricate web of functionally specialized agencies for the collection and assessment of security-relevant knowledge on behalf of the country's foreign policy and security and defence establishment, and for ensuring that the covert operations comply with laws and public policy. It is convenient for analytical purposes to characterize Canadian intelligence requirements by scope and function in terms of two distinct spheres of operations: security intelligence and foreign intelligence (Auditor General, 1996). Security intelligence relates to activities that could threaten Canada's domestic security, such as espionage, sabotage, foreign-influenced activities, or politically motivated violence, and is collected to help maintain public safety and protect national security. Foreign intelligence addresses the capabilities, activities, or intentions of foreign countries, organizations, or individuals, and is required to serve Canadian national interests, including its geo-strategic, economic, military, scientific/technological, environmental, and social policy objectives. There are also specialized organizations with mandates for intelligence assessment and for the oversight of the intelligence services. This chapter analyzes the evolution of Canada's intelligence community from the Cold War through to the war on global terrorism, highlighting its changing strategic and organizational thrust, operational agenda, targets, relations with allies, and its structure of accountability to government and Parliament. A concluding section considers future challenges for Canadian intelligence policy.

In Canada, responsibility for security intelligence is assigned primarily to the Canadian Security Intelligence Service (CSIS), a civilian agency established by statute in 1984 (CSIS Act), which took over that function from the Royal Canadian Mounted Police (RCMP). Canada never has had a dedicated foreign intelligence service of its own, unlike most other members of the North Atlantic Treaty Organization (NATO) and similarly situated middle powers like Australia and Sweden. Rather, Canadian activities in foreign intelligence collection are confined mainly to signals intelligence (SIGINT) on the part of the Communications Security Establishment (CSE), to certain CSIS activities abroad relating to Canada's security, and to the defence intelligence function of the Canadian Forces. Canada's own efforts in the domain of foreign intelligence are significantly augmented by exchanges of intelligence product with allies and partners under various international arrangements.

The end of the Cold War yielded a peace dividend in terms of vastly reduced defence budgets and military establishments generally. Nevertheless, as government budgets were cut back, the past decade has witnessed an upsurge in intelligence requirements and capabilities in response to a more challenging and more diffuse threat environment, coupled with far-reaching technological advancements in information gathering and processing. The aftermath of the 11 September terrorist attacks on the United States further prompted sharply increased appropriations of resources, federal and even provincial, for security and intelligence.

THE DIRECTION OF INTELLIGENCE POLICY

Intelligence informs many spheres of government decision-making and policy analysis. However, what distinguishes intelligence from other information resources is its sensitivity and intrusiveness, which precipitates collection by clandestine means as well as from open sources (Herman, 2001). The Canadian political system does not confer overall responsibility for security and intelligence on any single government department. By convention, the Prime Minister, as head of government, exercises broad high-level leadership in areas of major importance to the national interest, most notably international affairs, national unity and security, and economic and trade policy. The setting and co-ordination of policy directions for intelligence falls within this prime ministerial function (PCO, 2000). In particular, the Prime Minister chairs the annual Meeting of Ministers on Security and Intelligence and the cabinet decision-making process, appoints bureaucratic heads of the security and intelligence organizations, and from time to time takes personal charge of certain specifically sensitive issues. In October 2001, in the aftermath of the terrorist attacks on the United States, the government set up a high-profile Cabinet Committee on Security, chaired by then Minister of Foreign Affairs, John Manley, which was given an unprecedented mandate to co-ordinate and supervise Canada's counter-terrorism effort, including its intelligence component.[1]

The Prime Minister is supported in these responsibilities by the Privy Council Office (PCO), the central agency of the government of Canada. The Clerk of the Privy Council chairs the Interdepartmental Committee on Security and Intelligence, a deputy-ministerial body that deliberates on strategic policy and resource issues, reviews national security affairs, and makes recommendations to ministers and cabinet on intelligence matters, including the annual Meeting of Ministers on Security and Intelligence. The senior Canadian government official responsible for intelligence at the PCO, the Deputy Clerk, Counsel, and Co-ordinator of Security and Intelligence, supervises and co-ordinates the security and intelligence activities of all Canadian government agencies and departments and manages international intelligence relationships. The PCO houses two specialized intelligence-related secretariats reporting to the Deputy Clerk: a Security and Intelligence Secretariat dealing with policy matters and the Intelligence Assessment Secretariat, which produces integrated all-source assessments of political, economic, and strategic intelligence for the Prime Minister, cabinet, ministers, and senior officials.

Ministerial responsibility for the security and intelligence community is divided among several departmental portfolios, sometimes in curiously intricate ways. CSIS comes under the ministerial jurisdiction of the Solicitor General, Canada's senior law officer. In February 2001, the Solicitor General issued a revised compendium of Ministerial Directions to CSIS, a classified document setting out strategic guidelines and streamlining its policy and management framework (SIRC, 2001). CSE, for its part, has a bifurcated reporting relationship to the Deputy Minister of National Defence for financial and administrative issues and to the Deputy Clerk, PCO, on policy and operational matters. The Minister of National Defence has ministerial responsibility for defence and military intelligence (the mandate of the J2 division) and for the Office of Critical Infrastructure Protection and Emergency Preparedness. Intelligence and security units of other federal departments and agencies, such as Foreign Affairs and International Trade, Transport, Citizenship and Immigration, the Canada Customs and Revenue Agency, and the RCMP, report to their respective ministers.

The primary forum for collective ministerial participation in intelligence policy-making is the annual Meeting of Ministers on Security and Intelligence, where intelligence priorities for the security and intelligence community are determined. The relatively new cabinet Ad Hoc Committee on Security is likely to play a key role in the overall direction of Canada's intelligence effort and in deliberations over policy, organizational, and resource matters.

INTELLIGENCE AND THE POST-COLD WAR SECURITY AGENDA

In 1991, following the end of the Cold War, the federal cabinet for the first time issued a directive on intelligence priorities, setting out its urgent requirements for foreign intelligence collection (Auditor General, 1996). These priority requirements have been updated almost annually since then. Among the current priorities are international terrorism, ethnic and religious conflict, proliferation of weapons of mass destruction, illegal migration, transnational organized crime, economic counter-espionage, and trade intelligence. These priorities are given operational expression in the tasking assigned to the Canadian intelligence community. National Requirements for Security Intelligence are determined annually, including a general direction from cabinet about where CSIS should focus its efforts and setting out guidelines for its intelligence collection, analysis, and advisory functions. Current requirements for foreign intelligence collection imply the targeting by the intelligence services of neutral and friendly countries.

It is pertinent to note that the emergence of a 'new' post-Cold War threat environment has not displaced the more traditional threats to Canada's homeland security so far as the intelligence community is concerned. Canada remains vulnerable to threats of espionage or menacing conduct on the part of former adversaries like Russia, newly assertive powers like China and India, rogue states like Iran, Iraq, and Libya, or even ostensibly friendly countries (CSIS, 1997). For instance, clandestine French activities in support of Quebec separatism were closely monitored and countered by Canadian intelligence services (Black, 1996). Incidents have occurred in which aggressive foreign agencies, like those of Iran, tried to procure illegal weaponry and military technology, evade internationally mandated sanctions, and even foment civil unrest in Canada (SIRC, 2000). Canadian intelligence services also responded to security risks arising from attempts on the part of foreign governments to exercise improper influence on Canadian decision-making or public opinion, interfere with recent immigrants or homeland communities in Canada, or intrude on Canada's own communications systems (PCO, 2001).

The post-Cold War security agenda, for its part, has radically different implications for the functions of intelligence (Treverton, 2001). In responding to traditional threats the intelligence services are able to target specific countries or governments, but in the new threat environment there are numerous, vaguely defined, mostly non-state targets. Intelligence regarding traditional threats is typically scarce and difficult to acquire, and the most reliable sources tend to be available to the intelligence community; by way of contrast, information about the newly emergent threats tends to be widely dispersed among a multitude of sources, few of which are either reliable or owned by intelligence services. There are relatively few consumers—mainly security and defence officials—for traditional threat-related intelligence, while intelligence about the new threats has many prospective consumers across the departments and agencies of government.

Even prior to 11 September, international terrorism figured prominently in the threat assessments of Canada's foreign and domestic security intelligence services (CSIS, 1997). Many of the world's terrorist groups have established a presence in Canada, virtually all of them relating to ethnic, religious, or nationalist conflicts elsewhere in the world (CSIS, 1999; see also Chapter 8, this volume). Among the international terrorist organizations or fronts active in Canada are the Al-Qaeda network, Hezbollah and other Shiite Islamic terrorist organizations from the Middle East, the Palestinian Hamas, the Algerian Armed Islamic Group (GIA), Al-Jihad, the Provisional Irish Republican Army (IRA), the Liberation Tigers of Tamil Eelam from Sri Lanka, the Kurdistan Workers Party (PKK) from Turkey, and virtually every significant Sikh militant group from India.

These international terrorist organizations typically maintain a presence in Canada in order to raise and transfer funds, procure weaponry and material, set up operational sanctuaries, and support infiltration across the border to the United States or overseas. Cells of groups like Al-Jihad and GIA engage in financial fraud and theft, identity and document forgery, and people smuggling in support of their parent terrorist networks (Blatchford, 2001: A18–19). Reported links between the Al-Qaeda network in North America and the Montreal-based presence of the Algerian GIA exemplify this emergent globalized threat environment (Soloman, 2001; Sachs, 2001). The collection of intelligence on terrorist threats calls for new and challenging methods of penetrating tightly closed cells and loosely structured networks, and will have to depend on co-operation with partners and allies, not all of which will be governments (Treverton, 2001). The primary responsibility for counter-terrorist intelligence is vested in CSIS, working together with other pertinent government departments (e.g., Citizenship and Immigration, Department of Justice), the RCMP and local police forces.

Canada's foreign and security intelligence effort is also directed at the connection between transnational criminality, on the one hand, and terrorist racketeering and criminal collaboration with insurgency movements elsewhere, on the other. International terrorist groups have taken over legitimate businesses and even non-governmental organizations (NGOs) as a means of money laundering and in order to disguise their activities. Among the more notorious instances, the Liberation Tigers of Tamil Eelam established an underground network among Tamil sympathizers across Canada and also became extensively involved in racketeering to generate financing for their insurgency war in Sri Lanka (Porteous, 1996; Aryasinha, 2001; Chapter 8, this volume). Intelligence sources were instrumental in uncovering Middle Eastern organized criminal groups involved in transferring funds and stolen equipment to Hezbollah in Lebanon, including stolen vehicles (Bell, 2000). Criminal-terrorist syndicates were reportedly active in drug trafficking, immigrant smuggling, commercial fraud, and extortion from homeland residents in this country and elsewhere.

Transnational crime has been defined as a national security threat, thus warranting the attention of Canada's intelligence services. (Porteous, 1996). Organized criminal enterprises, which move money, people, and contraband, including drugs, across borders, Canada's included, seemed beyond the control of domestic law enforcement agencies alone. Moreover, some of the more insidious attempts at major international fraud, corruption, and financial manipulation were perceived as undermining the very foundations of legitimate governments, democratic institutions, and social order. By way of response, the governments of Canada and other allied countries decided to task their intelligence services with targeting transnational crime (CSIS, 1997). CSIS took on a role in combatting international criminal activity in Canada, primarily by providing access to international intelligence resources and producing analytical tools for law enforcement agencies (CSIS, 1995).

Canada participates in virtually the entire array of global and regional initiatives to counter the proliferation of weapons of mass destruction and their delivery systems (CSIS, 1997). By way of supporting its non-proliferation policy, Canada's security and intelligence community aims at identifying attempts by countries of proliferation concern to acquire Canadian weapons-related technology and expertise. One of the more alarming aspects pertains to students and researchers from countries suspected of seeking to achieve a capability in the production and deployment of weapons of mass destruction (WMD) enrolling in university programs in nuclear physics or other potentially militarized disciplines, a quarry calling for considerable dexterity and sensitivity in counter-intelligence operations (Smyth, 2002). Intelligence produced by Canadian agencies or obtained from their international sources helps keep the government and its allies alert to proliferation threats.

While the intelligence agencies never divulge operational targets or methods, various government reports, other disclosures, media accounts, and information from foreign sources provide some indication of the direction and purpose of Canada's intelligence activities.

INTELLIGENCE COLLECTION

The Canadian security and intelligence community deploys several specialized agencies for the collection and processing of intelligence of different types (PCO, 2001). The principal agencies include CSE for signals intelligence and communications security; CSIS for security intelligence and certain elements of foreign intelligence within Canada at the request of the Minister of National Defence; and J2 division of the Department of National Defence (DND) for defence and military intelligence. The RCMP also fulfills certain intelligence collection and investigatory functions, and works in co-operation with CSIS against transnational crime and in counter-espionage and counter-terrorism.

Communications Security Establishment

Most of the foreign intelligence provided to the Canadian government by virtue of Canada's own intelligence collection capabilities derives from signals intelligence collected by CSE or otherwise obtained through its international liaison arrangements. CSE is, arguably, the most secretive entity of the government of Canada— for decades the very existence of this SIGINT agency was unconfirmed; it had no statutory mandate, at least until recently; and virtually all details of its resources, objectives, and operations are still shrouded in official secrecy (Auditor General, 1996; Rudner, 2001). CSE collects signals intelligence by means of sophisticated, covert interception technologies designed to intercept terrestrial, microwave, radio, and satellite communications along with other electromagnetic emissions. In fulfillment of these foreign intelligence collection functions, CSE participates in international SIGINT sharing arrangements with the United States, the United Kingdom, Australia, and New Zealand within the framework of the UKUSA alliance.[2] CSE is also responsible for providing technical advice and guidance for protecting Canadian government communications and electronic data security.

Canadian signals intelligence operations during and after the Cold War may be considered in terms of four types of interception operations: local in-country, external in-country, long-range, and satellite communications, in accordance with the location and technologies deployed. Local interception operations were mounted within Canada to target communications to or from this country on the part of Soviet bloc diplomatic and consular missions,[3] trade and commercial offices, and organizations and individuals suspected of involvement in espionage or subversion (Cleroux, 1991). Radio transmissions from Soviet research stations in the Arctic were also intercepted, allowing intelligence analysts to monitor their scientific experiments (Bamford, 2001). By the early 1980s Canadian signals intelligence was pursuing economic targets of opportunity unrelated to security as part of Operation Aquarian, which aimed at foreign embassies and consulates, even those of friendly and allied countries. CSE intercepts were said to have been instrumental in enabling Canada to out-compete the United States in a US$5 billion wheat sale to China in 1981 (Livesey, 1998). Following the collapse of Communism in Europe and the end of the Cold War, a more variegated and volatile post-Cold War security situation has had a far-reaching impact on Canadian foreign intelligence requirements.

External in-country interception operations targeted communications to and from foreign countries at Canadian diplomatic posts, using US-supplied technologies. Microwave systems in most countries converge on their capital cities, rendering some of their most sensitive communications traffic vulnerable to embassy based interception operations. Embassy-based SIGINT stations were also effective for intercepting official car phone communications transmitted by short-range radio. The first such interception operation, Stephanie, was mounted from the Canadian embassy in Moscow beginning in the autumn of 1972, and ran for about three years (Frost and Gratton, 1994). A subsequent operation, Sphinx, was run in the late 1980s. Other external interception operations were reportedly conducted in Abidjan (Operation Jasmine), Beijing (Badger), Bucharest (Hollyhock), Rabat (Iris), Kingston, Jamaica (Egret), Mexico City (Cornflower), New Delhi (Daisy), Rome, San José, Costa Rica, Warsaw, and possibly Tokyo. All the intelligence collected by Canadian external-based interceptions was actually remitted to the US National Security Agency (NSA) for deciphering and analysis, since at the time Canada lacked a capacity to do this. For the want of cryptanalytical capability, Canada was unable to process the 'take' from its own external SIGINT collection efforts and had to rely on partners for this intelligence product (Robinson, n.d.; Rudner, 2001).

Apart from the Soviet bloc, the Canadian signals intelligence effort also sometimes targeted the communications of other countries whose foreign policy behaviour was considered inimical to Canada, and of those whose embassies or representatives were suspected of engaging in illegitimate political activities, inappropriate dealings with Canadian residents, support for subversive or terrorist groups, or illicit arms procurements. After the election of a separatist government in the province of Quebec, CSE reportedly began monitoring communications between the governments of Quebec and France (Black, 1996; Arnold, 1992). Such operations were ostensibly mounted by CSE itself, some say with support from SIGINT allies in Norway and the United States.

The development of space-based technologies since the 1960s has led to the deployment of sophisticated satellite systems for intelligence collection. Imagery satellites, for photographic and radar intelligence, were deployed first by the US and later by other countries, including France,[4] Russia, China, India, Israel, and Italy. However, the Americans and French are still the only countries to have developed a capability to intercept communications from space. Canada does not possess either imagery or SIGINT satellite capabilities of its own, but the UKUSA arrangement allowed CSE to share in satellite-based SIGINT collection and also to task—within certain parameters—US satellites to respond to specific Canadian foreign intelligence requirements.

The rapid expansion of satellite-based telecommunications traffic since the 1970s prompted the UKUSA partners to build a network of six satellite communications (SATCOM) interception stations in strategic locations in order to achieve global coverage. One of these operated under CSE aegis at Leitrim, Ontario, ostensibly targeted on Latin American PanAmSat communications links. To deal with the ensuing surge in raw intelligence collection, CSE undertook a revitalization and enlargement of its intelligence processing capacity and cryptanalytic capabilities. Early in 1985, CSE acquired its first supercomputer for cryptanalysis, a Cray X-MP/11. By the late 1990s, there were four satellite dishes operating at Leitrim. Personnel, likewise, had to be augmented and trained to analyze and disseminate the ensuing intelligence product. CSE staffing grew from around 600 people in the late 1970s to some 720 in the mid-1980s, and to about 900 by the end of the decade (Robinson, n.d.; Rudner, 2001).

By the 1990s, extensive refinements to UKUSA satellite interception technologies had made possible a virtually seamless global intelligence collection capability for the various modalities of signals intelligence collection: local in-country, external, high-frequency long-distance, and space-based. This integration and meshing of SIGINT technologies reached its zenith in the tightly integrated and networked interception and processing system known as Echelon (Campbell, 1999).[5] Highly secret still, the Echelon system is able to process and sort through vast flows of telecommunications traffic to or from most parts of the world and identify specifically targeted messaging. The great challenge confronting CSE and its partners has been the tremendous influx of intercepts that can overwhelm existing capacity to synthesize and analyze raw communications intelligence into readily usable product.

At the operational heart of this integrated SIGINT processing and networking system is the Echelon 'Dictionary', a specialized, powerful computer system having the capacity to store a comprehensive database on designated organizations or individuals, including names, topics of interest, addresses, telephone numbers, and other criteria for target identification (Bamford, 2001). While CSE may not have its own Echelon Dictionary computer, according to reports this networking infrastructure enables Canada to access readily other UKUSA partners' facilities. The reciprocal sharing arrangement under UKUSA gives each partner of the SIGINT organization virtually automatic access to interception modalities, but not necessarily to particular intelligence products.

In the wake of the 11 September attacks, Canadian intelligence reportedly intercepted encrypted communications among international terrorist networks warning of renewed terrorist assaults on the United States (Seper, 2001). This intelligence was forwarded to American authorities, who subsequently invoked a heightened state of alert. Although publicly credited to CSIS, it seems likely that the interception operation originated with CSE, probably through the Echelon network (Simmie, 2001). Under the new counter-terrorism legislation enacted in 2001, Bill C-36, CSE has been empowered, subject to authorization by the Minister of National Defence, to monitor communications to or from Canada specifically for the collection of foreign intelligence.

Canadian Security Intelligence Service

CSIS is a civilian security intelligence agency. Historically, the primary concerns of Canadian security intelligence related to Communist subversion and espionage and to perceived threats of separatist violence in Quebec. The cabinet intelligence directive of 1991 led to a refocusing of CSIS efforts more towards counter-terrorism, economic espionage, weapons of mass destruction, and foreign-influenced activities. In fulfilling its mandate, CSIS investigates, analyzes, and advises government departments and agencies on activities suspected of constituting threats to Canada's national security.

International terrorism is currently perceived to be the dominant threat to Canada's domestic security. Canada's open society and the presence of large, identifiable homeland communities from societies in conflict create a distinctly attractive arena for international terrorist networks. While most acts of political violence in Canada have been extensions of foreign conflict, individuals and institutions in this country have been targeted by rogue states and terrorist organizations in order to intimidate adversaries or gain public attention for their cause (Bell, 2001a; Edwards, 2001; Landy, 2001). Al-Qaeda reportedly plotted a bomb attack on Jewish neighbourhoods in Montreal (Matas, 2001: A1). Other Islamic militants set up Internet sites registered in Canada for recruiting and promoting an international, violent 'jihad' (Bell, 2001d: A1). Efforts to monitor and control such activities in Canada seem to have been impeded by lax immigration, citizenship, and passport procedures, as demonstrated by the Ahmed Ressam case (Bell, 2001b).[6]

CSIS legislation gives it the authority to investigate the activities of any group, organization, or person suspected of constituting a threat to the security of Canada (SIRC, 2000). This targeting authority is governed by policies and procedures that control the operational methods and investigatory techniques to be used. CSIS also investigates foreign government activities deemed detrimental to Canadian national interests or public safety, such as interference with ethnic and dissident communities in Canada. There have been instances where foreign operatives, like those of Iran, attempted to intimidate dissidents in Canada, threatened ethnic groups, or orchestrated public demonstrations to gain attention for their cause (SIRC, 2000). By way of responding to emergent terrorist threats, CSIS is taking steps to improve and expand its analytical skills, knowledge resources, and investigatory capabilities regarding distant conflict situations in the Middle East, Eastern and Central Europe, Asia, and Africa.

Large-scale mass movements of people, sometimes involving political, religious, or economic refugees and sometimes combined with the growth of transnational criminal activity, generate social, economic, political, and, by implication, security challenges. Migrant smuggling has become a lucrative endeavour for transnational criminal groups. While the intelligence component of Citizenship and Immigration Canada has the responsibility to forewarn of attempts at illegal migration, CSIS plays a role in the security screening of prospective immigrants and refugee claimants. Staff shortages and work overload have meant that CSIS can take as long as two years to complete these background checks on new arrivals, leaving a chink in the armour of Canada's security (SIRC, 2001). However, even when alerts are indicated, the record suggests that the refugee determination process has not worked adequately in checking and excluding suspected terrorist operatives from Canada (Blatchford, 2001).

The security and intelligence community has devoted increased attention to the phenomenon of illicit transnational fundraising and money laundering on behalf of international terrorism. At the Halifax Summit of the Group of 8 (G-8) countries (see Chapter 10, this volume) commitments were made to combat international terrorism by curbing the misuse of charitable, social, and cultural organizations for fundraising. Canada was slow to enact legislation, but in the aftermath of 11 September, in anticipation of further changes to the law regarding the suppression of terrorist financing, new regulations were introduced in October 2001 to block money transfers to terrorist organisations. The intelligence capabilities of the Canada Customs and Revenue Agency (CCRA) are also being reinforced to counteract abuses of charitable status for financial resource mobilization by international terrorist networks.

Cyber-based threats to Canada's communications and information infrastructure are among the increasingly complex challenges to critical national infrastructure with which CSIS must contend, in conjunction with the Office of Critical Infrastructure Protection and Emergency Preparedness (CSIS, 2001). CSIS identified a looming threat from information warfare waged through 'weapons of mass corruption' at the disposal of rogue countries and international terrorist organizations, such as the Provisional IRA, the Spanish Basque Euskadi ta Askatasuna (Basque Fatherland and Liberty) (ETA), the Kurdish PKK, and militant Islamics (Bell, 2001c).

Defence Intelligence
The institutional centrepiece of Canada's defence intelligence capability is the J2 division at DND. J2, with a staff of approximately 500, is responsible for providing the Canadian Forces (CF) with all-source strategic, military, and security intelligence, imagery (in co-operation with the CF Photographic Unit) and counter-intelligence (in conjunction with the CF National Counter Intelligence Unit). Activities include the provision of political, strategic, and tactical intelligence to CF commanders and the deployment of Intelligence, Geomatics, and Imagery detachments for CF operations, the dispatch of Intelligence Response Teams to support peacekeeping missions, and

the provision of counter-intelligence force protection to operational missions. Defence intelligence products are also shared with other components of Canada's security and intelligence community and government departments, as well as with selected allies.

The Strategy 2020 strategic capability plan for the Canadian Forces assigns high value to information and intelligence capabilities among its 'capability goals' (DND, 2000). Future scenarios stipulate that the CF must be capable of operating alongside allied or coalition partners in international operations, while retaining an autonomous capability to function domestically. Information and intelligence capabilities for peace support and other operations other than war must relate to situations of far greater complexity and indeed ambiguity than the traditional combat operations for which these systems were designed.

The military intelligence architecture of the CF is closely integrated, for operational purposes, with allied, and especially American, systems. DND is developing a Canadian Electronic Warfare Command and Control Program, an automated architecture for information processing and distribution designed for interoperability with the US and other allied systems and capable of offering commanders a common understanding of their mission environment. In addition, the CF will have to continue supporting other government departments and agencies in security and intelligence-related matters, such as Canadian Forces Information Operations Group support for CSE.

INTERNATIONAL ALLIANCES AND LIAISON

Intelligence alliances are among the most intimate, enduring, and secretive of international security arrangements. The Canadian security and intelligence community is highly dependent on its alliances and international liaisons for access to foreign intelligence sources, in particular, given the absence of a dedicated foreign intelligence service. International partnerships have proven to be especially relevant to SIGINT, where collaboration among allies has been of great value for extending the scope and depth of geographic coverage. Other international arrangements been put in place for sharing intelligence on a more specialized issue-oriented or institutional basis. These intelligence alliances generate significant operational synergies and cost-sharing advantages; however, they also have profound implications for Canadian foreign policy and security and defence planning.

The UKUSA Alliance

For more than 50 years, the little-known United Kingdom–United States Security Agreement on communications intelligence co-operation, the UKUSA alliance, has been the keystone of Canadian intelligence policy and its single most important asset (Bamford, 2001; Andrew, 1994; Richelson and Ball, 1985). As early as 1945, Canada's intelligence chiefs were determined that the country's independent SIGINT effort should be enhanced in order to gain a place in postwar co-operation among allies in the realm of communications intelligence (Wark, 1997). As the Cold War intensified, earlier bilateral arrangements with the US and Great Britain culminated in 1948 in the formation of a closely knit, plurilateral Anglo-American SIGINT alliance—UKUSA—involving the US, the UK, Canada, Australia, and New Zealand. This alliance enables CSE to gain access to a shared global capacity to collect and deliver real time signals intelligence on foreign intelligence targets as tasked by the government of Canada.

The existence of this UKUSA alliance is still an official secret. Its architecture reportedly provided for a geographic division of responsibilities for regional coverage among the five partner countries' SIGINT agencies, coupled with a collaborative arrangement for intelligence collection, processing, and product sharing. This robust, tightly networked alliance of SIGINT agencies co-operated in global intelligence targeting, operational procedures, and transfers of SIGINT technologies, and provided full exchanges of intelligence product (Andrew, 1994; Richelson and Ball, 1985; Bamford, 2001). It has become an underlying principle of UKUSA that the partner countries do not target one another or their respective nationals. Later, certain other countries were included in a somewhat looser, more limited association as so-called 'third parties' to UKUSA, usually by virtue of bilateral arrangements with Britain (e.g., Sweden) or the US (e.g., Norway) (Richelson and Ball, 1984; van Buuren, 2000). The US and to a lesser degree the UK are the core contributors to this plurilateral SIGINT collection and sharing arrangement, with other partners like Canada serving as valuable auxiliaries.

Canada's role in the UKUSA alliance was valued not so much for this country's inherent capabilities in intelligence production as for the distinct geographic advantage that the country offered by way of SIGINT coverage of the Soviet Union, especially its Arctic and Far Eastern regions, and the adjacent Atlantic, Pacific, and Arctic Oceans

(Rudner, 2001). This contribution was of great strategic significance to UKUSA during the Cold War. Nevertheless, the alliance mechanism provided Canada with substantially more intelligence product from its allies, and especially from the US, on a far wider array of issue areas, than this country itself generated. Indeed, Canada's lamentable terms of trade in intelligence product were at times deprecated by its UKUSA allies (Aid and Wiebes, 2001). Yet, despite its meagre capacity to produce tradable intelligence, Canada's geography sustained its role in this most powerful of international intelligence alliances. This in turn provided Canada's security and intelligence community with intimate access to the highest-level policy councils of its American and British allies and with privileged recourse to the most sophisticated technologies for intelligence and defence generally, as well as access to a shared capability for global intelligence coverage.

Intelligence for Multilateralism: NATO and the UN

The UKUSA connection also had implications for Canada's intelligence role in other international security contexts. The alliance provided the impetus for Canada to become further involved in a tripartite Canada-UK-US (CANUKUS) intelligence grouping within NATO. NATO, as an organization, does not possess its own intelligence collection capability, and has only a limited capacity for analysis. Ordinarily, all of NATO's intelligence requirements are met from intelligence products supplied by member countries for the exclusive use of the alliance itself and for its constituent governments. During the Cold War, the CANUKUS grouping was said to have contributed the bulk of the input into the annual NATO Military Committee assessments of Soviet military power (Urban, 1996). The CANUKUS grouping furnished a preponderant share of NATO's overall intelligence requirements, mostly derived from SIGINT, including CSE product.

Since the end of the Cold War, NATO has taken upon itself 'peace support' missions in the Persian Gulf, in Somalia, and in the former Yugoslavia. These missions were not only 'out of theatre', but also involved NATO in new kinds of operations aimed at conflict prevention, peacemaking, peacekeeping, humanitarian aid, peace enforcement and peace-building (Nomikos, 2000). NATO has recognized that peace support implies a requirement for robust information and intelligence capabilities at operational and strategic levels, a task that imposed severe tensions on the traditional principles underpinning the alliance's intelligence system.

It has been a fundamental principle of NATO intelligence sharing up to now that none of the intelligence supplied to the alliance can be made available to non-member countries or to any international organization composed of non-member countries (Nomikos, 2000). This principle is also applicable to peace support missions involving NATO in coalition with other countries or international organizations, notwithstanding operational requirements for intelligence sharing (Berlin Information Center, 1994). Indeed, some of the highest-value elements of intelligence collected by sophisticated American surveillance technologies are not even shared with other NATO forces on the same alliance-led peace support missions. However, the Canadian Forces reportedly have enjoyed privileged access to this intelligence.

As a result of these tensions and conflicting requirements, the intelligence architecture for NATO-led peace support missions has become compartmentalized into a three-tier, differentiated access arrangement. The top tier is restricted to US forces and their most intimate UKUSA allies who share full access to American intelligence, surveillance, and reconnaissance capabilities as well as NATO resources. This includes the Canadian Forces. A second tier consists of other NATO allies who may acquire intelligence made available through the alliance mechanism, but without having access to reserved American-generated products. A third tier is composed of all other countries or international components, who are denied access to either NATO or American intelligence resources. This trifurcation of NATO's intelligence architecture militates against effective command and control of peace support operations and humanitarian missions involving coalitions with non-NATO countries, and has impeded the availability of tactical and operational intelligence even for Canadian participants.

Although NATO membership and UKUSA connections have benefited Canada in terms of intelligence access, this country's frequent involvement in peace support operations in coalition with non-NATO/non-UKUSA partners can sometimes place the Canadian Forces on the fault lines between these three tiers of compartmentalization.

UN peace missions, for their part, were historically ambivalent regarding intelligence requirements (Johnston, 1997; Smith, 1994). Inasmuch as the UN considers itself an essentially neutral, multilateral organization, 'intelligence systems' were not countenanced as part of UN-mandated peace operations, ostensibly due to their covert connotations (IPA, 1984). As far as the UN was concerned, intelligence was equated with espionage, and therefore considered a betrayal of the 'trust, confidence, and respect' deemed necessary for effective UN peacekeeping. Reflecting this view, Canadian military doctrine rejected the term 'intelligence' as being 'negative and covert', insisting instead that peacekeeping operations rely on a more principled access to 'information' that was 'impartial, trustworthy and overt' (Canadian Forces, 1992). The operational consequences of this aversion to intelligence have proved to be very problematic for Canadian Forces on UN peace support operations. In the words of General Lewis McKenzie, Canadian commander of UN Forces in Bosnia: 'we had absolutely no intelligence' (Nomikos, 2000).

The report of the Brahimi panel, a review of UN peacekeeping doctrine undertaken at the behest of the Secretary-General and published in August 2000, recommended that UN peace operations acquire a more robust and realistic mandate to achieve their objectives (United Nations, 2000). As a result the UN established an Information and Strategic Analysis Secretariat within the Department of Political Affairs (UN General Assembly, 2000) to collect and manage 'strategic information', an acceptable euphemism for intelligence. It remains to be seen whether and how this new-found acceptability of information and analysis at the strategic policy level will percolate down to the intelligence requirements at the tactical and operational levels of UN peace support missions.

International Liaison and Co-operation

Canada has engaged in bilateral intelligence liaison with many countries and, in relation to specific threats, co-operates with certain plurilateral groupings on a functional basis. Canada's intelligence services have working relationships with counterparts in most countries, and formal liaison relations exist with countries with whom there are common security interests (PCO, 2001). International liaison relationships serve to facilitate a bilateral exchange of intelligence information regarding specific security threats among the countries concerned, and currently tend to focus on international terrorism, transnational crime, drug trafficking, money laundering, financial fraud, people smuggling, and the proliferation of weapons of mass destruction. The attacks of 11

September led to a deepening of international co-operation in the intelligence domain, with dozens of countries proceeding to share information and collaborate in operations against suspected terrorists and terrorist cells and networks (Woodward, 2001). This intelligence coalition was just as important to the war against global terrorism as the diplomatic and military coalitions.

In Canada's case, much of its intelligence liaison is taken up with immigration matters and visa security screening (SIRC, 2001). Of the many bilateral arrangements currently in place, some 44 are considered to be 'dormant', i.e., inactive. In establishing liaison relationships, the record of the country and agency concerned is assessed and the ensuing arrangements must be compatible with Canadian foreign policy. CSIS recently curtailed the level of exchange activity with two foreign counterparts, in one case due to human rights concerns and in the other due to doubts about that agency's reliability and stability (SIRC, 2001).

Canada's dependence on alliance partners and liaison for a very large portion of its foreign intelligence renders these international connections somewhat sensitive and complex. As part of the UKUSA intelligence sharing arrangement, allied liaison representatives at the Intelligence Assessment Committee in PCO exchange assessment material and share insights. Similar procedures are in place in Washington, London, Canberra, and Wellington, although the British Joint Intelligence Committee sometimes excludes allied liaison officers from discussions on certain sensitive issues, in particular issues relating to European affairs (Urban, 1996; Rudner, 2002.) In the Canadian context, alliance partners not only provide a substantial share of the foreign intelligence input, but furthermore help shape the assessments that inform Canadian foreign and security policy perspectives. About a quarter of Canada's intelligence assessment product derives input from alliance partners, though allied participation tends to be somewhat asymmetric in practice. Typically, the US responds with comment on Canadian assessment material but does not ask for input into its own; the UK gives feedback to Canada and occasionally requests Canadian comment on its own production; Australia rarely requests comment but sometimes provides feedback on Canadian material; New Zealand infrequently shares either assessments or feedback with Canada.

The establishment of constructive liaison relationships has helped to curtail foreign intelligence activities in Canada on the part of some countries (SIRC, 2001). Yet liaison with the intelligence services of even friendly countries is always an ambiguous affair. There is a strong propensity among intelligence services to monitor neutral and even friendly countries, which can render international co-operation somewhat awkward (Aldrich, 2001). As it is said: 'There are no friendly secret services, only the secret services of friendly states.'

International arrangements for plurilateral co-operation and liaison among intelligence services tend to be highly secretive. The Kilowatt group was formed in the 1970s by Belgium, Canada, France, Germany, Ireland, Israel, Italy, Luxembourg, Netherlands, Norway, Switzerland, Sweden, and the UK to deal with Arab terrorism, alongside the Magnetron group to counter other (non-Arab) terrorist phenomena. These highly secretive groups are backed by integrated databases on terrorist organizations, operatives, methods, and links, which facilitate intelligence sharing and liaison among participating countries and enhance their counter-terrorism capabilities (Friedman and Miller, 1983).

In order to facilitate international operations against transnational criminality, the governments of Canada, the US, Australia, and various European countries set up a consultative forum, the International Law Enforcement Telecommunications Seminar (ILETS), to co-ordinate intelligence collection with law enforcement requirements. One of their pre-eminent concerns was to ensure that design standards for telecommunications equipment and software remain accessible to legal surveillance. Transnational commercial crime is especially vulnerable to SIGINT interceptions, given its inescapable dependence on electronic means of voice and data communications (Porteous, 1996). At the same time, this implicit opening of global telecommunications to covert interception aroused much consternation in the European Union, which considered this to be a significant threat to commercial interests and privacy rights (Rudner, 2002).

In addition to international liaison, Canada has also provided training programs for intelligence officers from other countries, helping to support, for example, the civilianization and professionalization of intelligence services in Latin American and former Communist countries.

INTELLIGENCE REVIEW AND OVERSIGHT

Canada's intelligence services are subject to two modes of oversight, parliamentary and institutional, or what may be termed 'executive accountability' as distinct from 'public accountability' (Whitaker, 1991). In principle, parliamentary oversight is intended to facilitate public accountability for intelligence activities by providing a modicum of policy transparency and financial and operational scrutiny by the House of Commons and Senate of Canada, consistent with the legitimate requirements for operational secrecy or national security. The mechanisms for executive accountability are designed to provide oversight through intra-governmental institutions that evaluate and review the activities of the intelligence services to ensure compliance with policy, performance, and statutory requirements. Unlike the United States, there is no legislative scrutiny of the security and intelligence community as a whole in Canada, only of the individual intelligence services, i.e., CSE and CSIS.

Like all other departments and agencies of the Canadian government, the security and intelligence community is accountable to Parliament through their respective ministers. Since details of intelligence budgets, targeting, international liaison, and operations are kept secret from Parliament, parliamentary oversight has been constrained by innate weaknesses in the legislative committee system coupled with the unwillingness of the government or the intelligence services to respond to scrutiny (Farson, 2000). Nor have the Canadian parliamentary committees demonstrated the breadth of purview, continuity, or access to sources comparable to their congressional counterparts or the British House of Commons Committee on Intelligence and Security.

The role of the Office of the Auditor General of Canada (OAG) bridges, in some respects, parliamentary and institutional oversight. Whereas the OAG is an independent body reporting directly to Parliament, its mandate relates specifically to bureaucratic management performance and value for money, rather than broader public policy or operational concerns. In 1996, the OAG conducted a first-ever audit of Canada's foreign and security intelligence services (Auditor General, 1996). That report disclosed serious deficiencies in the oversight of the foreign intelligence function in particular, inasmuch as no external or internal review processes were in place to provide systematic assurances to ministers that control and accountability mechanisms are working effectively (until the appointment of a CSE Commissioner in 1996). There has not yet been a second OAG audit of the intelligence community.

Canada's intelligence services are also subject to review by the oversight institutions of government, most notably the Security

Intelligence Review Committee (SIRC), the CSIS Inspector General, the CSE Commissioner, the Privacy Commissioner, and the Human Rights Commission, as well as to the provisions of the Access to Information Act (PCO, 2001). SIRC performs a threefold function: it is charged by the CSIS Act with providing Parliament and the public with an annual review of how CSIS has performed its duties and functions; it serves as a quasi-judicial tribunal with power to investigate complaints against CSIS; and it may be tasked to advise on issues under the Human Rights or Citizenship and Immigration Acts. The challenges of reconciling these functions can sometimes be 'intractable' (SIRC, 2000).

The Inspector General of CSIS reports to the Solicitor General and functions as an internal auditor to review CSIS operations and to monitor compliance with ministerial directives and the enabling statute. According to the CSIS Act, the Inspector General must submit to the minister an annual certificate assuring the minister of this compliance. In the past, tensions between the Inspector General and CSIS Director loomed large and impeded the performance of the internal review and monitoring functions (Farson, 2000). Indeed, between June 1998 and September 1999 the position of Inspector General was actually left vacant following the resignation of the incumbent. In contravention of the CSIS Act, no certificate was ever issued for 1998-9. The appointment of a replacement Inspector General, who happened to be the former Executive Director of SIRC, Maurice Archdeacon, was made in July 1999, and a certificate was eventually submitted in autumn 2000.

In 1996, the government moved to create another institutional oversight mechanism by appointing a CSE Commissioner with a mandate to review and report on CSE's activities with respect to compliance with the law. To date the CSE Commissioner has declined to appear before any parliamentary committee to be questioned about the annual reports, the role of that office, or CSE operations. Assurances have been given repeatedly in ministerial pronouncements and in reports of review agencies, such as that of the Privacy Commissioner, that Canadian SIGINT operations respect the laws of privacy and do not intentionally target Canadians, monitor their domestic private communications, or use alliance partnerships to circumvent the law (CSE Commissioner, 2001).

It is inherently difficult to assess the operational performance of intelligence agencies. The government's own assessment of the performance and value of its intelligence effort is manifested in its budget and staffing allocations to CSE and CSIS. While the precise budgetary appropriations to the two intelligence collection agencies remain classified, it is apparent that both CSE and CSIS underwent sharp cutbacks in expenditures and personnel during the early post-war period. For 2000-1, the disclosed budgets of CSE and CSIS were approximately \$106 million and \$194 million respectively, expenditure levels that suggest that intelligence fared better than most other federal departments and services in withstanding declining resource commitments. In the immediate aftermath of the terrorist attacks on the United States, the government provided an interim increase of almost \$47 million to CSE and CSIS to enhance their technical capabilities to collect foreign intelligence; \$37 million of this was to go to CSE for research and development and to upgrade its technology infrastructure. In early 2002 a debate has commenced within government circles and beyond about whether Canada should establish a dedicated foreign espionage agency, with CSIS claiming that it already has a mandate and a capability—given resources—to operate abroad in the domain of security intelligence. Whatever the outcome of this debate, it seems likely that Canada will be vastly expanding its budgetary commitments for intelligence capacity-building for the foreseeable future.

THE CHALLENGES AHEAD

The attacks of 11 September catapulted the intelligence community to the forefront of Canada's war against global terrorism. After decades of decline, the intelligence community is suddenly being given high-level policy attention, substantial additional resources—budgetary and personnel—and extended operational authority. In response to the global threat environment, the main intelligence services are undergoing a far-reaching role expansion, while other government departments, such as Citizenship and Immigration Canada and the CCRA, are significantly expanding their respective intelligence capabilities. As this transformation unfolds, Canada's intelligence community is likely to encounter four elemental challenges to its future capacity to respond to national security requirements: (1) the weak capacity for co-ordination of Canada's decentralized and diverse security and intelligence community; (2) the need to reconfigure its strategic approach to intelligence collection as between

human intelligence (HUMINT) and SIGINT methods; (3) the accommodation of intelligence collection exigencies to the principles of law
enforcement, privacy rights, and civil liberties; and (4) concerns
about international intelligence co-operation and coalition-building
with new and hitherto unlikely partners. Each of these challenges
invokes policy choices that will have an impact on the evolving role
and effectiveness of Canada's intelligence community.

Up until now, intelligence co-ordination among the various agencies and departments involved has been the responsibility of the
Privy Council Office and was rendered simple, in effect, by the stable, almost predictable adversarial dynamics of Cold War intelligence.
The emergence of new and more blatant security threats has resulted
in a pluralization of intelligence efforts, which now encompass a
wide array of agencies and departments, including such newcomers
as the Office of Critical Infrastructure Protection and Emergency
Preparedness, the CCRA, and the Financial Transactions and Reports
Analysis Centre along with such line departments as Citizenship and
Immigration. The existing co-ordinating arrangement, which works
primarily through periodic consultative meetings, is scarcely
equipped to ensure policy coherence and overarching operational
control over the security and intelligence community as a whole.

Resulting deficiencies in the co-ordination and exchanges of intelligence information between CSIS, Citizenship and Immigration
Canada, and the RCMP, for example, have reportedly impeded the
identification of suspect refugee claimants and immigrants
(Humpheries, 2001). A tighter fusion of the intelligence capabilities
of all components of Canada's security and intelligence community
is a prerequisite for operational effectiveness. It remains to be seen
whether the high-level policy co-ordination that the new ad hoc
Cabinet Committee on Security is intended to promote at the ministerial level will percolate downward into improved functional co-
ordination at the operational level.

Along with horizontal, interdepartmental co-ordination, the intelligence community is faced with a challenge of vertical, client-ori-
ented co-ordination. Both CSIS and CSE have worked on tailoring
their intelligence products to meet the precise requirements of users
(so-called 'customer relations'). Line departments and agencies
expect and demand real-time, customized information resources, so
that the value added of intelligence must derive from its timeliness,
reliability, and relevance. The effectiveness of intelligence is

predicated on close interaction between its producers and consumers (Treverton, 2001).

The development of highly sophisticated technical means of collection was, arguably, the most significant legacy of the Cold War for
intelligence. For Canada, this legacy was reflected in the preponder-
ance of resources devoted to technical means of intelligence collection and early warning, notably SIGINT and electronic surveillance.
However, advances in publicly obtainable communications technology and information security in the late 1990s were threatening to
erode the capabilities hitherto available to SIGINT. These technological developments tended to favour communications security over
interception, protection over penetration, and encryption over cryptanalysis (Singh, 1999; Bamford, 2001). The ability of CSE and its partner organizations to monitor communications traffic will become all
the more problematic as telecommunications systems shift over to
high-capacity optical fibre networks, which cannot be readily intercepted by current SIGINT technology.

In order for SIGINT to preserve its future effectiveness, massive
investment in costly and innovative technologies for interception and
cryptanalysis and analytical capacity-building will be called for.
Canada will have little option other than to look to the UKUSA alliance
for the SIGINT technologies necessary for its future foreign intelligence requirements. Indeed, Canada's dependence on its US intelligence connection will likely grow even more acute with respect to
some of the more sophisticated technical means, such as satellite-
based imagery (IMINT).

Were Canada to proceed to create for itself a foreign espionage
capability, it will have to develop a vigorous and competent HUMINT
potential. The HUMINT challenge will be to recruit and train operatives with the required linguistic and cultural proficiency as well the
tradecraft to run agents in sensitive and hazardous operations. In the
war on terrorism, intelligence efforts will have to be targeted against
relatively small and amorphous cells, elusive networks, obscure organizations, and suspect governments over prolonged periods of time
(Treverton, 2001). Recent experience suggests that terrorist methods
of communication may no longer be vulnerable to SIGINT interception. Intelligence collection will therefore have to concentrate on
offensive covert methods for penetrating suspect target groups
abroad and among homeland communities in this country. Given the
high value of the intelligence to be derived, the historical primacy of

SIGINT will likely make way to a more balanced fusion with this HUMINT effort to identify, penetrate, monitor, and counter the elusive terrorist threat. A related challenge pertains to the human resource requirements for HUMINT, as well as intelligence analysis and assessment. Some co-ordination with higher educational institutions may be called for to ensure that these human resource needs for international and interdisciplinary area studies, knowledge, and language proficiencies are met.

The intensified involvement of intelligence services in counter-terrorism and transnational crime risks blurring the boundaries with law enforcement and human rights (Treverton, 2001). The enactment of new and powerful counter-terrorism legislation in Bill C-36 has prompted concerns about how to sustain an acceptable balance between the requirements of national security and public safety, on the one hand, and privacy rights and civil liberties, on the other. It is pertinent to acknowledge in this regard that Canadian jurisprudence is more protective of privacy rights than is the case in many other legal systems, including that of the United States (Palango, 1998). To be sure, the CSE Commissioner has provided a reassurance regarding SIGINT, at least, that Canada does not use its international alliances to circumvent Canadian laws or to provide allies with communications they could not otherwise legally collect for themselves (CSE Commissioner, 2001). Yet, any transgression of legal prerequisites can jeopardize the gathering of admissible evidence for bringing alleged terrorists or other criminals to justice, thus compromising the role of intelligence in public policy.

Intense public and, indeed, parliamentary concern over the adoption of more formidable anti-terrorist legislation could challenge Canada's Parliament to perform a more vigorous oversight function regarding intelligence matters. The establishment of a House of Commons or Joint Parliamentary Standing Committee on Security and Intelligence could undertake a more comprehensive oversight role with respect to the security and intelligence community in its entirety than is feasible in the narrower and more limited departmentally focused structure of existing committees. This was recommended by the 1998 report of the Special Senate Committee on Security and Intelligence (Senate, 1998), but was never acted upon. In present circumstances, the formation of a more robust mechanism for parliamentary oversight could help to assuage public concern by providing greater transparency and reassurance about compliance with law and policy, while also serving to demystify the intelligence services by facilitating broader public understanding of their role and purpose.

International co-operation in intelligence collection and early warning has always played a pivotal part in Canada's foreign and security intelligence efforts. Certainly the UKUSA alliance has been a most valuable asset. Until recently, there was some concern in Canadian intelligence circles that European security and defence integration might conceivably induce Britain to join in a Eurocentric architecture for intelligence co-operation that would decouple the historical transatlantic partnership (Rudner, 2002). A British defection would be fateful for UKUSA, but would furthermore leave Canada singularly dependent on the US for much of the SIGINT that informs its foreign intelligence capability. Historically, the US had certain reservations about sharing sensitive intelligence product even with its most intimate alliance partners, including Canada (Aid and Wiebes, 2001). It is by no means certain, in these circumstances, that the US would wish to continue sharing intelligence resources and product so liberally on a purely bilateral basis with a junior partner like Canada.

The war on terrorism has impelled Canada and its allies towards extending the boundaries of international intelligence co-operation to countries with which such dealings would hitherto have been unthinkable. An urgent requirement for HUMINT sources on Islamic terrorism has created an environment conducive to exchanges of intelligence with governments in the Middle East and Central Asia, many of which are authoritarian or otherwise suspect (Ajami, 2001; Ungoed-Thomas, 2001). Exchanges of intelligence are reportedly taking place even with rogue countries like Iran, Libya, Sudan, and Syria, whose security services may have penetrated these networks and have information to trade (Rissen and Weiner, 2001; Rifkind, 2001). In return, countries like Canada may be asked to share sensitive information regarding exiles and opposition groups, or strategic intelligence about third countries (Woodward, 2001). The imperative for intelligence co-operation can sometimes make strange bedfellows; however, in present circumstances, the trading of intelligence with politically disparate, fundamentally adversarial regimes could have profound implications for foreign policy, civil society, and human rights in the Western democracies, as well as for regional security and democratic development in the Middle East itself.

The responses to all these challenges on the part of Canada's security and intelligence community will affect its future capabilities and effectiveness. There is some concern in international intelligence circles, which also may be shared by Canadians, that diverting intelligence assets towards purposes for which they were not intrinsically designed, such as law enforcement, can confound and weaken these efforts (Treverton, 2001). Even if Canada chooses to bolster its capacity to collect foreign intelligence significantly, whether by creating a dedicated espionage agency or by building on CSIS capabilities, this country will probably still have to depend on international co-operation and liaison to gain access to vital intelligence resources. The ultimate challenge for Canada's security and intelligence community will be to develop and sustain both the capacity—through its own capabilities and international co-operation—and the prowess to deal robustly with daunting future security taskings likely to be punctuated by elusive, multi-faceted, globalized threats.

NOTES

1. Members of the Cabinet Ad Hoc Committee on Security are: John Manley (chair and Deputy Prime Minister), David Colenette (Transport), Paul Martin (Finance), Art Eggleton (National Defence), Martin Couchon (Justice), Lawrence MacAulay (Solicitor General), Elinor Caplan (National Revenue), Denis Coderre (Citizenship and Immigration), and Stéphane Dion (Intergovernmental Affairs).
2. The UKUSA alliance refers to the United Kingdom–United States Security Agreement on communications intelligence co-operation. See below.
3. The Soviets returned the compliment by way of surreptitiously installing interception facilities in KGB residences in Ottawa and Montreal to monitor Canadian communications traffic. Moreover, a KGB post in New York was able to intercept communications between the Canadian permanent mission to the United Nations and Department of External Affairs.
4. France launched its Helios-1A, a photo-imaging (IMINT) satellite, in 1995. It was later disclosed that it carried piggyback an experimental Ceris (Characterisation de l'Environment Radio-electrique par un Instrument Spatial Embarque) small interception package said to be capable of monitoring satellite communication relays.
5. Echelon may have been a code word for this interception program, so that it is possible that this code word has been discarded and replaced with another, as often happens when classified intelligence operations have been compromised by publicity.
6. Ahmed Ressam, an Algerian living in Montreal under a suspended deportation order, was caught by US immigration authorities in December 1999 trying to cross into the US at a Washington state/BC border crossing with a trunkful of explosives. It later became known that Ressam intended to plant a bomb in the Los Angeles airport.

REFERENCES

Aid, Matthew, and Cees Wiebes. 2001. 'Conclusions', Special Issue on Secrets of Signals Intelligence During the Cold War and Beyond, *Intelligence and National Security* 16 (Spring): 313–32.

Ajami, Fouad. 2001. 'The Sentry's Solitude', *Foreign Affairs* 80, 6: 2–16.

Aldrich, Richard. 2001: *The Hidden Hand: Britain, America and Cold War Secret Intelligence*. London: John Murray.

Andrew, Christopher. 1994. 'The Making of the Anglo-American SIGINT Alliance', in Hayden Peake and Samuel Halperin, eds, *In the Name of Intelligence: Essays in Honor of Walter Pforzheimer*. Washington: NIBC Press.

Arnold, Gary. 1992. 'Officials Deny Report of Canada-France Spy Feud', *Ottawa Citizen*, 22 May.

Aryasinha, Ravindra. 2001. 'Terrorism, the LTTE and the Conflict in Sri Lanka', *Journal of Conflict Security & Development* 1, 2: 25–50.

Bamford, James. 2001. *Body of Secrets: Anatomy of the Ultra-Secret National Security Agency from the Cold War Through the Dawn of a New Century*. New York: Doubleday.

Bell, Stewart. 2000. 'Hezbollah Terrorists Favour Stolen Ontario SUVs', *National Post*, 17 Oct.

———. 2001a. 'Canada Grows as a Target for Terrorists', *National Post*, 18 July.

———. 2001b. 'No Way to Fight Terrorism', *National Post*, 18 July.

———. 2001c. 'Cyber-attacks Threaten Canada: CSIS', *National Post*, 18 July.

———. 2001d. 'RCMP Probing "Jihad" Web Sites', *National Post*, 18 Aug., A1.

Berlin Information Center for Transatlantic Security. 1994. *NATO, Peacekeeping, and the UN*. Berlin.

Blatchford, Christie. 2001. 'Canada and Terrorism: Programmed to Receive', *National Post*, 24 Nov., A18–19.

Black, Eldon. 1996. *Direct Intervention: Canada-France Relations 1967–1974*. Ottawa: Carleton University Press.

Campbell, Duncan. 1999. *Interception Capabilities 2000, the Report to the Director General for Research of the European Parliament*. Brussels: European Parliament, Scientific and Technical Options Assessment Program Office.

———. 2001. 'Fight Over Euro-Intelligence Plan', *The Guardian*, 3 July.

Canada, Office of the Auditor General. 1996. *The Canadian Intelligence Community: Control and Assessment*. Ottawa.

Canadian Forces. 1992: *Peacekeeping Operations, 1992*. Ottawa: Canadian Forces Publication 301 (3).

Canadian Security Intelligence Service (CSIS). 1995. *1995 Public Report and Outlook*. Ottawa.

———. 1997. *1997 Public Report*, Parts 1, 3. Available at: <www.csis-scrs.gc.ca/eng/publicrp/pub1997e.html>.

———. 1999. 'Trends in Terrorism, Perspectives', *CSIS Report 2000/01*. Ottawa, 18 Dec.

———. 2001. *Public Report 2000*. Ottawa.

Cleroux, Richard. 1991. *Official Secrets*. Toronto: McClelland & Stewart.

Communications Security Establishment (CSE) Commissioner. 2001. *Annual Report 2000–2001*. Ottawa: Public Works and Government Services Canada.

Department of National Defence (DND), Directorate of Defence Analysis. 2000. *Strategic Capability Planning for the Canadian Forces*. Ottawa: Department of National Defence.

Edwards, Steven. 2001. 'Ressam Eyed Canadian Targets', *National Post*, 6 July.

Farson, Stuart. 2000. 'Parliament and its Servants: Their Role in Scrutinizing Canadian Intelligence', *Intelligence and National Security* 15 (Summer): 225–58.

Financial Times (London). 2001. 'How Militants Hijacked the NGO Party', 12 July.

Friedman, Richard, and David Miller. 1983. *The Intelligence War: Penetrating the World of Today's Advanced Technology Conflict*. London: Salamander Books.

Frost, Michael, and Michel Graton. 1994. *Spyworld: Inside the Canadian and American Intelligence Establishments*. Toronto: Doubleday.

Hager, Nick. 1996. *Secret Power: New Zealand's Role in the International Spy Network*. Nelson, NZ: Craig Potton Publishing.

Herman, Michael. 2001. *Intelligence Services in the Information Age*. London: Frank Cass & Co.

Humpheries, Adrian. 2001. 'Caplan Made Promises She Could Not Keep', *National Post*, 3 Nov.

International Peace Academy (IPA). 1984. *Peacekeeper's Handbook*. New York: Pergamon Press.

Johnston, Paul. 1997. 'No Cloak and Dagger Required: Intelligence Support to UN Peacekeeping', *Intelligence and National Security* 12 (Oct.): 102–12.

Landy, Keith. 2001. 'Scale up the War Against Terrorism', *National Post*, 12 July.

Livesey, Bruce. 1998. 'Trolling for Secrets—Economic Espionage is the New Niche for Government Spies', *Financial Post*, 28 Feb.

Matas, Robert. 2001. 'How Al-Qaeda Hatched Plot to Bomb Heart of Montreal', *Globe and Mail*, 30 Nov., A1.

National Post. 2001. 'Defunding Terrorism', 8 Sept., A15.

Nomikos, John. 2000. 'Intelligence Requirements for Peacekeeping Operations', Research Institute on European and American Studies Working Paper, Athens, Greece.

Palango, Paul. 1998. *The Last Guardians*. Toronto: McClelland & Stewart.

Porteous, Samuel. 1996. *The Threat from Transnational Crime: An Intelligence Perspective*. CSIS Commentary #70. Ottawa: CSIS.

Privy Council Office (PCO). 2001. *The Canadian Security and Intelligence Community: Helping Keep Canada and Canadians Safe and Secure*. Ottawa.

Pugliese, David, and Jim Bronskill. 2001. 'Mounties Create Unit to Control Public Protest', *National Post*, 18 Aug., A2.

Richelson, Jeffrey, and Desmond Ball. 1985. *The Ties that Bind: Intelligence Cooperation between the UKUSA Countries*. London: Allen & Unwin.

Rifkind, Malcolm. 2001. 'Why the US Must Rely on Arab Intelligence', *The Times* (London), 8 Nov.

Rissen, James, and Tim Weiner. 2001. '3 New Allies Help CIA in its Fight Against Terror', *New York Times*, 30 Oct.

Robinson, Bill. n.d. 'Lux Ex Umbra: The Communications Security Establishment: An Unofficial Look Inside Canada's Signals Intelligence Agency'. Available at: <http://watserv1.uwaterloo.ca/~brobinso/cse.html>.

Rudner, Martin. 2001. 'Canada's Communications Security Establishment from Cold War to Globalization', *Intelligence and National Security* 16 (Spring): 97–128.

———. 2002. 'Britain Betwixt and Between: UK SIGINT Alliance Strategy Balancing Trans-Atlantic and European Connections', *Intelligence and National Security* (forthcoming).

Sachs, Susan. 2001. 'Merger Spread al-Qaeda Tentacles', *New York Times*, 21 Nov.

Senate of Canada. 1998. *Report of the Special Senate Committee on Security and Intelligence*, William Kelley, Chairman. Ottawa: Senate of Canada.

Security Intelligence Review Committee (SIRC). 2000. *SIRC Report 1999–2000*. Ottawa: SIRC.

———. 2001. *SIRC Report 2000–2001*. Ottawa: SIRC.

Soloman, John. 2001. 'Authorities Identify Six Terror Centers in US', *Jerusalem Post*, 18 Nov.

Seper, Jerry. 2001. 'FBI Alert Based on Coded Message', *Washington Times*, 1 Nov.

Simmie, Scott. 2001. 'Why Spy Agency Had a Key Role in Terror Alert', *Toronto Star*, 1 Nov.

Singh, Simon. 1999. *The Code Book: The Science of Secrecy from Ancient Egypt to Quantum Cryptography*. London: Anchor.

Smith, Hugh. 1994. 'Intelligence and UN Peacekeeping', *Survival* 36 (Autumn): 174–90.

Smyth, Julie. 2001. 'All Foreign Students Face Tougher Scrutiny', *National Post*, 22 Sept.

Treverton, Gregory. 2001. 'Intelligence Crisis', *Government Executive Magazine*, 1 Nov. Available at: <http://www.GovExec.com>.

Ungoed-Thomas, Jon. 2001. 'Beating the Terrorists: Egypt Used Torture to Crack Network', *The Times* (London), 25 Nov.

United Nations (UN). 2000. *Report of the Panel on UN Peace Operations* (Brahimi Report). A/55/305-S/2000 801, 21 Aug.

United Nations General Assembly. 2000. *Resource Requirements for the Implementation of the Report of the Panel on UN Peace Operations*. Report of the Secretary-General. A/55/507, 27 Oct.

Urban, Mark. 1996. *UK Eyes Alpha*. London: Faber & Faber.

van Buuren, Jelle. 2000. *Making Up the Rules: Interceptions versus Privacy*. Amsterdam: Buro Jansen & Jannsen Stichting Eurowatch.

Wark, Wesley. 1997. 'Cryptographic Innocence: The Origins of Signals Intelligence in Canada in the Second World War', *Journal of Contemporary History* 22: 639–65.

Whitaker, Reg. 1991. 'The Politics of Security Intelligence Policy-making in Canada: 1970–84', *Intelligence and National Security* 6: 4 (Oct.): 649–68.

Woodward, Bob. 2001. '50 Countries Detain 360 Suspects at CIA's Behest', *Washington Post*, 22 Nov., A01.

8

Blood Money: International Terrorist Fundraising in Canada

STEWART BELL

With its stately colonial buildings, ancient temples, and lush tropical gardens, Colombo seems an earthly paradise at first glance. But the scars of 18 years of ethnic conflict are not easily concealed. In the downtown business district, the skeletons of bombed office buildings line the streets near the Indian Ocean—memorials to the wave of terrorist attacks that have struck the city. Although far from the front lines of Sri Lanka's civil war, Colombo still has the uneasy feel of a city under siege. Military checkpoints slow traffic at intersections, armed soldiers hang from buses to prevent terrorists from planting bombs, and government buildings are guarded like fortresses, as are the homes of prominent politicians.

Concrete patches cover the corner of the Hotel Galidari that was bombed in 1997 by Tamil Tiger separatists targeting the American servicemen staying there. Outside the Prime Minister's house, a crevice is gouged in the wall where a Tiger operative detonated his suicide vest. Across the street, a black statue marks the spot where the Security Minister was standing when he was blown apart by a suicide bomber. The grass is scorched brown on the lawn where President Chandrika Kumaratunga was giving an election speech in December 1999 when a Tiger suicide bomber made an attempt on her life. 'Let's pray', says Rafeeq, a Colombo banker blinded in a 1997 terrorist attack on his downtown office building, 'that these types of things will come to an end.'

Colombo is the tropical capital of a Commonwealth democracy that has experienced a level of terrorism unimaginable to outsiders. It is also the most striking example of how terrorism and insurgency around the world are financed from Canada. Extremists within Canadian immigrant and refugee communities send millions of dollars abroad annually to bankroll political and religious violence, and despite warnings by police and intelligence agents, federal politicians in Ottawa largely ignored the problem for over a decade. Fundraising for terrorism was not outlawed in Canada until public outrage at the 11 September attacks and pressure from the Americans finally forced the government into action. The legislation came so late, however, that Canada had already become among the top sources of foreign currency for groups such as the Tamil Tigers.

The Liberation Tigers of Tamil Eelam, or LTTE, is a cult-like band of guerrillas that employs the gruesome tactics of terrorism. According to Canadian security agencies, the LTTE has assassinated more than 100 politicians, carried out more suicide bombings than all other militant groups combined, and murdered the democratically elected leaders of two nations, India and Sri Lanka (*Suresh v. Canada*, 2001). It is also, to a large extent, tacitly aided and financed by supporters in Canada. The Canadian Security Intelligence Service (CSIS) estimates that up to $2 million a year is clandestinely funnelled to the Tigers' military purchasing arm from front organizations in Canada (CSIS, 1999). But the total amount could be 10 to 20 times that sum once the proceeds of organized crime are factored in.

Since the days of Lester Pearson, Canadians have liked to think of themselves as international peacekeepers, the heroes in the blue berets. In Sri Lanka, and in countries such as Israel and even the US, Canada is seen increasingly as a war financier, supplying the cash and other support that sustain political and religious violence, keeping self-styled freedom fighters outfitted with weaponry, and ensuring a continued surfeit of misery for civilians and soldiers alike. Through negligence and indifference, the Canadian government has permitted virtually every major terrorist organization to operate within its borders.

From South Asia to the Middle East, there is hardly an insurgency in the world that is not financed at least in part with Canadian currency. The Al-Qaeda group of Osama bin Laden, Al-Jihad, Hamas, the Sikh militant groups in India—all have a presence in Canada. So do the Kurdistan Workers Party (better known by the acronym PKK), Hezbollah, Colombian rebels, and the Armed Islamic Group of Algeria. 'With perhaps the singular exception of the United States', said CSIS director Ward Elcock, 'there are more international terrorist groups active here than any other country in the world' (Elcock, 1998).

Canada's failure to disrupt the terrorists on its soil has resulted in major security problems for Canada's neighbours and some of its closest allies. Canadian-based terrorists have been arrested in the US, Britain, France, Jordan, Algeria, Pakistan, Azerbaijan, and other nations (Bell, 2001). It has also caused severe troubles within Canada's refugee communities, where militants have hijacked cultural organizations and religious institutions for their own ends. And it has helped create an international climate in which global terrorist organizations such as Al-Qaeda have thrived. Canada may not be the only nation that has been negligent on this front, but for a country its size, Canada harbours far more terrorists than it should, possibly more by proportion than any other Western industrial power. As a result, even as it has sought to portray itself as tough on terrorism, the reality is that Canada has become seen increasingly as a source of terrorism.

While federal politicians, including the Prime Minister, continue to deny that Canada is a terrorist 'safe haven', the problem is spelled out in stacks of Federal Court case files, immigration and refugee files, CSIS reports, RCMP intelligence briefs, Security Intelligence Review Committee reports, and records from criminal prosecutions in other jurisdictions, notably France and the US. Perhaps most convincing are the admissions of terrorists themselves, who have confessed not only to using Canada as a base for violence abroad but also to plotting attacks within Canada. When these fragments of intelligence are pieced together, they form a window into the terrorist underworld that operates within the country. Terrorist groups use Canada as a staging ground to plan and carry out attacks, as a base for hiding out before and after operations, and as a source of recruits. Most common in Canada are terrorist-bureaucrats, those involved in support activity, mundane but nonetheless crucial, that feeds the larger international organization. These activities include stealing and doctoring passports, purchasing *matériel* with military applications, spreading propaganda, political lobbying and pressure and, particularly, fundraising.

Like most Western nations, Canada was preoccupied with the Cold War when terrorist organizations began expanding their networks into Europe and North America. The bulk of RCMP, and later CSIS, resources were then devoted to counter-intelligence rather than counter-terrorism. But while Canadian agents were monitoring Soviet spies, ethnic conflicts in Iran, Turkey, and particularly India began spilling into the country, bringing with them elements of terrorist organizations. With the Soviet economy in collapse and the East bloc countries going their own way, insurgents and terrorists could no longer count on state sponsors to outfit them with money and weapons or give them hideouts. They were forced to create their own support networks within diaspora communities in the West.

FRONT ORGANIZATIONS

Terrorist fundraising is conducted partly through non-profit organizations that purport to be involved in various types of humanitarian or community work but that in practice serve as fronts for extremist groups. In some cases, these organizations may be involved in legitimate work that masks their clandestine support for extremist violence. Less often, the broader organization may be unaware that it is being used as a cover for illicit activities. Relief organizations, religious institutions, immigrant and multicultural groups, and religious schools have fronted for terrorism in Canada, as have businesses. Some have been funded by various levels of government.

Outside the extremist core, mainstream supporters of these fronts may have no idea the money they are donating—or a portion of it, at least—is being diverted to finance political or religious violence. The extremists convince their supporters that the money is going to widows and orphans, or other worthy causes. While some if not most of the collections may in fact end up financing legitimate work, a portion is tacitly laundered into violence. Such blending of accounts is a deliberate tactic designed to throw investigators off the scent of blood money.

Indeed, RCMP intelligence documents show that investigations into fundraising by Middle Eastern terrorist organizations have been frustrated by the fact that Hamas and Hezbollah are engaged in development, politics, and terrorism (RCMP, 2000). Such an unclear arrangement, where money is dumped into a central fund and drawn upon for both charity and violence, also serves to cover up or assuage the guilt of fundraisers and donors. Should they be questioned about their activities, they simply reply that they were giving money to humanitarian causes and had no intention of financing terrorism. Or they claim that, while some of the money might be used to pay for violent operations, the bulk goes to legitimate charity work.

Further, even if money does wind up in the hands of widows and orphans, as is the case with some Middle Eastern terrorist organizations, these are the widows and orphans of suicide bombers. Prior to setting off on their death missions, Palestinian suicide bombers are assured their families will be taken care of for life. These payments can be considered as encouraging terrorist violence. The US shut down the Holy Land Foundation, the largest Muslim charity in the Americas, in December 2001, partly because it was underwriting support payments to the wives and children of deceased suicide 'martyrs' (US Treasury, 2001).

In Canada, the first to make proficient use of fronts were Sikh militants in British Columbia, who took control of temples and community organizations in the 1980s and used them as a pulpit to advance the cause of Khalistan, the sought-after Sikh homeland in India. Temple worshippers in south Vancouver were subjected to weekly sermons on the evils of the Indian government and the heroics of the Khalistani fighters. Large sums of money began to flow to the Sikh militant forces from their Canadian supporters. A wing of the Babbar Khalsa was established in Kamloops, BC, by Talwinder Singh Parmar, a Punjabi-born farmer's son who came to Canada in the early 1970s and worked at a sawmill. The organization managed to secure charitable status from Revenue Canada. Parmar set up an office in Vancouver that was called the Consulate of Khalistan, where he handed out photos of himself in a warrior costume. Underneath was the inscription 'When all else fails, lifting the sword is justified.'

Enraged by the Indian government's 1984 attack on the Golden Temple at Amritsrar, the holiest shrine of Sikhdom, Parmar plotted his revenge, police believe. In 1985, bombs hidden in luggage were placed aboard two planes at Vancouver International Airport. One of the bombs exploded at Tokyo's Narita Airport, killing two baggage handlers. The other detonated aboard Air India flight 192 off the coast of Ireland, killing all 329 aboard. Parmar was killed in a 1992 shootout with Indian police in the city of Jullandhar. After Parmar's death, according to a CSIS report, Ajaib Singh Bagri became the de facto leader of the Babbar Khalsa. Also known as Ajaib Singh Khalsa, Bagri has been charged with first-degree murder in connection with the Air India bombing, as has Ripudaman Singh Malik. It was not until 1996 that the Canadian government finally stripped the Babbar Khalsa of its charitable status.

In 1998 a Sikh newspaper editor was shot to death outside his house, apparently for his writings on the Khalistan issue. That same year, Canadian intelligence was still reporting on Babbar Khalsa activities. 'Sikh militants in North America are a source of financial support for terrorist activities in India', CSIS reported. 'In Canada, Service investigation has revealed that funds are raised through the collection of monies from Sikh communities in Canada and transferred to the leadership based in Pakistan and India' (CSIS, 1998).

Meanwhile, another independence effort was spilling into Canada. The Kurdistan Workers Party, or PKK, was established by Abdullah Ocalan in 1978 to agitate for an ethnic Kurdish state, to be known as Kurdistan, which would include parts of Turkey, Iraq, Iran, and Syria. At the Second Congress of the PKK in 1982, a long-term strategy was forged, which envisioned a build-up to a full-scale uprising in 2000. An important part of the plan was the killing of 'collaborators', mostly Kurds who did not adhere to Ocalan's hard-line militancy. Almost 2,000 were killed between 1984 and 1991, some of them in Europe. Money to pay for the 'struggle' was extorted from exiled Kurds—$24 million in 1992 in Germany alone. Because of Turkey's location on the fringe of Europe, countries such as Germany and France took in most of the Kurdish refugees, but Canada became an important part of the international PKK network in the early 1990s and was used as a source of funds and a safe haven for militants who had overstayed their welcome in other Western countries.

Hanan Ahmed Osman, also known as 'Helin', came to Canada in November 1994 using a false British passport. During a customs search, officers found she was carrying photos, documents on PKK military and political strategy, and a map of NATO installations in

Turkey. A diary was also found, containing notes taken during PKK training, CSIS alleged. Helin was deported but a second agent, Aynur Saygili, soon arrived to take her place. She claimed refugee status, but would not answer detailed questions and refused to speak to CSIS agents. She quickly took on a leadership role within 'PKK circles', according to CSIS. Police and immigration officials raided the Kurdish Cultural Centre in Montreal in May 1996 to arrest Saygili. CSIS believes both agents were sent to take control of the PKK's Montreal fundraising operations (*Saygili v. Canada*, 1997).[1] PKK supporters rioted outside the Greek embassy in Ottawa following Ocalan's 1999 arrest in Nairobi, injuring a police officer, but the Kurdistan movement appears to be in disarray with its leader in jail in Turkey.

The World Tamil Movement (WTM) office in Scarborough occupies the second floor of a strip mall, overlooking a row of shops selling South Asia wares—jewellery, saris, fish, and meat. The red and yellow banner draped in the window bears a distinctive emblem: the head of a roaring tiger. The LTTE logo is the only outward hint that the office is affiliated with ethnic violence half a world away. The WTM is the principal Tamil Tigers support organization in the world as well as in Canada. A secret list of 'LTTE front organizations in Canada' compiled by the Canadian intelligence service lists the WTM at the top, along with the Ellesmere Road address of the strip mall, as well as seven other non-profit associations in Toronto, Ottawa, Montreal, and Vancouver: the Tamil Eelam Society of Canada, Tamil Rehabilitation Organization, Federation of Associations of Canadian Tamils (FACT), Tamil Co-ordinating Committee, Eelam Tamil Association of British Columbia, World Tamil Movement (Montreal chapter), and the Eelam Tamil Association of Quebec (CSIS, 1999).

'The LTTE operates like a multinational corporation', a CSIS report says. 'This network consists of commercial companies and small businesses set up in Malaysia, Singapore, Bangladesh, China and some Western countries' and includes 'political offices, procurement offices, aid and humanitarian organizations located in at least 40 countries worldwide' (CSIS, 1999). The global support structure is so complex and so well organized that it is sometimes called Tigers Inc.

As the LTTE began to recognize Canada's potential as an offshore base, it dispatched a veteran operative to take control. Manickavasagam Suresh arrived in Canada on 5 October 1990 to co-ordinate the Tigers' crucial Canadian branch. He was an early LTTE member, joining in 1978, and was later assigned to help with the

Tigers' expanding international network, at first in the Netherlands and then in Toronto, where he took over as co-ordinator of the World Tamil Movement and FACT. Suresh lied about his past to Canadian immigration officials and was accepted as a refugee on 11 April 1991 (*Suresh v. Canada*, 2000).

The WTM was registered as a non-profit society in Canada in 1986, listing its purpose as serving the needs of Tamils in lobbying government and raising funds 'for charitable organizations serving the Sri Lankan Tamils, particularly destitute refugees'. The WTM did not conceal its support for the Tigers. Suresh himself admitted that 'there is no doubt that the WTM has close contacts with the LTTE'. He also admits that 'fundraising for the LTTE was done publicly by the WTM' (*Suresh v. Canada*, 2000). Even so, the group managed to secure a $19,000 grant from the Ontario government in the early 1990s.

The LTTE operates a taxation system in Canada that extorts money from Tamil families and businesses. The RCMP reported in 1999 that 'new Tamil refugees in Canada are traditionally contacted by Tamil Tigers from organizations [that] promote LTTE interests and collect funds. LTTE sympathizers in Canada are under pressure to provide funding to the Tigers in Sri Lanka. All Tamils are encouraged to donate 50 cents each day to the LTTE.' The door-knocking is legendary. It is done by avid Tigers supporters, and those who decline to hand over money are threatened and intimidated. Their homes are sometimes vandalized. While some Tamils donate money voluntarily because they support the independence movement, many others do so out of fear that they or their families will be harmed.

Fundraising also takes place at large rallies. A box wrapped in the red Tamil Tigers flag is typically passed around and money is stuffed inside. At schools and temples in Toronto and Montreal, the rallies have featured men and youths in camouflage uniforms carrying mock assault rifles. Donations are collected and Tamil Tigers paraphernalia and propaganda are sold. Law enforcement officials say the money goes to Tamil community organizations, which send it to the LTTE. Liberal MPs have also turned up at the fundraising events, in one case on a school stage where men in military uniforms carried replica weapons.

While terrorists often rely on rallies and charity events to raise money, legitimate businesses have played an increasingly important role in fundraising. According to Canadian intelligence, the LTTE's chief procurement officer established two import-export companies in Toronto to launder money raised by the World Tamil Movement and other fronts back to his base in Thailand. 'Although there are no official profit figures available for these companies there is some indication that they are highly lucrative and the LTTE are becoming increasingly dependent on these types of ventures to supply their war coffers' (CSIS, 1999).

The global weapons network is so successful that there are fears it could become a template for other terrorist and insurgent forces. What is unique about the Tigers is that, by behaving, in turn, like an international corporation and an organized crime syndicate, they have been able to build a frighteningly potent fighting machine. They have done so almost completely on their own, without the assistance of a benevolent state sponsor. Hezbollah has Iran to keep it armed; Al-Qaeda had Pakistan and Osama bin Laden. Aside from some initial assistance from India, the Tigers have done it alone, and if they can do it from the relative isolation of northern Sri Lanka, so can any other extremist organization determined to cause mayhem.

Canada is also a key base for terrorists active in the Islamic holy war that struck suddenly against the US when hijackers rammed loaded passenger planes into symbols of American economic and military power. Police, intelligence, and immigration documents describe a wide array of individuals and organizations scattered across Canada that have in common a singular cause: the promotion of radical Islamic beliefs through terrorist violence. Some are loosely connected to Osama bin Laden and his group, Al-Qaeda, while others simply share his mission of punishing the non-Islamic world of 'infidels'. But there are also those that Canadian investigators have tied directly to bin Laden, the Saudi-born millionaire. Canadian-based Islamic terrorist cells have provided significant support to the bin Laden-led international jihad over the years. Money raised in Canada has financed bin Laden's network; equipment with military uses has been bought here; passports have been stolen and forged to help Islamic militants move freely; operations have been planned; terrorists have hidden out; and Internet sites have been registered in Montreal and Toronto to promote the jihad.

Canada is probably not the most important offshore base in the bin Laden empire. Britain, France, Germany, and the United States also have extensive cells. But as the closest US neighbour, with a long, undefended border and a remarkably relaxed attitude towards national security threats, Canada has become a logical staging point for attacks against Americans, as the Ahmed Ressam case aptly demonstrated.[2]

During the 1979–89 Soviet war in Afghanistan, dozens of front organizations were established by mujahedeen guerrillas and their backers to move money to finance the 'jihad'. Following the Soviet withdrawal, when bin Laden created Al-Qaeda to wage an international holy war, those fronts became tools of terrorism, used to finance operations in many countries (CSIS, 1996). Among the organizations that intelligence agents believe was used by Al-Qaeda was Human Concern International (HCI), an Ottawa-based aid group engaged in humanitarian work in Pakistan. CSIS alleges that the Pakistan director of HCI, an Egyptian-born Canadian citizen named Ahmad Khadr, used the organization to funnel money for terrorism (*Re Jaballah*, 2001).[3] After the Egyptian embassy in Islamabad was bombed in 1995, killing 17, Khadr was arrested for allegedly financing the operation by Al-Jihad operatives. He was later freed by Pakistani authorities but CSIS believes he was involved in the plot, and he was subsequently listed by the United Nations as one of bin Laden's top associates. In the terrorist fundraising crackdown that has followed 11 September, several front organizations with ties to Islamic terrorism have been publicly identified, most notably the Holy Land Foundation, which had been fundraising in Canada for Hamas partly through the Jerusalem Front, and the Islamic Association for Palestine.

The Canadian system has played right into the hands of political extremists. Migrants can be remarkably vulnerable when they first arrive in a new country. They are disoriented, unfamiliar with the way things work. The government directs them to heavily politicized immigrant societies with agendas extending well beyond their mandate to provide language and settlement services, as well as 'humanitarian aid' to their countries of origin. The bulk of these non-profit organizations are ethnic-based, serving one particular migrant group, and as a result they have been vulnerable to being taken over by those with political agendas originating in their homelands.

ORGANIZED CRIME

As Western countries have begun to crack down on terrorist fundraising activities, realizing they are the lifeblood of terrorism, extremists have increasingly turned to organized crime to earn their blood money and launder it overseas. Police are now finding that organized crime investigations lead more and more to associates of terrorist groups rather than to mobsters or bikers. 'We used to have a pretty good feel for the motivation of these guys', said a Canadian police officer with extensive organized crime experience. 'Whoever they were—Russians, Mafia, Asians—it came down to money. Now at the end of the money trail, you never know what you're going to find. Has it been gobbled up by an insurgent army somewhere, or ploughed into explosives, or just old-fashioned laundering to buy a gangster a new house?'

In June 1998, the Sûreté du Québec, Canada Customs, and the RCMP conducted a series of raids as part of an investigation into auto theft in Ontario and Quebec. What they uncovered was a Lebanese-based crime ring in Quebec that was stealing luxury cars in Montreal, Ottawa, Toronto, and Halifax and exporting them to Russia, Western Europe, Africa, and the Middle East, where they were sold for about US $40,000 each. 'It appears that 10 per cent of the profits of this organization were funneled to a terrorist organization', the RCMP stated in an intelligence report called Project Sparkplug (Mogck and Therrien, 1998). The terrorist group in question was not named, but subsequent RCMP documentation suggests the money was going to the Lebanese Hezbollah. Indeed, high-ranking Hezbollah members are said to travel in luxury cars such as Lincoln Navigators stolen in Canada (RCMP, 2000).

The Ressam case also showed the tendency of terrorists to support their operations with organized crime. Shortly after arriving in Canada as a refugee claimant, Ressam and other members of his Montreal-based cell began stealing. At first it was petty theft. Ressam worked as a pickpocket at department stores, targeting elderly ladies. Later, he would hang out at airports and steal baggage. By the late 1990s, the Montreal cell was engaged in full-scale organized crime, operating a ring that stole cellular phones and laptop computers from the downtown business district, and that also extorted money from Muslims outside mosques. The crime cell was headed by Karim Said Atmani, a mujahedeen fighter who participated in the Afghan and Bosnian wars. He was the 'right-hand' of Fateh Kamel, a Canadian citizen believed to be a major player in the international Islamic terrorist movement (Kamel et al., n.d.).

Crime proceeds are a crucial source of funds for the Tamil Tigers. Street gangs composed of former rebel fighters serve as enforcers for the LTTE in Toronto. In the 1990s, Toronto police began noticing growing numbers of calls to investigate violent crimes in which the common denominator was that both the victims and the criminals were of Sri Lankan origin. They suspected a new organized crime group was emerging, bringing with it the same problems they had encountered when Asian-based crime first came to Canada in the 1980s. Motives, witnesses, and suspects were elusive and language and cultural barriers were frustrating investigations. In response, the Tamil Task Force was established, at first as a pilot project but then as a regular part of the police intelligence unit, working closely with the RCMP and Immigration Canada.

The Task Force soon discovered that Sri Lankan organized crime had its roots in South Asia. The key players, rival gangs called the VVT and A K Kannan, were aligned with warring Tamil factions back in Sri Lanka. A.K. Kannan, which has an estimated 300 members, derives its name from the AK-47 military assault rifle, the preferred weapon of Tamil guerrillas. A.K. Kannan's main rival is the VVT, short for Valvedditurai, the birthplace of the Tigers movement as well as its leader, Vellupillai Prabhakaran. The VVT is the principal pro-LTTE gang in Canada, with a strength of 350 to 500. The gang leaders are current or former Tiger guerrillas and remain loyal to the rebels, serving as their money-collectors and street muscle in Tamil neighbourhoods of Toronto. A Tamil-owned video store that remained open during Black July, a day of remembrance for the LTTE, was threatened by a gang that later set fire to the business. In 1993, a Tamil newspaper editor who had criticized the Tigers was assaulted and seriously injured. A firebomb struck the Tamil Resource Centre in Toronto in 1994. The following year, police arrested a man and seized a firearm in connection with a plot to kill a visiting Sri Lankan government official (RCMP, 1986).

'Members of the VVT will act as enforcers for the political representatives of the LTTE in Canada', the Tamil Task Force said in its February 1998 report. 'Extensive links and associations between the VVT and LTTE are common knowledge in the Tamil community' (Metro Toronto Police, 1998). The officer in charge of the RCMP's Immigration and Passport section in Milton said the 'Tamil Tigers control every aspect of Tamil gang life in Toronto.' Niranjan Claude Fabian, one of the top-ranking VVT leaders, has been identified by Toronto police as a former LTTE assassin. Fabian joined the gang shortly after arriving in Canada from Sri Lanka in 1990. Another high-ranking VVT leader,

Sri Ranjan Rasa, also arrived that year and made a refugee claim, saying he had been abducted and tortured by Indian peacekeeping troops and the Sri Lankan military, which suspected he was a member of the LTTE. The Immigration and Refugee Board accepted his claim on 8 July 1991. During a subsequent police search, Toronto officers found several photos of Rasa wearing camouflage gear, carrying weapons, and standing in front of the LTTE flag.

In addition to the two main gangs, there are a number of smaller ones, including the Jane Finch Gang, Kipling Gang, Sooran Gang, Seelapul Gang, Mississauga Gang, and the Gilder Tigers—all pro-LTTE factions loyal to the VVT. Three gangs—Udupiddy, Tuxedo Boys, and Silver Springs—are against the Tamil Tigers and pledge their loyalty to A.K. Kannan (interview). RCMP Sergeant Fred Bowen alone has referred over 200 Tamil gang members to the Immigration department for deportation. All told, there are an estimated 1,000 gang members (Bowen, n.d.). Toronto police and the RCMP estimate there are from 5,000 to 8,000 trained Tamil guerrillas in Toronto alone. 'These persons are known to have had extensive paramilitary training in the use of automatic weapons, hand to hand combat, Russian RPGs (rocket-propelled grenades) and other offensive weapons and substances', the Task Force reported. 'Many of these have been used in the Greater Toronto Area to carry out their projects' (Metro Toronto Police, 1998).

The gang extortion racket in Canada, in which pro-LTTE crime groups collect 'donations', is imported from the homeland, where the Tigers initiated a taxation system on families, businesses, and criminal enterprise in the areas under their control. Tamils in Toronto often complain about gang youths who go door to door at night collecting money, often with threats. Aside from extortion, the Canadian gangs have been involved in home invasions, kidnapping, attempted murder, passport theft, counterfeiting, fraud, auto theft, and murders. The gangs take turns attacking each other's hangouts in drive-by shootings, usually using sawed-off shotguns, a deadly turf war that has turned parts of Toronto into a shooting gallery.

Police have had poor success tackling the gangs. The gangs respect what one officer describes as a 'bond of silence', a tacit agreement that neither side will go to police if it is victimized. As a result, gang members are charged but seldom convicted. Non-gang members are also unwilling to come forward or testify as witnesses. Those who do are often threatened. Tamils in Toronto are told explicitly not to go to police to report crimes because doing so might hurt the cause of Tamil separatism, both politically and financially, and could result in the withdrawal of government funds to non-profit organizations, the RCMP says. One gang circulated a flyer in the Tamil language offering a reward to anyone who could help locate Crown witnesses. On the few occasions that witnesses have testified against gang members, other gangsters have sat in the courtroom holding up photos of the witnesses' children and elderly relatives. 'Many of the Tamils in the Greater Toronto Area live in fear of the gangs and the various extremist groups living in their communities and few will testify or complain to the police', an RCMP report asserts (RCMP, 2000).

This silence in the name of self-preservation is a trait imported from Sri Lanka, where Tamils dare not speak up for fear of retribution from the LTTE. The gangs, particularly the VVT, have served to keep a lid on community opposition to the LTTE and its front activities in Canada. The Tigers want to keep the appearance that Tamils are united in their support for the Eelam separatist struggle. But like any ethnic group, Sri Lankan Tamils are divided over such issues as independence and the use of violence. The threat of gang violence, however, has succeeded in silencing dissent. The other role of the gangs has been, of course, to raise money for the cause. The consistent pattern of Tamil gang activity has been its unflinching devotion to money-making schemes. 'The gangs are doing anything for money', says Sergeant Bowen (Bowen, n.d.).

An RCMP intelligence team set up to study the used of organized crime by Tamil extremists reported in 1999 that it had 'found strong connections between the LTTE and organized crime, specifically street gangs, in Toronto and Montreal. There is clear evidence to support the relationship and that the money involved is being funnelled to the LTTE for extremist purposes in Sri Lanka.' The RCMP report 'backs up the connections and indicates large numbers of LTTE members have a presence in Canada and connections to the criminal gangs—and in many cases are members—for monetary and enforcement purposes.' The RCMP also found evidence that gang members were being recruited in Sri Lanka for gang activity in Canada (RCMP, 2000).

One of their most shocking money-making schemes surfaced in May 2001, when the Ontario Labour Relations Board revealed that two VVT members with criminal records had been hired by a metal works company shortly before its 90 employees were to vote on whether to form a union. Gang members known as Kuti and Kodi began working at the company, which makes steel doors and frames, on 6 November 1998, the day the union filed notice it was holding a certification vote. The two gangsters threatened to kill employees if the union vote was successful.

'If the company wins, no problem', Kuti told one worker. 'If the company loses, you will not live thereafter. You will not be alive. Tell the others also.'

'You don't know me', he went on. 'I will do what I've said.'

'If the union wins you will be killed outside. We won't do anything now, but if the union wins we will do it.'

Following a complaint by the United Steelworkers of America, the Labour Relations Board did not determine who was responsible for the 'brief campaign of terror', but said 'at the end of the day it does not particularly matter who specifically in management was involved. What matters, and what I think is obvious from the evidence, is that Kuti and Kodi were recruited by the company's management to discourage the Sri Lankan employees from voting for the union' (Labour Relations Board, 2001). The LTTE's willingness to engage in union-busting shows that terrorist-affiliated gangs are a threat not only to the democratic institutions of Sri Lanka, but also to those of Canada. When terrorist extremists become guns for hire, renting their reputations and ruthless tactics to the highest bidder, that constitutes a startling attack on democracy.

IMPLAUSIBLE DENIAL: CANADA'S OFFICIAL COUNTER-TERRORISM POLICY

A few days after suicide terrorists rammed loaded passenger planes into the World Trade Center, Jean Chrétien stood in the House of Commons to make a remarkable statement. 'I am not aware at this time', the Prime Minister said, 'of a cell known to the police to be operating in Canada with the intention of carrying out terrorism in Canada or elsewhere.' It was a confounding pronouncement because Canada's intelligence, police, and immigration services had been warning the government for years that the world's major terrorist groups had all established offshore bases in Canadian cities, and that they were using Canada as a staging ground for political and religious violence around the world.

In addition to whatever top-secret reports and memos had circulated in Ottawa with this message, the Canadian Security Intelligence

Service, since the fall of 1998, had posted several public reports on its Web site warning that terrorists were setting up shop in the country. The warnings were explicit and increasingly urgent. The CSIS Director testified before a Senate subcommittee that 'terrorist groups are present here whose origins lie in virtually every significant regional, ethnic and nationalist conflict there is' (Elcock, 1998). By July 2001, CSIS was advising that the threat of a terrorist attack involving Canadians had never been greater, and that radical Islamic groups were a particular concern—a warning that would take on precision barely two months later in New York. And then there was the Ressam case, and the arrest of his Canadian cell mates who had plotted to bomb a Jewish neighbourhood in Montreal, which supplied ample evidence of the threat posed by Canadian-based terrorist and support cells.

During the 18 months preceding the 11 September attacks, the Prime Minister was asked again and again in Question Period why his government was not addressing the threat of terrorism. In their responses, Liberal ministers evaded substance and feigned outrage, branding the opposition racist, anti-Canadian, and anti-immigrant. Not once did the government acknowledge what its own counter-terrorism agents were saying in publicly available documents: that the country had been infiltrated by the world's most violent organizations. Anyone who reads newspapers could come up with the names of at least a dozen suspected members of the bin Laden organization who have operated out of Canada. Prime Minister Chrétien and his government, it seems, were the only ones who were not aware. The federal counter-terrorism policy, it seems, was official denial. After the US Justice Department identified two Tunisian-born Canadian citizens as Al-Qaeda members who had professed their desire to die for the cause, Bill Graham, the newly minted Minister of Foreign Affairs, was quick to claim that this 'doesn't make us a haven for terrorists' (*Toronto Star*, 2002).

The most favourable explanation is that this denial was strategic, that the Liberals did not want to tip off the terrorists that they were being watched, thereby forcing them deeper underground. That seems highly unlikely, however, especially considering the very agencies charged with safeguarding national security have been publicly reporting for several years the existence of Canadian-based terrorists. It is also possible the senior ranks of the Liberals had not been properly briefed on the threat, that there was some problem with the flow of intelligence from agencies such as CSIS to the cabinet and Prime Minister. But that also seems only a remote possibility, particularly in light of the substantial public reporting on the issue that has taken place since the spring of 2000 (see Chapter 7, this volume).

The most believable explanation is that the Liberals have sought to politicize the issue of national security for their own electoral gain. The Liberal strategists, whoever they are, seem to have concluded that national security measures could be perceived as immigrant-bashing, costing them the support of ethnic communities. By painting opposition calls for anti-terrorism measures as motivated by racism, the Liberals hoped to secure their lock on major urban ridings with large concentrations of immigrants. Bolstering this theory is the fact that Liberal rhetoric in the House of Commons on this issue was most heated in the months just before the last election. The Liberals may also have fallen for the ploy by front groups that were crying racism over national security measures. What the policy-makers in Ottawa failed to grasp was that Canada's ethnic communities are the main victims of terrorists seeking money and support for homeland conflicts.

To make matters worse, some Liberal MPs openly support groups such as the Tamil Tigers. Liberal MP Jim Karygiannis has attended Tamil Tigers support functions. Paul Martin and Maria Minna were guest speakers at a May 2000 dinner hosted by the Federation of Associations of Canadian Tamils, despite warnings that the group was a front for the Tigers. 'I do not believe that Canadians want their country to be known as a place from which terrorist acts elsewhere are funded or fomented', CSIS Director Elcock testified in 1998. 'We cannot ever become known as some R and R facility for terrorists. In other words, and I will be as blunt as I can be, we cannot become, through inaction or otherwise, what might be called an unofficial state sponsor of terrorism.' But one might argue that Canada, through its long-standing parliamentary inaction, has already become an unofficial terrorism sponsor.

Public outrage over the 11 September attacks and lobbying by Washington at last forced the government to pass anti-terrorism legislation banning fundraising and outlawing violence committed in the furtherance of religion and politics. But why did it take so long? The US did so in 1996, Britain in 2000. These laws did not prevent the attacks in New York and Washington, but they may well have prevented others, and they appear to have mitigated the damage somewhat, as suggested by the case against Zacarias Moussaoui, the so-called twentieth hijacker whose participation was apparently thwarted by his arrest. At least the US and Britain acknowledged the threat and were doing what they could. Faced with the same threats and warnings, Canada's ruling parliamentarians did nothing, and to that extent they shoulder a share of responsibility for the attacks of 11 September.

The Supreme Court of Canada upheld the government's already existing counter-terrorism policies on 11 January 2002, when it threw out challenges to the Immigration Act and ruled that dangerous terrorists can be deported even if they might be tortured in their homelands. The Court dismissed arguments by Suresh that fundraising and otherwise supporting violent organizations are a form of free expression and free association protected by the Charter of Rights and Freedoms. The Supreme Court also said that supporting terrorism abroad from within Canada was indeed a threat to Canada's national security. 'It may once have made sense to suggest that terrorism in one country did not necessarily implicate other countries. But after the year 2001, that approach is no longer valid', the Court said.

The Canadian government now has tools at its disposal that finally should enable it to take action against the terrorist organizations active within Canada, although refugee lobby groups have vowed to fight the new legislation in the courts. Whether the recent court ruling and laws will be effective remains to be seen. The problem is that Ottawa is so late into the game that terrorist groups are now deeply entrenched into Canadian society, so deeply that ridding them from the country may well be impossible.

NOTES

1. The CSIS brief submitted to the Trial Division of the Federal Court of Canada in the case of Aynur Saygili can be found in *Saygili v. Canada (Minister of Citizenship and Immigration)*, [1997] F.C.J. No. 287, Court File No. DES-6-96.
2. Ahmed Ressam, an Algerian living in Montreal under a suspended deportation order, was caught by US immigration authorities in December 1999 trying to cross into the US at a Washington state/BC border crossing with a trunk full of explosives. It later became known that Ressam intended to plant a bomb in the Los Angeles airport.
3. For the CSIS brief, see *Re Jaballah*, [2001] F.C.J. No. 1748 Docket DES-4-01.

REFERENCES

Bell, Stewart. 2001. 'Al Qaeda Operatives in Canada', *National Post*, 15 Dec.

Bowen, Fred, RCMP. n.d. Testimony before a refugee adjudicator.

Canadian Security and Intelligence Service (CSIS). 1996. 'Secret—Canadian Eyes Only', Ottawa, 31 July. (Released under Access to Information Act.)

———. 1998. Brief submitted to Federal Court of Canada in the case of Iqbal Singh.

———. 1999. *LTTE Front Organizations in Canada*. Research, Analysis and Production (RAP) Branch. Ottawa, winter.

Elcock. Ward. 1998. Testimony before the Special Senate Committee on Security and Intelligence, 24 June. Available at: <www.csis-scrs.gc.ca/eng/miscdocs/kelly_e.html>.

Federal Court of Canada. 1998. Department of Justice in the matter of a certificate in relation to Iqbal Singh, File DES-1-98. Ottawa.

Kamel, Fatehj, et al. n.d. Report of the prosecutor, Tribunal de Grande Instance, Paris.

Labour Relations Board of Ontario. 2001. Decision on Baron Metal.

Metropolitan Toronto Police. 1998. 'Tamil Organized Crime', Tamil Task Force Pilot Project Report, Toronto, Feb.

Mogck, Judy, and Josée Therrien. 1998. 'Project Sparkplug Report', RCMP Criminal Analysis Branch. Ottawa, 1 Sept.

Re Jaballah, [2001] F.C.J. No. 1748.

RCMP. 1998a. Information to Obtain a Search Warrant, in the case of Muralitharan Nadarajah, 15 Sept.

———, Criminal Intelligence Directorate. 1998b. *Report*. (Released under Access to Information Act.)

———, Criminal Intelligence Directorate. 2000. 'Middle Eastern and Tamil Criminal Extremism', 20 Jan.

Saygili v. Canada (Minister of Citizenship and Immigration), [1997] F.C.J. No. 287.

Suresh v. Canada (Minister of Citizenship and Immigration), [2000], 2 F.C. 592.

Toronto Star. 2002. 'Canada not a haven for terrorists: Graham', 26 June.

US Department of Treasury. 2001. Statement of Secretary Paul O'Neill on the Blocking of Hamas Financiers' Assets. Press release PO-837, 4 Dec. Available at: <http://www.treas.gov/press/releases/po837.htm>.

9

Canada and International Health:
A Time of Testing on AIDS

JOHN W. FOSTER

In 2001 Canada and Canadians began to face the devastating threat of AIDS with new interest and initiatives. Civil society organizations and various elements of the government found fresh ways to collaborate and some new resources. However, the overall response remains far from adequate and a central contradiction ruptures opportunities for coherence. In fact, much of the Canadian response is tied to a questionable objective—delaying and distorting impacts for those most at risk.

HEALTH FOR ALL

A remarkably clear call for a deep and radical renewal in global efforts to assure 'health for all' and universal access to the fundamental human right to health was issued as 2001 came to a close.

The Report of the Commission on Macroeconomics and Health, prepared for the World Health Organization (WHO), called for governments to make 'solemn commitments to reduce poverty and improve health', and 'to initiate and facilitate the global investments in health that can transform the lives and livelihoods of the world's poor' (CMH, 2001: 15).

The nature of the gap between current realities and the achievement of the human right to health, as well as the policy challenges facing governments, is vividly illustrated by the desperation and desolation resulting from the AIDS pandemic. The continuing inadequacies of the response to global health needs are clearly seen as well.

SETTING

The year 2001 saw the HIV/AIDS pandemic reach the centre of global attention, at least for a moment. The United Nations Secretary-General pressed the case for its urgency and the UN General Assembly Special Session on HIV/AIDS (UNGASS) took place in New York on 25–7 June. The G-8, meeting in Genoa, Italy, 20–2 July, took some notice of the issue, and a Global Health Fund (later termed the Global Fund against AIDS, Tuberculosis and Malaria or GFATM) was initiated.

Public outrage at the effects of the trade-related intellectual properties (TRIPs) regime in retarding access to essential drugs deepened and spread. Attacks on Brazil and South Africa for patent violations on essential drugs occurred.[1] The WHO and UN human rights bodies raised concerns and international non-governmental organizations (NGOs) campaigned with gusto. Amid growing North-South polarization on the issue, the World Trade Organization (WTO) met in Doha, Qatar, and made a political declaration on the TRIPs agreement and public health, noting 'the gravity of the public health problems afflicting many developing and least-developed countries' and the need for the TRIPs agreement to be part of the action taken 'to address these problems' (WTO Declaration, 2001).

As World AIDS Day was marked, deaths from AIDS verged on 22 million, with more than 40 million infected (I Update, 2001). More than half of these cases are in sub-Saharan Africa, and half of those infected contract the virus under age 25. The impact on the most economically active populations is intense. The UN estimates, for instance, that with 20 per cent infection, South Africa's GDP is already 17 per cent lower than it would be without AIDS.

The arrival of anti-retroviral (ARV) drugs in the 1990s and the rapid increase in survival rates and longer lives among those who could afford them, together with the ongoing search for vaccines, raise anew the issue of equity and access for all. Those advocating access confront the extension of patent protection regimes under TRIPs, negotiated at the WTO. While the large pharmaceutical corporations argue that in Africa 'patents are infrequently a barrier to accessing the medicine', US AIDS specialist James Love notes that the cheaper generic 'three-in-one' pill is blocked by Glaxo Wellcome's patents on Combivir in the 27 countries where the majority of the world's AIDS patients live, and that 74 per cent of those living with AIDS in Africa are in countries with at least two patents on ARV drugs. The British medical journal *Lancet* (18 Aug. 2001) argues that opening up drug markets to generic competition is 'so far the only proven way to bring drug prices down. In Brazil the price of AIDS drugs fell by 82 per cent over 5 years thanks to such competition.'

THE HUMAN RIGHT TO HEALTH

The 'right to health' is shorthand for rights cited in an extensive list of international human rights treaties and conventions, including the International Covenant on Economic, Social and Cultural Rights, the Convention on the Rights of the Child, the Convention on the Elimination of All Forms of Discrimination Against Women, and the Convention on the Elimination of All Forms of Racial Discrimination (Leary, 1994: 32–3). Canada is a party to virtually all the relevant agreements and has the responsibility, for example, to report progress periodically to the International Committee on Economic, Social and Cultural Rights.

Clearly, the right to health is not a *guarantee* of good health for everyone, but as phrased in one agreement this right is 'understood to mean the enjoyment of the highest level of physical, mental and social well-being', and in another 'good health' is defined as the 'highest attainable standard of physical and mental health'. Such definitions imply the provision of certain conditions that support the goal of good health, including a healthy environment and working conditions, specific maternal health provisions, and the opportunity for rest and leisure activities, as well as freedom from discrimination on grounds of race, religion, political belief, or economic or social conditions.

The extent to which the Canadian government has taken adequate account of the potential human rights impact of its many new trade and investment obligations is a vital question. The answer is by no means reassuring. The implications of the 'new generation' of trade and investment agreements, such as the World Trade Organization and the North American Free Trade Agreement (NAFTA), for commitments made in international human rights documents were not extensively examined or discussed in the mid-1990s when these agreements were set in place. The international battle over the proposed Multilateral Agreement on Investment (MAI) alerted many to the implications of the new economics. In recent years various non-governmental organizations—the International NGO Committee on Human Rights Trade and Investment (INCHRITI), the Federation Internationale des Droits de l'Homme, Canada's Rights and Democracy, and the HIV/AIDS Legal Network—have explored the relationship and the conflicts that can arise between these two sets of regimes. The UN human rights bodies have issued a number of general reports and studies on globalization and human rights as well as more specific declarations.

THE UNITED NATIONS RAISES THE FLAG

'This morning, I committed over $73 million for HIV and AIDS programming in Africa, the Caribbean, Asia and Central and Eastern Europe.' With this and a number of other commitments, Maria Minna, then Minister for International Co-operation, stated Canada's response to the UNGASS (Minna, 2001). To a considerable extent, the UNGASS was the high point in Canada's engagement with the issue in 2001. Initiated at the fall 2000 UN General Assembly, the June 2001 Special Session was prepared on a fast track. Minna headed the Canadian delegation, which also included officials from the Department of Foreign Affairs and International Trade (DFAIT), Health Canada, the Canadian International Development Agency (CIDA), and two NGO representatives, one of whom was a person living with AIDS. A number of Canadian AIDS service organizations (ASOs) and NGOs attended as observers with consultative status as well.

The UNGASS developed a Declaration of Commitment that recognizes human rights as essential in all areas of the response to AIDS. It commits participating governments to the development, by 2003, of multi-sectoral national strategies and financing plans involving civil society, with the full participation of people living with AIDS, and to national periodic reviews of progress in implementing the commitments. The Declaration calls for at least one full day annually at the General Assembly to review progress.

The Canadian HIV/AIDS Legal Network, in evaluating the UNGASS, paid tribute to 'the leadership role played by Canada in the process, and of the important contribution of the Canadian NGO movement both in providing practical technical guidance and moral weight to ensure that respect for human rights and sound public health principles continue to underscore the response to the epidemic globally' (Health Canada, 2001: 26).

Canada's role gained relatively high marks from non-governmental organizations engaged in processes of pre-UNGASS consultation and preparation. Canada, Malaysia, and Brazil were the only countries to place non-governmental representatives on their delegations as early as the first preparatory committee. The effective use of the NGO representatives in the inter-delegation negotiations, preparation of statements, and the overall approach was also appreciated, although it had clear limits. The leadership of the delegation's effective head, Ross Hynes of the Canadian Permanent Mission to the UN, in pursuing the issue of access and participation for gay and lesbian representatives was termed particularly courageous (personal interview). The appointment of the former Canadian UN Ambassador, Stephen Lewis, as one of the UN Secretary-General's Special Representatives, and the crisp and forceful statements he was able to make in his new work were also cited by participants as a catalytic contribution of Canadian origin.

THE FUND

The UNGASS Declaration estimates that an overall target of annual expenditure on the epidemic should reach US $7–10 billion in low- and middle-income countries and 'other countries experiencing or at risk of experiencing rapid expansion' by 2005. In addition to calling for increases in national budgets, research, and debt relief, the Declaration supports the establishment of a global HIV/AIDS and health fund to include contributions from both the private and public sectors. It calls for a 'worldwide fund-raising campaign aimed at the general public as well as the private sector' (Health Canada, 2001: 16).

CIDA claims at least partial parentage for the Fund, having convened a donors' meeting in January 2001 to discuss its establishment. Again in June, Canada co-convened a meeting of 200 stakeholders in Geneva to advance the project. While the up-front advocacy of the Fund by the Secretary-General led many to believe it was under the aegis and control of the United Nations, the Fund is a donor-led project. By autumn 2001, it had become the Global Fund To Fight AIDS, Tuberculosis and Malaria, with a Transitional Working Group (TWG) of 39 members (including Canada) seeking to establish the governance and operation of the new body by 15 December 2001. CIDA officials played an important role in both consultation at home and representation in Fund development abroad. Domestic, regional, and international consultations among NGOs and AIDS service organizations demonstrated the avid interest of the non-governmental community and elicited a significant number of recommendations and proposals for the various aspects of the Fund's priorities, governance, and operations. Canadian ASO representatives, including Toronto-based Richard Burzynski of the International Council of AIDS Service Organizations, were among the non-governmental representatives taking part in the TWG.

The development of the Fund could lead to a reinforcement of skepticism about new and separate instruments. There has been significant tension between North and South over such governance issues as the donors' desire for a veto and the achievement of a simple double (North and South) majority.[2] The threat that the US Congress would simply withdraw contributions from the Fund if the North was not given what it viewed as appropriate political control was recurrent.

A further fear was repeatedly expressed regarding the use of the funds raised, as the US pressed to have even the limited pledged funds devoted to the purchase of brand-name pharmaceuticals. Médécins Sans Frontières, Oxfam, and others believed that if the purpose of the Fund is to save lives and not to give taxpayers' money to shareholders, it should always be spent on the most affordable medicines and other health commodities. In the case of AIDS, for example, triple-therapy costs five times less from companies producing generic drugs in India than from pharmaceutical companies in the West.

Although Canadian government participants in the Transitional Working Group organized periodic consultation with the non-governmental community, they ran into trouble in December 2001 when they attempted to conclude negotiations without a Canadian NGO representative at the final international sessions. In general, however, the CIDA representatives in the Fund negotiations got high marks for a reasonable and focused approach.

The Fund has some extremely positive characteristics. It was designed to include a channel for rapid response, while other more sizable and carefully designed projects were developed. Despite difficulties that might have been expected, it brought together several international specific disease-related communities and networks: AIDS, malaria, and tuberculosis, each with its own urgencies, approaches, and history. From its inception, the Fund also engaged civil society representatives in design and governance.

At the time of the UNGASS, the Fund had a fresh image and a firm commitment to do something concrete and significant, and to do it in a new way. By late 2001, however, complaints were heard among non-governmental observers that it had already bogged down and was developing its own bureaucratic complexities, and that the level of contributions, from Canada among others, was far below the annual targets as well as being less than our capability.

Canada pledged US $100 million over four years, the US pledged three times that amount, and the Gates Foundation offered an amount equal to Canada's. The total reached by 21 October 2001 was US $1.497 billion. *The Lancet* noted that this was equivalent to sub-Saharan Africa's debt repayment costs for 6 weeks, hardly what the doctor had ordered and far short of the $10 billion annual target the UN cited as necessary (MSF, 2001).

For World AIDS Day, 1 December 2001, a group of leading Canadian non-governmental AIDS service and research bodies cited Canada's response as 'abysmally' short of commitments at UNGASS and elsewhere. The Canadian contribution, spread over four years, amounts to '$1.25 a year per person', stated Ralf Jurgens, executive director of the Canadian HIV/AIDS Legal Network, 'less than the price of a cup of coffee' (Canadian AIDS Society et al., 2001).

The fear, expressed in a variety of non-governmental as well as governmental quarters, is that the Fund was a 'flavour of the month' for 2001, particularly for the G-8 in Genoa. As the big players move towards the G-8 in Kananaskis, Alberta, in 2002, other priorities and photo opportunities may transcend the issue of follow-up and fulfillment of the vision for the Fund. A new pledge to Africa or education or increased security will emerge, new dollars will be committed, and the inadequacies of the Fund will remain unaltered.

THE DECLARATION AT DOHA

While the WTO Ministerial of 9–14 November 2001 in Doha, Qatar, took a relative back seat in media preoccupied with 11 September and the 'war' against terrorism, the key threat to the success of the talks was the dispute over the effect of the TRIPs regime on human rights and on access to essential medicines for AIDS and other diseases. The debate had emerged internationally the previous year in disputes between the United States and South Africa and Brazil regarding the nature and urgency of the AIDS pandemic, the availability of affordable generics, patent protection, and related issues. It continued in such theatres as a joint WTO-WHO consultation in 2001, the UNGASS, and meetings of the WTO's TRIPs Council. The latter, meeting in September in Geneva, received a declaration from 52 developing countries asking 'that the WTO guarantee that nothing prevents countries from protecting public health'. These countries requested protection against economic sanctions and other pressures when they implement public health protection measures 'such as use of cheap copies of expensive patented drugs'. They argued that the TRIPs agreement failed to provide genuine guarantees that public health protection would have priority and be free from sanctions from powerful governments defending the interests of multinationals (Healthgap, 2001).

In response, Canada, along with the US, Australia, Switzerland, and Japan, argued that patents were not a danger to public health, accepting, it appeared, the arguments of a spokesperson for a large German pharmaceutical firm, who stated at the time that 'more flexibility in TRIPs would be disastrous for continued investment in research and development in AIDS.'[3] The TRIPs defenders admitted that countries have a right to take measures necessary to address public health concerns, but at the same time they insisted that the TRIPs agreement took priority. Spokespersons for Brazil and South Africa indicated that whenever they have tried to put public health first, countries such as the US, Switzerland, and Canada have threatened legal battles and sanctions. The developing countries (and Norway) pressed for recognition at Doha that 'nothing in the TRIPs agreement shall prevent members from taking measures to protect public health.' When Canada and the United States later began to contemplate setting aside TRIPs commitments to contract the emergency use of generics against a possible terrorist attack using anthrax, a Brazilian trade negotiator commented that this 'added a lot of weight to our argument'. Both before and after Doha, spokespersons for the TRIPs defenders, instead of dealing directly with the issue of death and destruction caused by the pandemic, turned their fire on developing countries with generic drug producers—India, Brazil, Thailand, Egypt—arguing that they were simply arguing for their own selfish interests and had 'hijacked' the issue in favour of their own generic producers (Olson, 2001; *Third World Resurgence*, 2001; author interviews).

The developing countries were joined by a highly articulate international campaign for change led by Médécins Sans Frontères, Oxfam International, and a variety of AIDS-related non-governmental organizations. Pressure in Canada was considerable, but the trade-centred position remained solid (author interviews; Oxfam, 2001). Canada and its associates argued that existing flexibilities within the TRIPs regime obviated the need for change and that patents were part of the solution. Concerns were expressed about exhaustion of patents, and particularly about 'parallel importing' and the fear of 'seepage' into northern markets if cheaper drugs were permitted in the South. The issue of how and when a health emergency exists— therefore permitting measures like compulsory licensing of generics, parallel importing, and so on   continued to be debated, with both sides recognizing that even the chronic case of South Africa was not thought to merit emergency action until late into its crisis. Informing the debate was the growing consciousness that from the point of view of the United States, the existing TRIPs regime needed to be further strengthened by imposing so-called 'TRIPs+' conditionalities on countries, which are likely to retard further essential action on access or to increase its costs.

The upshot of the debate was a political declaration regarding TRIPs and public health at the Doha Ministerial, not the 'carve out' for public health in the TRIPs regime that critics had sought. Some non-governmental advocates, among them Oxfam and Médécins Sans Frontières, cried victory. James Love of the Washington-based Consumer Project on Technology stated that 'it is a road map for using the flexibility of the TRIPs agreement to protect public health' (Love, 2001). But he also noted that it did *not* modify the agreement, was not legally binding, and did not provide, through provision for parallel imports, a solution for the poorer countries that lack domestic production capacity and represent a significant proportion of infections in Africa. Why was this latter provision delayed for further consideration in the TRIPs Council until later in 2002? 'A small group of wealthy countries blocked agreement on this at Doha', states Canadian trade analyst and WTO critic Scott Sinclair (Sinclair, 2001).

Cecilia Oh of the Malaysian-based Third World Network spoke in measured tones. The declaration was a 'good first step' (quoted in Love, 2001). Sanctions and corporate pressures should cease. The governments of developing countries need to implement domestic measures. Non-governmental advocates must commit themselves to continue to work 'tirelessly' to defend public health priority and ensure access, utilizing the political declaration to this end.

DISCONNECT BY DESIGN?

Many voices in the policy community—both inside and outside government—argue for increased 'policy coherence' in response to crises like that represented by AIDS. There is considerable evidence of attempts to ensure both horizontal and vertical coherence in aspects of Canadian policy. Health Canada, CIDA, and others have various means to consult and co-ordinate on policy and Canada's international response to the crisis. Opportunities for what might be called 'vertical' consultation with non-governmental organizations and experts are relatively frequent, if not always clear in impact.

The lengthy activist-engaging battle against AIDS and the related policy and financing debates have given impetus to a variety of consultative mechanisms and practices, particularly on the part of Health Canada. A Minister's Council on HIV/AIDS has involved non-governmental experts in meetings on policy and implementation. The Inter-Agency Coalition on AIDS and Development and the International Council of AIDS Service Organizations were invited to consult regarding preparations for UNGASS. The Minister's Council has pressed the Minister of Health to take up specific interdepartmental issues with the Minister of Immigration and the Solicitor General, and also has cited interdepartmental coherence and co-ordination as an issue of concern. A Working Group on International AIDS includes representatives of Health Canada, CIDA, and DFAIT, along with a series of non-governmental representatives, and meets quarterly.

The Trade ministry also has a variety of consultative mechanisms with business, as well as some with NGOs. It consults other departments in the process of preparing negotiations. The extent to which it integrates into its considerations Canada's long-standing human rights commitments, including the priority of the right to health, remains obscure. It can be argued that two separate processes operate, one organized around trade policy, the other around health concerns, and that in any joust the trade focus will prevail. The legal priority or trump quality of human rights obligations appears in such circumstances to be ignored or sidelined.

After some years of recommendations from non-governmental advocates, the Standing Committee on Foreign Affairs and International Trade, under then chair Bill Graham (now Minister of Foreign Affairs), recognized the difficulties thrown up by potentially conflicting international commitments. In its review of the 2001 Quebec City Summit the Committee's first recommendation stated that, 'given the importance of the question of the enforceability of obligations in the fields of human rights, labour standards, the environment and the protection of cultural diversity, and the lack of agreement as to whether they may best be enforced through inclusion in trade agreements or by other means, the Committee recommends that the Government of Canada study the question of how these obligations may best be enforced, and table its findings with the Committee by April, 2002' (SCFAIT, 2001).

Participants in the Canadian delegation at UNGASS note that, while information and dialogue flowed freely on most issues, in the case of access to medicines a curtain was dropped. While NGOs might contribute to statements on other issues, on access and intellectual property the briefing notes and the government line were confidential and took precedence.

What is different about access to medicines? Very simply, say participants, it's a trade issue rather than a health issue. In a recent series of articles, Paul McGregor of the *Ottawa Citizen* detailed the creation of strong patent protection legislation and regulation in Canada by the Mulroney government. While the Liberals in opposition roasted the Conservatives for ensuring high drug prices, which would cause 'festering wounds . . . on . . . Canada's poorest citizens', once in power they actually strengthened the protections to large pharmaceutical corporations. Behind this continuity and a series of shifting excuses—for example, innovation or encouraging research and development in Canada—is a sizable team of lobbyists for multinational pharmaceutical corporations. As the spokesperson for the competing generic firms argues, 'for every lobbyist we can hire, they've got seven' (McGregor, 2001, 2002).

Whether the current regime is in the interests of Canadians is as significant as its role in retarding an effective and cost-efficient response to the AIDS pandemic internationally. The Romanow Commission on the future of medicare may address the issue, which has already held back a national pharmacare program as well as forced several provinces further to restrict provincial drug assistance plans. In the fall of 2001, the drug access issue erupted on front pages, including that of the *New York Times*, when Health Canada, at the height of the anthrax terror scare, placed a sizable order for the generic anti-anthrax drug Cipro with generic manufacturer Apotex, even though the antibiotic was under a Bayer patent. While then Health Minister Allan Rock beat a quick retreat, the initiative 'showed the basic flaw of the patent system by valuing intellectual property over the immediate health needs of Canadians', and contributed to an emerging debate over the issue in the United States (McGregor, 2002).

Canada's response to the crisis—at least in terms of access to essential drugs—remains firmly anchored to the trade docket and to the interests of the multinationals. While this position is characteristic of several developed countries, it is not universal. In the preparations for the Doha WTO Ministerial, Norway, which often finds common cause with Canada in a variety of international fora, was associated with the developing-country position, while Canada argued against change and defended a narrower interpretation of TRIPs.

CANADA'S RESPONSE: A BRIEF ASSESSMENT

Canada is a leader in the global response to the challenge of AIDS, and on occasion, as at the UNGASS in June 2001, its traditional commitment to human rights and inclusion breaks through and new ground is opened internationally. Canada's overseas development agency, CIDA, has made significant efforts to develop and give priority to an AIDS strategy, and in partnership with academic and NGO partners CIDA has contributed to valuable research, experimentation, and community-based programming abroad. But Canada's overall levels of assistance remain far below our capability.

A variety of governmental actors have worked hard to consult and engage concerned non-governmental actors, including people living with AIDS, in policy formation, representation in international negotiations, and the formation of global responses. In many cases these initiatives offer models to the international community. Non-governmental bodies are providing some remarkable leadership at home, in developing countries, and in international aid and AIDS service networks engaged in education, advocacy, and service provision.

The size and multiplying impact of the AIDS pandemic, however, confront Canada and other nations with atypical and profound challenges, which raise significant questions about our trade, aid, debt relief policies, and fundamental priorities. The question that emerges regards the moral compass at the national and international level and the urgency of reviewing the overall priorities expressed in Canadian policy. This is, simply, a life and death matter.

HUMAN RIGHTS RESTATED

Canada's official position on the issue of intellectual property rights going into the Doha Ministerial was one of 'balance'. A departmental summary from DFAIT stated that 'intellectual property rights represent a balance between the need to provide incentives to spur innovation and the benefits derived by society to have maximum access to new creations.' It admitted that the issue of access has been of 'particular interest to Canadians recently', but that 'the provision of drugs and therapies is a complex question involving patent rights, the establishment of systems to deliver and monitor drug usage, cost and alternative mechanisms to finance drug purchases by developing countries.' DFAIT sidestepped the key issue of the massive impact of AIDS, and while there are references to patent rights, a 'balancing' reference to the human right to health is absent (DFAIT, 2001).

The counter-argument to the constant refrain regarding the priority of TRIPs has been made by a variety of human rights experts and organizations. For example, Canada has ratified the Covenant on Economic, Social and Cultural Rights, and guidelines for its interpretation indicate that the government has obligations of conduct and of result. If it supports measures inconsistent with these rights—and one could argue a clear conflict between the results of the application of TRIPs and the objective of the fulfillment of the human right to health for all—it is in violation of its commitments. A government is also in violation if it fails to regulate third-party activities so as to prevent them from violating human rights. It is also in violation if it fails to take account of its human right obligations in entering into bilateral or multilateral agreements with other states, international organizations, or multinational corporations (Foster, 2001).

THE CHALLENGE OF HEALTH FOR ALL

Access to affordable quality medicines is not the only issue. Medicine alone cannot be treated as a silver bullet or isolated from the over-all context of providing basic health support to developing countries and poor populations. In September 2001, the Canadian Public Health Association (CPHA) convened a meeting of clinicians and public health experts with experience in various parts of Africa and in India to consider the appropriate conditions for the introduction of anti-retroviral drugs in resource-poor settings (CPHA, 2001). The consensus from this meeting emphasized the importance of the training and availability of counsellors and testing services, and the short-term priority of targeting women who have taken part in mother-to-child transmission prevention programs and HIV-positive women sex workers. The CPHA report is laced with the fear that a rush to buy anti-retroviral drugs, at whatever price, will divert funds from the support of basic health services, and that application of the drugs inadequate or poorly directed fashion will encourage the development of resistances and new forms of the virus. What is fundamental, the report argues, is the development of the necessary health-care infrastructure to support the provision of anti-retroviral therapy to all in need. This, the report admits, 'will take years, even if it is attacked with unprecedented vigour'.

The static, if not regressive, trends in the provision of official development assistance (ODA) by donor countries, the continued crisis in debt relief and forgiveness of developing-country debt, the recurrent currency and financial crises of a variety of countries, and the implementation of 'Washington consensus' policies by the World Bank and the International Monetary Fund all play a part in undermining the immune capacity of large populations and in limiting the effective response to the threat of disease in developing-country and poor populations worldwide.

It is in this context that new Canadian initiatives must be evaluated, whether in levels of ODA budgeted, special showcase funds for

African development, or topping up to respectable levels the ongoing Canadian contribution to the Global Fund. The role of non-governmental, academic, and AIDS service agencies based in Canada is significant both in service delivery and in policy consultation and advice. The recent report of the Commission on Macroeconomics and Health restates the challenge from the point of view of economic policy and possibility. It provides a renewed context and challenge illustrating the concrete feasibility of considerable steps, not only in the combat against AIDS, but towards health for all.

IF WE WERE WILLING . . .

In a reflection on his discovery of 'big pharma' in writing his most recent best-seller, author John le Carré, building on proposals made by Tina Rosenberg of the *New York Times,* suggests a proven approach: 'let the World Health Organization treat global AIDS in the same way that UNICEF has treated global vaccination, which saves 3 million lives a year and prevents crippling diseases in tens of millions more.' The cost might be $3 billion a year, or roughly the profit of one transnational pharmaceutical firm, Pfizer (Le Carré, 2001).

Canadian diplomat Stephen Lewis brings the point home. In Africa and the developing world in general, the drugs to which we have access in the rich North are unavailable to those who represent 95 per cent of new infections, dooming them to a 'gruesome and painful death . . . . But it's worse, much worse. Neither the pharmaceutical companies who have the drugs, nor the governments who have the money, nor the governments who could amend their laws to make cheap generic drugs available, are prepared to prolong or rescue African lives.' Lewis challenges governments, like that of Canada: 'if we had the political will, there is no question that we have the money. Then why isn't it being done? And because it's not being done, why doesn't it amount to murder? Mass murder' (Lewis, 2001).

NOTES

1.   A group of 39 transnational drug corporations represented by the Pharmaceutical Manufacturers' Association of South Africa took the government of South Africa to court challenging South African legislation permitting compulsory licensing and parallel importing of drugs related to treatment of AIDS and other diseases. On 19 April 2001, under considerable international and domestic pressure, the companies unconditionally dropped their lawsuit. The second dispute was a

complaint lodged by the United States against Brazil at the World Trade Organization arguing that Brazil's industrial property law imposed conditions in conflict with Articles 27.1 and 28.1 of the TRIPs regime. Under considerable public pressure at home, the US dropped the complaint in mid-2001.

2.   To give some element of democratic as distinct from donor definition to the Fund, a number of southern and NGO/ASO participants fought for a decision-making process requiring approval of decisions by simultaneous majorities in both southern and northern groups of voting members, rather than a majority of donors or a simple majority of all.

3.   Rolf Krebs, chairman of German drug giant Boehringer Ingelheim, as quoted in Khalil Elouardighi, 'Feedback on the TRIPs council' e-update, 20 Sept. 2001, circulated by the Health Global Access Process Coalition.

REFERENCES

The author conducted a number of personal interviews with officials of the Department of Foreign Affairs and International Trade and Health Canada, took part in several CIDA-sponsored consultations, and undertook interviews as well as with NGO and ASO representatives involved in each of the three main theatres of debate and action examined in this chapter.

Bahadur, Chandrika. 2001. 'TRIPs, HIV/AIDS and Access to Drugs: A Background Paper'. New York: UNDP.

Canadian AIDS Society et al. 2001. 'Canada's Response to HIV/AIDS Falling Short Domestically and Internationally', news release issued by Canadian AIDS Society, CATIE, Canadian Treatment Action Council, Canadian HIV/AIDS Legal Network, Inter-Agency Coalition on AIDS and Development, Canadian HIV/AIDS Clearing House, Canadian Association for HIV Research, and the Canadian Aboriginal AIDS Network, Ottawa, 29 Nov.

Canadian Public Health Association (CPHA). 2001. *The Opportunities and Challenges of Introducing Anti-Retroviral Therapy (ART) in Resource-Poor Settings: A consensus statement by organizations delivering AIDS projects for the Canadian International Development Agency (CIDA)*. Ottawa.

Commission on Macroeconomics and Health (CMH). 2001. *Macroeconomics and Health: Investing in Health for Economic Development*. Report of the Commission on Macroeconomics and Health. Geneva: World Health Organization.

Department of Foreign Affairs and International Trade (DFAIT). 2001. WTO 2001 Consultations: Doha (Qatar) Ministerial Meeting: Intellectual Property Rights— Information Paper.

Dommen, Caroline. 2000. *Raising Human Rights Concerns in the World Trade Organization: Actors, Processes and Possible Strategies*. Geneva: World Health Organization.

Elliott, Richard. 2001. *TRIPs and Rights: International Human Rights Law, Access to Medicines, and the Interpretation of the WTO Agreement on Trade-Related Aspects of Intellectual Property*. Toronto: Canadian HIV/AIDS Legal Network & AIDS Law Project, South Africa, Nov. Available at: <www.aidslaw.ca>.

———— and Marie-Helene Bonin. 2001. *Patents, International Trade Law and Access to Essential Medicine*. Ottawa and Montreal: Médécins sans frontières/Canadian HIV-AIDS Legal Network.

Foster, John. 2001. 'Beyond Trade and Death: Notes for remarks to the Second People's Summit of the Americas: Forum on the State Withdrawal and Equitable Redistribution of Wealth'. NSI/ICAD, 17 Apr.

Health Canada. 2001. *Report on the United Nations General Assembly Special Session (UNGASS) on HIV/AIDS, New York, NY. June 25–27, 2001*. Ottawa: International Affairs Directorate, Health Policy and Communications Branch, Health Canada, June. Available at: <www.hc.gc.ca/datapcb/iad/ih-e.htm>.

Healthgap. 2001. 'Feedback on the TRIPs Council', Geneva, 20 Sept.

House of Commons, Standing Committee on Foreign Affairs and International Trade (SCFAIT). 2001. *Balance, Transparency and Engagement After the Quebec Summit: Report of the Standing Committee on Foreign Affairs and International Trade*. Ottawa, June.

I Update. 2001. 'HIV/AIDS. 40 million infections, 22 million dead', *Development Information Update*, 5. Evercreech, Somerset.

Leary, Virginia. 1994. 'The Right to Health in International Human Rights Law', *Health and Human Rights* 1, 1 (Fall). Available at: <www.hsph.harvard.edu/fxbcenter/journal.htm>.

Le Carré, John. 2001. 'In Place of Nations', *The Nation*, 9 Apr.

Lewis, Stephen. 2001. 'J'accuse: The West is Willfully Turning Its Back on the Greatest Human Tragedy of Our Age', *Globe and Mail*, 26 Jan.

Love, James. 2001. 'Some Views on the Draft Declaration on the TRIPs Agreement and Public Health', Doha. Consumer Project on Technology, 13 Nov., e-circular.

McGregor, Paul. 2001. 'Drug makers' war on generics: How powerful lobbyists help brand-name firms fight competition', *Ottawa Citizen*, 14 Oct.

————. 2002. 'Patent play by the multinationals: Take two patents . . . and call me next year: The never-ending war to redraw Canada's arcane patent laws', *Ottawa Citizen*, 20 Jan.

Mann, Jonathan M., Lawrence Gostin, Sofia Gruskin, Troyen Brennan, Zita Lazzarini, and Harvey V. Fineberg. 1994. 'Health and Human Rights', *Health and Human Rights* 1, 1 (Fall). Available at: <www.hsph.harvard.edu/fxbcenter/journal.htm>.

Médécins Sans Frontières (MSF). 2001. 'Health and human rights', *The Lancet*, 18 Aug.

Minna, Maria. 2001. 'Canadian Statement to the Special Session of the United Nations General Assembly on HIV/AIDS delivered by Maria Minna, Minister for International Cooperation, New York, New York, June 25, 2001', in International Affairs Directorate, Health Policy and Communications Unit, Health Canada, *Report on the United Nations General Assembly Special Session (UNGASS) on HIV/AIDS, New York, NY. June 25–27, 2001*. Ottawa: Health Canada. Also available at: <www.hc-sc.gc.ca/datapcb/iad/ih-e.htm>.

Naim, Moises. 2002. 'The Global War for Public Health: Interview with Gro Harlem Brundtland', *Foreign Policy* (Jan.-Feb.): 24–36.

Olson, Elizabeth. 2001. 'Drug Issue Casts a Shadow on Trade Talks', *New York Times*, 2 Nov. Available at: <www.nytimes.com/2001/11/02/business/worldbusikness/02DOHA/html>.

Oxfam. 2001. *Priced out of Reach*. Oxford.

Sinclair, Scott. 2001. e mail Re: Clarification on TRIPs declaration, 14 Nov.

Stratfor. 2000. *The Economics of AIDS*. Available at: <www.stratfor.com>.

Third World Resurgence. 2001. 'Patents and Profits', various articles, July, 131–2.

World Trade Organization (WTO). 2001. 'Declaration on the TRIPs and Public Health', adopted on 14 Nov. WT/MIN(01) Dec/2 20 Nov.

10

Canada as a Principal Summit Power: G-7/8 Concert Diplomacy from Halifax 1995 to Kananaskis 2002

JOHN KIRTON

In its definitive 7 February 1995 statement on Canadian foreign policy, the government of Prime Minister Jean Chrétien began with the bold assertion: 'Canada can further its global interests better than any other country through its active membership in key international groupings, for example hosting the G-7 Summit' (DFAIT, 1995: 9). Seven years later, as Canada prepares to host the old G-7 and the new G-8 Summit in Kananaskis, Alberta, on 26–7 June 2002, many Canadians could legitimately question their Prime Minister's grandiose claim. Those with long memories note that it was issued just before Canada last hosted the summit in Halifax in June 1995, an event with little visible lasting impact and followed some months later by a Quebec referendum the separatists almost won. Casual summit watchers are hard-pressed to identify any made-in-Canada achievements at subsequent summits, leaving the media to portray summits as glorified global photo-ops with little substance and lots of show.

As Canadians watched violence, injury, and death at the July 2001 Genoa Summit, they could easily conclude that G-7/8 summits brought more risks than rewards. Indeed, when the shock of the 11 September attacks on North America aroused fears that terrorists might join anarchists in an assault on the Kananaskis Summit, Alberta Premier Ralph Klein demanded that it be cancelled or at least banished to anywhere else. As Canada assumed the G-7/8 chair at the beginning of January 2002, the media joined the critical chorus, declaring that the estimated $200 million cost of staging a summit that would attract 30,000 protesters and require 6,000 police officers was too much to pay for 'a meeting that produces little more than bland sentiments and scenic photo opportunities' (*Toronto Star*, 2001: A38; Harrington, 2001: A31). When Jean Chrétien suddenly shrunk his summit from its usual three days to only two, and it appeared President George Bush might not spend even one night on the Kananaskis mountaintop, more Canadians began to wonder, 'why bother at all?'

In their opposing attitudes Jean Chrétien's government and skeptical Canadians stand at opposite ends of long-standing debates about Canadian foreign policy, Canada's role in the G-7/G8 Summit, and the contribution of the G-7/8 to global governance. The debate about Canadian foreign policy portrays Canada in a range of ways: alternatively, as a fading power destined to depend on an imperial America or anonymous markets in a globalizing age (Doran, 1996), as a middle power exercising limited influence through the broadly multilateral institutions of 1945 (Keating, 2002), or as a 'foremost' or 'principal' power exhibiting effective global leadership through select major power clubs such as the G-7/8 (Eayrs, 1974; Dewitt and Kirton, 1983; Hampson and Molot, 1996; Black, 1997–8). In the debate about Canada's role in the G-7/8 in particular, Canada is seen, alternatively, as abandoning the United Nations' liberal internationalism for the G-7's neo-liberalism, as merely 'being there' to bask in the limelight, as exercising 'initiative without influence', as having selective internal impact, or as effectively engaging as an equal in the 'diplomacy of concert' (Kirton, 1995).

In the larger debate over the role of the G-7/8 in global governance, the competing models of G-7/8 success implicitly assign Canada a distinct place (Kirton and Daniels, 1999: 5). The 'false new consensus model' suggests the G-7/8 has abandoned efforts to control now ungovernable globalized markets and assumes that a small, exposed Canada has joined in this neo-liberal 'Washington consensus'. The 'American leadership model' argues that G-7/8 success comes only when the US is able and willing to lead and is supported by a 'strong second' that leaves Canada out (Putnam and Bayner, 1987). The model of 'democratic institutionalism' asserts that success comes when popular and committed G-7/8 leaders work through international institutions they control or create; this perspective allows Canada a 'niche diplomacy' role (Kokotsis, 1999; Ikenberry, 1993). Finally, the 'concert equality' model suggests that all members, including Canada, act as full and equal principal powers within a globally effective G-7/8 concert (Kirton, 1989, 1993, 1995a).

A review of Canada's record of G-7/8 diplomacy from Halifax to Kananaskis reveals that Canada has in fact come close to living up to Jean Chrétien's far-reaching claim. During the last seven-year summit cycle,[1] Canada has proven to be a foremost rather than a fading power, a G-7/8 leader rather than a laggard, and an accomplished principal power practitioner of the diplomacy of concert. It has moved beyond supporting market-friendly, America-led initiatives for greater globalization, or mediating to secure a summit consensus for its own sake, to exercising influence of a defensive and increasingly offensive kind. The ambitious agenda and objectives Canada has set for the Kananaskis 2002 Summit, and its initial efforts to realize them, suggest this trend towards effective Canadian G-7/8 leadership will continue. However, since the G-7/8 Summit ultimately depends on the leaders who design and deliver it, Canadian success depends crucially on whether Jean Chrétien himself will prove to be a foremost rather than a fading Prime Minister at Kananasksis.

Canada's growing leadership in the G-7/8 flows largely from several trends in the post-Cold War, rapidly globalizing, post-11 September world. These trends highlight the character of the G-7/8 as a concert among equals. The addition of Russia, and thereby the creation of a new G-8, has increased the predominant capabilities of the G-7/8 in the world, equalized capabilities among members within the still select club, and given Canada an enhanced rank. Intensifying globalization has rendered the US, Japan, and other G-8 members as vulnerable to global forces as Canada has long been. The 11 September attacks have deepened and broadened this sense of common vulnerability, reinforced the global centrality of

G-7/8 institutions in responding to such common enemies, and placed a premium on Canada's role as incoming chair. With their international experience and domestic political strength, Jean Chrétien and Paul Martin are in a strong position to make Kananaskis a major success, should they display the energy, flexibility, and vision required for global governance in the new twenty-first-century world.

AN OVERVIEW OF CANADA'S SUMMIT CONTRIBUTION

Canada's growing position as a principal summit power can first be seen in the available systematic evidence on the performance of the G-7/8 since its 1975 start. This evidence strongly suggests that Canada acts increasingly as an equally influential principal power.

Canada has been a substantially and increasingly successful summit host. The master grader of summit performance, Nicholas Bayne, has awarded the G-7 a C for Canada's first summit at Montebello in 1981, C- for Toronto in 1988; and B+ for Halifax in 1995 (Bayne, 2000: 195). Canada's average grade of C+ places it at the overall summit average. The evaluation of the Halifax Summit makes it the third-best in the history of this forum and the first-ranked in the third hosting cycle (Kirton and Takase, 2002).

This portrait is confirmed by a count of the specific, actionable, future-oriented commitments or concrete decisions that each summit produces (Kokotsis, 1999).[2] Pierre Trudeau's Montebello Summit produced 40 such commitments, while Brian Mulroney's Toronto Summit dropped to 27. The first summit that Chrétien hosted, at Halifax in 1995, produced 76 such decisions, making it considerably more productive than the Italian-hosted Naples Summit the year before (Kirton and Takase, 2002).

Canada, along with most summit members, has secured to a relatively high degree its priority objectives at each of the annual summits since 1995 (G-8 Research Group, 2001). Canada has an average grade of B+ and ranks in the top half of summit participants as a country that has never put in a performance below B-. On two occasions it has been tied for first place (measured in terms of attaining its summit goals).

Canada also complies with its summit commitments to a high and rising degree. More importantly, it has been joined in this regard in recent years by its more powerful partners. From 1975 to 1989 Canada ranked second as a faithful complier, with a score well above the average of summit members (von Furstenberg and Daniels, 1991). From 1988 to 1995, Canadian and US compliance with G-7 sustainable development and Russian assistance commitments showed Canada's score rise, with the US joining it in the high compliance club (Kokotsis, 1999). From 1996 to 2001 Canada again displayed a strong compliance record and again ranked second-highest in the group (G-8 Research Group, 2001). Of greater importance, however, is the soaring compliance level of most other summit members, as all members now keep their word and bear their share of burden in putting collective commitments into effect.

Canada has also made a substantial contribution to the institutional development of the G-7/8 system. Canada mounted a major program to secure wider acceptance of the international institutional reforms the G-7 approved in 1995 (Smith, 1996). At the ministerial level, Canada's 1981 Montebello Summit created the Trade Ministers Quadrilateral, the first stand-alone G-7 forum for ministers not regularly involved at the summit itself (Cohn, 2001). In 1994 Canada hosted a G-7 conference on financial assistance for Ukraine in Winnipeg. In December 1995, in Ottawa, Canada founded the G-7's Ministerial Meeting on Terrorism, a body that has met nine times since. More recently, Canada has done much to found, chair, and shape the G-20 forum of finance ministers and central bankers, in part by hosting its second ministerial meeting in Montreal in October 2000 and its third in Ottawa in November 2001 (Kirton, 2001a, 2001b).

CANADA'S SUMMIT DIPLOMACY, FROM HALIFAX 1995 TO GENOA 2001

A more detailed examination of Canadian diplomacy from Halifax in 1995 to Genoa in 2001 confirms this portrait. Canada's contribution can be charted against the three major clusters of roles that countries play in the G-7/8. The first cluster is that of a *supporter* of American initiatives and the neo-liberal policies demanded by the market in a globalizing age. The second is that of *mediator* between the conflicting initiatives of other members, in support of a consensus that may bear no particular relevance to distinctively Canadian concerns. The third is that of a *leader* that seeks and secures support from any and all summit members for distinctively Canadian preferences, interests, values, and visions of world order.

The leadership cluster[3] contains eight specific roles that run along a scale from four defensive ones through to their four offensive equivalents. In the defensive realm, the first role is *vulnerability compensation*—securing support from summit partners to compensate for national vulnerabilities. The second is *anti-priority prevention*—to deter damage to national priorities, interests, and values. The third is *defensive G-7/8 positionalism*—to prevent the erosion of Canada's place in the G-7/8 system and thus in global governance. The fourth is *anti-principle prevention*—to deter the adoption of principles, norms, rules, and decision-making procedures antithetical to Canada's distinctive national values and conception of a desirable world order.

Moving to the offensive realm, the fifth role is that of *global system stabilizer*—investing a proportionate share of resources to help others and the G-8 stabilize the global system in response to crisis and critical systemic needs. The sixth is that *of national priority adopter*—advancing and securing support for initiatives that advance Canadian policy priorities. The seventh is *G-7/8 system builder*—acting to build and broaden G-7/8 institutions in ways that reinforce both Canada's place within it and the place of the G-7/8 in global governance. The eighth and last leadership role is that of *national principle pioneer*—having the G-7/8 adopt and implement principles to strengthen and reshape global governance in accordance with Canada's distinctive national values. Against this framework, a review of Canada's G-7/8 diplomacy over the seven years since 1995 reveals relatively few supporter or mediator roles. It further shows a steady shift from exercising defensive to offensive leadership, culminating in successes in building the G-7/8 system and in shaping the global order.

Halifax 1995 is often judged to be a successful summit for its review and reform of the United Nations, Bretton Woods, and other international institutions, its handling of the delicate issue of Russian participation, and its advance of Canadian priorities such as sustainable development, the linkage between development assistance and excessive military expenditure, and the G-7 implementation review (Bayne, 2000; Smith, 1996; Boehm, 1996). The institutional review was actually launched by President Clinton at Naples in 1994, and this, along with the other Canadian accomplishments, had little lasting impact. Jean Chrétien's most distinctive contribution at that time was to maintain the singular summit focus on the issue of international institutional reform amid other claims in the autumn of 1994, and to find a formula for making this a far-reaching review. Canada also practised anti-priority and anti-principle prevention, saving the 1995 summit from disruption by a US–Japanese trade dispute over autos and from an ambitious last-minute US neo-liberal initiative for an 'Open Markets 2000' program.[4] At the end of its year as host, Canada served as a G-7/8 system-builder by creating the G-8 Ministerial Meeting on Terrorism.

Canada's most striking success at Halifax actually came on the invisible but ultimate issue of Quebec's separation from Canada. At Halifax, Canada had all members rally around to maintain Canada as a major power and hence a member of the club. Held on the eve of the initially envisaged date for the referendum on Quebec separation, the summit saw French President Jacques Chirac behave in such a way as to lend no comfort to the Quebec separatists, and to offer considerable support to the federalist cause. Originally slated for Quebec City, the hosting of the summit in Atlantic Canada, from where Canadians had shipped out twice in the twentieth century to help liberate France, conveyed a multi-layered message about how a separated Quebec would be cut off, and France along with it, from a globally positioned and engaged Canada. The message was driven home on the summit's first night when Jean Chrétien instantly rearranged the carefully planned schedule so the G-7 leaders could endorse a sudden initiative from Chirac on Bosnia, where French and Canadian troops had gone together in the G-7 vanguard in the spring of 1992. It was hardly surprising that Quebec's separatist politicians, considering their diminished chances at the polls as the road to and through Halifax unfolded, delayed their referendum until the autumn.

At Lyon in 1996, with a deficit-ridden Canada still reeling from its near-defeat in the 30 October 1995 referendum, the premium on vulnerability compensation remained. Canada was thus eager to show it was a full partner, as the G-7's only other francophone member, in the priorities set by France. These priorities, especially popular in francophone Quebec, were development, official development assistance (ODA), debt relief for the poorest, and Africa. Here Chrétien's Canada found it easy to be at one with France. A second area of successful defence concerned a rapidly downsizing and democratizing Russian, which shared Canada's preoccupation with combatting separatist forces. On the specific issue of Russia's G-7 participation, Canada, acting as anti-priority preventer, solved its difficulties by helping involve Russia so as to ensure victory for democratic forces in Russia's presidential elections, reassuring Ukraine and the many Canadians of Ukrainian origin that Ukraine would not be left behind, and closing Ukraine's Chernobyl reactor and strengthening nuclear safety in ways that protected the image and commercial prospects of Canada's CANDU program and nuclear non-proliferation objectives. Here nuclear-laden France and Russia served as sympathetic soulmates. A third accomplishment, taking Canada tentatively into the offensive realm of the G-7/8 system-builder, involved helping President Clinton secure his sudden need for anti-terrorist initiatives by extending the recently constructed anti-terrorism ministerial forum into a new Lyon Group.

At the 1997 Denver Summit of the Eight, with Quebec separation receding, Canadian prosperity and fiscal surplus returning, and Russia's arrival elevating Canada's summit rank, Canada was better positioned to go on the offensive (G-8 Research Group, 1997). However, America's booming economy, its triumphalist faith in its model for sustained growth, and its prerogatives as host constituted a formidable countervailing challenge. Canada, as supporter, endorsed host Bill Clinton's system-building initiatives to include the Russians as virtually a full participant in the summit and to advance an African agenda. Canada also acted as a defensive positionalist summit system-saver. Faced with a prospective European walkout over Clinton's invitation for the leaders to attend a social event wearing cowboy costumes he had provided, Chrétien broke the ice by declaring that he would attend but wear his own, all-Canadian cowboy attire. As anti-priority preventer Canada secured communiqué language that protected its position on the divisive climate change issue. Offensively, Chrétien skilfully secured acceptance from many hitherto reluctant leaders to accept a key Canadian order-building priority—the Convention on Anti-Personnel Landmines generated by the Ottawa Process.

Three weeks after Denver, Thailand devalued the baht, precipitating a two-year global financial crisis that by September 1998 had bankrupted American hedge fund long-term capital management (LTCM) and threatened to drive a liquidity-short US economy into financial collapse (Kirton, 2000a). On the road to Birmingham in 1998, Canada stopped the G-7 from having the International Monetary Fund (IMF) amend its Articles of Agreement to affirm the neo-liberal principle of capital account liberalization. As a system stabilizer Canada offered financial support to Thailand when its regional partners no longer could. It also joined with G-7 partners during the grim summer and autumn of 1998 to save the global economy and a now vulnerable America from collapse (Kirton, 1999a). At Birmingham, Canada supported the British in creating a permanent G-8 Summit and in having the leaders meet without attending ministers, in an informal setting, for an agenda focused on three major themes (Kirton and Kokotsis, 1998). Canada also worked effectively with Britain and France to further advance the Lyon-generated initiative for debt relief for the poorest countries. When nuclear explosions in Asia disrupted the carefully constructed summit agenda, Chrétien was assigned the role of contacting Pakistan to urge restraint on the G-8's behalf.

At Cologne in 1999, Canada worked with host Germany and a flexible array of partners to advance its key priorities (Kirton et al, 2001). It joined with the German 'red-green' coalition government headed by Gerhard Schroeder as a national principle pioneer to affirm a new Cologne consensus on socially sustainable globalization. Joined by Britain and France, Canada gave this new approach as a national priority adopter real life with further significant advances on debt relief for the poorest nations. As a national principle pioneer, it joined Britain to push for a G-7 and then G-8 consensus on using ground combat forces to complete the liberation of Yugoslavia's province of Kosovo, a threat that led to the voluntary withdrawal of Yugoslav forces from the territory and the end of the threat of genocide there. During the year Canada, as a system builder, joined with Germany and Italy to lead the G-8 into a new program on conflict prevention.

At Okinawa in 2000, Canada sympathized with host Japan's desire to focus on development and information technology and to have the latter theme presented in a development-friendly rather than American-proposed neo-liberal guise (Kirton and von Furstenberg, 2001). However, Canada made little progress in securing further debt relief or in devising a food safety regime that protected Canada's investments in genetically modified organisms. As a national principle pioneer, Canada did help the G-8 endorse the principle of cultural diversity. Canada was also able, as a national principle adopter, to convert the December 1999 foreign ministers' agreement in principle on conflict prevention into actionable decisions in five specific fields, largely composed of those where Canada's human security agenda had been in the lead.

At Genoa in 2001 Canada worked in tandem with the Italian host to devise a two-year agenda to culminate in Canada's year as summit host. Canada's objectives centred on poverty reduction, debt relief, combatting infectious disease, bridging the digital divide, forging the trade-development link, and conflict prevention. Despite Genoa's deadly distractions, Canada helped the summit focus on Africa, create a multi-billion dollar Global AIDS and Health Fund, and highlight the needs of developing countries in multilateral trade liberalization. It succeeded as a G-7/8 system builder by having the G-8 leaders appoint personal representatives for Africa, under the chair of Canada, to spearhead a dialogue and partnership premised on a new development paradigm. The report received from the Digital Opportunity Task-Force similarly emphasized bridging the digital divide. G-8 leaders directed that an action plan aimed at implementation be devised for discussion at Kananaskis. Canada worked with Italy and Germany to expand the G-8's work on conflict prevention into the environmental and gender fields.

EXPLANATIONS FOR CANADA'S GROWING G-7/8 CONTRIBUTION

Canada's increasingly successful practice of first defensive and then offensive leadership roles during the fourth summit cycle is well explained by the core components of the 'concert equality' model of G-7/8 performance, as refined to account for individual country performance within the summit system. Its application to current conditions also suggests favourable prospects for Canada's performance as host in 2002.

The first factor, 'concerted power', has been enhanced by the post-Cold War, rapidly globalizing, post-11 September system that has emerged during the past seven years. Since 1995, the global predominance of the G-7/8 has expanded due to Russia's admission as a full and now robustly growing member of a new G-8 and the downsizing of major emerging economies in the 1997–9 global financial crisis. Within the G-7/8, members' capabilities have become more equal with the revival of Russia, the relatively strong growth of Canada and Britain, the plunge of the United States into a sharpened recession since 11 September, the further fall of a long stagnant Japan, and a significant economic slowdown in third-ranked Germany. Only a return to explosive US growth or a soaring US dollar in the first half of 2002 could disturb this dynamic. In fact, the US economy appeared to have begun to turn out of the doldrums in the spring of 2002.

The most dramatic trend has been the equalization of vulnerability within the G-8. Over the past 20 years flows of foreign direct investment have knit G-7 members ever more tightly together (Kirton, 1999b, 2000b). The September 1998 collapse of LTCM and the 11 September terrorist attacks in New York and Washington have now made the US as vulnerable in its homeland as its less capable G-8 partners have long been. A cascade of successive shocks has also made the US aware of its comprehensive vulnerabilities. The 1997–9 financial crisis that affected the US and recent crises in Turkey and Argentina have led America to recognize its need for its G-7 partners and the international financial institutions they control. The terrorist assault on the World Trade Center on 11 September 2001, following the World Trade Center bombing of 1993, brought the fact and fear of vulnerability to the US in its deadliest form. Since G-7/8 leaders have personally faced the threat of an Al-Qaeda terrorist assault at their summits since 1996, they know first-hand how vulnerable they all are to this common enemy.

Within this configuration of capabilities, vulnerabilities, and systemic shocks, Canada occupies a relatively favourable place. During the fourth summit cycle Canada entered the upper tier of G-7/8 members in terms of economic growth and restored its fiscal surplus; indeed, it is now the only G-7 member in the black. As the G-8's earliest and deepest adapter to globalization (Doern and Kirton, 1996), and with a floating exchange rate, Canada experienced little new vulnerability from overseas financial crises. Moreover, the 11 September attacks left Canada as the only G-8 member not to have experienced a terrorist attack on its soil.

The second key factor in making the G-7/8 an effective concert is constricted participation. The restricted membership has remained, even with the addition of Russia as a member since 1997–8 and the slow expansion of European Union (EU) involvement in the system. Relevant here have been the continuation of the G-7 Summit and the 1998 emergence of a way for seamlessly moving from G-7 to G-8 at a single summit. This formula will continue at Kananaskis, where members will decide whether Russia will get the opportunity to host its first real G-8 summit in 2003. Limited and balanced representation at the summit has also largely been constant throughout the fourth cycle, with only the Dutch Prime Minister joining the regulars in

1997. For Kananaskis, the Spanish Prime Minister will be added for the first time as the representative of the EU Council.

Limited and balanced outside participation has also been a feature of the fourth cycle. The G-7 has brought a much broader array of international organizations and countries to the event, thus increasing its political legitimacy, sensitivity, and functional expertise. The outsiders have offset the Eurocentricity of Russian membership and brought a global perspective. This trend should continue at Kananaskis, through an outreach event involving leaders from Africa and the heads of global institutions, although with the summit now reduced to two days there are limits to the effective dialogue that can take place.

The depth and breadth of G-7/8 ministerial institutions have increased significantly during the fourth cycle. Since 1992 the G-7/8 has bred six new and stand-alone ministerial institutions. Since 1995 these have involved outside countries and organizations and members of civil society, just as the official-level bodies of the G-7/8 increasingly have included representatives from outside the summit nations. The 1999 birth of the G-20 and the Financial Stability Forum has also furthered the G-7's global outreach (Kirton, 2001b).

These changes in G-7/8 involvement have been of particular advantage to Canada. The addition of Russia, as noted above, has improved Canada's rank and given it a new coalition partner with compatible interests, particularly on issues related to natural resources. Canada has had a historically close relationship with the Dutch, while the presence of the Spanish at Kananaskis will mark the end of the Canadian–Spanish turbot war tensions that hung over the Halifax Summit in 1995. Canada has been well placed in the multilateral institutions and with the countries that have participated in the summit from 1996 onward. It will welcome the African leaders to Kananaskis as fellow members of the Commonwealth and la Francophonie. Finally, Paul Martin's skilfully executed role as the seminal chair, twice host, and lead architect of the G-20 has afforded Canada a powerful international institutional instrument for shaping global order.

The third factor of common purpose has also been enhanced by the systemic changes of the past seven years. Within the G-7/8, the 1996 and 2000 presidential elections in Russia and Russia's 1999 response to G-8 pressure over Kosovo and Chechnya showed that Russia was internalizing the deeper democratic and foundational G-7 norms of respect for human rights. The advent in the 1990s of electorally created change in the governing party in Japan also deepened the practice of democracy there. Globally, the legitimacy and effectiveness of the G-8 has been enhanced by the completion of the democratic revolution in all of Europe, the advent of democracy in Indonesia, and the maintenance of democracy in all of the Americas outside Cuba. Also useful have been the admission of China to the WTO and the broad acceptance by poor countries of development strategies based on integration with the international economy and its institutions.

The 1990s also broadened and deepened the shared systemic perspective and sense of responsibility among G-7/8 members. Whereas the 1994 Mexican meltdown was largely left to the United States and Canada (Kirton, 1995b), the Asian financial crisis of 1997–9 saw all G-7 members transcend regionalism to offer the supplementary financial support to save the most afflicted countries and the global system from the worst effects of this crisis. In 1999 Russia abandoned its traditional identity as a defender of Slavic Yugoslavia to accept the G-7 consensus to inject ground forces for combat to complete the liberation of Kosovo from Slobodan Milosovic's Serbian forces. More broadly, Japan has now deployed peacekeeping forces to distant regions and has sent its naval forces to the distant Indian Ocean. The strong support among all G-8 countries for the war against terrorism in Afghanistan and the weak support for this American-led initiative outside the G-8, suggest that this shared sense of systemic responsibility is deeply grounded in the leaders and citizens of the G-8 (Walton, 2001: A13).

In recent years a shared political philosophy among summit leaders has also arisen, in the form of a third-way centrist coalition, led by former US President Clinton, Britain's Prime Minister Tony Blair, Germany's Prime Minister Gerhard Schroeder, Italy's prime ministers, and Canada's Chrétien (with only France's Chirac representing a formerly dominant right). This prevailing third-way coalition culminated in a shift at the Cologne Summit of 1999 from a dominant neo-liberal ideology towards a more socially sustainable approach to globalization (Kirton and Freytag, 2001) and, consequently, an emphasis on cultural diversity and on the need to combat the digital divide. However, the more recent arrival of US President Bush and Prime Minister Sergio Berlusconi of Italy in 2001, and of Russia's Vladimir Putin the previous year, together with the advent of a reformist Prime

Minister, Junichiro Koizumi, in Japan, has now produced a more even division. This philosophical divide did not detract from the Genoa Summit, nor is there much evidence that such divisions are fatal for summit success (Kirton, 1989). Nonetheless, Jean Chrétien's will and skill in bringing George Bush into the existing consensus will do much to determine the fate of the Kananaskis Summit.

Yet, even here there are deeper ties that bind. Canada was in the G-7 vanguard in supporting human rights, including over Hong Kong in 1997 and 1998 and in regard to Kosovo in 1999. Although Canadians are evenly divided on whether the 11 September attacks were on America alone or on America and its allies, including Canada (*Maclean's*, 2002: 38), apart from Americans, of course, Canadians generally have been the most supportive, among the citizens of G-8 countries, for the US-led military campaign in Afghanistan and are among the more active of those supporting the use of their own armed forces in the campaign.

The fourth factor of political control by popularly elected leaders has also made for successful summitry. In recent years the G-7/8 has had little electoral uncertainty and leader inexperience to distract it. In the year leading up to June 2002, it is likely that only France's Chirac will face a personal national electoral test. His re-election would make the Kananaskis summiteers a relatively experienced group, with no newcomers at all at the table. The general domestic popularity of all G-7/8 leaders has also contributed to past performance and is a promising condition for success at Kananaskis.

Jean Chrétien will be the unrivalled dean of the club at Kananaskis, having been in national-level electoral politics since 1963 and having attended his first G-7 Summit as Canada's Finance Minister in 1978. Offering strong support at the Finance Minister's level is Paul Martin, who is the only G-7 finance minister to have been at all meetings since 1994. Both men won their third majority mandate in 2000 and are not due for another electoral test for the three years. More broadly, the experience of leaders at Kananaskis tends to run in an offsetting fashion to the distribution of relative capability among their countries, with the leaders of the US and Japan coming to Kananaskis with only one year of G-7/8 experience.

Chrétien should also come to Kananaskis with a large measure of domestic support. Support for separation in Quebec has plummeted. Having long faced a divided opposition distracted by the need to recover from internecine warfare and a leadership campaign,

Chrétien sports unusually high and stable personal and party approval ratings. Moreover, recent polling suggests that Canadians continue to support and trust the G-7/8 Summit. A Strategic Counsel poll of 1,200 Canadians taken in late November 2001 indicates that, unlike Alberta's Premier Klein, 77 per cent of Canadians want the Kananaskis Summit to continue, compared to only 23 per cent who say it should be cancelled. A majority 63 per cent blame the anti-globalization protestors, and only 13 per cent blame the police, when violent confrontations between the two take place (*Maclean's*, 2002: 39).

CANADA'S CONCERTED RESPONSE TO 11 SEPTEMBER 2001

Given these favourable conditions, it was understandable that Chrétien's immediate reaction to the terrorist attacks in the United States on 11 September was to mobilize the G-8 forum to design and deliver a collective response. Within the G-8 Canada was second only to Britain in the speed and size of its military contribution to the American-led campaign against the Taliban and Al-Qaeda in Afghanistan. Canada also worked to make the broader linkages, in finance, global growth, the natural environment, African poverty reduction, post-conflict reconstruction and elsewhere that would prevent the threat from recurring once the current anti-terrorism campaign was won. At the same time, Chrétien remained determined that the 11 September terrorists would not hijack the G-7/8 Summit agenda agreed to at Genoa, and that Kananaskis would unfold the way he had long felt it should (Anderson, 2001).

The day after 11 September, Chrétien, along with Italian chair Sergio Berlusconi and Russia's Vladimir Putin, publicly called for the G-8 to be used as the dominant vehicle for politically defining Canada and its allies' response. Chrétien brushed aside Ralph Klein's suggestion that Canada's G-8 meeting be cancelled or moved. Having sent the initial signal, Chrétien then left subsequent initiatives largely to his major ministers.

On 12 September, G-7 finance ministers issued their first of several statements condemning the attack, offering condolences to the victims' families, pledging to prevent disruption to the global economy, and promising to provide liquidity as required. In the following weeks, Finance Minister Paul Martin and his colleagues moved quickly to strengthen the efforts of the G-7/8 against terrorist financing, which had begun in 1989 with the establishment of the Financial

Task Force but whose implementation had been sluggish. By mid-December 2001, 196 countries and other jurisdictions had expressed support for the campaign against terrorist financing, 139 had issued blocking orders, and US deputy treasury secretary Kenneth Dam had expressed his satisfaction with current G-8 and G-20 efforts to share financial intelligence (Dam, 2001).

Canada's most prominent display of G-8-centred leadership came from Paul Martin, in his hosting in Ottawa on 17–19 November of the G-20, the IMF's International Monetary and Financial Committee (IMFC), and the Development Committee of the IMF and World Bank (Kirton, 2001a). While 11 September had led most multilateral institutions, including the UN, IMF, and World Bank, to cancel their scheduled summits or ministerial meetings, G-7 finance ministers moved with minimal delay to hold their regular meeting in Washington. When India, as the host of the G-20, cancelled its scheduled November 2001 meeting, Paul Martin stepped into the breach. In a short six weeks, despite security anxieties and the desire of IMFC's chair, Gordon Brown, to hold the meeting in his native Britain, Canada hosted the otherwise stranded forum in Ottawa. This effort enabled Canada to take an unprecedentedly deep, broad, and action-oriented G-20-created consensus on terrorism financing and have it approved and moved into implementation by the more broadly based and operational Bretton Woods twins, the IMF and World Bank. Moreover, Canada had the G-20 adopt as an agenda and approve far-reaching conclusions in regard to combatting financial terrorism and furthering two other Kananaskis Summit priorities—generating global growth and reducing poverty in developing countries.

In the foreign policy sphere, the G-8 foreign ministers' meeting traditionally held on the eve of the opening of the UN General Assembly on 30 September took place, along with the delayed UN session, in New York on 11 November 2001. The discussion at the dinner was devoted entirely to the war against terrorism and developments in the Middle East. With US and alliance forces having just reached the outskirts of Kabul, US Secretary of State Colin Powell freely shared the latest developments with his G-8 colleagues. Among other things, the group discussed the question of how to put Osama bin Laden on trial should he be captured. At the end of December, G-8 foreign ministers again sprung into action, issuing under Russian leadership a collective statement calling on India and Pakistan to move back from the brink of a terrorist-inspired conflict in Kashmir.

In the security sphere, Canada suggested to its G-8 colleagues, following its 1995 Halifax experience, that it host a G-8 meeting bringing together ministers responsible for security and foreign affairs. As the year ended, the suggestion had not been taken up. However in late November, the G-8's group on terrorism met. This group was now fused with the Lyon Group, and the G-8 group on non-proliferation was charged with determining how it could contribute to the anti-terrorism campaign.

In the defence sphere, Canadian leadership was shown in the early, large contribution of Canadian naval, air, and ground forces that Canada dispatched to assist the US coalition in Afghanistan and the Persian Gulf. Canada extended its contribution in December with the deployment of long-range patrol aircraft, and again in January when it sent combat ground troops to the Kandahar front. The calculus behind Canada's investment was well captured in then Foreign Minister John Manley's memorable phrase, 'You can't sit at the G8 table and then, when the bill comes, go to the washroom' (Wells, 2001).

THE ROAD TO KANANASKIS

As Canada moved into its position as 2002 chair of the G-8 Summit system, it acted steadily, if slowly, to shape the event in its preferred image. Reinforced by his attachment to the Montebello model of 1981 and his vindication in sticking to the previously endorsed agenda in 1995, Chrétien struggled to deliver a small, informal, private summit focused on reducing poverty in Africa.

Amid the violence of the Genoa Summit, Chrétien acted on his instinct to switch Canada's 2002 summit from its intended site in Ottawa to Kananaskis, Alberta. The move was inspired by the civil society protest and violence and the terrorist threats at Genoa, the way the media and leaders reacted to these events, the desire to give western Canada its turn as G-8 host, and his desire to reproduce the Montebello model on the mountaintop. This meant an isolated retreat-like setting, small delegations of no more than 30 per country, maximum informal dialogue among leaders, minimum pomp and ceremony, most of the critical or unmanageable media kept far away, and no serious participation by civil society. Chrétien even chose to dispense with the traditional carefully prepared concluding communiqué that authoritatively informs the world of G-8 decisions.

To deliver his summit, Chrétien appointed Robert Fowler as his personal representative for both the G-8 and for the parallel African dialogue. Fowler, a senior, skilled Canadian diplomat, had been at Montebello and at Genoa as Canada's ambassador to Italy, and also had been involved in Africa. As Canada's ambassador to the United Nations Fowler had recently led the international community in constructing a regime against the illicit diamond trade that fuelled Africa's wars.

At the final meeting of senior G-8 officials hosted by the outgoing Italian chair in early December 2001, Canada proposed that Kananaskis should avoid a diffuse, comprehensive agenda. Rather, the meetings should focus exclusively on the three themes of combatting terrorism, generating global growth, and reducing poverty in Africa, with other subjects left for the separate pre-summit meetings of G-7/8 ministers. These include ministers of finance on 7–8 February in Ottawa, labour on 25–7 April in Montreal, environment on 12–14 April in Banff, and energy on 2–3 May in Detroit, as well as the others on trade, finance (in Victoria), and foreign affairs.

Canada sought to convey three major messages at Kananaskis. The first is that the world must go beyond the decades-old philosophy of development to ensure that recipients, civil society, and private-sector actors participate fully in the process. The second is that medium-term prospects for growth in the G-7 and global community are good, that productivity-enhancing structural policies to sustain growth are needed, and that alternative approaches for different regions and countries may be required. The third is that G-8 and global commitments on combatting terrorism must be fully implemented, must be comprehensive, and must be backed by the capacity-building required to ensure their effectiveness.

In delivering its first priority of reducing poverty in Africa, Canada began by taking seriously the proclamation of African leaders in their New Plan for African Development (NEPAD) that they represented a new generation with new domestic commitments and new approaches to development. The challenge was to have the G-8 and Africa agree on a new paradigm and find the real resources to make it work. This required having the IMF and World Bank, in their poverty reduction strategies, invite recipient countries and their citizens to take ownership, review lending conditionality so as to restrict the costly paper and personnel burden imposed on developing countries, and review the program for highly indebted poor countries.

Canada sought to emphasize recipients' responsibilities, notably good governance through the rule of law, civil society participation, more egalitarian social policy, sustainable development, an educated workforce, and a sound banking sector.

Canada recognized the need to raise new resources to finance development, both by enhancing the levels of traditional ODA and by instituting innovative global mechanisms. Aware of the large bill required to rebuild Africa, hoping to inspire its G-8 colleagues and others to do more, and led by Chrétien's directive not to forget Africa, Canada increased ODA spending by $1 billion in its December 2001 budget and added a special fund for Africa of an additional $500 million, to come from year-end surpluses over the following three years. On the larger challenge Canada noted the favourable response that British Finance Minister Gordon Brown's proposal for a US $50 billion trust fund for Africa was starting to receive. Canada also took a close analytic look at several other suggestions: a Tobin tax,[5] a new allocation of special drawing rights, a carbon tax, an air travel tax, an armaments tax, and a return to the Pearsonian aid targets of the 1960s that the public and private sectors pledged to meet. Canada's strategy, along with that of the US, was to move in an integrated fashion from the spring 2002 United Nations Conference on Financing for Development in Monterrey, Mexico, through the Kananaskis Summit to the 'Rio-plus-10' World Summit on Sustainable Development in Johannesburg in September 2002.

In financing development, Canada favoured in principle President Bush's idea of having the International Development Agency (IDA) give money as grants rather than as long-term concessional loans. A Canadian financial analysis showed that the approach was affordable. However, since the Europeans strongly resisted it, Canada foresaw a compromise that yielded a significantly larger portion of IDA funding given in pure grant form.

Another element of the Canadian approach was to continue, through the G-7 process, Canada's long-standing effort to construct a regime for private-sector participation in response to financial crises. Here Canada could now build on the formal G-20 agreement to have G-20 deputies conduct a detailed operational study of issues such as how to immunize countries from domestic lawsuits in the face of an international 'standstill' mechanism, and to determine who would serve as the neutral arbiter in making a standstill mechanism work. The December 2001 debt default by Argentina, the world's largest ever, infused the Canadian thrust with broader support.

On the theme of generating growth, Canada sought to emphasize that, beyond Japan, the fundamentals were sound for good medium-term growth. Thus, more attention needed to be paid to enhancing productivity, especially as the costs incurred as a result of the anti-terrorism campaign were now being priced into the G-7 economic systems. The events of 11 September generated expenditures and all national policies, the Canadian government believed, should be scrutinized for their contribution to productivity, which had the potential to raise growth levels on a permanent basis. An emphasis on productivity could help resolve the existing debate between Europe and the US over whether fiscal integrity or fiscal stimulus was most needed now to boost growth. The success of trade ministers at the World Trade Organization (WTO) meeting in Doha in launching a new round of multilateral trade liberalization talks was welcomed as an important element in productivity-based global economic growth.

The final theme of combatting terrorism included pressing for implementation of the G-20 Action Plan on Terrorist Financing. In this instance Canada would follow the G-7/G-20/IMF strategy to make the new regime fully global and devoid of holes. In contrast to France and Italy, who sought to ensure compliance by relying on sanctions alone, Canada urged the need for capacity-building as well. Representing the Commonwealth Caribbean in the international financial institutions and recalling the time and trouble it took to develop its own system of financial tracking, Canada sought to mobilize ODA, technical assistance, and human assistance to developing countries, including emerging markets.

Taken together, these three themes represented one of the more ambitious agendas put forward by a summit host. While terrorism and growth were imposed by an unforgiving world on a relatively unaffected Canada, the insistence on highlighting poverty reduction in Africa showed Canada's leadership in setting the agenda and its de facto alliance with its summit soulmates in Japan, Italy, Britain, and France. Should Canada be able to maintain the momentum, backed by its December 2001 budget funds as a global system stabilizer, and act as a national principle pioneer to create a new North-South paradigm for development, it would finally deliver the dream of Pierre Trudeau and his ministers at Montebello in 1981 and produce a vision for a new global order designed on Canadian ideals.

As the 26–8 June 2002 Kananaskis Summit drew near, systemic, societal, and global forces offered favourable conditions for the realization of the Canadian agenda. Yet substantial risk factors remained. The first was whether an international crisis would erupt that did not fit easily into the predefined thematic trilogy. The second was whether the African leaders could agree—among themselves and with the G-8—on a credible new development paradigm in time for its anointment at Kananaskis. The third was whether Chrétien could convince his neighbour, President Bush, to come to Kananaskis for the entire summit and make Canada's preferred agenda appeal to the President's rather different concerns. The fourth was whether Chrétien could convince the media, civil society, and the Canadian public, so cut off from the summit, that three genuinely productive summits—with the African leaders, the G-7, and the G-8—could be held in the space of two days. And the fifth was whether Jean Chrétien could mobilize the personal energy and enthusiasm to secure from his summit partners the painful compromises required to put his far-reaching plan into effect. While no one was prepared to say that Canada was a principal summit power with a fading Prime Minister, as 2002 unfolded there were doubts as to whether Chrétien on his mountaintop would have the vision and vigour that Trudeau had at Monetbello in his day.

NOTES

1. Summits are hosted in seven-year cycles that began in 1975. The first cycle ran from 1975 (at Montebello) to 1981, the second from 1982 to Toronto in 1988, the third from 1989 to Halifax in 1995, and the fourth to Kananaskis in 2002.
2. Although G-7/8 and other meetings often are dismissed as 'talk shops' or places where states merely mouth vague generalities, such commitments prove these international gatherings are important decision-making fora whose participants are fully prepared to have their subsequent implementing behaviour monitored and assessed against hard criteria.
3. The leadership role demonstrates that the G-7/8 is a concert of equals in which any member, even the weakest, can successfully veto and initiate successful proposals.
4. The 'Open Markets 2000' program was a proposal by President Clinton that the G-7 endorsed at Halifax. This called for a new round of multilateral trade liberalization in which participants would agree to open their markets by the year 2000.
5. Speculative currency trading in 'hot' (short-term) money has potentially devastating effects on poorer nations. By marginally increasing the cost of currency trading by instituting a transaction fee, the so-called Tobin tax proposed by

economist James Tobin would stabilize the volatility induced by capital flight, thereby reducing the risk of a debt crisis. Advocates estimate that $50 billion to $300 billion could be raised annually to fight poverty.

REFERENCES

Anderson, David. 2001. 'Notes for an address by the Honourable David Anderson, Minister of the Environment, to the Canadian Institute of International Affairs', Ottawa, 27 Oct.

Bayne, Nicholas. 2000. *Hanging In There: The G7 and G8 Summit in Maturity and Renewal.* Aldershot: Ashgate.

Bergsten, C. Fred, and C. Randall Henning. 1996. *Global Economic Leadership and the Group of Seven.* Washington: Institute for International Economics.

Black, Conrad. 1997–8. 'Taking Canada Seriously', *International Journal* 53 (Winter): 1–17.

Boehm, Peter. 1996. 'There Was a Summit in Halifax', *Bout de Papier* 13 (Spring): 5–7.

Campbell, Don. 2002. 'A Canadian Perspective on the Birmingham Summit'. Available at: <www.G8.utoronto.ca>.

Canadian Foreign Policy. 1995. 'Canada and the 1995 G7 Halifax Summit: Developing Canada's Positions', special issue, 3 (Spring).

Cohn, Theodore. 2001. 'Securing Multilateral Trade Liberalization: International Institutions in Conflict and Convergence', in John Kirton and George von Furstenberg, eds, *New Directions in Global Economic Governance: Managing Globalization in the Twenty-First Century.* Aldershot: Ashgate, 189–218.

Dam, Kenneth. 2001. 'Hunting Down Dirty Cash', *Financial Times,* 12 Dec., 17.

Department of Foreign Affairs and International Trade (DFAIT). 1995. *Canada in the World.* Ottawa: Canada Communications Group, Feb.

Dewitt, David, and John Kirton. 1983. *Canada as a Principal Power.* Toronto: John Wiley.

Doern, G. Bruce, and John Kirton. 1996. 'Foreign Policy', in Doern, Leslie Pal, and Brian Tomlin, eds, *Border Crossings: The Internationalization of Canadian Public Policy.* Toronto: Oxford University Press, 237–64.

Doran, Charles. 1996. 'Will Canada Unravel?', *Foreign Affairs* 75 (Sept.–Oct.): 97–109.

Eayrs, James. 1975. 'Defining a New Place for Canada in the Hierarchy of World Powers', *International Perspectives* (May–June): 15–24.

Frechette, Louise. 1995. 'The Halifax Summit: A Canadian Perspective', *North American Outlook* 3 (June): 7–13.

G-8 Research Group. 1997. 'Country Performance Assessments for the Denver Summit: Overall Scores'. Available at: <www.g7.utoronto.ca/g7/evaluations/1997denver/overasmn.htm>.

———. 2001. *Analytical Studies.* Available at: <www.g8.utoronto.ca>.

Gotlieb, Allan. 1987. *Canada and the Economic Summits: Power and Responsibility,* Bissell Paper No. 1. Toronto: University of Toronto Centre for International Studies.

Hampson, Fen, and Maureen Molot. 1996. 'Being Heard and the Role of Leadership', in Fen Hampson and Maureen Molot, eds, *Canada Among Nations 1996: Big Enough To Be Heard.* Ottawa: Carleton University Press, 3–20.

Hajnal, Peter I., and John J. Kirton. 2000. 'The Evolving Role and Agenda of the G7/G8: A North American Perspective', *NIRA Review* 7, 2 (Spring): 5–10.

Harrington, Carol. 2001. 'G-8 Summit security costs to top $100 million', *Toronto Star*, 27 Dec., A31.

Ikenberry, John. 1993. 'Salvaging the G7', *Foreign Affairs* 72 (Spring): 132–9.

Keating, Tom. 2002. *Canada and World Order: The Multilateralist Tradition in Canadian Foreign Policy*, 2nd edn. Toronto: Oxford University Press.

Kirton, John. 1989. 'Contemporary Concert Diplomacy: The Seven-Power Summit and the Management of International Order', paper prepared for the International Studies Association annual conference, 29 Mar.–1 Apr., London, England.

————. 1993. 'The Seven Power Summit and the New Security Agenda', in David Dewitt, David Haglund, and Kirton, eds, *Building a New Global Order: Emerging Trends in International Relations*. Toronto: Oxford University Press, 335–57.

————. 1994. 'Exercising Concerted Leadership: Canada's Approach to Summit Reform', *The International Spectator* 29 (Apr.–June), 161–76.

————. 1995a. 'The Diplomacy of Concert: Canada, the G7 and the Halifax Summit', *Canadian Foreign Policy* 3 (Spring): 63–80.

————. 1995b. 'The G7, the Halifax Summit and International Financial System Reform', *North America Outlook* (June).

————. 1997. 'Le Role du G7 Dans Le Couple Integration Regionale/Securite Globale', *Etudes Internationales* 28 (juin): 255–70.

————. 1998. 'The Emerging Pacific Partnership: Japan, Canada, and the United States at the G-7 Summit', in Michael Fry, Kirton, and Mitsuru Kurosawa, *The North Pacific Triangle: The United States, Japan and Canada at Century's End*. Toronto: University of Toronto Press.

————. 1999a. 'Canada as a Principal Financial Power: G-7 and IMF Diplomacy in the Crisis of 1997–9', *International Journal* 54 (Autumn): 603–24.

————. 1999b. 'Economic Co-operation: Summitry, Institutions and Structural Change', in John Dunning and Gavin Boyd, eds, *Structural Change and Co-operation in the Global Economy*. Cheltenham: Edward Elgar.

————. 2000a. 'The Dynamics of G7 Leadership in Crisis Response and System Reconstruction', in Karl Kaiser, Kirton, and Joseph Daniels, eds, *Shaping a New International Financial System: Challenges of Governance in a Globalizing World*. Aldershot: Ashgate, 65–94.

————. 2000b. 'Deepening Integration and Global Governance: America as a Globalized Partner', in Tom Brewer and Gavin Boyd, eds, *Globalizing America: The USA in World Integration*. Cheltenham: Edward Elgar.

————. 2001a. 'Guiding Global Economic Governance: The G20, the G7 and the International Monetary Fund at Century's Dawn', in Kirton and George von Furstenberg, eds, *New Directions in Global Economic Governance: Managing Globalization in the Twenty-First Century*. Aldershot: Ashgate.

————. 2001b. 'The G20: Representativeness, Effectiveness and Leadership in Global Governance', in Kirton, Joseph Daniels, and Andreas Freytag, eds, *Guiding Global Order: G8 Governance in the Twenty-First Century*. Aldershot: Ashgate.

———— and Joseph Daniels. 1999. 'The Role of the G8 in the New Millennium', in Michael Hodges, Kirton, and Joseph Daniels, eds, *The G8's Role in the New Millennium*. Aldershot: Ashgate.

————, Joseph Daniels, and Andreas Freytag, eds. 2001. *Guiding Global Order: G8 Governance in the Twenty-First Century*. Aldershot: Ashgate.

———— and Ella Kokotsis. 1998. 'Revitalizing the G7: Prospects for the 1998 Birmingham Summit of the Eight', *International Journal* 53 (Winter): 38–56.

———— and Junichi Takase, eds. 2002 (forthcoming). *New Directions in Global Political Governance: The G8 and International Order in the Twenty-First Century*. Aldershot: Ashgate.

———— and George von Furstenberg, eds. 2001. *New Directions in Global Economic Governance: Managing Globalization in the Twenty-First Century*. Aldershot: Ashgate.

Kokotsis, Eleanore. 1999. *Keeping International Commitments: Compliance, Credibility and the G7, 1988–1995*. New York: Garland.

Maclean's. 2002. 'Maclean's Year-End Poll: Since September 11', *Maclean's* 114, 53 (31 Dec. 2001–Jan. 2002).

Putnam, Robert, and Nicholas Bayne, eds. 1987. *Hanging Together: Co-operation and Conflict in the Seven-Power Summit*, 2nd edn. London: Sage Publications.

Smith, Gordon. 1996. 'Canada and the Halifax Summit', in Fen Hampson and Maureen Molot, eds, *Canada Among Nations 1996: Big Enough To Be Heard*. Ottawa: Carleton University Press, 83–94.

Toronto Star. 2001. 'Summit too costly', 28 Dec., A38.

von Furstenberg, George, and Joseph Daniels. 1991. 'Policy Undertakings by the Seven "Summit" Countries: Ascertaining the Degree of Compliance', *Carnegie-Rochester Conference Series of Public Policy* 35: 267–308.

Walton, Dawn. 2001. 'Support for U.S.-led war high in G-7, low elsewhere', *Globe and Mail*, 22 Dec., A13.

Wells, Paul, and Sheldon Alberts. 2001. 'We don't pull our weight: Manley', *National Post*, 5 Oct.

Wolfe, Robert. 1995. 'Should Canada Stay in the Group of Seven', *Canadian Foreign Policy* 3 (Spring): 47–62.

11

In Search of a Hemispheric Role: Canada and the Americas

In the year prior to the tragic and dramatic terrorist attacks on New York and Washington in September 2001, Canada and the United States placed a high degree of importance on hemispheric affairs, in particular pressing forward with the agenda on the Free Trade Area of the Americas (FTAA). Canada has also played an increasingly significant role in the Organization of American States (OAS). César Gaviria, OAS Secretary-General, observed at Prime Minister Jean Chrétien's presentation to that body in February 2001 that Canadian entry into the OAS in 1990 has 'reinvigorated the Organization, providing a new perspective on—and a new approach to—the inter-American system' (OAS *Weekly Press Reports*, 1 Feb. 2001).

Canada was a major player early in the decade in the establishment of the OAS Unit for the Promotion of Democracy. Elections Canada has been an important contributor to electoral reform and the mechanics of electoral operations in the Americas during the past decade, and in June 2000 Canada hosted the General Assembly of the OAS in Windsor, Ontario, and the controversial Summit of the Americas in Quebec City in April 2001, building on the agenda-setting of the first two summits, in Miami in 1994 and Santiago in 1998. At Windsor, Canada was a leading nation in establishing a new democracy fund and in urging member countries to engage in resolving the Peruvian political crisis (Cooper and Legler, 2001). Free trade, the conclusion of a democracy provision in the Quebec City Summit declaration, the stimulation of economic development in the Americas, and the social agenda, which was identified as 'Realizing Human Potential' at Quebec, and the civil society dissent from the globalization trends—these were issues that attracted the attention of leaders, the media, and the general public through mid-2001.

Canadian foreign policy towards the Americas during the Liberal government of Prime Minister Jean Chrétien has tended to vary in substance and tone according to who held the position of Minister of Foreign Affairs. This chapter encompasses the years of transition from Lloyd Axworthy to John Manley.[1] Axworthy was strongly committed to the pursuit of a human security agenda in the Americas and elsewhere, with the result that his approach, notably where relations with Cuba were concerned, frequently irritated US officials. He brought a definitive ideological approach to Canadian foreign policy, somewhat reminiscent of Woodrow Wilson's approach in the United States during and after World War I. Like Wilson, Axworthy was an academic with a sophisticated knowledge of world affairs. That knowledge, combined with a high level of energy and commitment to the issues he addressed, contributed to a very active several years in the Foreign Affairs ministry. Axworthy was quite proactive in the Americas, travelling to such troubled countries as Cuba and Colombia to emphasize that Canada had a role to play in the region that was distinct from that of the US. His emphasis was on improving the human condition in the Americas, with a focus on social and economic development, enhancing environmental conditions, and containing narcotics traffic by means short of escalated military conflict. There was also a reasonably clear demarcation of focus on policy towards the Americas between Axworthy and Prime Minister Chrétien, with the Prime Minister concerned primarily with trade expansion.

Axworthy's retirement from public office in the fall of 2000 and the appointment of former Ministry of Industry John Manley represented a change in style and substance. Manley's approach was pragmatic, non-ideological, less anti-military, less overtly antagonistic to the United States, and concerned more with the basic issues of expanded trade in the Americas, including the FTAA, than with Axworthy's human security agenda. Indeed, the term 'human security' gradually receded from the prominence it had enjoyed in the language of the Department of Foreign Affairs and International Trade.

The terrorist attacks in September 2001 marked a fundamental shift in the focus of leaders and the public. After 11 September the print and electronic media were consumed with the war that the US and its coalition, including Canada, waged against the Taliban government of Afghanistan for harbouring Osama bin Laden. The Israel–Palestine conflict also intensified in that period. Fear of terrorist attacks, including a significant preoccupation with biological and chemical warfare that was triggered by an anthrax scare in the fall of 2001, displaced much of the normal daily business of both North American governments and pushed the 'Americas' agenda off the front pages and onto the cold back burners of Canadian and American leaders.

Although the issues had shifted, the Organization of American States and its members immediately became engaged in the larger conflict, much as they had in the Cold War years. In 2001, however, there was even more solidarity with US goals. Only a week after the attacks, Secretary of State Colin Powell called on the Foreign Ministers of the Americas meeting at the OAS to strengthen the Inter-American Committee against Terrorism. OAS Secretary-General Gaviria, former President of Colombia, called for unified action to combat terrorism, suggesting apocalyptically that 'if we do not punish terrorism, it will take over our lives in every corner of the universe' (OAS *Weekly Press Reports*, 5, 21 Sept. 2001). The OAS invoked the collective security and reciprocal assistance provisions of the 1947 Rio Treaty, on the grounds that the attack on the United States was an attack on all the states of the Americas. The foreign ministers also adopted several other resolutions calling on all states to collaborate in identifying, capturing, and punishing terrorists and their sponsors. At the same time the resolutions stressed that the war on terrorism should be conducted with respect for law, human rights, and democratic institutions.

Canada, though a member of the OAS, is not a signatory to the Rio Treaty. In practice, this made no discernible difference in the

Canadian response to the US war on terrorism. Foreign Minister Manley's language at the September 2001 meeting of hemispheric foreign ministers was as strong as Gaviria's. Manley contended that it was 'critical' that the 'international community stand united against terrorism and its perpetrators. There can be no cracks in our defence—no rifts to exploit, no vulnerabilities to embolden the terrorists' (DFAIT, 2001a). Manley suggested on that occasion that the states of the Americas could contribute to the war on terrorism in a variety of ways, including financial regulation, enhanced co-operation among law enforcement and security agencies, and promotion of the newly adopted Inter-American Democratic Charter.

This chapter is concerned primarily with the role of Canada in the Americas prior to the events of September 2001, but it is critical to understand that the ground shifted substantially thereafter. Not only did Canada join the US military operation against the Taliban and Al-Qaeda, but it was also affected by the general anxiety over terrorism since there were demonstrable links of the 11 September terrorists to Canada (see Chapter 8). In addition, Canadians were preoccupied with the anthrax scare and with the debate over the impact of tightened security on traditional civil liberties. The economic recession that deepened in the fall of 2001 was a further distraction from the previously heightened interest in Canada's relationship with Latin America and the Caribbean. As much, therefore, as issues such as the FTAA and economic and social development in the Americas remained important goals for Canadian officials, they lost both momentum and attention in late 2001.

In the course of the year 2000, the main concerns of Canada in the Americas were expanded trade, democratization, and such security concerns as narcotics traffic, small arms trade, regional instability, threats to democracy, and the need for continued attention to improved social and economic conditions in Latin America and the Caribbean. There was particular concern as a new century began that the trend towards democratization and away from militarism had slowed and that some democracies were extremely fragile. The message from Latin America in the course of 2000 was a mixed one. On the one hand, Mexico appeared to be on the verge of a new era with the defeat for the first time in 70 years of the PRI (Institutional Revolutionary Party) by Vicente Fox, the charismatic leader of the National Action Party. Fox attracted significant media coverage in North America and elsewhere in the hemisphere in the course of the election campaign and in the year that followed his inauguration. Fox's presidential victory seemed to usher in a new democratic era in Mexico, although he was hampered by the absence of control over the Mexican Congress. Fox was pragmatic, and committed to moving forward with a range of reforms to alleviate corruption, promote further privatization, expand trade and investment opportunities, and work with other hemispheric leaders in an effort to resolve outstanding conflicts.

On the other hand, several instances of slippage on the democratic front in the course of 2000–1 underlined the fragile nature of democratic institutions in the hemisphere. A political crisis in Peru in 2000, which resulted in new elections and the departure from the country of reformist President Alberto Fujimori, challenged the capacity of the OAS to respond. Hugo Chavez's presidency in Venezuela seemed to be a return to old-style Venezuelan *caudillismo*. Thousands of well-heeled Venezuelans fled to the United States with their investments. Chavez further undermined his credibility by lending support to the Colombian Revolutionary Armed Forces (FARC) and by flaunting his personal affection for Fidel Castro. In Argentina, the political alliance that had brought Fernando de la Rua to power fragmented as the country slipped into a deep recession and financial crisis early in 2001.

The Castro government in Cuba continued to be a disappointment to Canada at the turn of the century. In spite of considerable Canadian economic and diplomatic support for the Castro regime, including, in contrast to the hard line taken by the Clinton and Bush administrations, highly publicized official visits to his government by Prime Minister Chrétien and Lloyd Axworthy, there were no improvements in the Cuban government's human rights record, and little movement occurred towards a market economy or towards political liberalization. Official Canadian attitudes to the Castro government thus noticeably cooled as the policy of constructive engagement failed to bring about the desired changes, either in the Cuban government's human rights record or in shifting the Cuban economy towards a more market-oriented regime.[2] With the retirement of Axworthy, Canada has also been less vocal in its criticism of US policy towards Cuba, at a time when the Bush administration and the US Congress have taken an increasingly hard line, including with the Cuban Solidarity Act of 2001 and by providing direct support to Cuban dissident organizations.

Canadian policy-makers have placed a high value on continued advances in democratization, and neither Cuba under Castro nor Venezuela under Chavez fits that goal. At the conclusion of his term as Permanent Representative to the OAS in July 2001, Ambassador Peter Boehm challenged the organization and its leaders to put a stronger emphasis on political democracy, human rights, and judicial dispute and post-conflict resolution issues. Boehm made a strong impact on the OAS during his four-year term, serving on the Permanent Council and the Special Committee on Inter-American Summits Management. He was also a key figure in organizing the Windsor OAS General Assembly in June 2000. His successor, Ambassador Paul Durand, in his first address to the OAS indicated that Canada believed that the OAS would be judged by its effectiveness in implementing the stated objectives of the summits. Ambassador Durand insisted that the Inter-American Democratic Charter, drafted for the Quebec City Summit, was at the heart of the OAS mandate (OAS *Weekly Press Reports*, 22 Aug. 2001).

TRADE AND INVESTMENT

Eliminating or at least significantly reducing tariff barriers and restrictions on foreign investment has been a major goal of hemispheric governments since the first Summit of the Americas in 1994. In 1999 the 34 member nations of the OAS produced more than $11 trillion (US) in goods and services, but there was only $2.7 trillion in cross-border trade. Proponents of the goal of achieving the FTAA by 2005 argue that this free trade agreement would link 800 million people, representing 15 per cent of the world's population. They also contend that free trade and investment would enhance democracy, improve human rights, alleviate poverty, and advance the objective of controlling narcotics traffic.

Canada's trade with Latin America remains a minor component of overall Canadian trade, while trade with the US continues to be overwhelmingly the most significant to the Canadian economy. The US share of Canada's hemispheric trade in 2000 was 98.4 per cent in the area of exports and 92.7 per cent in imports. Canada has historically also had a negative balance of trade with the FTAA countries (except for the United States), and that deficit has grown over the past two decades from approximately $300 million in 1980 to more than $12 billion in 2000. A significant proportion of the deficit stems from trade with Mexico, the result of the growth in imports from that country since the conclusion of the North American Free Trade Agreement (NAFTA). Nonetheless, Canadian merchandise exports to the region enjoyed a substantial increase in 2000 as the result of a recovery from financial and economic problems that plagued much of the area in 1998. As a result, Canadian merchandise exports to Central and South America increased by 8.7 per cent and 12.3 per cent, respectively; exports to countries with which Canada has free trade agreements—Mexico, Costa Rica, and Chile—increased even more dramatically, by 26.5 per cent, 25.2 per cent, and 23.6 per cent, respectively.

Canada has significant trade with only six Latin American countries: Mexico, Brazil, Colombia, Venezuela, Argentina, and Chile. In 2000, those countries absorbed 81 per cent of Canada's total exports to the FTAA countries (save for the US), and Canadian imports from the same countries constituted more than 90 per cent of Canadian imports from the region (save for the US). To place Canada–Latin American trade in global perspective, however, Latin America purchased only 1.15 per cent of Canada's merchandise exports in 2000, down from a peak of 1.7 per cent in 1997. Canadian merchandise exports to the six key Latin American countries in 1997 were valued at more than $5.1 billion, in contrast to $4.7 billion in the year 2000. On the import side, Latin American exports to Canada in 2000 increased 11 per cent at the same time that imports from the US declined from 76.3 per cent in 1999 to 73.7 per cent in 2000 (DFAIT, 2001b: 19, 30–4).[3]

The patterns of Canadian foreign direct investment (FDI) indicate the importance of the western hemisphere to Canadians. Canadian industries and financial institutions have been well established in Latin America since early in the twentieth century and that tradition has been maintained. In the mid-1990s, Brazil was the largest Latin American recipient of Canadian FDI, followed by Mexico, Argentina, the Dominican Republic, and Chile. In 1992 Canada ranked sixth among G-7 countries in terms of FDI in Latin America. In individual Latin American countries Canada was a major source of FDI, in 1989 ranking second in Bolivia, Peru, and the Dominican Republic, fourth in Chile and Colombia, fifth in Brazil, sixth in Argentina and Mexico, and seventh in Venezuela (Burgess, 2000: 110).

Between 1990 and 2000 Canadian FDI in a number of Latin American economies underwent a significant increase. In Argentina, for instance, Canadian FDI increased from $123 million in 1990 to

$3.6 billion in 2000. In Chile it showed a similar increase, from $265 million in 1990 to $5.5 billion in 2000. Investment in Brazil increased from $1.7 billion in 1990 to $4.7 billion 10 years later (Statistics Canada, 2001).[4]

Proponents of the FTAA view the region as having considerable potential for expanded Canadian trade and investment opportunities, although from a Caribbean and Latin American perspective the main appeal is access to the large and lucrative US market. The FTAA initiative was officially launched in 1998 with a broad focus on negotiations leading not only to free trade but also to a higher degree of economic integration. In 1998 and 1999 Canada served as chair of the FTAA negotiations, followed by Argentina. The initial drafts of the agreement proposed tariff cuts on approximately 7,000 products, ranging from orange juice to rolled steel, but subsequent discussions have been far more comprehensive, including telecommunications, electronic commerce, and intellectual property rights. Specifically, and as a reflection of its scope, the FTAA is divided into nine separate areas: market access, investment, services, government procurement, dispute settlement, agriculture, intellectual property rights, subsidies and anti-dumping and countervailing duties, and competition policy. In addition, the FTAA as envisaged would include all of the disciplines of the World Trade Organization (WTO) and the powers of the failed Multilateral Agreement on Investment (MAI).

In spite of what appear to be desirable goals, the American nations made only marginal progress between the Santiago and the Quebec City Summits in moving the free trade agenda forward. A variety of factors accounted for the lack of progress, not least of which was the inability of the Clinton administration to obtain fast-track authority for trade agreements and the administration's general lack of political effectiveness following the series of personal scandals that marred President Clinton's second term. A second factor has been the lack of support for the FTAA from some of the Caribbean and Latin American countries, in particular the smaller economies of the Caribbean and Central America. There is also a perception among a number of Latin American countries, including major economies such as Brazil, that there may be more to be gained through adherence to the WTO and a global approach than in a regional trading organization and agreement such as the FTAA. Financial crises in Brazil and then in Argentina, which had an impact

on the international financial community, also served to divert attention from the FTAA. The massive financial and political crisis that hit
Argentina in 2001, culminating in two changes of government and
a moratorium on its $132 billion foreign debt, not only compromised
progress on the FTAA but also put in doubt the viability of Mercado
Común del Sur (Mercosur). The fact that Canada served as chair of
the Trade Negotiations Committee in the period leading up to the
Quebec City Summit was, nonetheless, a reflection of the leadership
role that Canada was able to play on trade issues. Canada promoted
a reasonably uniform trade policy in the Americas in spite of the
existence of a number of regional free trade or common market
organizations such as Mercosur, the Andean Pact, the Caribbean
Community (CARICOM), and the Central American Common Market.

As much as there has been official and business support for the
FTAA, there was also public opposition to what some considered an
excessive concentration on trade at the expense of a broader social
and economic agenda. Foreign Minister Manley was thus careful in
the months leading up to the Quebec City Summit to stress that
'while the FTAA remains central to our collective effort to promote
economic growth and expand prosperity, the Summit is not just
about trade. Our commitment to economic integration is not just
about the FTAA. We are equally concerned with how we reduce
poverty, promote equity, create more opportunities for enterprise,
and share in the benefits of growth, manage migration, and prepare
for, and mitigate the impact of, natural disasters.' Manley argued that
economic integration and the protection of the rights of workers and
the environment were not incompatible goals (Manley, 2001).

Manley's reassurances did little to quell opposition to the FTAA
from the so-called People's Summit of the Americas at Quebec City
in April 2001, a loose coalition of individuals and organizations called
the Hemispheric Social Alliance, constituting 'the voices of unions,
popular and environmental organizations, women's groups, human
rights organizations, international solidarity groups, indigenous, peas-
ant, student associations and church groups.' One of the press
releases from the People's Summit was headlined 'No to the FTAA!
Another Americas is Possible' (People's Summit, 2001). The release
contended that the FTAA was a neo-liberal project that was 'racist and
sexist and destructive of the environment. We propose to build new
ways of continental integration based on democracy, human rights,
equality, solidarity, pluralism and respect for the environment.'

This popular opposition to the FTAA has been in marked contrast to the official support from governments in the hemisphere. Nonetheless, in spite of the rhetorical support for the FTAA from governments, it has remained an elusive goal. There have been precious few real gains. It was not until several months after the Quebec City Summit of the Americas that the FTAA Secretariat even released a negotiating text. Canadian authorities were among those who pressed for its publication in order to offset public criticism about its alleged contents. The text released in July 2001 was, as DFAIT officials indicated, a 'preliminary compilation of ideas, proposals and negotiating positions from the 34 countries taking part in the FTAA negotiations'. The DFAIT news release noted, realistically, that 'most of the material is in square brackets, meaning there is no consensus on its elements' (DFAIT, 2001c).

The difficulty in achieving real consensus on the precise terms of the FTAA reflects deep-seated divisions among the countries of the Americas, with Canada and the US the most committed and vocal supporters of the agreement. The smaller economies of the Caribbean and Central America have had the same reservations about the FTAA that they did about the potential impact of NAFTA; their economies remain too small for their exports to compete in local or international markets against the major exporting and manufacturing economies of the hemisphere. It is also unclear what the fate of regional trading organizations such as CARICOM would be under the umbrella of an FTAA. At the same time, several of the developing economies in the Americas have viewed access to the lucrative US market as a key goal in the FTAA, similar to Mexican objectives at the time of NAFTA. Ecuador provides a good example. It remains highly dependent on commodity exports such as bananas, and for some years there has been a conflict between the European Union and the United States over banana imports, with the result being protectionist tariffs that have had a negative impact on banana exports from Ecuador. On a national level, Canada has been interested in pursuing NAFTA-like agreements with Latin American countries along the lines of the 1996 bilateral agreement with Chile. Brazil has not been receptive to Canadian initiatives among the Mercosur countries, but there have been more positive responses from the Andean Group. Among the Central American countries Costa Rica was the first to conclude an agreement (FOCAL, 2000).

The FTAA has consequently become something of a lightning rod in the Canadian and international debate over what opponents see as the agenda of international capitalism and its government allies and supporters view as an opportunity to break down tariff and investment barriers, protect intellectual property rights, promote democratic institutions, and in the process alleviate pervasive poverty and inequality of access to public services such as education. The jury remains out on the veracity of the arguments of the more extreme proponents and the more extreme antagonists.

CRISIS IN PERU

The importance of Canadian membership in the OAS was underlined in the course of 2000 by the significant role that Canada played in resolving the political crisis that gripped Peru when President Alberto Fujimori challenged tradition by seeking a third presidential term. The elections in April of that year were roundly criticized and failed to provide President Fujimori with the requisite 50 per cent of the popular vote, with the result that a second round of voting was necessary in June. The main challenger, Alejandro Toledo, withdrew from the contest on grounds that the election process was unfair, given the extent of the government's control over the electoral machinery. There was considerable international sympathy for Toledo's position, with the result that the June 2000 elections that returned President Fujimori to office were marred by controversy and widely viewed as lacking legitimacy. Foreign Minister Axworthy and then Secretary of State for Latin America and Africa, David Kilgour, expressed strong concern over the Peruvian government's decision to proceed with the June elections in spite of the national and international criticism and the decision of the OAS to withdraw its electoral observers from the country. The Canadian ambassador to the OAS, Peter Boehm, indicated to the OAS Permanent Council that Peru's electoral process did not meet standards expected by the international community (DFAIT News Release, 26 May 2000).

The Peruvian situation received prominent attention at the OAS General Assembly meeting in Windsor in June 2000. Resolution 1753 of the General Assembly mandated sending a mission to Peru involving Axworthy, as chair of the General Assembly, and Secretary-General Gaviria. An advance mission led by Boehm and Fernando Jaramillo, the Chief of Staff of the OAS Secretary-General, visited Peru for several days in late June. This interim mission and the subsequent high-level mission found a government and political community deeply divided. Mission members met with a wide range of government and opposition political groups, non-governmental organizations, representatives of civil society, including organized labour, and prominent individuals. The mission obtained agreement from all sides that there should be reforms in the administration of justice to strengthen the rule of law and ensure the separation of powers among the branches of the national government; freedom of expression for individuals and the media; electoral reform to ensure transparency and to mitigate the control of the national government over the electoral machinery and process; and reform of the intelligence services and armed forces to ensure civilian control. At the same time, the mission stressed that Peruvians had responsibility for ensuring that reforms were implemented and recommended as a target date for their completion the municipal elections in 2002 (OAS *Weekly Press Reports*, July 2000).

The OAS initiative in Peru was controversial given the long-standing Latin American opposition to any intervention, individual or collective, in the internal political affairs of a member country. There were advances in the 1980s and 1990s in OAS agreements towards the incorporation of the principle of collective intervention, beginning with the Protocol of Cartagena in 1985, which amended the OAS Charter and increased the OAS obligation to 'promote and consolidate representative democracy', to which the Protocol added the critical qualifier 'with due respect for the principle of non-intervention' (Cooper and Legler, 2001: 105). The Cartagena Protocol did not specify the means that should be used to achieve its objectives, but this deficiency was gradually rectified over the next decade, with amendments providing for collective action, rapid response to crises, and the threat of suspension for nations whose governments have been overthrown by force. Nevertheless, there has been a consensus against the use of external military force to deal with internal political confrontations. This opposition to military intervention has given momentum to Latin American institutional collaborations, in particular the Rio Group. Formed through a coalition of the former Contadora Group and its supporting countries (Colombia, Venezuela, Mexico, Panama, Argentina, Brazil, Peru, and Uruguay), the Rio Group has focused on democracy as a criterion for membership and has not involved the United States or the OAS. With a former coup leader, Hugo Chavez, as President, Venezuela has lost much of its credibility as a democratic force, but Brazil under President Fernando

Cardoso has undertaken significant initiatives, serving as a joint co-ordinator, with Canada, of the OAS Summit Working Group on Democracy and Human Rights.

There was thus considerable precedent for collective action by the OAS in Peru as the political crisis deepened in mid-2000. The relative lack of focus on Latin America by the Clinton administration, with the exception of activity in the areas of narcotics, immigration, and free trade, also provided an opportunity for Canada and the major Latin American countries to play a more significant brokering role in the hemisphere. Nor was Canada encumbered by the historical legacy of US military intervention in the region.

The Peruvian crisis provides an effective example of how Canada has been able to assume a leadership role on some inter-American issues and to do so in collaboration with other Latin American countries, in the process enhancing its credibility in the region. When Fujimori was inaugurated in late July 2000 amid considerable ongoing controversy, Lloyd Axworthy, in his capacity as head of the high-level mission, called on all parties to exercise restraint during the inauguration and noted that Canadian officials were in Peru to observe events as part of Canada's 'ongoing commitment to democracy in Peru' (DFAIT News Release, 27 July 2000; Cooper, 2001).

Fujimori's tenuous hold on political power was further eroded in September, when Valdimiro Montesinos, the head of the national security organization (SIN), was accused of corruption, violation of human rights, and arms trafficking. The OAS mission was informed that intelligence officers had attempted to bribe members of the opposition in Congress in order to give the government a majority. Opposition political leaders informed the mission that they were suspending their participation in the mission dialogue until those responsible for the illegal conduct had been appropriately sanctioned. The mission reported that, if President Fujimori's government did not respond quickly and effectively to the conduct of these public officials, it would be difficult to re-establish the democratization process. Fujimori announced that there would be new elections for both Congress and President and that he would not be a candidate. He also dissolved the security agency. Yet the crisis deepened as further revelations highlighted the depth of corruption in the administration. In mid-November Fujimori travelled to Japan from a meeting of Asia-Pacific leaders in Brunei and faxed a resignation to the Peruvian Congress. Congress rejected the resignation and voted to remove him from office, appointing Valentin Paniagua, the President of Congress, as interim President. Paniagua in turn appointed Javier Perez de Cuellar, the former UN Secretary-General and Fujimori's opponent in the 1995 presidential election, as Prime Minister.

The fate of Valdimiro Montesinos remained a point of friction, including between Canadian officials and the OAS. Montesinos fled to Panama following the revelations of his conduct, and Canada successfully opposed Secretary-General Gaviria's initial inclination to have Panama grant Montesinos asylum. Equally urgent and sensitive was the need to bring together a wide range of competing political groups in order to defuse the crisis. Peruvian and other international figures credited Ambassador Boehm and Foreign Minister Axworthy with pressing Peruvian government officials into accepting the role of non-governmental and civil rights groups in the negotiations, and Canadian embassy officials were instrumental in gaining the participation of wide-ranging groups, including government, at the *mesa de dialogo* (negotiating table). Between the establishment of an interim government and new elections in mid-2001, the OAS and the high-level mission worked with Peruvian officials to improve the conditions under which new elections would be held, signing an agreement in February 2001 to send an OAS election monitoring mission with experience in election observation, electoral training, and election administration.

The appointment of John Manley as Minister of Foreign Affairs occasioned no shift in the Canadian role in Peru. In June 2001 Alejandro Toledo, Fujimori's opponent the previous year, won a narrow victory and assumed power, the first person of Amerindian origin to become President of Peru. The crisis passed and an election-sanctioned transfer of power took place. As much as it can accurately be stated that free elections in themselves do not guarantee a democracy, the Peruvian situation in 2000–1 went some distance towards the restoration of democratic principles. Canada's role in that process was significant.

NATIONAL SECURITY ISSUES

The Canadian approach to national security in the Americas has drawn a close link between security and democratization. National security has been defined very broadly to include a range of issues, from guerrilla warfare and narcotics traffic to poverty, forced human migration, and refugee pressures. In addition to its bilateral activities in the area of national security, Canada has been a member of the OAS Committee on Hemispheric Security since its establishment as a permanent committee of the OAS, and has been a regular participant in the Defence Ministerial conferences, the most recent of which were held in Brazil and Chile (Stevenson, 1996; Sinclair, 1997).

Even in the aftermath of the terrorist attacks on New York and Washington on 11 September 2001, Canadian security concerns in the Americas have focused on two major and related national security issues: the illicit narcotics trade and the danger of an expanded guerrilla war in the Andean region. The international effort to control narcotics traffic has engaged Canadian diplomatic, police, and military forces in collaborative efforts with the United States and other countries of the Americas. Closely related to the narcotics issue has been Canadian and international concern over the possibility of an expanded regional war in the Andean countries resulting from the US effort under a multi-billion dollar aid package, Plan Colombia, to enhance the capacity of the Colombian national police and armed forces to contain and destroy the narcotics industry. As the supplier of 80 per cent of the world's cocaine and of two-thirds of the heroin now consumed in the US, Colombia has been the main target of US and Canadian anti-narcotics policies. Since the US and Colombian government announcements of their objective of a harder line and military approach to controlling the narcotics industry, there has been increased concern that such confrontation would also inevitably involve the dominant Colombian guerrilla forces, FARC and the smaller ELN (National Liberation Army), as well as the right-wing paramilitary forces led by Carlos Castaño, given their close ties to the narcotics industry as one of their main sources of funding.

The Canadian government was not openly critical of the US approach, but there were concerns, shared with other critics of the Plan, including Great Britain and France, that an aggressive military campaign against the narcotics industry would involve the guerrillas, intensify the military conflict within Colombia, and drive guerrillas over the borders with neighbouring Panama, Ecuador, Peru, Brazil, and Venezuela. Canadian diplomats consequently continued to focus on such major issues within Colombia as the hundreds of thousands of people displaced by rural violence (Randall, 2001).

Canada and Colombia intensified their bilateral relationship in the course of 2000–1. President Pastrana's official visit to Ottawa was the first official visit to Canada by a Colombian President. Foreign Minister Axworthy and International Trade Minister Pierre Pettigrew both paid official visits to Colombia, and the Colombian government sought preferential access to Canadian markets for its merchandise and service exports to encourage economic development in an economy that has been in serious recession for several years and to offset the unfavourable balance of trade Colombia has with Canada. There was also increased Canadian public interest in Colombia, driven by concerns over human rights, narcotics, and the guerrilla war. Even *Maclean's* magazine carried a rare article on the Canadian ambassador in Bogotá, and the House of Commons Standing Committee on Foreign Affairs and International Trade established a subcommittee to conduct hearings on human rights and development issues in Colombia (Human Rights Subcommittee, 2001; *Maclean's*, 2001: 38).

Canadian investment in Colombia has been significant, especially in the natural resource sector and in telecommunications. Canadian FDI in Colombia in 2001 was approximately $5 billion. In 2000 Alberta alone exported nearly $50 million in goods and services to Colombia. There are approximately 1,400 Canadians living and working in the country. The presence of large, frequently Alberta-based companies such as Alberta Energy Company, Nexen, TransCanada Pipelines, and Enbridge has made Colombian security a concern to Canadian business, especially those, like the energy companies, that have to operate in more remote areas of the country where they are vulnerable to guerrilla and paramilitary activity. According to one estimate, security accounts for approximately 20 per cent of a company's operating budget in Colombia, and concern for security was heightened further in the fall of 2000 by the kidnapping in Ecuador near the Colombian border of Canadian oil workers employed by Edmonton-based United Pipelines (*Oilweek*, 2001: 4).

With a comparative lack of military power, Canada has chosen to play the more traditional role of peacemaker in Colombia, in the course of 2000–1 working with the United Nations representative in Colombia and participating in the Facilitation Commission for the Peace Process. The Commission, which has had the support of both the Pastrana government and FARC leaders, includes representatives of Canada, Sweden, France, Cuba, Mexico, Norway, Spain, Italy, and Switzerland. In the spring of 2001, Canada also considered a request to participate in international verification of the demilitarized zone between FARC and the Colombian government. Beyond formal involvement in peace negotiations, Canada has co-operated with the Colombian armed forces to enhance human rights education for cadets. There is also a program for co-operation through the RCMP with Colombian police to address the problem of narcotics traffic and to encourage addiction treatment programs.

Canadian initiatives have been positive ones but, like their Colombian counterparts, they have produced only marginal results. Government–FARC negotiations made virtually no progress, and in July 2001 the Colombian government turned to a new group of peace commissioners. Assassinations, kidnappings, violence, and the growth and export of narcotics continued to hamper the capacity of the government to establish an effective rule of law.

THE QUEBEC SUMMIT AND ITS AFTERMATH

In April 2001 Canada hosted the third Summit of the Americas in Quebec City. Involving the heads of state and government from the hemisphere, the Summit met amid intense security in light of the extensive violence that had occurred at the WTO meetings in Seattle and the stated intent of anti-globalization groups to protest the FTAA. Although much of the extensive media coverage focused on the dissenters who were outside the controversial steel-wire fencing that surrounded the conference site, inside there was a substantial effort on the part of the Canadian government to lead a dialogue with representatives of civil society. This had been an objective of senior Canadian foreign policy-makers for several years prior to the Summit. In the course of 2000 organizations such as the Canadian Centre for Foreign Policy Development and the Canadian Foundation for the Americas (FOCAL) sponsored workshops, conferences, and discussion groups on aspects of inter-American relations, with a focus on such themes as democratization and governance, indigenous peoples, educational reforms, free trade, small arms trade and control, and regional security. Senior government officials, including the Secretary of State for Latin America and Africa, the Assistant Deputy Minister (Americas), and ultimately the Prime Minister's personal representative for the Quebec City Summit, participated in these sessions and also made presentations on university campuses across the country in the months leading up to the Summit.

The message was clear. The Chrétien government seriously wished to broaden the consultative base for foreign policy-making on inter-American affairs (CCFPD, 2001). Only a few months prior to the Summit, the Prime Minister outlined for a special session of the OAS the outcomes that Canada sought at Quebec City. Human security continued to provide the conceptual parameters of Canadian policy objectives. 'Canada', Chrétien suggested, in as inclusive and politically correct a statement as any speech writer could concoct, 'wishes to see a clear and forceful commitment to strengthening democracy and fostering social inclusion . . . which extends to our democratic institutions, our electoral machinery, and the impartiality of justice; to protecting human rights and freedom of expression; to fighting drug trafficking and corruption; to empower local governments and safeguard the rights of minorities, indigenous peoples, migrants and the disabled; and make the strongest possible pledge to promote the legal, economic and social equality of women and men.' The Prime Minister indicated that the Canadian government believed that information technology was a key tool in enhancing knowledge throughout the Americas and that narrowing the 'digital divide' would improve access to information and increase productivity (Chrétien, 2001).

In the months leading up to the Quebec City Summit, Canada was active in a number of ministerial meetings. Hemispheric ministers with responsibility for such areas as trade, transport, energy, gender, education, labour, justice, finance, environment, and health already met regularly. In early 2001 there were four pre-Summit ministerial meetings, those on finance and the environment hosted by Canada, and a post-Summit ministerial on labour in October. The Canadian Parliament also hosted the first Inter-Parliamentary Forum of the Americas in Ottawa in the spring of 2001, which produced recommendations on co-operative action to combat corruption and narcotics traffic, promote economic integration, reduce poverty, enhance environmental protection, and support cultural diversity (Manley, 2001).

The Declaration and Plan of Action for the Quebec City Summit was intended to provide a coherent and balanced agenda organized around three main themes: strengthening democracy, creating prosperity, and realizing human potential. What received most public attention was the commitment on the part of the Summit presidents and prime ministers to collaborate to strengthen and protect democratic institutions in the Americas. With some irony, adoption of the Inter-American Democratic Charter did not occur until the day of the terrorist attacks on New York and Washington. An effort to have the Charter adopted failed at the June 2001 meeting of OAS foreign ministers in Costa Rica, and it was not until the Lima meeting in September that there was agreement on wording. The Charter includes a provision for a member state to lose its right to participation in the OAS in the event of an 'unconstitutional alteration or disruption of the democratic order' in that state. Removal of a state's right to OAS participation requires a two-thirds majority vote by member states. The Charter also broadened the definition of democracy to include social rights, freedom of expression, and subordination of military and police forces to civilian authority, but it failed to specify the procedures for OAS suspension of a member state if democracy were overthrown or seriously threatened or to enumerate the precise abuses that would justify such action, such as electoral fraud or military interference in civilian affairs. Equally significant was the fact that the Democratic Charter does not apply to membership in the FTAA, with the result that in theory it would be possible for a member country to be suspended from the OAS but continue to enjoy its participation in hemispheric free trade, if that goal is ever achieved (Knox, 2001: A9; OAS, 2001b).

OAS member states failed to agree on the democracy clause at the San José, Costa Rica, meeting of the General Assembly, but a working group was established to bring a document forward at the September meeting in Peru. At San José, Canada supported the establishment of a mechanism to fight corruption in the Americas, following up on the Inter-American Convention against Corruption adopted at Caracas in 1996. Manley committed the Canadian government to a $50,000 allocation to support the anti-corruption initiative. He announced an additional $540,000 commitment to a range of projects that directly support recommendations contained in the Quebec Summit Plan of Action. Canada was the leading proponent of many of the agenda items, all of which are intended to strengthen democracy, reduce corruption, encourage judicial reform, and facilitate the participation of civil society in policy formation. The projects to which Canada was making this allocation included the OAS Peace Fund and the Strengthening Democracy Fund; the Justice Studies Centre of the Americas; the promotion of corporate social responsibility in the Americas; work of the Unit for the Promotion of Democracy to enhance the quality of electoral operations; the establishment of a network of national human rights institutions in the Americas; and a round table for citizens' groups (DFAIT News Release, 4 June 2001).

The OAS Peace Fund and the Strengthening Democracy Fund, to which Canada has contributed, were established at the 2000 Windsor General Assembly. The goal of the Peace Fund is to assist in the peaceful resolution of territorial disputes; the purpose of the Strengthening Democracy Fund is to preserve, strengthen, and consolidate representative democracy in the Americas. The Justice Studies Center of the Americas is based in Santiago and was established as the result of the Santiago Summit in 1998. The Canadian contribution to the Center was to assist in the design and implementation of an electronic information system that will provide extensive information about the operation of the hemisphere's judicial systems. Canada has been the leading country in supporting the corporate social responsibility agenda in the OAS. Its $100,000 contribution in 2001 was intended to facilitate discussion of the issues—including such matters as human rights and labour and environmental standards—relating to corporate social responsibility among government, non-governmental organizations, and the private sector. The Canadian contribution to the Unit for the Promotion of Democracy was intended to support a seminar on improving how elections are held, including such issues as political party registration, political party access to media and funding, campaign financing, oversight and dissemination of election results, and transparency and accountability in electoral systems. The Canadian contribution to the Network of National Institutions for the Protection and Promotion of Human rights was aimed at improving communications among human rights commissioners and ombudsmen, as well as agencies and institutions responsible for the promotion and protection of human rights.

An additional Canadian agenda item at San José was the focus on a landmine-clearing program for Central America, an issue on which Axworthy provided strong international leadership and that remained a Canadian goal following his retirement. The main focus of the Costa Rica discussion was on Central America. The OAS resolution noted the progress made by Nicaragua in mine demarcation, the fact that Honduras had destroyed its stockpile of anti-personnel mines, and congratulated Peru and Ecuador for their decision to conduct mine-clearing operations along their borders. The Costa Rica resolution instructed the Unit for the Promotion of Democracy to continue its technical assistance and to obtain contributions from member countries for the elimination of anti-personnel landmines from the hemisphere (OAS Press Release, 5 June 2001).

CONCLUSIONS

The past two years have been significant, indeed dramatic, in the relationship between Canada and its hemispheric neighbours. If there was any skepticism in 1989, when Canada joined the OAS, about the extent to which Canada had become a nation of the Americas, the leadership that it has shown in the region over the past several years should have dispelled those doubts. The ties of tradition, culture, and economics that Canada has long enjoyed with Europe, especially Great Britain, have been overshadowed by the bilateral relationship with the United States and by the promise of closer linkages with the Americas. That Canadian shift has been a true sea change, one that would not have been predicted in the earlier Cold War years. The enhanced importance of Latin America to Canada is now reflected in so many small and large ways in Canadian society, including the increased teaching of Spanish in Canadian schools, the impact of Latin American immigrants and their children on Canadian society over the past 20 years, and the increasing significance of economic ties between Canada and the countries of the Americas. That shift also accounts for the greater importance in Canadian politics and public opinion of such issues as regional security in the Andean countries, the FTAA, human rights in the Americas, and narcotics traffic. One can anticipate that those 'American' issues will only continue to assume a greater place in Canadian political consciousness in the next several years.

NOTES

1. Bill Graham succeeded John Manley as Foreign Minister after this chapter was written. Graham has a strong interest in the hemisphere, was Chair of the Inter-Parliamentary Forum of the Americas, and is a fluent Spanish speaker. He is likely to push the hemispheric connection, recognizing that 11 September has altered Canada's foreign policy priorities.
2. For a discussion of Canada's recent policies towards Cuba, see Grenier (2000).
3. Brazil and Mexico are Canada's main Latin American markets. Exports to those countries are composed primarily of vehicles, aircraft, vessels, and associated transportation equipment, machinery/mechanical appliances, electronic equipment, live animals, wood pulp and paper products, mineral products, chemicals, and audiovisual equipment.

4.   The Canadian investment position in Latin America has to be placed in comparative perspective, however, since Canadian FDI in the United States dwarfs that in Latin America, representing $154 billion in 2000.

REFERENCES

Armstrong, Sally. 2001. 'Our Man in Bogota', *Maclean's*, 4 June, 28–31.

Bothwell, Robert. 2000. 'Lloyd Axworthy: Man of Principle', *National Post*, 19 Sept., A18.

Burgess, Bill. 2000. 'Foreign Direct Investment: Facts and Perceptions about Canada', *Canadian Geographer* 44 (Summer): 98–113.

Canadian Centre for Foreign Policy Development (CCFPD). 2001. *Canadian Voices: The Americas*. Ottawa.

Canadian Foundation for the Americas (FOCAL). 2000. Policy Paper, 21 Jan.

Chrétien, Jean. 2001. 'Canada's Goals for the Summit of the Americas', *Canadian Speeches* 15 (Mar.–Apr.): 15.

Cooper, Andrew F. 2001. 'More Than a Star Turn: Canadian Hybrid Diplomacy and the OAS Mission to Peru', *International Journal* 56 (Spring): 279–96.

———— and Thomas Legler. 2001. 'The OAS Democratic Solidarity Paradigm: Questions of Collective and National Leadership', *Latin American Politics and Society* 43 (Spring): 103–22.

Department of Foreign Affairs and International Trade (DFAIT). 2000–1. News Releases. Available at: <www.dfait-maeci.gc.ca>.

————. 2001a. 'Notes for an Address by the Honourable John Manley to a Consultative Meeting of the Foreign Ministers of the Organization of American States', Washington, 21 Sept. Available at: <http://198.103.104.118/minpub/Publication.asp?>.

————. 2001b. *Trade Update 2001: Second Annual Report on Canada's State of Trade*. Ottawa, May.

————. 2001c. 'Minister Pettigrew Announces Release of Draft FTAA Negotiating Text', Press Release no. 94, 3 July. Available at: <www.dfait.gc.ca>.

Grenier, Yves. 2000. 'Our Dictatorship: Canada's Trilateral Relations with Castro's Cuba', in Maureen Appel Molot and Fen Osler Hampson, eds, *Canada Among Nations 2000: Vanishing Borders*. Toronto: Oxford University Press, 247–73.

Kilgour, David. 2001. 'Notes for an Address by the Honourable David Kilgour (Secretary of State for Latin America and Africa), at the First Canadian Open Business Forum on Building Corporate Social/Environmental Responsibility', Calgary, 8 Mar.

Knox, Paul. 2001. 'OAS Agreement to Protect Democracy Needs Teeth, Critics Say', *Globe and Mail*, 11 Sept., A9.

Manley, John. 2001. 'Summit Goals Vital to Canada', *Canadian Speeches* 15 (Mar.–Apr.): 14–17.

McKenna, Peter. 1995. *Canada and the OAS: From Dilettante to Full Partner*. Ottawa: Carleton University Press.

Oilweek. 2001. 'Canada Takes Different Approach to Colombia Problem', 28 May, 4.

Organization of American States (OAS). *Weekly Press Reports*. Available at: <www.oas.org>.

————. 2001a. Special Session of the Permanent Council of the Organization of American States, 5 Feb.

————. 2001b. Special Session of the General Assembly, Press Release, 11 Sept. Available at: <www.oas.org/charter/docs>.

Pettigrew, Pierre S. 2000. 'Trade Protectionism would hurt Canadians more than most others', *Canadian Speeches* 14 (May–June): 10–15.

Randall, Stephen J. 2001. 'Canadá, Estados Unidos, Colombia y la seguridad hemisférica', in Marta Ardila, ed., *Colombia y la seguridad hemisférica*. Bogotá: Universidad Externado, 23–42.

Sheck, Conrad (Deputy Director, Inter-American Division, DFAIT). 2001. 'Summit of the Americas: DFAIT Overview', 14 May.

Sinclair, Jill. 1996. 'Canada's International Security Policy', in Harold Klepak, ed., *Natural Allies? Canadian and Mexican Perspectives on International Security*. Ottawa: Carleton University Press, 155–68.

Statistics Canada. 1997. *Canada's International Investment Position, 1926–1996*. Ottawa: Minister of Supply and Services.

————. 1998. *Canada's International Investment Position, 1997*. Ottawa: Minister of Supply and Services.

————. 2001. *Canada's International Investment Position, 2000*. Ottawa: Minister of Supply and Services.

Stevenson, Brian. 1996. 'Cooperative Security and Canada's Role in Inter-American Security Reform', in Harold Klepak, ed., *Natural Allies? Canadian and Mexican Perspectives on International Security*. Ottawa: Carleton University Press, 133–54.

Subcommittee on Human Rights and International Development of the Standing Committee on Foreign Affairs and International Trade. 2001. Minutes of proceedings of meeting no. 2, 21 Mar. Available at: <www.parl.gc.ca>.

United States Congress. 2001. Bill 5.894: 'Cuban Solidarity Act of 2001'. Available at: <www.congress.com>.

12

Trapped: Brazil, Canada, and the Aircraft Dispute

JEAN DAUDELIN

The bilateral relationship between Brazil and Canada is hostage to a dispute about subsidies for the production of aircraft. The reason is straightforward: the companies involved, Embraer in Brazil and Bombardier in Canada, are more important economically and politically for their respective countries than the bilateral relationship itself.

This chapter examines the emergence and development of this asymmetry. In a first section, it looks at the growing weight of Embraer and Bombardier in their respective countries' political economies. Each company is presented and its growth is located in its specific political, economic, and (for Brazil) military context. This section shows that Embraer has developed into the most important exporter in Brazil, the one whose fate is the most consequential for the government and its economic model. Bombardier, while not as important in Canada, is nonetheless shown to be an economic powerhouse with a very strong political hand, thanks in part to its presence and visibility in Quebec. Distinct histories notwithstanding, the result in each case is similar: both companies entered the 1990s as political and economic heavyweights.

The second section explores the evolution of the bilateral relationship since the early decades of the century, when the two countries were financially linked through the presence of a massive natural resources and infrastructure conglomerate, the Brazilian Light and Traction Company, later to become Brascan. That honeymoon saw each country become a significant economic partner of the other. The narrow basis of that relationship, however, was never more obvious than in Brascan's departure at the end of the 1970s, which drastically shrunk the relationship and paved the way for a decline in trade and investment that, relative to each country's connections to the rest of the world, continues to this day. In that second phase, the two countries also took diverging paths in the world economy, with Canada deepening its ties to the United States, and Brazil diversifying away from the latter to become a truly global—if still relatively small—power. The third period is paradoxical, as Canada 'rediscovers' the Americas, including Brazil, but in a way and with an outlook that largely conflicts with Brazil's hemispheric ambitions and with its economic and political objectives. This third period also sees the multiplication of small incidents, all of which contributed to the further weakening of bilateral ties. In sum, since the end of the 1970s the once significant relationship between Brazil and Canada has crumbled, leaving very little but lofty abstractions about common natural size, similar gross domestic products (GDPs), a shared hemisphere, converging values, middle-powerdom, and multilateral impulses. As the 'air war' between Bombardier and Embraer developed, the hollowness of this discourse would become perfectly obvious.

The third section examines the dogfight per se, beginning with the first salvos, followed by the full-fledged World Trade Organization (WTO) process. The chapter then looks at some of the key directions the affair could take. The impotence of the WTO in this case is also examined, and its sources and consequences discussed. A short conclusion emphasizes the limited ability of political and diplomatic initiatives to re-establish and consolidate a healthy bilateral relationship. It suggests that, as Canada's global reach fades, this kind of foreign policy hostage-taking is likely to flourish, as the number of bilateral relationships that truly matter goes down precipitously.

THE TRAPPERS: BOMBARDIER AND EMBRAER IN THEIR NATIONAL CONTEXTS

Fifteen years ago, no one could have predicted that Bombardier and Embraer would find themselves in tense competition over the sale of aircraft. Bombardier had just dipped a toe into the aerospace business, with the acquisition in 1986 of Canadair, and Embraer was a state-controlled aerospace firm, heavily indebted, with no globally competitive flagship. Indeed, its survival was totally dependent on government handouts. In little more than a decade, these two companies would become major players in the global aerospace industry, competing for third place among aircraft makers—admittedly very far behind Airbus and Boeing—and dominating its fastest-growing market: that for 50- to 70-passenger regional jets.

In the process, the Brazilian and Canadian governments played a central role in the companies' rise, and in each case the companies became political monsters whose interests simply could not be attacked without politicians and even governments taking important risks. It is the story of that process that we will now outline.

Embraer

Embraer is arguably Brazil's most powerful company. 'If Embraer goes bankrupt, the government falls', a Brazilian diplomat confided to the author in the fall of 2000 at a particularly tense moment of the confrontation. The ultimate validity of that statement notwithstanding, the fact that such a thought could even be entertained by a well-informed public servant is a good indicator of the political weight Embraer has acquired in recent years.

The Empresa Brasileira de Aeronáutica (EMBRAER) was formally established in August 1969 as a state venture under the responsibility of the Air Force ministry. It was part of the effort of the military government, then into its most repressive phase but also presiding over a period of extremely fast growth, to increase Brazil's industrial capacity and transform it into an economic powerhouse (Bernardes, 2000:159–63; Silva, 1998: 209–58). This project was framed into the broader 'national security doctrine' of the military government, which conceived industrialization and development, particularly in the area of infrastructure, as strategic assets enabling the country to exploit fully its large size and massive resources and therefore to claim its rightful place in the Western world as a key player in its defence against Communism.[1] From the outset to the present, the security mandate of Embraer was conceived broadly and the company developed mostly dual-use aircraft that enabled territorial control and facilitated transportation in remote areas, particularly in the Amazon.

Embraer's dependence on the Brazilian government was nearly total. Through investments in research and development, government procurement, and export subsidies, the Brazilian state carried the company through its first 20 years. Such dependence and Embraer's limited ability to gain a foothold in global markets left it vulnerable when the state, after years of economic crisis and instability and confronted by a severe fiscal crisis, proved unable to maintain its support. Heavily indebted, the company was slated for privatization and put on sale in 1994, becoming the main symbol of Brazil's new-found commitment to freer markets and economic liberalization. Meanwhile, however, it had developed a new project for a regional jet, the ERJ 145, that would prove a major commercial success and for the first time enable Embraer to compete for and win major contracts in global markets.

As this consolidation took place, the company became untouchable. The current political weight of Embraer has four main bases. The first is purely economic, since the success of the ERJ 145 has made the company Brazil's largest exporter. Its quick expansion, moreover, consolidated its position as the core of the country's high-tech sector and its most important source of high-wage, highly qualified jobs.

Second, Embraer has never abandoned its position as the dominant player in Brazil's military-industrial complex. While Brazil's defence budget is limited, even by low Latin American standards, the company's existence has enabled the country to keep a critical part of its military equipment procurement at home. Not only do Embraer planes, from ALX and Xavante jets to the turbo-prop Tucano, represent the mainstay of its air force, but modified versions of the ERJ 145 are also used as part of the monitoring system set up to control the country's hinterland, which borders all the countries of South America except Ecuador and Chile. Brazil's intention to renew its fleet of combat jets in the coming years also put Embraer in the limelight as a necessary partner to any major firm interested in the contract. The decision of a consortium of France's largest military contractors to take a 20 per cent stake in Embraer must be understood in that context.[2] The production by Embraer of an aircraft like the Mirage 2000, which is one of the options currently being considered, would represent a massive boon for the company, opening up lucrative avenues of exports to third countries. Moreover, this specific contract—worth $700 million (US)—is only one of a series of initiatives to modernize the Brazilian air force, most of which involve the possible purchase of planes from Embraer. Valued at US $3 billion, the program as a whole was explicitly linked by the press to the government's determination to help the company overcome the post-11 September downturn.[3]

The third basis of Embraer's political clout flows from the government's still heavy investment in the company—in spite of all the fuss about its privatization, only one among its major national owners is a truly private company. The Bozano-Simonsen group, a financial conglomerate, currently controls 40 per cent of the voting shares of the company. Two large public-sector pension funds, whose investment decisions are made by the government, Sistel and Previ, control a further 20 per cent. The government itself, finally, kept a 'golden share', which gives it a veto on the company's defence investments, on changes to its 'social mission', and on shareholding control (Bernardes, 2000: 256–60; Jubany, 1998, ch. 3). There is nothing arm's-length, in other words, in the relationship between the Brazilian government and Embraer.

Paradoxically, however, another source of Embraer's leverage lies in its being the foremost symbol of Brazil's success in the privatization program, the proof that liberalization does indeed work for the country, contrary to what the many critics held at the time. This is profoundly intertwined, moreover, with the idea that Brazil can play in the 'First Division', that it is not only a producer of resources and agricultural products but also a competitive player in one of the most technologically advanced market niches. At stake, in other words, is Brazil's only real foothold in the new economy, its image in the world, and the soundness of its economic options of the last decade. This is a great deal indeed and, as a result, the political consensus behind Embraer is difficult to overestimate.

Bombardier

Bombardier is the closest thing Canada has to an Embraer. The grip it has on the government is not quite as tight, but it is certainly sufficient to constrain severely the range of options open to Canadian policy-makers, especially but not exclusively when the Liberal Party is in power.

The company was born 60 years ago in Valcourt, a small town in Quebec's Eastern Townships, the work of Joseph-Armand

Bombardier, a clever engineer and mechanic who invented the snowmobile. For a while, the brand name of Ski-doo became synonymous with the product and, to this day, Bombardier's snowmobiles are among the best in that market. Over the years, Bombardier diversified, first into other recreational vehicles, from all-terrain vehicles and motorcycles to jet skis, then into subways and trains—a field in which it now claims first place in the world—and later still, albeit to a limited extent, into military vehicles and jeeps.

Beginning with its involvement in rail equipment, Bombardier's business model was structured around government incentives, government subsidies, government contracts, government-led export promotion, and government 'tied aid' to developing countries. It must be noted that few if any large aerospace and public transportation companies have taken a different path. Hence, 'the Bombardier story', to use the title of a recent book on the company (Macdonald, 2001), is quite representative of the whole industrial segment. However, not all such companies have proven so adept at turning government support and subsidies into profitable and sustainable business ventures. At that game, arguably, Bombardier has few peers.

The company's involvement in the aircraft business started in 1986 when it bought Montreal-based Canadair from the federal government, which had in turn bought it in 1975 from General Dynamics when the US-parent company decided to close down the factory. The federal government took on Canadair's $1.2 billion debt and sold the company, and its promising Challenger business jet, for $120 million. To get things rolling and barely a week after the deal was announced, the government chose Canadair for a $1.7 billion contract to maintain the Canadian Forces' newly acquired McDonald-Douglas CF-18. Massive government injections of funds would also be involved in two of the three other acquisitions that consolidated Bombardier's position in the aerospace business. In 1989, it acquired Belfast-based Shorts Brothers PLC under favourable conditions offered by Margaret Thatcher's Conservative government and, in 1992, Ontario-based de Havilland, this time with support from Bob Rae's New Democratic Party provincial government. In the meantime, Bombardier had acquired Wichita-based Learjet, again in a moment of great vulnerability but this time without government support. The company thus found itself, after barely six years, in control of a broad if somewhat ailing aircraft conglomerate. Shortly after, Bombardier launched its most successful aircraft, the 50-seat

Regional Jet, developed in part thanks to a joint $86 million grant from the federal and Quebec governments. In 1996, its share of the regional aircraft market had surpassed 40 per cent. The company's sales exploded along with that market, but Bombardier was unable to increase or even maintain its market share, essentially because of the success of a Brazilian competitor, which also happened to be heavily supported by its own government.

Government support was crucial to Bombardier's emergence as an aerospace giant and to its maintenance of that status in a highly competitive global market. Such support can be explained by a number of factors. The first is the sheer size attained by Bombardier, which ranks among the country's top exporters and employs about 40,000 Canadians, mostly in Ontario and Quebec. It is true that aerospace represents only about 50 per cent of the total revenues of the company, but in 2001 it generated 85 per cent of its profit (Macdonald, 2001: 259). The success of that division, in other words, is crucial for the health of the company, and, to the extent that aircraft development and sales depend on public monies, the government would be hard put to cut them off.

The case for subsidies has been contested, but to no avail. Beyond the sheer size of the company and of its workforce in Canada, that failure has two additional sources. One has to be access to government, at various levels. Although left undocumented, for obvious reasons, there is a broadly shared understanding that Laurent Beaudoin, long-time president of Bombardier, had direct access to Prime Minister Jean Chrétien and especially to his Chief of Staff, the former mayor of Quebec City, Jean Pelletier. Moreover, Beaudoin's successor as President and CEO of Bombardier, Robert Brown, is a former military officer who rose to become associate deputy minister at the Department of Regional Industrial Expansion—the federal government's industrial subsidy shop—before joining the company as head of the aerospace division, where he remained for much of the 1990s (Yakabushi, 2000). Finally, much has been made, especially in Brazil, of Bombardier's contributions to the Liberal Party's coffers, which, between 1992 and 1998, were higher than those of any other company.[4] It would be easy, however, to exaggerate the weight of these arguments, since few world-class Canadian companies would not be found among contributors to the Liberal Party, and many enjoy similar access to the Prime Minister's Office and the higher reaches of the bureaucracy, without necessarily getting as much in return.[5]

As in the case of Brazil, a second key factor is probably political and symbolic. Montreal-based Bombardier is the undisputed star of Quebec companies, the foremost—if not only—multinational company that French-Canadian and Québécois nationalists can claim as their own. At the same time, the company and Beaudoin himself did not shy away from taking a stand in the independence debate, stating bluntly during the 1995 referendum campaign that he could not assure Quebecers that Bombardier would stay in Montreal if Quebec became independent. Obviously, from Ottawa's standpoint, this was as good as gold and no doubt was worth as much support as the company might need on the international front. Moreover, this time through a Canadian nationalist lens, the government simply could not let down the company that saved the country's aerospace industry; the memories of the Avro Arrow jet fighter, the well-advanced development of which was abandoned by the Diefenbaker government in 1959, remain vivid.[6]

For these reasons, Bombardier has become so powerful politically that the government has little ability to cross it. For a number of reasons, however, Bombardier's position is significantly less strong than that of Embraer in Brazil. There is a counter-lobby in Canada; Bombardier has many enemies, especially among journalists, commentators, and politicians from western Canada, who see it as the epitome of the government's overwhelming commitment to central Canada (see Macdonald, 2001: 245–51), but also, more generally, in the significant phalanx of free traders that one finds throughout the country, in the media, in the business community, and even within the government itself.[7] The regional dimension of the Bombardier issue is particularly significant; with a Liberal Party that has little support west of Ontario, one can see clearly that a change in government at the federal level, while not necessarily devastating given the dependence of *any* majority government on central Canada, could have significant consequences for Bombardier. Embraer, meanwhile, is virtually immune to political changes at the federal or state levels in Brazil.

THE PREY: A FADING RELATIONSHIP

Given the political weight of the companies involved, a significant impact on bilateral relations was to be expected. Yet, those relations have become so strained and problematic in recent years that the plane fight left little in its wake.

Canada's presence in Brazil goes back more than a century. For much of that period it centred on resources and infrastructure, and was dominated by a single company, Brazilian Light and Traction, later to become Brascan, under which name the company continues to operate. The weight and influence of the 'Light', as it was known then, could hardly be overestimated (McDowall, 1988): Brascan was nicknamed 'the octopus' and at the end of the 1950s it was possibly the biggest firm in Latin America (Sharp, 1994: 85). Even today, electricity bills in the state of Rio are paid to the 'Light', a legacy of the role played by the company in setting up the electricity grid of southeastern Brazil. The Light was obviously a significant political player, and for a long while it remained at the core of the bilateral relationship, a fact reflected by the presence among its local representatives of such political luminaries as Jean-Louis Gagnon and Mitchell Sharp, who was vice-president before running for office the first time. Both were important members of the Liberal Party establishment for much of the post-war period (Gagnon, 1998: 324–8; Sharp, 1994: 85–7).

As befits a relationship so strongly centred on one company, the quasi-total withdrawal of Brascan in 1978 was a massive blow to what looked like a significant economic relationship. For a while, indeed, it appeared that the two countries' economies were quite tightly linked: in the 1970s Brazil came to represent 10 per cent of the total stock of Canada's investments abroad and was by far its most important economic partner beyond the US, Europe, and Japan. When Brascan sold its energy business to the government, the book value of Canadian investments in Brazil fell precipitously to 2 per cent of its global investment stock, where it remains to this day. Trade, similarly, has declined in relative terms to negligible levels, now representing about 1 per cent of Canadian imports and exports.

While the material basis of the relationship shrank dramatically, nothing emerged to take its place. The hardening and turning inward of the military regime (Sennes, 2001; Soares de Lima, 2000: 71–2), especially between 1968 and 1979, made Brazil highly unreceptive to Canada's attempt at developing more diversified foreign relations through the 'Third Option' policy. When Brazil appeared ready to change its mind, at the end of the 1970s and the beginning of the 1980s, little remained to salvage in the relationship. Brazil would soon have little to offer foreign investors since, with the rest of the South America, it would soon be plunged into a 'lost decade'. Canada's so-called rediscovery of the continent, beginning in the

1990s, had little impact on its relationship with Brazil, which remained mired in economic instability until then Finance Minister Fernando Cardoso's Real Plan in 1996. Beyond the lack of interest that stemmed from Brazil's continuing economic mess, and contrary to Canada's naive view, Brazil did not see Canadian involvement in the region as a good sign. Indeed, it became clear that Canada saw itself as a kind of intermediary between the region and the United States, a position that Brazil, since at least World War II and possibly since the beginning of the century, had claimed for itself—however unsuccessfully. Above all, Canada's cheerleading of the Free Trade Area of the Americas (FTAA) process and its very efficient move to set up and prepare the negotiation machinery worked against Brazil's attempt to slow down the hemispheric project while it built up a negotiation coalition of its own (Jubany, 1998: 60–78). Finally, Canada's stand on labour and environmental standards, which are widely perceived in Latin American trade circles as covers for northern protectionism, was indistinguishable from that of the US. As such, the Canadian position was seen in Brazil as proof that, far from playing the role of facilitator or bridge-builder, the 'gringo from the far north'[8] was little more than a gringo, period.

Even if Canada's multilateral hemispheric policy had met with Brazil's approval, which it did not, a series of events conspired to keep the substance of the relationship inconsequential when it was not frankly confrontational, and the public tone and press coverage of the relationship were negative. The first such event was the arrest in 1989—and quick condemnation to 28 years in prison—of two Canadians involved in the kidnapping of a Brazilian businessman. To the Brazilian media and public, it was an open-and-shut case. Denying any guilt, however, Christine Lamont and David Spencer found support in Canada among their families and, soon, among provincial politicians in British Columbia and New Brunswick. Well-covered visits by Canadians and denunciations of Brazil's judicial system in the Canadian press kept the wound open until 1996, when documents discovered in Nicaragua confirmed the couple's long involvement in terrorist activities.[9]

That affair was just subsiding when Canada and then Brazil brought the Bombardier–Embraer case to the WTO. Meanwhile, however, new tensions were generated by the cancellation of a contract worth $125 million between Bombardier and Embraer for the provision of turboprop aircraft to the Bombardier-managed North Atlantic

Treaty Organization (NATO) Flying Training in Canada (NFTC) program, at a former military base in Moose Jaw, Saskatchewan. That project, worth $2.8 billion, was given to Bombardier by the federal government without any tendering process. It held the promise of 'saving' a military base in an economically depressed area that defence cuts apparently condemned. Embraer's participation was terminated unilaterally and the contract given instead to US-based Raytheon. While the details of the affair are still muddled,[10] the loss to Embraer and to Brazil was crystal clear: the plane involved, Embraer's Super Tucano, was to be bought also by the Brazilian army, and with the NATO seal of approval, potentially by other countries, which opened up commercial possibilities for the company and promised substantial savings for the cash-strapped Brazilian government. Needless to say, the development of the affair during the summer and fall of 1997 did nothing to ease tensions between the two companies or the two governments.[11] With supreme irony, press reports recently suggested that the unreliability of Raytheon's Harvard II planes purchased by Bombardier had significantly affected the program (Leblanc, 2000: A1).

The Moose Jaw episode is closely related to another embarrassment—the very public refusal by the Brazilian government to sign, in the name of Mercosur, a Trade and Investment Co-operation Arrangement (TICA) with Canada. Such an agreement, while extremely limited in scope, was important to Canada as a symbolic building block of its hemispheric trade and investment strategy and as a show of interest towards Brazil and its Mercosur partners (Jubany, 1998: 18–25). The TICA signing was to be the Brazilian highlight of a high-level government-private sector visit to Mexico and South America, at the beginning of 1998—one of the earliest 'Team Canada' ventures. The government's decision to go ahead and try to corner the Brazilians into signing the TICA while Team Canada was in São Paulo backfired badly; Brazil's Foreign Minister, Luis Felipe Lampreia, not only refused very publicly to sign but also explicitly linked that decision to Bombardier's decision (Leal, 1998: A6).[12]

Finally, at the beginning of 2001, and at a moment when the tone of the confrontation about aircraft subsidies had gone up significantly, Canada suspended the import of beef from Brazil and had all Brazilian meat products removed from supermarket shelves, alleging risks of mad cow disease. With Canada charged with surveillance in that area for the three NAFTA countries, imports of Brazilian meat products by Mexico and the United States also had to be suspended, although both countries expressed reserves about the severity of Canada's decision and, significantly, did not order a recall of products already on sale on their markets.

The reaction in Brazil was overwhelming and unanimous. The country is an agricultural superpower, it has the biggest cattle herd in the world, and it is traditionally a major meat and meat product exporter. In addition, it was getting the upper hand over a hoof-and-mouth infection that had frozen its exports and, above all, it had never had a single case of mad cow disease, either in native cattle or in imported ones (as had Canada). Finally, cattle ranchers dominate the multi-party Bancada Ruralista or Rural Coalition in Brazil's Congress, the most powerful political coalition in Brasilia. The decision of Canada's health authority, coming in the middle of a heated phase of the aircraft confrontation, became the proverbial last straw.[13] No conclusive evidence was ever produced suggesting that the two affairs were related or that health authorities had in any way been pressured to take that decision—which, for that matter, would have made little if any political sense. Ever since, nonetheless, diplomats from both sides have been trying to improve relations but Canada's benign image in Brazil, already undermined, lay in ruins.

Arguably, an accumulation of events such as these would strain any bilateral relationship and it did throw Brazil–Canada relations into the doldrums. It would be wrong, however, to limit the analysis to those skirmishes, for there are deeper reasons for the diminishing of the relationship between the two countries, reasons that militate against the establishment of a meaningful partnership in the foreseeable future.[14] These reasons explain the importance that the incidents reviewed took on and constitute a drastic limitation on the capacity of the two governments to find a basis of understanding to transcend the plane fight.

The reality is that the two countries have been going through quite divergent processes of integration into the global political economy. While Brazil was going global, Canada was turning North American; in both cases, it meant that the bilateral relationship was becoming increasingly irrelevant.

This diverging pattern starts in Brazil. Beginning with a strategic intervention in the troubled period that followed the establishment of Brazil's First Republic, in 1888, and strongly favoured by an aggressive alliance policy under then Foreign Minister Barão Rio Branco, the United States had been the primary focus of Brazil's foreign relations up until the mid-1960s. Then, after reaching its apex at the beginning of the military regime, the bilateral relationship, if it never really soured, became ever less 'special' (Soares de Lima, 2000). Much of the military regime period was marked by a turning inward of the country, with a concentration on the full exploitation and development of its own potential, a self-centring whose pre-eminent symbol was the Amazonian development policy of the regime. In terms of foreign policy, this meant primarily a disengagement from global affairs. It is only with the full beginning of the civilian period, in 1989, that Brazil really opened up to the world again. By that time, however, the world really meant the world, and Brazil emerged from isolation with a very diversified foreign policy and commercial outlook, which it has maintained since. As much in trade as in political relations, Brazil's foreign policy follows three important axes: the US, the EU, and South America, with an emphasis on the Southern Cone. In addition, it has significant commercial links with Asia and a special relationship with Japan, related among other things to the presence in the São Paulo area of a significant immigrant community from that country. Brazil has also had an active diplomatic presence in southern Africa, primarily in the former Portuguese colonies of Angola and Mozambique, where it has, for instance, concentrated its peace-keeping involvement (Sennes, 2001).

While Brazil has been globalizing, Canada has become ever more North American. In spite of its activism at the UN and in western hemispheric circles, Canada has seen its economy become essentially integrated with that of the United States. The Canada–US Free Trade Agreement and then NAFTA institutionalized and deepened an integration whose foundation had already been established by massive investment flows and whose foremost expression had been the integrated production lines of the auto sector (Molot, 1993). The depth of that economic integration played a key role in what Doern, Pal, and Tomlin should probably have called the 'North Americanization' of Canadian public policy over the last two decades (Doern et al., 1996). Finally, the political and military actions set in motion by the attacks of 11 September on the US appear to be leading to a quick extension of that integration process (Hart and Dymond, 2001), now to include immigration, domestic security policy, and defence.

More than ever in its history, Canada's involvement outside North America has become essentially symbolic. This even applies to its more muscled military manifestations, as in Kosovo and Afghanistan, which cannot be disentangled from Canada's political and security relationship with the United States.

When Brazilian and Canadian diplomats speak of economic and political multilateralism, in other words, the first group refers to a field in which their country and government have important and growing stakes, and the second to an increasingly abstract concept to which they certainly are attached, but largely by inertia, and whose relevance to the economic and political future of the country is limited. Brazil is no power yet, but it certainly is going global. Canada's power is fading, and it is going North American. These diverging paths leave increasingly less space for converging policies and interests.

STRUGGLE IN A BIRDCAGE

Given the larger context of the relationship between Canada and Brazil, the air war per se is essentially irrelevant, because the constraints are such that neither of the governments had policy space or even incentives to look for some.

The first salvos were fired by Canada in 1996, shortly after Bombardier had lost another important contract for regional jets to Embraer. The Canadian government asked for a panel to be struck by the WTO to examine Brazil's Programa de financiamento às exportações (PROEX: Program of support to exports). Brazil struck back a few months later, in 1997, asking the WTO to look at Technology Partnerships Canada and the Canada Account programs of Canada's Export Development Corporation (EDC), a Crown corporation. In decisions made public in 1998, the WTO sent both countries back to their corners, requesting modifications to PROEX and to both Canadian programs. The two countries came back a few months later, each challenging the compliance of the other with the WTO decision. New panels were struck in 2000, and in the end Canada passed the exam and Brazil did not. The Canadian government requested the right to impose tariffs on Brazilian goods entering Canada that would amount to the value of the damage inflicted on Bombardier.[15] The WTO acquiesced to a compensation of $2.065 billion over six years, (WTO, 2000: 26), the biggest such redress it had allowed in its admittedly short history.

Canada's victory proved Pyrrhic. The value of the compensation was such that it would have cut Canada's imports from Brazil in half during the period covered. As we saw, however, Canada is so insignificant a market for Brazilian products that even if it had reduced Brazil's exports, sacrificing Canada on Embraer's altar would have been an easy political choice for the Brazilian government. When the next bidding war came up in 2001, for a contract to Air Wisconsin, it was clear to both Bombardier and Canadian authorities that Embraer's bid would once again be sweetened by the Brazilian government. Canada thus moved in with financing subsidies of its own that proved substantial enough to win the contract for Bombardier.[16] Immediately, Brazil took the case to the WTO, whose decision, announced in February 2002, in the main condemns Canada. At the time of this writing, negotiations are underway between the two countries to resolve the issue, but a likely follow-up is a new request for damages, this time on the part of Brazil. Were the WTO to be agreeable, and it is likely to be so, compensation will be sought by Brazil. If acted on this time, which in turn is likely given the anti-Canada mood of the Brazilian public and political class and the coming general elections in Brazil, this will lead to retaliation by Canada, which would finally act on its threat and impose the punitive tariffs permitted by the WTO in 2000. In the meantime, Canada also subsidized the sale by Bombardier of 75 regional jets to Northwest Airlines, a move that should lead to a new complaint by Brazil. The way things are going, in other words, it looks likely that commercial and political relations between the two countries could well be crippled for some time into the future. Once that happens, any remaining incentive for either side to limit its use of subsidies will also have vanished altogether.

What we have is a clear instance of a prisoner's dilemma: the companies have too much at stake to lose the next contract, and they have too much influence over their respective governments for their requests for subsidies to be turned down. Hence the trap. Now, as game theorists would put it, and as Canadian and Brazilian taxpayers and government officials know only too well, the current 'solution' is, to say the least, suboptimal, and the quest for a way out is open. We will now review some of the alternatives that appear to exist and indicate which ones among them are likely to materialize.

The first possibility is for the game to become unsustainable to both governments. This could happen for two reasons: direct economic cost or negative implications for one or both countries' global trade interests. The cost of current and future financing is difficult to assess, but even a worst-case scenario appears to be sustainable. Using as a base the estimate arrived at by the WTO arbitrators to decide the level of compensation Canada would be allowed to impose on Brazil (about $1.8 million per plane), assuming subsidies for about 200 regional jets, and factoring in the movement of both companies towards larger and more expensive planes, the cost of the subsidies can be estimated at between $360 million and $500 million per year. This is not pocket money, but it certainly remains within the range of possibilities for the governments of two of the world's biggest economies.[17] This might not even change, moreover, were the WTO to agree with Brazil's request for $ 6.4 billion in compensation following the latest condemnation of Canada because such massive sanctions would be so disruptive to even Brazilian importers that they are unlikely ever to be imposed. As the São Paulo newspaper *Valor Econômico* (2002) put it, the two countries find themselves back to square one in the exact same game.

The risks for the parties in continuously bringing cases to the WTO could also be construed as strong pressure on the current game, since the members of the global trade regime have a vested interest in seeing the decisions of the organization respected and are thus likely to band together against violators. Before the February 2002 decision against Canada, this reasoning appeared to apply only to Brazil's policy. In fact, interviews I have done suggest that Bombardier itself has been trying to engineer such a reaction. The attitude of Canadian officials also implies that they share that view. This argument was put best, during a television interview, by William Dymond, from the Centre for Trade Policy and Law at Carleton University, who argued that the price Brazil will end up paying is just too much to bear over time. That view, however, overlooks at least three things: one is the domestic politics of Embraer subsidies, which, as I have demonstrated, leave no room for the government to manoeuvre; the second is the significantly self-contained character of the Brazilian economy, which, not unlike that of the US, depends primarily on domestic demand, a situation drastically distinct from Canada's massive dependence on foreign—read US—markets; the third is the broad understanding of Brazil's situation among WTO members, and most importantly the support it gets from emerging industrial powers, for whom the rules under which Brazil has been condemned create a disadvantage in relation to exporters from developed countries.

To understand that situation, one must go back to the functioning of Brazil's program, PROEX. Under its various guises, it involves a grant from the Brazilian government to an institution, Brazilian or foreign, that *might* use it to lower the interest it charges to the buyer of an Embraer plane—and is obviously expected to do so. Canada's accusation was that the resulting interest rates were lower than those allowed by the Organization for Economic Co-operation and Development (OECD)'s commercial interest reference rates (CIRRs), which the WTO adopted as the reference for credits that were to be exempted from the general ban on export subsidies. This argument is based on the second paragraph of item 'k' of the Marrakesh Treaty that concluded the Uruguay Round. That clause, already buried in Annex I of the Treaty ('Illustrative List of Export Subsidies'), does not even mention the OECD and refers only implicitly to its 'Arrangement on Guidelines for Officially Supported Export Credit'.[18] It is, however, the little hole through which much of existing export subsidies now go, and the key to both Brazil's and Canada's arguments before the WTO since 1996.

Brazil's first line of defence was that the financial institution chosen was not legally compelled to use the money to lower the interest rate it charged a borrower wanting to buy an Embraer aircraft. The second defence was that PROEX in fact conformed to the OECD criteria. The third line is the key: Brazil argued publicly that the use of the OECD rules was an expression of the 'asymmetries of globalization' that the WTO locks in, ignoring 'the difference that exists between countries, especially as to the interest rates offered to companies, a key factor of their competitiveness' (Lafer, 2001). As we saw, the WTO, keeping to the text of the agreement, would have none of it, and condemned the government's use of PROEX in these instances.[19] The point, however, is that Brazil's stand cannot but get sympathy from the more industrialized among the developing countries. Like Brazil, most of them appear to have been unaware of the full implications of that clause for their export subsidies programs, namely, that much of their 'export-oriented' industrial strategy would be subjected to a set of rules devised by a club of which they were not a member.[20]

For these reasons, the promised 'systemic' sanctions are unlikely to materialize, at least in the case of Brazil. Canada's situation is trickier, after its latest move was sanctioned by the WTO (D'Cruz and Gastle, 2002: 33), because, contrary to Brazil, it is a full-fledged member of the OECD. In the end, however, and this also applies to Brazil, Canada is likely to bet on a general understanding among WTO members that this particular dispute is a special case and that the country's attitude in this case cannot be construed as a challenge to the regime as a whole.

In other words, neither financial cost nor systemic pressure appears likely to 'free' the game. Other options have been touted, however. It has been suggested, for instance, that the real way out is to close the game by establishing an informal cartel and effectively dividing up the market. This could simply involve lowering the level of subsidies in such a way that the number of orders end up relatively well distributed—and obviously leaving the WTO out of it. That option, which could lead to an elimination of the subsidies altogether, is certainly open, but it is clearly illegal and the degree of secrecy required from both private sector and government players would make the arrangement highly unstable. In addition, given US antitrust statutes, the risks entailed would be momentous, since the Clayton Act and the Wilson Tariff Act enable the US government to treble the damages suffered by their companies, which, in the absence of subsidies, would likely see the price of the aircraft they buy rise (Gastle, 2002).

Finally, I would suggest that there is a third option, which might already be emerging. It involves a massive broadening of the game through the full consolidation of the global aircraft industry. In one such scenario, Embraer could be taken over, in full or part, by the Airbus group, and Bombardier by Boeing. As we saw, there are already openings in that direction with the French aerospace consortium taking a stake in Embraer. The recent demise of British Aerospace's regional aircraft program would facilitate that movement, as would the recently touted purchase by Bombardier of Germany's Fairchild-Dornier, the third player in the regional jet game. On the minus side, there are no reports of discussions between Bombardier and Boeing. Instead, the two companies are moving towards a direct confrontation in the 90–100-seater market. Still, with the post-11 September air transport crisis, the implications of which are still unclear for the regional jet market, things could move very quickly. Were one of the companies taken over, the other would have no choice but to look for a buyer, because neither Brazil nor Canada could take on the monster subsidizers that sponsor Boeing and Airbus.

Now, *pace* Brazilian and Canadian taxpayers, if such developments could free the bilateral relationship from a massive source of tension, the need to keep jobs at home would probably force their governments to keep subsidizing local facilities of the two companies.

CONCLUSION

Beyond this speculation, the crucial point is that none of these scenarios leaves much policy space to the Brazilian or Canadian governments. The choices will not be theirs to make, and in the meantime they will be hard-pressed to cut the subsidies. The two governments and their bilateral relationship have been taken hostage by the companies they have sponsored, and they will likely remain so until some outside intervention frees them.

As this chapter was finished Canada announced that it would not appeal the WTO decision and would try instead to resolve the dispute through bilateral negotiation. Indeed, a Brazilian newspaper proclaimed the coming end of the dispute (*Jornal do Brasil*, 2002). Such optimism appears utterly misplaced, for the trap is still there. Neither of the two companies can afford to lose the next few contracts, and if need be they will bring in their respective governments to help with subsidies—legally if possible, illegally if required.

Meanwhile, considerable effort is being made in both countries to insulate the bilateral relationship from the aircraft dispute and to find other areas of converging interests. The prospects for these efforts do not look good, however, for at least three reasons: the dispute has such domestic ramifications that it is unlikely the governments will be able to find areas of convergence that are both significant and immune from its shock waves; the companies have no interest in seeing their competition insulated from the broader relationship between the two countries, since a deeper and more diversified relationship would lessen their relative weight in the policy process;[21] finally, the deeper political economy of Brazil's and Canada's international relations is taking them along distinct and increasingly divergent paths.

Much keeps the two countries apart, and very little brings them together. The deepening of a strong bilateral relationship is not worth investing much in for either Brazil or Canada. In many ways, this has been reflected in the limited effort made thus far to build up that relationship. Such relative diplomatic indifference, accompanied by a respectful attitude, is probably the best option currently open to the diplomacy of both countries. Beyond that, there are tourism, culture, and music, which are not bad at all.

Finally, a note on hostage-taking that is closely related to the broader theme of this book: Canada's deepening North American-ization could be creating a standard game for its bilateral relationships with extra-regional countries, especially in the developing world. Every time a large Canadian multinational is involved, the bilateral relationship itself could be on the block for the simple reason that, politically, the preservation of that relationship is likely to have less weight in Canada than the multinational's interests. For a power, how-ever fading, that remains so proud of its multilateralist tradition, such a development would be quite disastrous.

NOTES

This paper has benefited from the lively meeting of contributors that the edi-tors organized and from the suggestions and critiques of Mario Marconini, François Roberge, Ted Hewitt, Annette Hester, Amancio Jorge Oliveira, Chuck Gastle, and Naomi Harrison. It also owes a lot to numerous discussions with Ed Dosman, Maureen Molot, and Florencia Jubany, and to short but pointed exchanges with Philippe Faucher and Michael Hart. Thanks to all.

1.   The nationalism of the Brazilian military regime was rooted in a Cold War out-look; although after 1967 this did not imply a subservient relationship to the United States; anti-Communism was internalized. For the classic statement of that doctrine, see Golbery do Couto e Silva (1981).

2.   Aerospatiale Matra, Dassault Aviation, Snecma, and Thomson-CSF described their involvement as a 'strategic alliance'. Press release by the European Aeronautic Defence and Space Company EADS, 25 Oct. 1999. Available at: <www.eads.net/sml/intl/press/archiv/foundingpartners/aeromatra1999/19991020_bozano.xml>. According to the Brazilian press, Dassault and Embraer have submitted a joint bid for the air force jets. *O Estado de São Paulo*, electronic edition, 3 Oct. 2001.

3.   According to *O Estado de São Paulo* (Augusto, 2001), 'The Air Force will help the company overcome the crisis that forced it to dismiss 14 per cent of its employees.' *O Estado* also specifies that 'in the reequipment plans of the Air Force, only two aircraft cannot be substituted by Embraer planes: the Buffalo transport plane . . . and the Chinook helicopter.'

4.   See *Valor Econômico*, electronic edition, 9 Feb. 2001.

5.   Philippe Faucher first planted a doubt in my mind about the weight of this widely touted factor.

6.   Although having lost some of its emotional charge, the case remains a *cause célèbre* in nationalist circles of English Canada. For examples of the imposing litterature it has generated, see Dow (1997) and Campagna (1992).

7. A case in point is the sympathy with which Brazil's accusations were received in the press when it held that a meat import ban imposed by the government, allegedly for health reasons, was in fact linked to the Bombardier-Embraer affair. For a view that is surprisingly typical of the press treatment of the affair, see *National Post* (2001).

8. To use the famous title of J.C.M. Ogelsby's (1978) pioneering book on Canada's involvement in the Americas.

9. See Vincent (1995) for the whole affair, whose final point was only reached in November 1998, when the two kidnappers were transferred to Canadian prisons.

10. Originally, the main competitor of Embraer's plane, the Super Tucano, was produced by Pilatus, a Swiss company. While the project was being set up by Bombardier, however, Pilatus was bought by Raytheon, one of the biggest military contractors in the United States, which quickly secured a contract to provide trainers to the US Air Force. From then on, the pressure on Bombardier was probably overwhelming, as the profitability of the Moose Jaw venture depended on European countries sending their pilots, a proposition much less interesting if the training was to be realized on a different airplane than that of the US Air Force. Cf. Jubany (1998: 19–20).

11. See the NFTC press releases of 23 Apr. 1997, where Embraer is mentioned as a partner in the venture; 4 Nov. 1997 (NR-97.057), when no aircraft manufacturers are mentioned; and 18 Dec. 1997, when Bombardier announces the agreement with Raytheon.

12. In her careful examination of that episode, Florencia Jubany argues convincingly that the Bombardier issue was not the sole or even the main reason for Brazil's decision, which she traces primarily to Brazil's discontent with Canada's aggressive stance on the FTAA (Jubany, 1998: 78–84). This is strongly supported by the fact that Brazil rallied behind Argentina when the latter signed the agreement a few months later for Mercosur. This has little bearing on our reading of the affair, however, as the TICA episode, particularly the public attempt to force the Brazilians' hand, clearly compounded the tensions existing between the two countries.

13. The episode was front-page news in every Brazilian newspaper in the first three weeks of February 2002. See the electronic editions of *Valor Econômico* and *O Estado de São Paulo*, 5–8 Feb. 2002, for samples. See Daudelin (2001) for a brief analysis of the Canadian side of the affair.

14. This dimension is neglected in Jubany's more optimistic take on the bilateral relationship (Jubany, 1999).

15. All the documents relevant to Canada's complaint before the WTO are under the dispute number DS 46. Those that refer to Brazil's complaint about Canada are under the numbers DS 70 and 71.

16. This should be understood literally and implies nothing about the potential outcome of the competition in the absence of subsidies.

17. See section 3, 'Calculation of the present value of the subsidy', of World Trade Organization, 'Brazil—Export Financing Programme for Aircraft: Recourse to Arbitration by Brazil under Article 22.6 of the DSI and Article 4.11 of the SCM Agreement, Decision by the Arbitrators' (WT/DS46/ARB, 28 Aug. 2000), 23–6.

18. Cf. *The Results of the Uruguay Round of Multilateral Trade Negotiations* (Geneva: WTO, 1994), in particular articles 1 and 3 of the Agreement on Subsidies and Countervailing Measures (pp. 264 and 266), and especially item (k) of Annex I, 'Illustrative List of Export Subsidies' (p. 306).

19. Significantly, the WTO concluded in August 2001 that PROEX was not *as such* illegal, arguing that it could be used in way that would be consistent with OECD rules. It reached the same conclusion, for that matter, about the EDC as a whole and Investissement Québec in its January 2002 decision: while condemning their use in the specific cases examined, it ruled that the programs *as such* were not illegal.

20. Brazil's Foreign Minister, Celso Lafer, who has been for a while his country's ambassador to the WTO, admitted as much: 'During the Uruguay Round negotiations, Brazil was not exporting aircraft; as a result, it did not measure the risk involved in that footnote to the treaty' (Lafer, 2001). A member of Brazil's negotiating team during the last stages of the Uruguay Round confirmed that this one had 'slipped through'. The last stages of the Uruguay Round negotiations took place during a very peculiar period of Brazil's history, and possibly the one when all-out liberalization gained the most support from the political class and large parts of the public. Trade liberalization was basically associated with modernity and Brazil's access to the realm of the 'serious countries'. Dismissing much of the country's past industrial policy, the first fully democratic government of Brazil since the 1960s was busy deregulating, eliminating import tariffs, and supporting global trade liberalization. In addition to that broad openness, limited resources meant that a small mission needed to cover all the bases, which goes a long way towards explaining how this measure slipped through.

21. A case in point is the attitude of Embraer in the face of the wave of goodwill coming from Canada following the WTO decision. As reported in the *National Post* (9 Feb. 2002, electronic edition), 'an executive with Embraer said the Canadian government could not be trusted to negotiate fairly in the latest talks, which are set to resume by April.'

REFERENCES

Augusto, Antônio. 2001. 'Embraer terá contrato de US$3bi com a FAB', *Estado de São Paulo - Estadão.com.br*, 10 Oct.

Bernardes, Roberto. 2000. *EMBRAER. Elos entre Estado e Mercado*. São Paulo: Editora Hucitec.

Bueno, Clodoaldo. 2000. 'Relações Brasil-Estados Unidos (1945–1964)', in José Augusto Guilhon Albuquerque, ed., *Sessenta Anos de Política Externa Brasileira (1930–1990)*, vol. 3, *O Desafio Geoestratégico*. São Paulo: Núcleo de Pesquisa em Relações Internacionais da Universidade de São Paulo.

Campagna, Palmiro. 1992. *Storms of Controversy: The Secret Avro Arrow files Revealed*. Toronto: Stoddart.

Cervo, Amado Luiz, and Clodoaldo Bueno. 1992. *História da Política Exterior do Brasil*. São Paulo: Editora Ática.

Daudelin, Jean. 2001. 'A Loucura da Vaca Louca', *Valor Econômico* (São Paulo), 2 Feb., A10.

D'Cruz, Joseph, and Charles M. Gastle. 2002. *An Expedited Arbitral Mechanism May Be Required to Resolve the Aircraft from Brazil/Canada Dispute*. Saskatoon: Estey Centre for Law and Economics in International Trade.

Doern, G. Bruce, Leslie A. Pal, and Brian W. Tomlin. 1996. *Border Crossings: The Internationalization of Canadian Public Policy*. Toronto: Oxford University Press.

Dow, James. 1997. *The Arrow*, 2nd edn. Toronto: James Lorimer.

Drache, Daniel, and Nirmala Singh. 2001. *The First Seven Years of the WTO and Canada's Role at the Centre Stage: A Report Card on Trade and the Social Deficit*. Toronto: Robarts Centre Research Papers, York University, 18–26.

Gagnon, Jean-Louis. 1988. *Les Apostasies*, Tome II, *Les dangers de la vertu*. Montréal: Editions La Presse ELO.

Gastle, Charles M. 2002. 'Brief Introduction to United States Antitrust Statutes', Toronto, unpublished manuscript.

Golbery do Couto e Silva. 1981. 'O Brasil e a Defesa do Ocidente', in *Conjuntura Política Nacional, O Poder Executivo & Geopolítica do Brasil*, first published in 1958. Brasilia, Rio de Janeiro: Editora Universidade de Brasilia, Livraria José Olypio Editora.

Hart, Michael, and William Dymond. 2001. *Common Borders, Shared Destinies: Canada, the United States and Deepening Integration*. Ottawa: Centre for Trade Policy and Law.

Jornal do Brasil 2002. 'A briga entre Brasil e Canadá pelo mercado de aviação regional está acabando'; 'Canadá opta por acordo com o Brasil', 20 Feb., electronic edition.

Jubany, Florencia. 1998. 'Canada and Brazil in the 1990s: The Aircraft Dispute and the Free Trade Area of the Americas', M.A. thesis, The Norman Paterson School of International Affairs, Carleton University.

———. 1999. *Shall We Samba? Canada-Brazil Relations in the 1990s*. Ottawa: Canadian Foundation for the Americas.

———. 2001. *Getting Over the Jet-Lag: Canada-Brazil Relations 2001*. Ottawa: Canadian Foundation for the Americas.

Lafer, Celso. 2001 'Notas Taquigráficas do Depoimento do Ministro Celso Lafer no Senado, (13 de março de 2001)', Ministério das Relações Exteriores, Assessoria de Comunicação Social, Informação à Imprensa, no 92, 14 Mar. 2001, in *RelNet, Relatório no 015/2001*, 15 Mar.

Leal, Luis. 1998. 'Canadá impaciente com indefinição do Brasil', *Gazeta Mercantil* (São Paulo), 17–18 Jan. 1998, A6.

Leblanc, Daniel. 2001. 'Troubles plague Bombardier NATO deal', *Globe and Mail*, 16 Aug., A1.

Macdonald, Larry. 2001. *The Bombardier Story: Planes, Trains and Snowmobiles*. Toronto: John Wiley & Sons.

McDowall, Duncan. 1988. *The Light: Brazilian Traction, Light and Power Company Limited, 1899–1945*. Toronto: University of Toronto Press.

Molot, Maureen Appel, ed. 1993. *Driving Continentally: National Policies and the North American Auto Industry*. Ottawa: Carleton University Press.

National Post. 2001. 'Beef baloney', 13 Feb.

Ogelsby, J.C.M. 1978. *Gringos from the Far North*. Toronto: Macmillan.

Organization for Economic Co-operation and Development (OECD). 1998. *Arrangement on Guidelines for Officially Supported Export Credit.* Paris: OECD.

Sennes, Ricardo. 2001. 'O Brasil e o Mantenimento da Paz', paper presented at the conference 'The Price of Peace: Political Economy of Peace Operations', Montreal, 30 Nov.–1 Dec.

Sharp, Mitchell. 1994. *Which Reminds Me . . . A Memoir.* Toronto: University of Toronto Press.

Silva, Ozires. 1998. *A Decolagem de um Sonho. A História da Criação da EMBRAER.* São Paulo: Lemos.

Soares de Lima, Maria Regina. 2000. 'As relações do Brasil com os Estados Unidos: 1964–1990', in José Augusto Guilhon Albuquerque, ed., *Sessenta Anos de Política Externa Brasileira (1930–1990)*, vol. 3, *O Desafio Geoestratégico.* São Paulo: Núcleo de Pesquisa em Relações Internacionais da Universidade de São Paulo.

Valor Economico. 2002. 'Brasil e Canadá voltam à estaca zero', 28 Jan.

Vincent, Isabel. 1995. *See No Evil. The Strange Case of Christine Lamont and David Spencer.* Toronto. Reed Books.

World Trade Organization (WTO). 2000. 'Brazil—Export Financing Programme for Aircraft: Recourse to Arbitration by Brazil under Article 22.6 of the DSI and Article 4.11 of the SCM Agreement, Decision by the Arbitrators' (WT/DS46/ARB, 28 Aug.).

Yakubushi, Konrad. 2000. 'Bob Brown in Command', *Report on Business Magazine*, 27 Oct., electronic archive.

13

Canada and the Commonwealth

W. DAVID MCINTYRE

Under Prime Minister Jean Chrétien Canada has been less engaged in the Commonwealth than in the days of Diefenbaker, Pearson, Trudeau, or Mulroney. Canadian political leaders were absent from at least two significant enterprises in 2001. Canada was not selected as a member of the High-Level Review Group (HLRG) charged with advising heads of government on new directions for the twenty-first century, and the Health Minister had to send a deputy to the innovative 13th Commonwealth health ministers' meeting in November 2001. Canada is one of the 'Group of Three' (along with Britain and New Zealand) to have been represented at all the summit meetings since 1887. It is one of the 'ABC Members' (Australia, Britain, Canada) that together always provide over half the association's funds. But Canada's non-inclusion in the HLRG prevented Chrétien—one of the nine longest-serving Commonwealth leaders in 2001—from being among the 10 heads of government who were supposed to provide an update for the Harare Declaration of 1991 and the Millbrook Action Program of 1995.

This absence, not of Canada's choice, was probably unfortunate. The Commonwealth heads of government meeting, planned for Brisbane in October 2001, was postponed at the last minute in the aftermath of the 11 September terrorist attacks in the US. But such information as became available about the draft report of the HLRG indicated that it gave a less than a clear mandate and direction for the Commonwealth in the new millennium and failed to address some of the Commonwealth's most glaring problems. Apart from a salutary emphasis on youth, serious attention to the 'digital divide', and some suggested streamlining of the intergovernmental infrastructure, there was disappointingly little about giving the organization more teeth for dealing with violations of Commonwealth principles or about engaging with the expertise and the concerns of 'civil society'. Some matters, such as sport, private business, education, the need for better public awareness, and the improvement of Commonwealth meetings, were largely ignored. An overall impression was gained of minor tinkering and reiteration of platitudes. Although some of these gaps were filled in the report endorsed at the heads of government meeting in March 2002, this did not address clearly the basic dilemmas of the Commonwealth.

STRUCTURE AND SOFTWARE

The Commonwealth is a voluntary association of 54 independent states that consult and co-operate in matters of common concern and recognize Queen Elizabeth II as their symbolic head of state. It is the oldest, and least understood, political association of states. Second only to the UN in size of membership and geographical spread, it is unique among international bodies for the width and depth provided by its voluntary and sporting aspects—its people-to-people links. The biennial summit meetings are the oldest, largest, and longest regular meetings of heads of government and they now constitute the premier forum for the small states that make up the majority of the member countries. At a pre–heads of government meeting seminar in Johannesburg in 1999, Charles van der Donckt, from the Policy Planning Staff of DFAIT, said that common heritage and language were the 'software' that enables the Commonwealth network to function (van der Donckt, 1999: 32). As Canadian Senator Gildas Molgat put it, at the opening of the 14th Commonwealth Education Ministers' Conference at Halifax in November 2000, the 'glue' that binds the Commonwealth 'is to be found in a shared heritage, with the resulting similarity of institutions, governing structures, education systems, and approaches to civil society, and by a shared language' (Molgat, 2000).

If Margaret Ball's analogy of an iceberg is used, only the tip is visible (Ball, 1971: 78–9). This comprises the quadrennial Commonwealth Games, the Queen as Head of the Commonwealth, and, occasionally, the heads of government meetings. Most of the organization is hidden below the waterline of public and media attention. This includes regular official, ministerial, and regional meetings, the permanent infrastructure of intergovernmental organizations (IGOs), and the Secretary-General. These constitute the *official Commonwealth*—historically the most familiar aspect. However, there is now much more to command our consideration, partly stemming from the growing complexity of international relations induced by environmental, human rights, health, gender, and social issues. Thus, the *voluntary, unofficial Commonwealth* of non-governmental organizations (NGOs), known as 'civil society', has been given an increasing role since the early 1990s when the phrase 'People's Commonwealth' gained currency. In Canada, the association of NGOs with policy-making was unusually enhanced by Foreign Affairs Minister Lloyd Axworthy (Rooy, 2001: 253–4). Large claims have been made more recently for the private sector, or *corporate Commonwealth*—private investment, corporate business management, and public/private partnerships. There has been optimistic talk of a 'Commonwealth business culture'. As the new century opened, the future balance between these three elements—official, voluntary, and corporate—was uncertain and the HLRG did not resolve the issue.

THE VISIBLE TIP

Of the few visible elements, sport is by far the most popular. The Commonwealth Games, for the majority of people, is their only point of knowledge about the Commonwealth. In addition, more continuously popular team sports that engage the enthusiasm of millions include cricket and rugby football, where most of the leading protagonists are Commonwealth countries. In this sporting Commonwealth, Canada has always been in the lead (although not in cricket and rugby). The first 'British Empire Games' was held in Hamilton, Ontario, in 1930. The first 'British Empire and Commonwealth Games' (and the first to be televised and to stage a parallel physical education congress) was in Vancouver in 1954. The first 'Commonwealth Games' (and the first to include a Commonwealth Arts Festival) was at Edmonton in 1978 (Dheensaw, 1994). Canadian contingents to the Games are always among the largest. After Victoria, BC, won the bidding to host the 1994 Games, the Canadian government was so concerned for the future of the Games (and, possibly, embarrassed by the resentments caused by the rejection of New Delhi's bid) that it ensured that the future of the Games was placed on the agenda of the Kuala Lumpur heads of government meeting in 1989. This led to a Working Party, later the Commonwealth Committee on Co-operation Through Sport (CCCS), chaired by Roy McMurtry, former High Commissioner in London and Associate (later Chief) Justice of Ontario, with Anne Hillmer, a former head of the International Sports Relations section of the Department of External Affairs, and a member of the Canadian Olympic Association, as executive secretary.

Throughout the 1990s the CCCS presented eloquently argued biennial reports to heads of government on the importance of sport for individual values and personal character-building, for identity-building at the national level, and, more recently, for health and economic development. Some governments were persuaded to give assistance to the Commonwealth Games Federation to ensure the continuation of the Games and new sports were added. The four most developed member countries made sports assistance part of their regional development aid programs. In Canada's case, the instrument was the Commonwealth Sport Development Program, which gave aid for infrastructure and for projects with youth, women, and girls. In the Canadian-supported Mathare Youth Sports Association in Kenya, footballers also became involved in youth leadership, environmental cleanup, and HIV/AIDS education (CCCS, 1999: 19–22).

The theme most often promulgated by the CCCS was that sport was the only point of identification with the Commonwealth for the vast majority of people and it was an activity that engaged loyalties across the generations and from presidents to peoples. Roy McMurtry's relinquishment of the chair and Anne Hillmer's untimely death, in 2001, marked the end of an era for the CCCS and the end of Canada's leadership. For some time, Australia had been eager to take the lead. There was a delay because of the postponement of the heads of government meeting, but in January 2002 the Secretary-General called on the Australian Sports Commission to provide the Chair and Secretariat for the CCCS.

Second in visibility and popular awareness after the Games is the Head of the Commonwealth (McIntyre, 1991: 244–61). Queen Elizabeth II is, of course, also Head of State of Canada and another 15 of the member states, but the majority of the members are republics. A long-standing campaign for a republic in Australia received a setback in 1999 when the option of a republic with a President elected by Parliament was outvoted in a referendum. At least two New Zealand prime ministers have declared themselves to be republicans, but the issue appears to have been shelved for the duration of the present reign. In Canada, by contrast, debates about the monarchy have always been less significant than those about the future of Confederation, but the issue surfaces periodically. In May 2001 Foreign Affairs Minister John Manley restated his objection to a 'foreign' head of state and suggested that 'people realize that it's an institution that is a bit out-of-date for Canada to continue with.' This was passed over by the Prime Minister's Office as a personal view and with the statement that 'Canada has no intention of opening up a debate on the future of the monarchy' (Ingram, 2001: 489).

More importantly, the Head of State issue has to be separated from the Head of the Commonwealth issue. Although 'common allegiance to the Crown' was once tenaciously held as the ultimate bond of the Commonwealth, it was quite suddenly dropped in 1949 to accommodate independent India's wish to remain in the Commonwealth as a republic. By the London Declaration leaders of the Commonwealth agreed to accept 'The King as the symbol of the free association of its independent members and as such the Head of the Commonwealth' (Communiqués 1, 1987: 29). Some vital words in this formula were provided by then Foreign Minister Lester B. Pearson. By the end of the twentieth century, 32 of the 54 members were republics and six had their own traditional rulers.

Although republican status does not affect membership, the very different question of the succession to the headship came to the surface in the 1990s. Two views on this are possible. One holds that the headship went with the Crown—that acceptance of the symbolic Head of the Commonwealth in 1949 was simply a verbal substitute for 'common allegiance to the Crown'. The other view holds that the headship is personal. The 1949 Declaration referred to the 'King' and not the

'Crown'. The only precedent is not helpful. In 1952, when George VI died, Nehru, Prime Minister of India, the only republic of the day, sent a telegram of condolence to Queen Elizabeth II in which he welcomed her as the new Head of the Commonwealth (*Times*, 9 Feb. 1952). The others agreed, even though the mechanisms by which they did so have not been divulged. Recent controversies about the heir to the throne have led to discussion about the headship succession. This was further complicated by the report of an Intergovernmental Group on Criteria for Commonwealth Membership in 1997 (on which Canada was represented). The Group was set up at the Auckland heads of government meeting in 1995, after Cameroon's and Mozambique's accession to membership had puzzled many people, who then were bemused by applications to join from Rwanda, Yemen, and the Palestinian Authority. The Intergovernmental Group's report, which was endorsed by the Edinburgh heads of government meeting of 1997, listed the criteria for membership under three categories: historic links (through earlier British rule or an administrative link with another member); adherence to Commonwealth values (summarized in the Harare Declaration of 1991 as democracy, human rights, good governance, and the rule of law); and adherence to certain Commonwealth 'norms and conventions', one of which was acceptance of the 'British monarch as Head of the Commonwealth' (Collinge, 1996: 279–86). This last phrase, which appeared to downgrade Canada and the other 14 nations besides the UK that recognize the monarch as the Head of State, was not specifically mentioned in the communiqué approved by the heads of government.

Although some senior officials believed that the endorsement of the criteria report had secured the succession of Prince Charles, it is likely that most heads of government did not understand this, as they did not discuss the details of the report as opposed to the blander communiqué. Thus, the question of succession to the headship remained an issue on the eve of the golden jubilee of Elizabeth II's reign. In June 2001, the Commonwealth Secretary-General, Don McKinnon (former deputy to a republican-inclined New Zealand Prime Minister), appeared to lend support to the 'personal title' interpretation when he said the future of the headship would have to be the subject of consultation at the time of the Queen's death. By the time that this happens, it could be that a symbolic head will not be deemed necessary or immediate consensus for continuation may be achieved as part of the accession formalities.

The third element of the visible Commonwealth is provided by the biennial heads of government meetings, which, since 1971, mostly have been held in various large convention centres in cities around the Commonwealth, including Ottawa (1973) and Vancouver (1987). Canadian prime ministers—Laurier, Borden, King, Diefenbaker, and Pearson—had made notable contributions to earlier Commonwealth conclaves. In the era of meetings of heads of governments, Canada has pioneered improvements to these meetings. Pierre Trudeau resolved that for the Ottawa meeting more informal procedures would preclude long set-piece speeches, and he arranged the first weekend retreat for heads of government and spouses only—trying to recapture the spirit of informal weekends in earlier days at Chequers, the country home of British prime ministers. Brian Mulroney pioneered the shorter meeting at Vancouver in 1987. Only five days were allocated to match the Francophone Summit in Quebec in the same year. After a brief return to week-long events, the meetings during the 1990s lasted three and a half days. At Vancouver in 1987 there was a 'Small States Exposition' and a foreign ministers' panel before a student audience, in addition to the formal meeting. These prefigured, in part, the Commonwealth 'People's Forums', which were tried in 1997, 1999, and 2001.

Canada tends to send strong, efficient, well-briefed, but not excessively large delegations. In the past their press conferences have been the most informative available. One could guess that recommendations for streamlining the business of these meetings and reducing some of the excessively pretentious delegations will have figured in the Canadian submission to the HLRG. Yet accident may have achieved such reform more effectively. The postponement of the Brisbane meeting in October 2001 and the subsequent organization of a truncated meeting at Coolum Beach, Queensland, in March 2002 suggest a permanent move towards simpler retreat-like meetings, detached from NGO jamborees (and possible anti-globalization demonstrations), and with much of the main business transacted by preliminary officials' meetings.

THE HIDDEN ELEMENTS: OFFICIAL COMMONWEALTH

Beyond the spotlight of popular and media attention, the ongoing work of the official Commonwealth is pursued in the periodic meetings of ministers, officials, and experts and through the intergovernmental organizations. Many ministerial meetings take advantage of gatherings of major international agencies. The HLRG first met in New York at the time of the UN General Assembly in September 2000. Finance ministers meet before the annual meetings of the World Bank and IMF, health ministers before the World Health Assembly. Triennial meetings of law, education, and (only recently) health ministers meet in parallel with larger professional conferences. There are also meetings of ministers responsible for labour, agriculture, women's affairs, the environment, youth, and science. The 14th Education Ministers' Conference at Halifax, in November 2000, was combined with a Parallel Symposium and Trade Fair on 'Commonwealth Knowledge Solutions' involving 400 representatives of NGOs and education institutions. The ministers reviewed the education work of the Secretariat, made pledges of money for the Commonwealth of Learning (COL), and adopted, for the first time, a general statement on rights of access to education and called on all Commonwealth agencies to enhance these rights (CCEM 14, 2000). In the following year the Commonwealth Consortium for Education, consisting of a group of 12 organizations, was created to try and achieve an adequate voice with the HLRG.

Canada has played a leading role in the most powerful ministerial organ created in recent years—the Commonwealth Ministerial Action Group (CMAG), set up in 1995 at the time of Nigeria's suspension from membership as a mechanism for dealing with 'serious and persistent violations' of the Harare principles. Building on the experience of the Committee of Foreign Ministers on Southern Africa, set up in 1987 under the chairmanship of Secretary of State for External Affairs Joe Clark, Canada took a lead at the 1995 heads of government meeting in pressing for a stringent approach to the problem of 'errant states'. Prime Minister Chrétien, along with President Nelson Mandela of South Africa, was a strong advocate of the Millbrook Action Program and Canada was given one of the eight initial seats on the CMAG (Communiqués 2, 1997:156–9). The Group concentrated first on undemocratic violations by Nigeria, Sierra Leone, and Gambia. Canada's membership in the CMAG was renewed in 1997 and 1999. In response to the military coup in Pakistan in October 1999, when the elected government of Nawaz Sharif was overthrown by General Pervez Musharraf, the CMAG moved fast to send a mission led by Lloyd Axworthy, who warned Musharraf that there were three options. Pakistan could be suspended from Commonwealth councils, suspended from membership, or expelled from the association. The

Axworthy mission recommended the first or 'lightest sentence'—suspension from Commonwealth councils, which was done on the eve of the Durban heads of government meeting (Durban Communiqué, 1999: 10). This meant that, as the postponed Australia meeting approached in 2002, a country that had acquired immense strategic importance in the post-September 2001 war against terrorism, and whose stability had become a key interest of many countries, was still excluded from Commonwealth discussions.

In 2000 the CMAG turned its attention to the military regime in Fiji, which was also suspended from Commonwealth councils, and to militia disorders in the Solomon Islands. Fiji was readmitted to the councils in December 2001 after new elections. Growing government violence and abuse of civil rights in Zimbabwe presented delicate procedural problems since there was a constitutionally elected government. The problem was initially raised only informally. Canada wanted a tougher line and supported a CMAG recommendation to the HLRG that the Commonwealth, using the Secretary-General's 'good offices', should investigate cases of 'perceived' violations of Commonwealth principles and not confine its attention simply to unconstitutional overthrow of governments. The CMAG specifically reiterated the possibility of expulsion from membership, but the HLRG adopted a blander formula. However, by its 20 December 2001 meeting, CMAG patience in the face of continued violence in Zimbabwe was exhausted. Agreeing that the situation constituted 'a serious and persistent violation' of the Harare principles, the CMAG resolved to place Zimbabwe on its formal agenda (CMAG 17, 2001: 2–3). At the 30 January 2002 meeting a move by Britain to suspend Zimbabwe from Commonwealth councils only received firm support from Australia and Barbados. The general view, supported by Canada, was that they would have liked to suspend Zimbabwe out of their sheer frustration, but that the CMAG could only do this in the event of a coup. Thus they simply called on the government of Zimbabwe to end violence and intimidation and conduct a fair election so that the people's voice could prevail (CMAG 18, 2002: 2). At the Coolum meeting in March 2002, Chrétien led off the discussion that dominated the leaders' retreat, but was unable to float a bridge-building formula. Britain and New Zealand called for suspension, but the only thing the leaders could agree on was to set up a troika of past, present, and future chairpersons (Mbeki, Howard, and Obasanjo) mandated to make a decision on behalf of the Commonwealth after the report of the Commonwealth observers of the Zimbabwe election. This was like shutting the stable door after the horse had bolted, and raised a real possibility that members would not necessarily follow a troika ruling. In the event, the Commonwealth observers wrote a damning report on the Zimbabwe election. After Mbeki and Obasanjo visited Harare and failed to persuade Mugabe to form a government of national unity, John Howard announced in London on 19 March the suspension of Zimbabwe from Commonwealth councils. It was the 'lightest sentence' under the Millbrook options, which include suspension of membership or expulsion. The contrast between the Commonwealth's response to Pakistan's bloodless coup in 1999 and two years of bloodshed and violence under Zimbabwean 'democracy' could not be more marked.

A big gap in the sequence of ministerial meetings relates to foreign ministers. A handful meet in the CMAG, as they did in earlier committees on southern Africa, but the only full meeting of foreign ministers was held in Ceylon in 1950, from which the Colombo Plan emerged. A proposal for regular foreign ministers' meetings was included in the HLRG report in 2002 (Commonwealth, 2002: 15).

Canada has always played a major role in support of the inter-governmental organizations, being the second largest contributor of funds after Britain. Their respective contributions come to 30 per cent and 25 per cent of the Commonwealth's budgets. Canada provided the first Secretary-General, Arnold Smith, from 1965 to 1975, whose chief institutional legacy is the Commonwealth Fund for Technical Co-operation (CFTC) (Smith, 1981). Moreover, for about 20 years, from the mid-1970s to the mid-1990s, Canada's contribution to the CFTC—the Commonwealth's largest single budget item—exceeded Britain's. The dollar value of Canadian contributions for the year 2000–1 was $26.3 million. This was made up of $4,923,000 to the Secretariat (19 per cent); $1,580,000 to the Commonwealth Youth Program (28 per cent); $12,000,000 to the CFTC (29 per cent). In addition, $2.1 million went to the COL, and Canada contributes $4,740,000 for scholarships. There is also a contribution of $250,000 to the costs of the Joint Office in New York for Permanent Missions to the UN from small states (DFAIT, 2001).

After the Secretariat, the second IGO, the Commonwealth Foundation, has a staff of little more than a dozen and, with a budget of only £2.6 million, is on an altogether smaller scale than the Secretariat. The Canadian contribution for 2000–1 was $1,360,000.

The Foundation's original role was to foster professional exchanges, and its great contribution was to encourage and support the growth of some 40 new associations. After its mandate was expanded in 1980 to include a large list of development, welfare, and cultural categories, it began to work with a much wider range of NGOs. Quadrennial NGO fora began in 1991 and in 1995 the Foundation promulgated *Non-Governmental Organisations: Guidelines for Good Policy and Practice.* It included the four-part definition of NGOs as voluntary, independent, not-for-profit, and not self-serving (Ball and Dunn, 1995: 19). This excluded professional organizations, but the Foundation did not stop supporting them.

The third major IGO—the Commonwealth of Learning—is located in Vancouver and receives grants from both the federal and British Columbia governments. In response to the drastic drop in student mobility caused by cost-recovery fee regimes during the 1980s in the traditional meccas of higher education (notably Britain), Lord Briggs (Chancellor of Britain's Open University) was charged to report on the possibilities of distance learning. His report proposing a 'University of the Commonwealth for Co-operation in Distance Education' was accepted by the Vancouver heads of government meeting in 1987. The British Columbia government offered a major grant in order to secure the venue of the COL. The idea was not for an institution to enrol students, but a brokerage house to build up and share expertise and information around the Commonwealth. The visionary goal, as stated by the Briggs Report, was that 'any learner, anywhere in the Commonwealth, shall be able to study any distance-teaching program available from any bona fide college or university in the Commonwealth' (Briggs, 1987: 50). The COL began work in January 1989, with Canada providing the second largest contribution after Brunei, but in its early years the COL was racked by controversy and plagued by insecurity of funding. The Brunei largesse was withdrawn at one point, as was the British Columbia grant. In 1993 the COL was reviewed by Ian MacDonald of York University, who subsequently became Chairman of the Board of Governors. The 'any learner anywhere' vision became somewhat muted as slender resources were concentrated on technical and vocational training, continuing education and professional development, open schooling, and non-formal education—all with emphasis on gender equality (Dhanarajan, 2001).

New funding arrangements were sought, and by the end of the 1990s these were determined at the triennial meetings of education ministers. The target of Cdn$5 million per year was to be met by three tiers of contributors. Of this total, $4 million would be contributed jointly by a tier comprising Australia, Britain, Canada, India, and New Zealand. At the start of the new century, Canada remained one of the largest contributors. To a revised $9 million total, agreed at the Halifax Education Ministers' Conference in 2000, $1.1 million came from the federal government and $1 million from the BC government.

THE VOLUNTARY COMMONWEALTH

Commensurate with their contributing a quarter of the Commonwealth's working budgets, Canadians show a high level of awareness of the Commonwealth. A DFAIT-sponsored poll in 1999 indicated a 66 per cent familiarity with the Commonwealth, which came second after the UN among international institutions (van der Donckt, 1999: 38). At the same time, Canadian voluntary organizations have always been prominent in the civil society dimension of the Commonwealth. Supplementing and re-enforcing the work of the IGOs and the official Commonwealth, the 'People's Commonwealth' of NGOs played an increasing role in the 1990s. It should not be forgotten, however, that these had been present from the start of the Commonwealth and represent a major part of its uniqueness. Indeed, the oldest NGOs—the Press Union (1909), the Parliamentary Association (1911), and the Universities Association (1913)—predated World War I. Dating from 1925, the pioneer women's organization (and the first NGO to incorporate 'Commonwealth' rather than 'Empire' in its title) was the British Commonwealth League, now Commonwealth Countries League (to which Canada's Imperial Order of the Daughters of Empire was affiliated) (McIntyre, 2001: 169–70, 178–9). The Royal Commonwealth Society (recipient of a $20,000 grant from the federal government in 2000–1) began as the Royal Colonial Institute in 1868. The Ottawa branch pioneered the youth heads of government meetings, which send their communiqués to their political counterparts.

One of the oldest and most prominently recognized organizations is the Commonwealth Parliamentary Association (CPA), which has always had strong support in Canada, where there are now 14 branches. CPA Secretary-General Arthur Donahue, a former Speaker of the Nova Scotia House of Assembly, reported in 1999 that one of the newest branches was from the Legislative Assembly of Nunavut

(Donahue, 1999). At the time of the 46th CPA Conference in London and Edinburgh in September 2000, there were 162 branches in national, provincial, and territorial legislatures. During the parallel conference of Commonwealth Women Parliamentarians in 2000, Canadian leadership was again evident from the report that bills before the Ottawa Parliament were now subject to 'gender analysis' to ensure the absence of discrimination. The Commonwealth Foundation's *Guidelines for NGOs* listed 2,000 organizations in Canada specializing in environmental issues alone (Ball and Dunn, 1995: 8).

With Foundation encouragement and support, some 40 new professional associations have been created since the 1960s. For about a decade, from the mid-1980s, the Foundation created a network of Commonwealth Liaison Units (CLUs) to link up NGOs at the national, regional, and pan-Commonwealth levels. But in 1993 the Secretariat appointed its own NGO Liaison Officer, who began to organize special accreditation for NGOs at Commonwealth heads of government meetings, where meeting rooms and documentation centres were also provided. Starting modestly with a dozen NGOs at Limassol, Cyprus, in 1993, this dimension had expanded in Durban in 1999 to 300 people from some 60 NGOs. In Edinburgh (1997), Durban (1999), and Brisbane (2001), large Commonwealth People's Forums were organized alongside the formal meetings, where hundreds of NGOs (not necessarily with a Commonwealth focus) ran mini-conferences, symposia, and exhibitions. The Brisbane 'Commonwealth Festival' went ahead, in a much truncated form, in spite of the postponement of the heads of government meeting.

The most significant endeavour of the 'People's Commonwealth' was the Foundation's largest research project—on Civil Society and Governance. The five-member Eminent Persons Panel included Maurice Strong, the environmental economist who headed Canada's external aid program from 1966 to 1971 and later became a special adviser to the UN Secretary-General. The study involved seeking the opinions of over 10,000 ordinary citizens in 47 countries. The results were reported and analyzed in *Citizens and Governance: Civil Society in the New Millennium*, which was tabled at the 1999 heads of government meeting. The researchers had asked three rather sophisticated questions: (1) What is your view of the 'good society' and to what extent does such a society exist today? (2) What roles are best played by citizens and what roles are best played by the state and other sectors in such a good society? What limits the playing of such roles in today's society? (3) What would enable citizens to play their role in the development of society more effectively in the future? A large part of the report consisted of quotations from the answers of ordinary citizens. These were often very moving, though, perhaps because Canada is a highly developed country, it did not provide quotable copy. The conclusions of the report ran counter to the free market, user-pays, privatizing, and globalizing orthodoxy of much recent official Commonwealth consensus. The message came through clearly that ordinary people are concerned about *basic needs* (economic, social, and physical security) and *association* in communities (including respect for culture, sharing, and caring), and that they wish to *participate* (in responsive and just government). People expect the state to be a *provider* of services and law, a *facilitator* of participation, and a *promoter* of equality and justice (*Citizens and Governance*, 1999: 75–8).

When this message was tabled at the Durban meeting in 1999, the heads of government seemed unprepared for it. They responded somewhat feebly by referring the report to officials for detailed consideration before the 2001 meeting. Yet the HLRG gave it scant attention and merely suggested that the Secretariat, the Foundation, and the Secretary-General should work out criteria for accrediting NGOs to ministerial meetings for approval in December 2002. Meanwhile, at the national and regional levels, an ongoing 'Citizenship and Governance' program went forward under the Foundation's leadership. In Canada, the project on the theme 'Venting to Inventing' was co-ordinated by Miriam Wyman, a consultant with Practicum Ltd who contributed a theoretical paper in July 2001 on citizen-centred governance and some of the barriers to achieving it (Wyman, 2001).

THE CORPORATE COMMONWEALTH

While the 'People's Commonwealth' began to come into its own to mobilize citizens and civil society, a new 'Star in the East' appeared in the second half of the 1990s in the optimistic role accorded to private business. The Commonwealth Private Investment Initiative (CPII) and the Commonwealth Partnership for Technology Management (CPTM) were launched at the Auckland meeting in 1995. Canada was one of 13 government participants in the CPTM, donating $100,000 per year. Bombardier Transportation was one of the 16 original corporate members (CPTM, 1994: 1). In 1996, a discussion paper by Australian Katherine West spoke of a 'Commonwealth business culture' comprising use of a common language, and comparable administrative and legal systems (West, 1996: 26–9). Building on the initiatives at the 1995 heads of government meeting, the British hosts went further in 1997 when the Edinburgh meeting was preceded by the First Commonwealth Business Forum. Here it was decided to create the Commonwealth Business Council. The themes of private investment, technology transfer, public-private partnership, and globalization dominated discussion in 1997 and 1999. The role of private investment and public-private partnerships in sustainable development were also seen to be dependent on good governance, a stable society, the rule of law, and equal opportunities.

In this way it could be said that in 1997 the political and economic tenets of the Harare Declaration were brought together and great faith was laid on the corporate Commonwealth, especially the role of the new information technologies, market forces, and the spread of private investment and business expertise. Such private-sector involvement in the ongoing work of the Commonwealth was associated with the Commonwealth finance ministers' first post–IMF/World Bank meeting, held in Ottawa in September 1998. A parallel meeting of the Commonwealth Business Forum took place, at which Finance Minister Paul Martin put forward a six-point plan to secure sustained growth, reduce the risk of financial crises, and take heed of the needs of the poorer countries (Martin, 1998: 33–8). While Canadian political and business leaders take part in this Forum, the government does not give financial support. This remains a truly private-sector enterprise. The Business Forum did not get a mention in the HLRG report.

THE IMPACT OF 11 SEPTEMBER 2001 ON THE COMMONWEALTH

The turmoil of 11 September came only three weeks before Commonwealth leaders were scheduled to meet in Brisbane. Some officials, media, and NGO representatives had already set out for Australia when it was announced that the Queen's visit and the Brisbane meeting were postponed. Prime Minister Chrétien was one of the key leaders, along with the British and Indian prime ministers, whose intimation that they could not leave their capitals tipped the balance against going ahead. A group of Caribbean prime ministers facing catastrophic drops in tourism also decided to stay at home. The Commonwealth finance ministers' meeting and the Commonwealth Business Forum were also cancelled. As noted above, the People's Festival and the Youth Forum went ahead in Brisbane, but with a much lower attendance and impact than had been hoped.

As well as the postponement of the meeting, the 11 September incidents dented Commonwealth credibility in other ways. The Commonwealth did not issue a statement condemning terrorism for more than a month after the event. The Secretary-General then called a Commonwealth Committee on Terrorism (of which Canada was a member). The CCOT formulated an action plan that was approved at Coolum in March 2002 by the heads of government, who pledged themselves to assist member countries in preparing model legislation and measures to trace, freeze, and confiscate terrorist assets. The postponement of the Brisbane meeting also meant that President Mugabe did not have to face his fellow heads of government, as he scheduled the Zimbabwe election for just after the Coolum meetings, thus contributing to a much-distorted meeting agenda. In general, the Commonwealth entered the new century facing a tri-sector dilemma, and remained uncertain of the relative roles of the official, voluntary, and corporate Commonwealths (McIntyre, 2001: 226–9). Yet the first major Commonwealth conference after 11 September exemplified a pattern that points to a possible resolution of the tri-sector dilemma. This was the 13th Commonwealth Health Ministers' Meeting held at Christchurch, New Zealand, in November 2001.

As well as representing a 'resumption of business' by the Commonwealth, this meeting of health ministers saw four innovations. First, it was preceded by an 'NGO Consultation', held at the University of Canterbury, where 41 pan-Commonwealth, regional, and national NGOs considered the major agenda items that the ministers were about to discuss and were listened to by the CHMM chair. Second, and building on the example of the education ministers in Halifax a year earlier, there was, for the first time at a health ministers' meeting, a parallel 'Commonwealth Health Symposium and Trade Fair' sponsored by Kensington Publications Ltd. Led by the Chairman of the Nuffield Trust, John Wyn Owen, the symposium considered health-care priorities, in particular, the role of new technologies. Third, the NGO Consultation and the parallel symposium were integrated with the ministerial meeting through joint panels, inter-sector reporting, and NGO and private-sector input into the communiqué. Fourth, the media were admitted freely for the first time to all meetings, including ministerial committees, except for a brief exclusion from a sensitive debate on one communiqué item.

Canada, although not represented by the Health Minister, had a prominent presence at this Christchurch meeting. When commitments of financial support for the Secretariat's Technical Support Group on Gender and Health were called for, Dr Jeannot Castonguay, the Parliamentary Secretary for Health, led the pledging with a Cdn$40,000 grant over two years. This was in marked contrast to the Australian and British representatives, who declined support. The ministerial committee on tobacco and health was chaired by Dr Judith Shamian, Executive Director of Nursing Policy in Health Canada, and a strong paper on Canada's smoking eradication programs was considered. The interaction of NGOs, professionals, administrators, and private-sector health providers with the ministers and officials in Christchurch was deemed to be stimulating and successful (CHMM 13, 2001). It adds positive re-enforcement to the 'civil society and governance' theme of the past four years in the Commonwealth, and is consistent with the UN's 'International Year of Volunteers' in 2001.

The events and aftermath of 11 September surely highlight the importance of the civil society dimension of the Commonwealth. Numerous civil society voluntary organizations work to enable people to grapple with the problems of globalization, poverty, disease, illiteracy, and poor housing, and, above all, to gain a sense of belonging and participation. A positive Canadian endorsement of the Commonwealth's role was made in 1999 when van der Donckt called it a 'flexible and decentralised instrument which does not demand constant political attention; it is a cost-effective co-operative framework which does not engulf vast amounts of public funds; it does not suffer from major structural characteristics which can paralyse its functioning under adverse political conditions' (van der Donckt, 1999: 33). The HLRG report, endorsed at Coolum in March 2002, for all its limitations, did look to enhance these assets: 'we seek a Commonwealth known, and valued by its peoples, [for its] response to their evolving needs and invigorated by a more focussed and productive partnership between governments and civil society' (Commonwealth, 2002: 2). The voluntary and corporate Commonwealths provide opportunities for involving people in constructive activities that can gain the ear of governments, rather than expressing frustration in destructive terrorist acts.

REFERENCES

Ball, Colin, and Leith Dunn. 1995. *Non-Governmental Organisations: Guidelines for Good Policy and Practice.* London: Commonwealth Foundation.

Ball, Margaret. 1971. *The Open Commonwealth.* Durham, NC: Duke University Press.

Briggs, Asa. 1987. *Towards a Commonwealth of Learning: A Proposal to Create the University of the Commonwealth for Co-operation in Distance Education.* London: Commonwealth Secretariat.

Commonwealth Committee on Co-operation Through Sport (CCCS). *Report of the 1999 Committee on Co-operation Through Sport.* London: Commonwealth Secretariat.

CCEM (14th Conference of Commonwealth Education Ministers). 2001. Communiqué in *The Round Table* (Halifax) 90, 358 (26–30 Nov.): 46–51.

CHMM (13th Commonwealth Health Ministers' Meeting). 2001. Communiqué, Christchurch, New Zealand, 29 Nov.

Citizens and Governance: Civil Society in the New Millennium. 1999. London: Commonwealth Foundation.

CMAG (17th Meeting of Commonwealth Ministerial Action Group on the Harare Declaration). 2001. Concluding statement, 20 Dec.

Collinge, John. 1996. 'Criteria for Commonwealth Membership', *The Round Table* 85, 339: 279–86.

Commonwealth. 2002. *Report of the Commonwealth High-Level Review Group to Commonwealth Heads of Government, Coolum Australia*, HGM (02) 9, 3 Mar.

Communiqués 1. 1987. *Commonwealth at the Summit*, vol. 1, *Communiqués of Commonwealth Heads of Government Meetings 1944–1986.* London: Commonwealth Secretariat.

Communiqués 2. 1997. *Commonwealth at the Summit*, vol. 2, *Communiqués of Commonwealth Heads of Government Meetings 1987–1995.* London: Commonwealth Secretariat.

CPTM (Commonwealth Partnership for Technology Management). 1994. 'Canada Country Task'.

Department of Foreign Affairs and International Trade (DFAIT). 2001. Table of contributions to Commonwealth organizations, 2000–1, courtesy of Department of Foreign Affairs and International Trade.

Dhanarajan, Gajaraj. 2001. *Reflections on Ten Years of the Commonwealth of Learning.* Vancouver: Commonwealth of Learning.

Dheensaw, C. 1994. *The Commonwealth Games: The First 60 Years, 1930–1990.* Auckland: Hodder & Stoughton.

Donahue, A. 1999. 'A Commonwealth of Parliaments', *The Parliamentarian* (Oct.): 359–64.

Durban Communiqué. 1999. Commonwealth Heads of Government Meeting, Durban. London: Commonwealth Secretariat.

Ingram, Derek. 2001. 'Commonwealth Update', *The Round Table* 90, 361: 489.

McIntyre, W. David. 1991. *The Significance of the Commonwealth 1965–90*. London: Macmillan, ch.14, 'Head of the Commonwealth'.

———. 2001. *A Guide to the Contemporary Commonwealth*. London: Palgrave.

Martin, Paul. 1999. 'Canada and the Commonwealth Business Forum', *The Round Table* 88, 349: 33–8.

Molgat, Gildas. 2000. Speech notes for opening of the 14th Commonwealth Education Ministers' Conference, Nov., courtesy of DFAIT.

Smith, Arnold, with Clyde Sanger. 1981. *Stitches in Time: The Commonwealth in World Politics*. London: André Deutsch.

van der Donckt, Charles. 1999. 'Examining the Commonwealth's Political Role: Constraints, Challenges, and Opportunities', in G. Mills and J. Stremlau, eds, *The Commonwealth in the 21st Century*. Johannesburg: South African Institute of International Affairs.

Van Rooy, Alison. 2001. 'Civil Society and the Axworthy Touch', in F.O. Hampson, N. Hillmer, and M.A. Molot, eds, *Canada Among Nations 2001: The Axworthy Legacy*. Toronto: Oxford University Press.

West, Katherine. 1995. *Economic Opportunities for Britain in the Commonwealth*. Chatham House Discussion Paper 60. London: Royal Institute of International Affairs.

Wyman, Miriam. 2001. 'Thinking about Governance: A Draft Discussion Paper', prepared for the Citizens and Governance Program, Commonwealth Foundation, July.

The Canada Among Nations Series

Canada Among Nations 1998: Leadership and Dialogue, edited by
Fen Osler Hampson and Maureen Appel Molot
019-541406-3

Canada Among Nations 1999: A Big League Player?, edited by
Fen Osler Hampson, Michael Hart, and Martin Rudner
019-541458-6

Canada Among Nations 2000: Vanishing Borders, edited by
Maureen Appel Molot and Fen Osler Hampson
019-541540-X

Canada Among Nations 2001: The Axworthy Legacy, edited by
Fen Osler Hampson, Norman Hillmer, and Maureen Appel Molot
019-541677-8

Canada Among Nations 2002. A Fading Power, edited by
Norman Hillmer and Maureen Appel Molot
019-541791-7